Effective Reading Strategies

Effective Reading Strategies

Teaching Children Who Find Reading Difficult

3RD EDITION

Timothy Rasinski
Kent State University

Nancy Padak
Kent State University

PEARSON

Merrill
Prentice Hall

Upper Saddle River, New Jersey
Columbus, Ohio

Library of Congress Cataloging-in-Publication Data

Rasinski, Timothy V.
    Effective reading strategies : teaching children who find reading difficult /
Timothy Rasinski & Nancy Padak.—3rd ed.
      p. cm.
Includes bibliographical references (p.   ) and indexes.
ISBN 0-13-112186-3
    1. Reading—Remedial teaching.   2. Developmental reading.   I. Padak,
Nancy.   II. Title.
    LB1050.5.R33 2004
    372.43—dc21

                                              2003012831

Vice President and Executive Publisher:
  Jeffery W. Johnston
Senior Editor: Linda Ashe Montgomery
Editorial Assistant: Laura Weaver
Production Editor: Mary M. Irvin
Production Coordination: Karen Ettinger,
  The GTS Companies/York, PA Campus
Design Coordinator: Diane C. Lorenzo

Cover Designer: Jeff Vanik
Cover Image: Getty
Photo Coordinator: Cynthia Cassidy
Production Manager: Pamela D. Bennett
Director of Marketing: Ann Castel Davis
Marketing Manager: Darcy Betts Prybella
Marketing Coordinator: Tyra Poole

Photo Credits: Cynthia Cassidy/Merrill, p. 97; Scott Cunningham/Merrill, p. 8, 16, 80, 137, 143, 200, 226, 266; KS Studios/Merrill, p. 2; Anthony Magnacca/Merrill, p. 36, 58, 108, 120, 154, 222, 229, 238; Pearson Learning, p. 211; Barbara Schwartz/Merrill, p. 42, 54, 132, 202; Anne Vega/Merrill, p. 11, 21, 102, 164, 191, 210, 247, 248, 258, 264; Tom Watson/Merrill, p. 180; Todd Yarrington/Merrill, p. 32, 246; Shirley Zeiberg/PH College, p. 245.

This book was set in Korinna by The GTS Companies/York, PA Campus, and was printed and bound by R. R. Donnelley & Sons Company. The cover was printed by Phoenix Color Corp.

Pearson Education Ltd.
Pearson Education Singapore Pte. Ltd.
Pearson Education Canada, Ltd.
Pearson Education—Japan

Pearson Education Australia Pty. Limited
Pearson Education North Asia Ltd.
Pearson Educación de Mexico, S.A. de C.V.
Pearson Education Malaysia, Pte. Ltd.

10 9 8 7
ISBN 0-13-112186-3

To all children who struggle in learning how to read, and to the dedicated and caring reading teachers who help them.

Preface

We have been working together for 15 years, teaching and thinking; talking with children, teachers, and parents; conducting research; providing professional development; and discussing reading and instruction with each other and with others—sometimes heatedly. We have struggled with many questions: What are the best ways to provide instruction for children who struggle as readers? How should their instruction differ from instruction for children who progress more typically? What insights can we glean from research? What are the proper roles of teachers and parents in instructional efforts? And how can we best communicate our ideas about corrective instruction to teachers—those in training and those already working with children?

This volume, like the two editions that preceded it, is our best current response to those questions and many others. It offers new instructional strategies for helping children in an informal, easy-to-read, yet scholarly approach. The ideas presented here have been tried and tested in studies of effective instruction and, more important, in our own classrooms and tutoring rooms and those of teachers we have known and worked with over the years.

Our Framework for Helping You with Struggling Readers

Many books offer ideas for helping struggling readers. Many espouse a highly analytic, diagnostic-prescriptive approach that results in a detailed recipe book of prescribed activities designed to remediate specific skills and subskills. These books include lists of skill activities aimed at remediating everything from medial vowel sounds to homonyms, to sequential comprehension difficulties. But such books pay little attention to the instructional context or how various activities might interact to form a coherent, logical, and effective whole.

Our book breaks with this traditional model. The instructional strategies and activities are arranged around general areas of focus, such as phonemic awareness, decoding, fluency, vocabulary, and comprehension. Because we built the framework of this book around broad-based areas of concern, you now have a framework on which to organize your own understanding and approach to remedial and corrective reading instruction. The instructional strategies and activities nurture and develop proficiency within that broad area rather than remediate any specific skill or subskill.

Generalized Strategies. The strategies can be generalized to many situations so that informed teachers can mold and modify them for their own teaching and learning contexts. As you work with these strategies, you will find they offer supported opportunities to experience reading success. We like to think of our descriptions of the instructional strategies as the raw material. Teachers use this raw material to meet their students' needs without lessening the effectiveness of the activities. Indeed, because our presentation assumes that informed, sensitive, and caring teachers will mold the strategies to fit their own instructional contexts, we expect the effectiveness of the strategies to be enhanced.

Teacher Voices. Because instruction depends heavily upon the context in which it occurs, we wanted you to hear the voices of teachers who have tried out these strategies in their own rooms. You will see how they perceive and provide corrective instruction, how they modify the strategies for their own use, what they like about the strategies, and why they choose them. We believe that, by reading about these teachers, your understanding of and insight into the activities will be deepened and enhanced.

Connecting Strategies to Make a Cohesive Whole. This book includes another unique feature—our attention to how different strategies might fit together in whole instructional packages or routines. We offer opportunities for wide and guided reading to help you form consistent and complete instructional routines that are predictable, successful, and effective.

New to This Edition

In this third edition, we have updated all the chapters by incorporating new research findings and describing new instructional activities. We have continued to address technological supports for children's literacy learning and have addressed some basic issues surrounding teaching reading to children whose first language is not English. In addition, newly added Appendix O provides a list of common words for instructional focus.

Perhaps the most significant addition to this edition, however, is the focus on scientifically based research in reading and learning to read. Since the 2000 edition of this book, the National Reading Panel (NRP) report has provided the research foundation for the reauthorization of the Elementary and Secondary Education Act, commonly called "No Child Left Behind." In this edition, we summarize NRP findings and provide a clearer focus on the research base for instructional strategies and other aspects of reading program development. We have woven these findings into a research-based approach that reflects an integrated curriculum with authentic and engaging reading.

Whether you use this book as a course textbook or a handbook for working with children in a classroom or clinic, you will find that it contains ideas, suggestions, and discussions that will help you be the best teacher you can be. This book is for you and for the struggling readers with whom you interact.

Acknowledgments

A book such as this is more than the product of any two individuals. We had help. Among those we gratefully recognize are Linda Montgomery, senior editor; Mary Irvin, production editor; Laura Weaver, editorial assistant; and Karen M. Keady, copyeditor, at Merrill/Prentice Hall, who shared our vision of a new type of book on corrective reading strategies and methods.

We also wish to thank our mentors, Jerry Zutell at The Ohio State University and Jane Davidson at Northern Illinois University, who have continued to influence our thinking and challenge us to consider problems in new ways. We are especially grateful for our own students—those who challenge us in our classes now and those who have graduated and are on their way to becoming conscientious teachers. These students and former students have continually provided us with fresh insights into working with children who find reading difficult.

We would be remiss not to acknowledge all of the teachers, principals, and other educators with whom we have had the privilege to work. Their collaboration provides us with ideas, insights, and inspiration into teaching reading. We wish to thank teachers from Akron, Canton, Chicago, ESU #3, Mobile, Palatine, Parkview Elementary in Wooster, Nordonia, Sonoma County, Sunbeam Elementary in Cleveland, Tallmadge, and other locations in Ohio and throughout the country. Each has contributed greatly to this book, and we sincerely appreciate their part in its development.

Finally, we acknowledge the contributions of our reviewers from this and previous editions for their careful reading and thoughtful comments: Carole L. Bond, The University of Memphis; Hazel A. Brauer, University of San Francisco; Mariam Jean Dreher, University of Maryland; Karen R. Cook-Enlow, Rio Linda Union School District; Joyce Kostelnik, Arizona State University West; Harry B. Miller, Northeast Louisiana University; Kouider Mokhtari, Oklahoma State University; Evangeline Newton, The University of Akron; Lucille B. Strain, Bowie State University; and Elizabeth Sturtevant, George Mason University.

We hope that everyone who has influenced our work—especially those teachers and children whose classrooms we have visited and whose stories we have told—will benefit from this book. In many ways, we can say that this is a book for teachers and children by teachers and children.

Timothy Rasinski

Nancy Padak

Discover the Companion Website Accompanying This Book

The Prentice Hall Companion Website: A Virtual Learning Environment

Technology is a constantly growing and changing aspect of our field that is creating a need for content and resources. To address this emerging need, Prentice Hall has developed an online learning environment for students and professors alike—Companion Websites—to support our textbooks.

In creating a Companion Website, our goal is to build on and enhance what the textbook already offers. For this reason, the content for each user-friendly website is organized by topic and provides the professor and student with a variety of meaningful resources. Common features of a Companion Website include:

For the Professor

Every Companion Website integrates **Syllabus Manager**™, an online syllabus creation and management utility.

- **Syllabus Manager**™ provides you, the instructor, with an easy, step-by-step process to create and revise syllabi, with direct links into Companion Website and other online content without having to learn HTML.
- Students may log on to your syllabus during any study session. All they need to know is the web address for the Companion Website and the password you've assigned to your syllabus.
- After you have created a syllabus using **Syllabus Manager**™, students may enter the syllabus for their course section from any point in the Companion Website.
- Clicking on a date, the student is shown the list of activities for the assignment. The activities for each assignment are linked directly to actual content, saving time for students.
- Adding assignments consists of clicking on the desired due date, then filling in the details of the assignment—name of the assignment, instructions, and whether or not it is a one-time or repeating assignment.

- In addition, links to other activities can be created easily. If the activity is online, a URL can be entered in the space provided, and it will be linked automatically in the final syllabus.
- Your completed syllabus is hosted on our servers, allowing convenient updates from any computer on the Internet. Changes you make to your syllabus are immediately available to your students at their next logon.

For the Student

- **Topic Overviews**—Outline key concepts in topic areas.
- **Strategies**—These websites provide suggestions and information on how to implement instructional strategies and activities for each topic. The Assessment topic also contains Practice Case Studies as well.
- **Web Links**—A wide range of websites that allow the students to access current information on everything from rationales for specific types of instruction, to research on related topics, to compilations of useful articles, and more.
- **Electronic Bluebook**—Send homework or essays directly to your instructor's email with this paperless form.
- **Message Board**—Virtual bulletin board to post or respond to questions or comments from a national audience.
- **Chat**—Real-time chat with anyone who is using the text anywhere in the country—ideal for discussion and study groups, class projects, etc.

To take advantage of these and other resources, please visit the *Effective Reading Strategies: Teaching Children Who Find Reading Difficult,* Third Edition, Companion Website at

www.prenhall.com/rasinski

Educator Learning Center: An Invaluable Online Resource

Merrill Education and the Association for Supervision and Curriculum Development (ASCD) invite you to take advantage of a new online resource, one that provides access to the top research and proven strategies associated with ASCD and Merrill—the Educator Learning Center. At **www.EducatorLearningCenter.com** you will find resources that will enhance your students' understanding of course topics and of current educational issues, in addition to being invaluable for further research.

How the Educator Learning Center will help your students become better teachers

With the combined resources of Merrill Education and ASCD, you and your students will find a wealth of tools and materials to better prepare them for the classroom.

Research

- More than 600 articles from the ASCD journal *Educational Leadership* discuss everyday issues faced by practicing teachers.

- A direct link on the site to Research Navigator™ gives students access to many of the leading education journals, as well as extensive content detailing the research process.

- Excerpts from Merrill Education texts give your students insights on important topics of instructional methods, diverse populations, assessment, classroom management, technology, and refining classroom practice.

Classroom Practice

- Hundreds of lesson plans and teaching strategies are categorized by content area and age range.

- Case studies and classroom video footage provide virtual field experience for student reflection.

- Computer simulations and other electronic tools keep your students abreast of today's classrooms and current technologies.

Look into the value of Educator Learning Center yourself

Preview the value of this educational environment by visiting **www.Educator LearningCenter.com** and clicking on "Demo." For a free 4-month subscription to the Educator Learning Center in conjunction with this text, simply contact your Merrill/Prentice Hall sales representative.

Contents

NOTE: Every effort has been made to provide accurate and current Internet information in this book. However, the Internet and information posted on it are constantly changing; therefore, it is inevitable that some of the Internet addresses listed in this textbook will change.

1

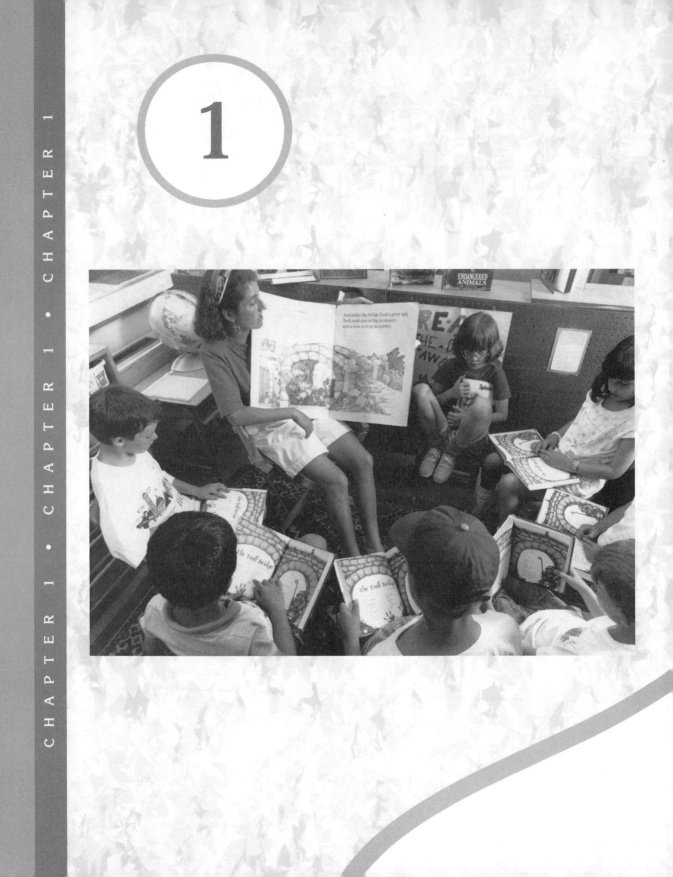

New Perspectives on Helping Students Become Literate

Despite great progress in understanding how children acquire literacy and in methods for teaching reading and writing, the field of literacy education continues to be dominated by multiple perspectives and approaches. Among theories about literacy acquisition, concepts such as *skills* and *subskills, psycholinguistics, bottom-up, top-down, automaticity,* and *interactive* are still debated, sometimes quite fiercely.

Like the various theoretical orientations to literacy, the methods of teaching literacy are equally diverse and equally debated. Terms such as *basal-oriented, skills* and *skills management, literature-based, linguistic, whole language, balanced, whole word, phonics, language experience, flexible grouping,* and *early intervention* are sometimes used to describe comprehensive literacy education programs as well as specific methods or components of literacy programs.

Given this variety, the authors of any book that attempts to describe and advocate certain approaches to reading and writing instruction must begin by providing the orientation that frames the book. Now, we do not wish to enter into the debate over best theories and theoretical orientations to teaching reading. We see merit in many theories and approaches, but we also see the limitations that each theory and each approach carries with it. The approach we advocate in this book derives from three key ideas that underlie many theories of literacy development and approaches to literacy education: authenticity, engagement, and essentials.

We know from the theories and work of John Dewey that learning is most powerful when it is connected to the world that exists outside of the classroom. To the extent that teachers can make their classrooms and the work that occurs in their classrooms reflect students' lives outside the classroom, the

3

authentic is the connection between the reader and personal experience

students are more likely to want to learn. This is what we mean by authenticity—what students read, how they read it, and how they respond to what they read (and write) must connect to the children's interests and lives, to the real world, and to other curriculum areas. After all, literacy is essentially a vehicle for enriching one's life and for helping one learn about the world in all its wonderful facets.

It's not enough, however, for reading and writing to be authentic. Students need to approach literacy tasks eagerly; they need to be *engaged*. Too many students live passive school lives. They allow school to happen to them. These students are less likely to take the initiative to employ reading and writing for their own purposes and pleasure.

Progress in becoming literate depends largely on the amount of time that students spend engaged in literate activity. If students struggle in reading and writing, one of the best ways to move them forward is to engage them in the literacy act. The teacher's job, then, is to engage students fully and completely in the task of learning to read—moving students away from responding in a passive and mechanical fashion and toward responding thoughtfully and with understanding and enthusiasm.

Authentic reading and writing lead to motivated reading. Motivated reading inspires engaged reading. Engaged reading results in improved reading. And improved reading leads to more authentic reading. In a sense, the reading and writing teacher's job is to "prime the pump," to motivate students to read so they will engage themselves in the task and bootstrap their way to full literacy.

A focus on the essential elements in reading suggests that specific competencies must be developed for students to experience success. The National Reading Panel (2000) has identified five essential elements: phonemic awareness, phonics or word recognition, reading fluency, vocabulary, and comprehension. To be successful in reading students must be competent in each of these areas. We agree. We argue that there is more to reading success than what is embodied in these five competencies, but we do recognize that these components are incredibly important. Moreover, students who struggle in reading usually experience difficulty in one or more of these areas.

Throughout this book you will see the ideas of authenticity, engagement, and essentials come through over and over. When essential reading strategies and skills are taught within a context of authentic reading for authentic tasks and in a context that challanges students to fully engage their cognitive and creative selves, those strategies and skills are likely to be internalized quickly and find use in students' school tasks and in their lifelong reading.

We begin then with the belief, almost a cliché nowadays, that people learn to read by reading. Several studies have documented that good readers read substantially more than less able readers during reading lessons and free reading time in school and at home. Findings from the National Assessment of Educational Progress (NAEP) for 1992, 1994, 1998, and 2000 (National Center for Education Statistics, 2001) found that fourth-grade students who read the most in school and home tended to be the highest achieving students in reading. Students who read the least were the lowest achievers. An international study of reading achievement among second- and eighth-grade students (Postlethwaite & Ross, 1992) found that the amount of reading at home and at school were two of the top three predictors of reading achievement. Clearly, reading success can only be achieved when students practice the reading skills, strategies, and competencies taught them—and this can be done only through reading.

Our next assumption is connected to the first. We believe that children are most likely to engage in reading when they perceive it as meaningful, instrumental, and/or enjoyable. When students see that reading is useful, playful, or interesting, they are more likely to pull out books, newspapers, or other written materials and read with purpose and passion.

Proceeding from this assumption, we believe that teachers, principals, schools, and parents must make reading meaningful and enjoyable for students. Teachers need to help students master and make sense of the written symbols on the page. Equally important, they need to help students develop a passion for reading—to see that reading can be as engaging as video games, watching sports on television, talking on the telephone, camping in the woods, playing soccer, collecting stamps or baseball cards, or any other activity in which students take pleasure and delight. In other words, students need to see reading as worth doing. Teachers can foster this attitude by sharing their own passion for reading—for example, by talking about their own reading, reading to students, recommending books, and listening with interest to students talk about personal reading.

In authentic, engaging, and essential reading classrooms, teachers create conditions and develop activities that inspire students to read wholeheartedly and enthusiastically. When students read willingly and teachers provide necessary instruction, assistance, modeling, support, and encouragement, students become more proficient readers. Because instruction is aimed at students' needs and interests, they see the importance of reading and remain active and engaged readers beyond the boundaries of the classroom. The teacher who subscribes to this authentic, engaged, and essential orientation, therefore, aims not simply to develop students who *can* read but those who *want* to read and *choose* to read.

The Essentials of Reading Instruction

Proficiency in phonemic awareness, word recognition, reading fluency, vocabulary, and comprehension are necessary competencies for success in reading (National Reading Panel, 2000). As such, these areas must be the focus of instruction. Students need direct, thoughtful, organized, and regular instruction in these areas in order to become readers.

Handwritten margin notes: Phonemic = think & manipulate sounds. Word recognition = ability to turn written word into oral word. Fluency = bridge between recognition & comprehension.

Phonemic awareness refers to the ability to think about and manipulate the sounds of language. Proficiency in phonemic awareness is necessary to profit from phonics and word recognition instruction. Word recognition is the ability to turn a written word into its oral representation. Clearly, reading requires word recognition. Fluency is a bridge between word recognition and comprehension. It is the ability to read accurately, expressively, meaningfully, with appropriate phrasing, and at an appropriate rate. Fluent readers need not think about each word as they decode it or sound it out; rather they recognize words in print automatically and so can devote their attention to the most important part of reading: comprehension. Vocabulary refers to the ability to know the meaning of words encountered in print. Comprehension refers to the ability to actively construct appropriate meaning from written text.

We think that these competencies are critical to reading success and must be taught. That is why we devote a chapter to the first four essential reading components and two to comprehension. We believe, too, that writing is an essential part of reading success. Thus, we devote a chapter to writing. But reading success entails more than these essential elements. In the next section we describe other components critical to successful reading instruction.

Authentic and Engaged Reading Classrooms

Teachers create conditions that make students want to read and want to learn to read in various ways. But nearly all these teachers share an excitement about reading. They are avid readers themselves and they share their enthusiasm with students, telling them about what they are reading, why they choose certain books, and how reading affects them. Teachers also communicate this enthusiasm by reading to their students every day. In effect, they are saying, "Reading is so important that I am willing to take the time to share with you some of the best stories and poems that I know. I want you to know about and enjoy these stories and poems, too." Students are much more likely to develop an enthusiasm for reading in an environment in which reading is treated as special and important.

A considerable amount of research supports this point. In one study, students in an authentic and engaging second-grade classroom read more in school and at home than children from a more traditional, skills-oriented program (Mervar & Hiebert, 1989)—by nearly 3 to 1! In another study, intermediate-grade students from a school with a long-standing tradition of authenticity and engagement had considerably better attitudes toward academic and recreational reading than children from a similar school that embodied a more structured, skills-oriented approach (Rasinski & Linek, 1993).

Some of the biggest differences in authentic and engaging classrooms are found between grade levels. In the primary grades, instruction focuses on introducing students to the printed word and stories. Because many activities at this level are group oriented, we would expect to find the teacher reading aloud and talking to the class about books every day. Groups of students would be reading oversized (big) books together. Usually the content of these books is patterned or predictable, which makes them easy and fun to read and read again. (See Appendix C for titles.) Bill Martin's *Brown Bear, Brown Bear* is one of the best examples of a patterned book. After several group readings in which the teacher points to words as they are read, most children can read the story on their own and begin to identify specific phrases, words, and word parts in the text and in isolation.

Language experience activities are also a large part of reading instruction at this level. In language experience students share an experience—for example, a field trip to a supermarket, a visit with the school principal, or a math or science activity. After a brief discussion of the experience, students dictate a text that summarizes what they learned or reflects their perceptions of the shared experience. As the children dictate, the teacher acts as a scribe, writing students' words on a large sheet of paper that hangs from the chalkboard. When the text is finished, students read and reread it, first with the teacher's help and later independently. Children read this text successfully because it is about an experience they have all shared, talked about, and composed. Once students are familiar with the text, the teacher may begin pointing out individual words and letters.

At this level we would also expect many opportunities for children to read and look at books on their own and with peers; write their own stories and make entries in personal journals; and read individually to and with the teacher, classroom aides, parent volunteers, and students from other classrooms and grades. When students begin to develop an affinity for reading and some proficiency in fluent reading, the teacher gives them even greater control over and choice about their reading.

Intermediate-grade students may engage in what many reading educators call readers' workshop (Atwell, 1987; see chapter 8). In readers' workshop most instructional time involves reading real books, primarily ones that students have chosen. Students' response to what they read is an important aspect of this approach. They may respond in their personal journals or write to their teacher and peers. In addition, they may recast the story in a poem, script, skit, or visual art form. Students also have many opportunities to discuss their reading with peers and teacher in an informal, accepting environment. Of course, teachers at all levels introduce students to unfamiliar books and literary genres by reading regularly to their classes.

The teacher's role in authentic, engaged, and essential reading and writing classrooms is far from traditional. Authentic, engaging, and essential teachers are coaches, encouragers, and explicit models of what it means to be a literate person. Just as students write books using the model of a book written by a distinguished author, students also model their development as literate people by watching and listening to their teachers. Teachers who love

Authentic, engaging, and essential teachers are avid readers themselves.

reading and demonstrate this passion to their students allow students an important view at what an engaged literate person looks like in the flesh.

In addition, effective literacy teachers constantly seek to improve themselves and their schools through staff development and support from administrators (Gaskins, 1998). Through self-improvement activities, teachers take ownership of their instructional programs and become more willing and able to make them work. Moreover, informed teachers make informed decisions about students, classroom instruction, and long-term goals and plans.

Corrective Reading in an Authentic and Engaged Context

We now have a good picture of authentic, engaged, and essential reading and writing instruction in regular classrooms. Less clear is how it works with students who experience considerable difficulty learning to read and require some adaptive instruction. Some people claim that this approach may be fine for students who learn to read in a normal manner and at a normal rate but will fail with those not making it. According to this way of thinking, these children need a more structured environment in which reading is divided into small, digestible units. Educators assume that students can better master smaller segments of reading as they work alone or in groups with other children who also have reading problems than they can deal with reading books and working with students of diverse ability. This approach is called a diagnostic–prescriptive model: Identify the specific skills in which the student exhibits the most difficulty, provide intensive remedial instruction in the deficient skill(s), often in the form of mindless drill and incessant worksheets, and (according to the theory that underlies this model) the student will achieve proficiency in reading.

The idea may sound good on paper, but in reality it doesn't work. Richard Allington and his associates have studied remedial, special, and compensatory reading instruction for several years (Allington, 1987, 2000; Allington & McGill-Franzen, 1989; Allington, Stuetzel, Shake, & Lamarche, 1986; Allington & Walmsley, 1995). They report that current approaches to remedial reading do little for struggling readers. Instruction tends to rely heavily on skill, drill, and worksheet activities focused on isolated words, sounds, and letters. Students have few opportunities to read materials of their own choosing. What they do read is usually chosen for them according to perceived reading level. Children work by themselves or with other struggling readers, and little of what they do in these special reading classes has any connection to what they are learning in their regular classrooms. Remedial instruction usually emphasizes word-perfect oral reading of uninteresting texts rather than acquisition of meaning from the text or development of attitudes and habits that will draw students to reading throughout their lives.

Allington argues that these approaches to remedial reading don't work well enough to justify their continued use. Students placed in special programs rarely leave or improve sufficiently. They tend to remain behind classmates who achieve at more normal rates. What usually changes in these students are their attitudes toward learning, reading, and themselves. They begin to see themselves as failures and to view reading as a meaningless and frustrating task—something to be avoided. Allington and others say that it is time to reinvent remedial reading.

Those taking a broader perspective on educational reform share a similar view. The Commission on Chapter I (now Title I) was formed to investigate the strengths and weaknesses of current programs and recommend alterations for reauthorization of the federal legislation that provides Chapter I funds for school-based compensatory and corrective reading programs. The commission's report describes typical remedial instruction: "Children in Chapter I learn and relearn discrete low-level skills. They rarely know what it is like to attempt interesting content or to use knowledge creatively. Rather than experiencing the joy of wrestling with ideas, children are more likely to spend their time circling m's and p's on dittos" (Commission on Chapter I, 1993). The Commission argued for remaking the federal program for remedial reading.

One way to reinvent remedial reading is to make instruction look, feel, and be more like authentic and engaged classrooms than skill-and-drill emporiums. The ideas and activities in this book are innovative and exciting approaches for helping students overcome their difficulty with and dislike of reading. Moreover, they are organized around components essential for reading success, areas that are often the source of difficulty for struggling readers.

Our university reading center gives children this kind of instructional experience. They read books of their own choosing as well as exemplary trade books and other material chosen by the teacher. They respond to their reading in creative ways—for example, by recasting their stories as scripts and performing them in readers' theater for their families. These children write every day in school and at home about topics of interest to them. While developing competency in the essential components of reading, they learn to like reading, understand that reading is enjoyable, and discover that it can help them in their own lives.

Parents see the difference this instruction makes for their children, and they are universally pleased. They tell us how their children hated to read before enrolling at our center. Today those children not only look forward to the center sessions but also insist on reading to and with their parents at home. Parents tell us that students who had previously refused to pick up a book, even when Mom or Dad told them to, now choose to read on their own.

Good instruction is good instruction, whether it's for children reading four levels above grade placement or for those who struggle with reading. If children learn to love reading and make good progress in learning to read in regular classrooms with an authentic, engaged, and essential orientation, then it makes sense that instruction with the same basic characteristics will work just as well for children who have trouble learning to read. Certain adaptations may be necessary, but we believe the principles that drive high-quality instruction in regular classroom settings are equally applicable in settings that address the needs of struggling readers.

Throughout this book we will describe various instructional strategies aimed at overcoming specific areas of difficulty in reading (such as attitude and motivation, phonemic awareness, word recognition, reading fluency, vocabulary, comprehension, and writing). Rather than precisely defined skills, these are broad areas essential to growth in reading. Difficulties in reading can often be attributed to problems in one or more of these areas.

Although we describe and recommend instructional practices, let us be clear at the outset that such instruction must occur within a larger framework of authentic literacy education. The strategies and practices we describe are generic and can easily be adapted and applied to nearly any instructional setting, with students of all levels of achievement, and with texts of any level of difficulty.

Principles of Authentic, Engaged, and Essential Corrective Instruction

These principles apply directly to corrective reading situations and establish a general framework for corrective reading.

Effective instruction uses authentic materials.

Use Authentic Texts and Other Reading Material

If we want children to read real books and other reading materials, they need plenty of opportunities to read such material in their corrective reading instruction. By reading real stories, poems, and essays, students learn that reading is enjoyable and has meaning in their lives. The workbooks and skill sheets of traditional remedial reading offer little enjoyment and satisfaction for students, and they certainly have questionable applicability to students' real-life reading. Skill sheets, if used, are best developed by the teacher and aimed specifically at whatever difficulty the student is experiencing.

Focus on the Essential Components of Reading

Struggling readers most likely experience difficulty in one or more of the essential components of reading: phonemic awareness, word recognition, reading fluency, vocabulary, and comprehension. Corrective instruction needs to focus squarely and rigorously on these essential components of reading and overcoming difficulties in components in need of development. Successful teachers of struggling readers develop intensive instructional routines that focus on the essential component that is the source of the student's reading difficulty, while at the same time providing independent and guided opportunities for students to put the essential component to use through real reading.

to use while learning modeling, practice

Maximize Reading of Connected Text

Students in traditional corrective reading programs often read little connected written discourse. Certainly, they read less than students in regular classrooms. Yet we know that quantity of reading is directly related to reading growth. We must create situations that make students want to read real books on their own, both in and out of school.

Provide for High Levels of Engagement

Not only do students need to read a lot, the nature of that reading should encourage high-level thinking. This requires that students read for their own purposes or purposes determined within the classroom community. Students need to read and write to solve their own problems and to satisfy their own hunger for enjoyment and learning.

Focus on Students' Motivation and Interest in Reading

Most students who have difficulty learning to read also dislike reading. They have experienced pain and frustration in their reading instruction and associate reading with unpleasant experiences. Corrective instruction must help students develop more positive images of reading and of themselves as readers. Teachers accomplish this by helping students achieve success in reading, by encouraging them to read real and personally satisfying materials, and by developing authentic and enjoyable instructional activities.

Make Connections

Purposes for reading and writing lie in the world around the students—their lived-in world and their school world. Students must read and write so as to make connections to their own world and the various content areas in the school curriculum. Students need to see that they can apply literacy to all areas of the curriculum and life.

Let Students Lead the Way

In traditional corrective reading classrooms, the teacher makes all the decisions about lessons for individual students, sometimes basing lessons on diagnostic test results or packaged instructional materials. Students have little voice in this process and often have difficulty making sense of lessons or connecting lessons to real reading situations. Consequently, motivation and interest can decline.

We can best foster motivation and interest when students are involved in reading and learning that they care about. By encouraging students to select their own reading material and inviting them to react, ask questions, and seek answers, we can help students control the purpose, content, and direction for their literacy experiences. Learning is easiest and most efficient under these conditions.

Be More Than a Teacher

Authentic and engaged teachers do more than teach. They model for students what they teach, and they demonstrate for students every day what a literate life looks like. They constantly encourage students to do their best, and they communicate to students their belief in them. Teachers engage students in real conversations about what they have read and written, not the kind of traditional discussion in which teachers read questions from the book and challenge students to "guess what's in my head." In many ways teachers become coaches, working closely with students not just through teaching but also through close support, encouragement, and modeling. In addition, authentic and engaged teachers constantly strive to grow as professionals through staff development activities, professional reading, and graduate coursework.

Provide Support When Needed

Students in corrective reading placements cannot read material with the same degree of fluency as more normally progressing students. Effective teachers are ready and able to provide support (or scaffolding) to make reading manageable and meaningful for students. This may mean reading to or with students before asking them to read the text on their own, ensuring that they have sufficient background knowledge to understand the text, checking that the text is sufficiently easy for them to read, or asking them to practice reading a passage at home with their parents before reading it at school. Readers should never struggle to the point of failure or frustration in any reading task or activity.

Sometimes support involves instruction in specific skills or strategies. But this instruction is neither the focal point of the curriculum as in traditional corrective reading programs, nor provided for all readers. Instead, teachers provide skill or strategy instruction as needed—only if they see that lack of a particular strategy or bit of reading knowledge is hampering a student's progress. That is, teachers make no assumptions about student need; rather, they take their cues from student performance.

Focus on Success

Traditional corrective reading programs are predicated on a deficit view of students. They assume that something is missing or wrong with a student, that instruction should fill in what's missing or correct what's wrong. This view focuses on weaknesses among readers—on what they *can't* do. We believe that teachers, on the other hand, need to focus on what students *can* do. Rather than think about students as remedial or view teaching as fixing what is wrong with learners, teachers should view students from a developmental perspective: They should believe that all students can learn and expect that they will. Such teachers base instruction on what students know and are interested in and what they can do.

Everybody's a Teacher; Everybody's a Learner

Authentic and engaged classrooms look little like traditional classrooms—no desks in rows, no isolated individual learners, no teacher behind a desk monitoring activity. Instead, students are learning from and with each other. Variety and choice are evident. And the teacher is a learner, too. Teachers learn about students by listening to and observing them in action; they value students and are genuinely interested in their thoughts and opinions. Together, teachers and their students strive to create a learning community where everybody's a teacher and everyone learns.

Involve Parents

Reading is best learned when it is practiced at home as well as at school. Ideally, students read any time, any place. Making parents aware of what is going on in the school and encouraging them to help their children at home in ways that complement school instruction will reinforce and multiply instructional effectiveness. Moreover, involving parents usually makes them greater stakeholders in their children's education and increases their support for and satisfaction in the job that schools do. Effective reading instruction demands that teachers inform parents and involve them in substantive ways in their children's development as readers.

Know Your Students; Track Their Progress

Effective teachers know their students. They know their likes and their dislikes. They know what motivates students and they are aware of what tends to turn students away from engaged learning. Teachers should observe their students closely, question their students often, and use this information to guide instruction.

Progress in reading should be monitored regularly. Brief but regular assessment aids teachers in determining instructional effectiveness and guides them in altering instruction when necessary. In this book we describe several approaches for helping teachers learn about their students and track their reading progress.

A New Direction for Teaching Struggling Readers

Authentic, engaging, and essential instruction is a legitimate approach for helping children who experience significant difficulty when learning to read. This book was written to introduce classroom and specialist teachers of students with reading difficulties to instructional strategies that fit within this orientation. In it we provide descriptions of instructional strategies and activities. As we suggested earlier, however, these strategies are not aimed at remediating any particular or precise skill such as learning consonant blends, mastering sight words, or determining the main idea of a paragraph. Rather, the strategies we present are organized under general areas of concern that can be diagnosed simply by listening to children read and respond to questions about the reading, observing children within the classroom during instruction and recreational reading times, talking with children about how they perceive and feel about reading, and talking with parents and teachers about how they perceive the children's progress and interest in reading. Our major topics include the broad areas of phonemic awareness and word recognition, interest in and motivation for reading, reading fluency, vocabulary development, and comprehension.

Although teachers will find these strategies useful for helping children learn to read, we do not intend them to be implemented in any prescriptive or lockstep manner. Rather, we recommend that teachers become familiar with the strategies and modify them for use within their own instructional settings. Not all strategies work the same way for all students or teachers. Informed teachers will take the essence of strategies they believe have the greatest potential for success; fit them to the needs and interests of their students; and combine them with other strategies to create complex and integrated lessons that synergistically support children's reading while engaging children in authentic, interesting, and enlightening literacy experiences.

We encourage teachers to use the strategies creatively to develop effective lesson formats, but we recommend implementing them with a high degree of consistency. From one day to the next, the general lesson format should be consistent yet used with a variety of texts. This consistent application of effective instruction will minimize lost time, make lessons secure and predictable for students, and ultimately lead to significant gains in reading. Successful reading programs such as Reading Recovery or Paired Reading owe a large part of their success to the consistent application of instruction as well as the incorporation of strategies that engage students in real reading.

We encourage our readers to use this book as a handbook or reference guide. It is not a book to be read during a university course in corrective reading and then forgotten. It is meant to be read, reread, and consulted frequently as teachers search for instructional strategies that make reading real for students and help them overcome the difficulties and failures they have experienced in past attempts to become successful readers.

2

The Instructional Framework

Sarah, a 7-year-old, finds reading difficult. Yet when we chatted with her about reading, she said, "Well, it's hard sometimes, but it's not boring. Reading is fun mostly. It's sort of like taking a vacation in your mind." Sarah's comments make it clear that despite her struggles, she considers reading meaningful and satisfying. When we visited her classroom, we found out why. Every day, Sarah reads and writes in an instructional atmosphere that reflects the principles about literacy learning that we outlined in chapter 1.

Betsy, a reading resource teacher, shared with us her views about reading and learning to read: "When I have a student who appears to be at risk, my questions to myself are simple: What does the child know? What can the child do? Given the answers to these questions, how can I adjust my teaching to support the child's learning? I no longer focus on what's wrong with the child. Instead, I examine my instructional program, the strategies and materials I use." Betsy adapts her instruction to respond to her students' interests and needs rather than expecting them to adjust to her agenda. The framework that guides her instruction provides students with daily opportunities to succeed as readers and writers in meaningful and satisfying ways.

In this chapter we explore issues that Betsy and teachers like her encounter in their attempts to foster literacy learning. First, we address several general aspects of instruction that affect what and how students learn. Then we describe concrete aspects of the instructional environment, such as the creation of predictable routines. Together, these ideas and activities provide a conceptual and practical framework that helps instruction realize principles of literacy learning.

create predictable routines!

Accommodation

Betsy's comments focus on a critical concept for developing an effective instructional framework: accommodation or environmental responsiveness to students' needs. Accommodation does not involve letting kids off the hook, lowering standards, or anything of the sort. It is simply an acknowledgment that students have their own interests and needs, and that teachers can use these to create personal learning environments.

Suppose you're interested in developing an accommodating instructional environment. The first step, and it's a big one, is to consider how you think about the teaching–learning process. Years ago, many people believed that teaching was simply a matter of transmitting knowledge from someone who had it to someone who didn't. As we argue in chapter 1, however, learning involves construction of knowledge, not its transmission. Learning is something we do *with* students, not *to* or *for* them.

Gordon Wells (1986) describes constructivism in the literacy learning classroom:

> Knowledge [is] constructed afresh by each individual knower, through an interaction between the evidence (which is obtained through observation, listening, reading, and the use of reference materials of all kinds) and what the learner can bring to bear on it. The teacher arranges the situations—or encourages those that the children themselves have set up—and so has considerable control over the evidence that the learners encounter. But teachers cannot control the interpretations the children will make. (p. 116)

Those who think of teaching and learning in this constructivist way believe that students must make their own meaning as readers and writers. Rather than tell students what a story means, for example, they create learning environments that support students as they figure out the story for themselves. This sort of accommodation (or environmental responsiveness) reflects students' conceptual and instructional needs and beliefs. Let's take a closer look at these two areas.

Students' Conceptual Needs and Beliefs

During the past three decades, literacy scholars have done a great deal of talking, thinking, and researching about the importance of students' conceptual schema (what they already know about a topic they are going to study or read about). We know that effective teaching–learning environments must accommodate and build on knowledge students bring with them to the classroom. Therefore, the question isn't *if* accommodations are necessary but *how* to accommodate and what implications such accommodations have for larger curricular issues. When teachers begin thinking about accommodations, they often become concerned about time. It takes time to teach from a

[handwritten margin notes:] Teachers have some control over the evidence the students encounter but can not control the outcome or interpretation. Don't tell! Construct meaning

constructivist perspective, time for students to think and talk about what they already know, and time for them to embed new learning in their established network of ideas. As teachers, we have to decide if time spent this way is worth it.

Deb struggles with the issues of accommodation and time in her fourth-grade classroom (Watson & Konicek, 1990). She once began a science unit about heat by asking her students to brainstorm a list of things that give off heat. In addition to the sun, stoves, and their bodies, the children mentioned sweaters and hats. (After all, they had been hearing "put on your warm clothes" for years.) So Deb, sensing a need to address students' conceptual beliefs, said, "What could we do to find out which things give off heat?"

The children decided to wrap sweaters and scarves around thermometers. After 15 minutes, the thermometer readings hadn't changed. But rather than changing their beliefs, the children decided that the thermometers hadn't been wrapped up long enough. They resolved to keep the thermometers wrapped up overnight and predicted three-digit temperatures by morning.

By the next morning, nothing had changed. Deb asked students to write about the experiment in their science journals. They wrote entries such as, "We just didn't leave them in there long enough," and "Maybe some cold air got in them somehow." So the testing went on, with children hypothesizing, designing ways to find out (including sealing the items in large plastic bags so that cold air couldn't seep in), and reflecting on the results of their experiments.

After three days, Deb realized that the children had given up their old beliefs but had yet to replace them with new ones. So she wrote two statements on the chalkboard: "Heat can come from almost anything, even sweaters and hats. We are fooled when we measure heat because cold air can get inside," and "Heat comes mostly from the sun and our bodies. Heat is trapped inside winter clothes that keep our body heat in and cold air out." The children decided which theory made sense to them and wrote reasons for their choices in their science journals. Some were still puzzled, so Deb said, "What could we do to find out?" The children went out to recess with thermometers in their hats to test this new hypothesis.

In their commentary about Deb's experience, Watson and Konicek (1990) note the following:

> [If she had begun the unit] in the usual way, she might never have known how nine long Massachusetts winters had skewed her students' thinking. . . . [Students] would have learned a little about the sources of heat, a little about friction, and how to read a thermometer. By the end of two weeks, they would have been able to pass a simple test . . . but their preconceptions, never having been put on the table, would have continued, coexisting in a morass of conflicting ideas about heat and its behavior. (p. 680)

By viewing teaching and learning as a cooperative construction of knowledge rather than as its transmission, Deb enabled her students to learn about sources of heat. She was satisfied with her decision to accommodate children's conceptual needs, but she worried about the time it took to do so. In her journal she noted, "The kids are holding on to and putting together pieces of what they know of the world. But the time we are taking to explore what kids think is much longer than if I just told them the facts" (Watson & Konicek, 1990, p. 682).

Learning involves conceptual change. To teach for conceptual change, we establish instructional frameworks that stress relevance; involve lots of predicting, testing, and confirming; and offer consistent opportunities to talk things through with others. This issue of talk, especially talk supported by a "more knowledgeable other" (the teacher or parent), is critical to establishing effective literacy learning environments.

Exploratory talk helps children learn to use language to aid their thinking. Eventually this talk becomes "inner speech" (Vygotsky, 1962). Supported talk or discussion guides students in the way they think, solve problems, and perform other school-related tasks. With support from peers and the teacher, children perform much more than they can independently (Vygotsky, 1978). The story of Deb and her students illustrates all these principles in action.

Authentic experiences, whether in the classroom (such as the ones Deb provided for her students) or outside it (such as field trips), offer students opportunities to develop new concepts and refine old ones. To some extent, the teacher's or students' related readings can achieve the same purpose. In any event, instruction focused on conceptual change should offer students plentiful opportunities to share what they know, think, and have learned. Of course, this takes time. But teachers like Deb have decided that the time spent is worth it because such accommodations allow students to make productive use of what they already know as they try to make sense of or understand how their world works.

Students' Instructional Needs and Beliefs

Surely, creating an instructional environment that accommodates students' academic needs makes sense. We invite students to read and write and observe them carefully as they do. We look for ways to support students' growth as literacy learners. We also look for ways to challenge students, to offer them opportunities to stretch and grow in an atmosphere that promotes success. These two notions, *challenge* and *support*, describe frameworks that effectively accommodate students' instructional needs.

Students' instructional beliefs, their assumptions about how one "does school," are equally important to the creation of supportive and successful instructional frameworks. Educational anthropologist James Heap (1980) calls these beliefs *cultural logic*. He says that people develop expectations, based on their experiences, about what to do and how to behave in certain cultures (such as classrooms) and use these beliefs to guide future actions. We think he's right. Consider, for example, the story of Johnny:

Johnny came to our summer reading program at the end of second grade because his parents and teachers were concerned about his reading. He had made no progress, they said; he wasn't an independent reader. Johnny's tutor, Janine, verified his lack of independence. He knew what he knew, but he lacked strategies for solving problems in reading. For example, his only word-recognition strategy was to make wild guesses based on the first letters of unknown words.

So Johnny and Janine spent some time working on word recognition strategies that summer. She taught him how to use context by asking questions such as, "What word would make sense there?" She encouraged him to skip unknown words when he encountered them and then reread the sentence, looking for familiar words or word parts within unknown words. At the end of the summer program, Janine suggested that Johnny dictate a list of strategies to try when he encountered an unknown word. She hoped the list would remind him of his options as a reader. Here's his dictation:

When I Get Stuck

1. You can skip them and then go back.
2. You can think about what's happened so far.
3. You can look at the pictures.
4. You can sound it out.

At the end of the summer program, Janine suggested that Johnny dictate a list of strategies to try when he encountered unknown words.

After Johnny completed the dictation and Janine read it back to him, they had the following conversation:

Johnny: [points to items 1–3] Did you know about these before?

Janine: Yes.

Johnny: Where did you learn about them?

Janine: At school.

Johnny: You know, [my teacher last year] only knew about how to sound it out.

Janine: Oh.

Johnny: Well, she should learn about them. They work better, and they're easier, too.

We don't know how Johnny drew the conclusion about his teacher, but we suspect that he came to it honestly by constructing knowledge based on his classroom experiences. We have known others like him—students who think that their goal as readers is to say all the words correctly. In fact, a study of intermediate-grade students' perceptions of reading (Henk & Melnick, 1998) found that most children characterized good reading as "automatic, error-free, and rapid" (p. 71). Only one third of these children mentioned anything about comprehension in their descriptions. Although successful reading is no doubt characterized by fluency, ignoring comprehension is a mistake. The point is that students' experiences in school cause them to draw conclusions about "doing school" and about what they should do as readers and writers. Depending on their nature, these conclusions can hinder learning, as they did for Johnny.

Classrooms based on the principles outlined in chapter 1 and this chapter will reduce the possibility of students' drawing harmful conclusions about what reading and writing are and what readers and writers do. Teachers and students must share assumptions about the purposes and goals of literacy activities and individual literacy lessons. For example, if students believe their responsibility is only to produce error-free oral reading, complete assignments, or answer the teacher's questions, the intended learning may or may not take place.

Instructional responsiveness to students' needs—or accommodation—involves conceiving of learning as the construction of knowledge, both content knowledge and procedural knowledge. In many ways, this instructional responsiveness is at the heart of effective teaching. When we understand learning as the construction of knowledge, we also understand the importance of instruction that invites students to behave as real readers and writers and to complete tasks that spark genuine student interest in inquiry. Most of all, we know the importance of signaling that we care about what students know, think, say, and learn. We convey many of these understandings to our students subtly—by the questions we ask, the way attention is focused in the classroom, and our choice of instructional routines. In all ways, we signal to students that the classroom is a community of learners.

Developing Communities of Learners

Adults may perceive reading as a solitary activity, but in classrooms, reading is "a very social activity, deeply embedded in interactions with teacher and peers" (Cazden, 1981, p. 118). We know that literacy instruction should foster meaningful interactions with texts and among participants. But we also know that students determine what they should do and how they should participate in lessons by drawing conclusions about the tasks they are asked to perform. As Johnny's story illustrates, they may sometimes draw conclusions that we do not intend.

One conclusion we do want students to draw is that they should cooperate rather than compete. In competitive situations, difficulties cause distress, particularly if everyone else seems to be coping well. This may lead struggling readers to "believe that reading is a contest they will never win" and to "become more concerned about avoiding failure and embarrassment than with learning to read" (Winograd & Smith, 1987, pp. 307, 308). Moreover, scores, numbers of stories read, or other measures of reading often become more important in students' minds than the actual process of reading, their reactions to reading, or what they are learning as they read.

A competitive classroom atmosphere can actually cause students to make counterproductive decisions about participating in lessons. For example, students whose comprehension instruction consists of providing the right answers to the teacher's questions may decide that silence or "I don't know" responses are safer than risking failure. Having chosen this route, students' minds are free to wander, and little further learning can take place. Over time, all these decisions become part of children's beliefs about being a student.

Activities that foster cooperative involvement and joint problem solving are much better alternatives (Ames, 1992; Turner & Paris, 1995). Students in cooperative situations, are likely to view problems as challenges for group consideration instead of indications of their own inability. In addition, cooperation leads to better learning (Spurlin, Dansereau, Larson, & Brooks, 1984). Instruction based on active, cooperative participation among groups of students can support the development of a community of learners within classrooms.

What is a community of learners? Dictionaries tell us that *communities* are unified bodies of individuals with common interests who share ownership and jointly participate in community activities. Families are communities, as are groups of friends. Classrooms can be communities, too, if the instructional framework invites learners to participate actively, share responsibility, explore issues of common interest, and interact cooperatively.

The ownership aspect of communities is also important. Community members can ordinarily make some decisions about if and how to become involved in community activities. Classroom communities should also feature choice. For example, students should frequently choose what to read, how to respond to their reading, and whether they wish to work alone or with others. Of course, individual community members don't make all the decisions about involvement; so in classroom communities the teacher has choices, too. In fact, balance between teacher choice and student choice is one feature of a supportive instructional framework. In classrooms, learning is most assuredly a social activity. To foster the development of literacy learning communities, we must promote authentic, cooperative interactions among students. We must expect active involvement and invite student choice.

How Much Time on What Kind of Task?

Time is another important factor to consider in establishing a framework for instruction. Deb's young students showed her the value of taking time to teach for conceptual change. Time available for reading is equally important. For example, in the mid-1980s, Anderson, Hiebert, Scott, and Wilkinson (1985) reported that students in basal-dominated classrooms spent up to 70% of their reading instruction time completing worksheets. That does not leave much time for reading, reflecting, discussing—all the things we know lead to reading growth. Indeed, much research (e.g., Allington, 2002; NAEP, 2000; Postlethwaite & Ross, 1992; Rupley, Wise, & Logan, 1986) indicates that time spent reading correlates highly with reading achievement. This certainly makes sense. To grow as readers, students need opportunities to read, and they need to be accountable for how they use this time. So in planning instruction, teachers must carefully consider how much time to make available for reading and how students will account for their reading time.

The focus of attention, especially during reading instruction, is another issue related to time. One careful study of two 30-minute reading lessons revealed that students in a high-ability group spent three times as much time on task (that is, reading and discussing what they'd read) as students in a low-ability group (McDermott, 1978). Allington's (1977, 1984) research found a similar dearth of contextual reading for less able readers. These substantial differences must affect reading growth.

Other studies have shown that teachers' discussions with better readers tend to focus on text meaning, but discussions with poorer readers tend to focus on decoding (Allington, 1978, 1980; McDermott, 1978). As a consequence, better readers spend more time reading, thinking about their reading, and sharing their thoughts with others. In contrast, less able readers focus on the mechanics of reading while paying little attention to what the reading means or how they might respond to it. And students are aware of these differences. In their study of intermediate-grade students' perceptions about "good readers," Henk and Melnick (1998) note, "Children demonstrate a remarkable sensitivity not only to subtle variations in the way they and others are called upon, but also to the amount of time individuals are allowed for responding to questions or sharing their ideas" (p. 72).

Thus, instructional environments can differ, even for students in the same classroom, with regard to how time is spent. Like others (for example, Good, 1987), we believe that these differences are cause for concern. Too often, struggling readers participate in lessons that emphasize mindless decoding, rote drill, and meaningless practice. Given our knowledge of the reading process and ways to support reading growth, we believe that this sort of instruction does more harm than good. In fact, it can lead to what Keith Stanovich (1986) calls the "Matthew Effect," a sort of rich-get-richer and poor-get-poorer situation in which the environment supports continued growth for good readers but actually thwarts growth for those who find reading difficult. Instead, instructional frameworks for children who experience difficulty in reading should feature an abundance of time to read and write for meaningful, interesting, student-selected purposes.

Establishing Instructional Routines

Part of the solution to the problems we have identified lies in instructional planning—specifically, the creation of predictable routines that together constitute daily opportunities for reading and learning to read. *Routines* are blocks of time during which a predictable set of activities regularly occur. Routines allow teachers to maximize the amount of time spent on instruction and minimize time spent on giving directions, explaining procedures, and maintaining order. To some, the word *routine* connotes boredom. That is not so in student-centered, constructivist classrooms. The routines we describe in this section—read-aloud, independent reading, choice time, and mini-lessons— are anything but dull.

Read-Aloud

Read-aloud should be an instructional routine in all classrooms, including those for struggling readers. The benefits are many. Listening to an interesting text read well is a pleasure for us all. In fact, both younger and older students report that teacher read-aloud motivates them to read (Ivey & Broaddus, 2001; Palmer, Codling, & Gambrell, 1994). In addition, the literature read to them helps students encounter new ideas, words, and concepts as well as interesting characters, situations, and places. Another advantage of reading aloud, especially for struggling readers, is that it familiarizes students with the style and form of written language. It also provides students with a model of what fluent reading should sound like. Often poor readers have only other poor readers for models of expressive oral reading. Finally, a special time for daily read-alouds powerfully demonstrates that reading is a worthwhile activity, important enough to include in the busy instructional schedule.

Virtually any interesting material can be read aloud—fiction or nonfiction, picture books or chapter books, poetry, articles, letters, and so on. And read-alouds need not be restricted to story time. Mary Beth frequently reads aloud to her students with learning disabilities. "We have story time every day," she says. "But I also read to students during science and social studies, sometimes just a paragraph or two and sometimes an entire selection. Not just nonfiction either; I look for poetry and fiction related to the concepts that we're working on. Sometimes the kids bring things in. Reading aloud in the content areas is a great way to foster additional learning and to give students access to information that they couldn't read independently."

Instructional routines certainly need not be static or prescriptive. In fact a good routine offers some flexibility in implementation. Mary Beth's friend and colleague Kelly has used read-aloud for years, but last year she decided to expand on it occasionally. On Fridays when she reads to her students she asks them to enjoy the story but also to listen for interesting or unusual words or phrases. After the reading, the students talk about these words. Kelly makes sure she also adds a few words from the story and expands on any words the children may not know well or whose meaning is not totally clear.

During the weekend she thinks about how these words can be used in word sorts, games, and other instructional activities that focus on decoding and understanding the words. Then, on Monday, students put the words on cards. Throughout the week, students spend a few minutes each day practicing, sorting, or otherwise playing with the words. On Friday the routine begins anew.

"I only use this different approach to read-aloud on Fridays," Kelly says. "By October students know what to expect. But what's so great about this routine is that the students get wonderful opportunities to study words that come from stories they have experienced. Since they choose the words, they feel a sense of ownership over them. I know that this activity has increased their sensitivity and understanding of how words work. When I see them using the words in their own writing and speech, I know they are developing an appreciation for words."

Kelly's expansion of the read-aloud routine works well for her class. Read-aloud and other instructional routines permit an almost limitless number of expansions.

Time for Independent Reading

Just as every day includes time devoted to the teacher reading aloud, so, too, should students have daily opportunities to read material of their own choice for their own purposes. To develop feelings of comfort and success as readers, students need consistent opportunities to behave as readers—to read. Toward this end, we recommend self-selected *independent reading* time as another regular instructional routine. These periods of time when everyone, often including the teacher, reads, are known as Sustained Silent Reading (SSR), Drop Everything And Read (DEAR), Hooked On Books (HOB), or Super, Quiet, Uninterrupted, Independent Reading Time (SQUIRT).

Recreational reading—in and out of school—relates to reading achievement: The more we read, the better we read. Abundant recreational reading has been linked to higher achievement test scores, vocabulary growth, and more sophisticated writing styles (for example, see Block & Mangieri, 2002). Moreover, as little as 15 extra minutes of reading appears to make a difference, especially for struggling readers (Taylor, Frye, & Maruyama, 1990). In describing their "Hooked on Books" buddy-reading program, teachers Meryl Menon and John Mirabito (1999) report that children's book selection strategies became more sophisticated: "Our students think about what makes any book worth reading, and they comment orally and in writing about characters, events, and the author's writing style. Parents tell us children read more at home. . . . [N]onreaders have become readers" (p. 194). Thus, both researchers and classroom teachers have documented the benefits of independent reading time.

Harry introduces independent reading time to his first graders on the very first day of school. Initially, children read for only 2 or 3 minutes, but by the end of the year, they read for 20 to 30 minutes each day. He begins with such a brief time period because he wants the students to be successful: "Everyone can hang in for a couple of minutes. After a week or so, I gradually increase the time." Two rules govern independent reading time in Harry's classroom: Children must be quiet and may not leave their seats. Children's desks are arranged in clusters, and Harry puts an extra stack of books on each cluster of desks so that children can easily select other books if they need or want them. Harry often reads during this time as well. "My reading sends the message to the kids that 'reading is so important that I want to do it with you.'"

Independent reading time always concludes with a brief sharing session so that children can read interesting parts of their books aloud, talk about what they have read, and offer evidence that they spent their reading time well. (See Figure 2.1 for other quick response activities.) Harry also tells his students about what he's reading—what he likes, what difficulties he has encountered, and so forth. "I consider myself a model for the children," Harry says. "Just reading is an important part of this, and so is responding to what I am reading. But sharing tough spots is equally important, I think. The kids need to learn that everyone—even adults—has trouble with reading from time to time."

Of course, Harry's students can choose to read and choose what to read at other times during each school day, too. "But this is a time when we all have our noses in books at the same time," Harry says. "We enjoy it, the kids get good practice, and I think it goes a long way toward helping children develop the 'reading habit.' In fact, I really know they're hooked when they start groaning about having to stop reading. That's music to my ears!"

- Use sticky notes to mark interesting passages, places where the author describes some aspect of instructional interest (characters, setting).
- Ask several students to "say one thing" or "say something I learned" about their books.
- Ask students to write interesting words on sticky notes. Make a chart for the classroom called "Interesting Words We Read Today."
- Play "Around the Room": Announce some aspect of stories (time, location, protagonist, etc.) and have students tell just this about their books.
- Use large sticky notes to review books from the classroom library. Keep these notes inside book front covers so others can refer to them.
- Ask students to rate their books with a number of "stars" by raising their hands. (Or keep large sheets of chart paper posted in the classroom for this purpose.) Ask them to write a rationale for this rating in their reading journals.
- Create bookmarks for students to use: "This is the problem in the story" or "This is the funniest part" or "This is my favorite character." Students make notes on the bookmarks as they read.
- Ask students to e-mail their pen pals (or parents) about their books.
- Select four students' names. Each goes to a corner of the classroom to talk a bit about his or her book, read a short selection, do a "commercial" for the book, and so on. Other students divide among the four.
- Ask students to write in their reading journals: "What happened in my book today" or "What's going to happen next" or "My favorite character is . . . ," or other general prompts.

Figure 2.1
Quick Response Activities

Some teachers wonder if independent reading time will be frustrating for struggling readers. After all, they are asked to sustain an activity that has proved troublesome for them in the past. We have found just the opposite: Even the most reluctant readers eventually find success. They begin trying to read because they know that reading is their task at hand. As they experience success, their interest in reading grows, as does their confidence in themselves as readers. In other words, success breeds success. Teachers can support this cycle of success by beginning with short time periods, ensuring a plentiful supply of interesting reading materials at a variety of difficulty levels, and clearly communicating that everyone reads during independent reading time.

Choice Time

A third block of daily time should be devoted to choice, a time when students can make their own decisions about what they wish to do as readers or writers.

During *choice time,* students can do whatever they want as long as their activity relates somehow to reading or writing, so many different literacy activities may occur simultaneously.

Choice time is fun to observe in classrooms because students are so productively busy with such a variety of tasks. Some read or write alone, and others read or write together. Some perform or share their work, and others prepare to do so. "If you don't look carefully, choice time can appear chaotic," says Brenda, a fifth-grade teacher. "And I suppose, in a way, it is. But all you have to do is talk to the kids to see that they are meaningfully engaged and interested. Boy! Talk about time on task!"

Some teachers and students establish informal rules for choice time. For example, they might decide to reserve certain portions of the classroom for children who need silence or establish a procedure for seeking the teacher's assistance. (Brenda's students list their names on the chalkboard, and she works down the list in order.) Other teachers prefer less initial regulation, opting to see if problems arise and inviting students to develop solutions if they do.

Because students are involved in a variety of activities during choice time, the teacher's role varies, too. Bobbi Fisher (1991), a kindergarten teacher, describes her role during choice time:

> I have six primary functions during choice time: (1) to set up the environment, (2) to facilitate the routine, (3) to teach, (4) to act as audience, (5) to kid watch, and (6) to enjoy the children. . . . [M]ost of the children are practicing independently or with peers, and I work with individuals and small groups of students . . . , although sometimes my role is to be an audience while children are performing or sharing their work. During part of each day I watch children and conduct formal or informal assessments, and occasionally I [simply enjoy myself] as a member of the classroom community. (p. 70)

Choice and response are critical features of all three routines we have discussed. During read-aloud and independent reading, students exercise choice over reading materials; during choice time, they also select their own activities. Response, encouraged in all three routines, helps students comprehend and elaborate on what they have read in personally meaningful ways. Moreover, students learn to behave as readers by exercising choice, responding to what they have read, and finding success as readers.

Mini-Lessons

Many teachers develop other routines, such as time for whole-group instruction or for using the strategies and techniques that we describe throughout this book. *Mini-lessons* about specific topics are useful as well. A mini-lesson is a short, focused instructional session that can introduce a new strategy or help students solve a problem they have encountered recently in their reading.

[handwritten margin note: I think it's important that teachers engage in this time & not use it to do their work or sit on their computers (wrong message)]

mini lesson w/ whole
starts or one specific
focuses on discussion of
ends w/ strategy
usefulness

Topics for mini-lessons often come from what learners need. The lessons themselves typically begin with the whole, focus on some part, and end with a discussion of the usefulness of the new strategy or information. A great thing about mini-lessons is that they can fit naturally within other instructional routines. Suppose, for example, that the teacher makes a significant mistake during read-aloud. This would be a good time to teach a mini-lesson about when and how to employ the strategy of rereading.

Betty makes frequent use of mini-lessons in her Title I instruction. Not long ago, for example, her upper-grade students were conducting library inquiry projects. "I noticed lots of kids just flipping through the pages," Betty says. "At first I thought they were just wasting time, but then I realized that they didn't know how to use tables of contents or indexes." So Betty taught a mini-lesson. She began with the whole—in this case, a brief discussion of students' frustrations about their inability to use the reference books. She then told students about tables of contents and indexes and demonstrated their usefulness by using overhead transparencies taken from a book. Next, pairs of students practiced using tables of contents and indexes in books from the school library. Betty concluded the lesson by asking students how knowledge of tables of contents and indexes might help them. "The whole lesson took no more than 10 minutes," Betty says, "but the students really learned, probably because the topic was immediately useful to them."

Amy teaches strategies through mini-lessons as well. Her routine involves a mini-lesson on Monday followed by the creation of a "Strategy of the Week" poster to hang outside the classroom door. During independent reading time each Tuesday through Friday, children use sticky notes to keep track of times when they use the strategy that Amy has taught—visualizing, inferring, repairing comprehension, and so forth. Then on Fridays, the class assembles all the notes, looks for patterns among them, and prepares the "Strategy of the Week" poster. "Children love sticky notes," she says, "so I use them to help children think about strategies and apply them to their reading."

Planning instruction in terms of routines helps teachers focus on what's important and ensures that classroom time will be well spent. Routines also help students, a predictable instructional environment fosters independence. Students can go about the business of reading and writing rather than always waiting for the teacher's directions.

Creating a Literate Environment

Creating a literate environment involves everything that we have addressed thus far in this chapter. Two other aspects of the physical environment can also affect opportunity to learn: room arrangements and availability of materials. Support, interest, variety, and choice are important concepts to remember when making decisions about either aspect, because environments that reflect these concepts both encourage and facilitate literacy learning.

Room Arrangements

Think of effective room arrangements as "user friendly." Rooms should be organized so that students can read and write independently and efficiently. This means easy student access to reading and writing materials and well-defined areas for certain types of activities, such as a classroom library area or a corner where resources and editing supplies are available. Display areas, such as bulletin boards, celebrate children's work and promote books and reading. Even promotional materials should be student designed and made.

Everything about the room arrangement should foster the notion of student ownership of the classroom and their reading. Some of the most exciting and lively rooms we have visited, places in which children engage in real learning, have students' work displayed on tables, walls, and ceilings in the classroom; in the hallway; outside the principal's office; and, in some cases, outside the school itself. What a message this sends to children, parents, and the community about what goes on in school!

Although the specifics of room arrangement may depend on students' ages and curricular issues, the overall organization should promote group inquiry, encourage independence and responsibility, and cultivate student interest. Many classrooms feature reading centers and writing centers as special places. Reading centers have comfortable places to sit, nooks and crannies for curling up with a good book, bookshelves and book displays, and so on. It's amazing what a rug, a few pillows, and a rocking chair can do.

Writing centers have all the materials students need for writing organized for ready access. Classroom computers and writers' reference books are also typically located in writing centers. Other areas of the classroom, such as areas for read-alouds or sharing, may support both reading and writing as well as instruction in other curricular areas.

We believe every classroom should have some form of *word wall*. A word wall is simply a bulletin board, sheet of chart paper, or other portion of a classroom wall dedicated to words the class is studying. Word walls can be composed of high-frequency words, words related to phonics generalizations or word families (e.g., *hat, cat, sat*), content words (e.g., words related to geometric shapes), or interesting words that students select from their reading. Words on word walls are practiced and discussed regularly. Word walls remind students that words are important, that word study can be fun and fascinating, and that the study of words is the work that happens in classrooms. (Additionally, word walls solve for teachers that age-old problem—what do I do with this bulletin board?)

Classroom setups are important because they, too, can support or hinder students' learning. Like so many other decisions we make as teachers, room arrangements reveal what we believe about how children learn and the best way to support their learning. Bolted-down desks in straight rows reveal one set of beliefs; classrooms arranged as a variety of interest centers where students' interests and work are taken seriously and celebrated reveal another.

Materials should be
conveniently available so that
students have easy access to
what they need.

Materials

A literate classroom environment offers a wide range of authentic materials
for reading and writing. Materials should be conveniently available to allow
student readers and writers easy access to what they need.

Reading materials for beginners of any age should support and encourage them in their quest for meaning. Predictable materials are especially
effective because it is easy to determine what will come next, both what the
author is going to say and how it will be said. Students' own dictations are
predictable because dictations contain familiar language and students already
know the content. Pattern literature is predictable for a variety of reasons,
including repetition, use of familiar concepts, match between illustrations and
text, and use of rhythm or rhyme. (A starter list of pattern literature is provided in Appendix C.) Both types of materials provide a familiar, dependable
context for beginning readers.

Likewise, materials for developing readers should also be supportive
and encouraging. Because reading interests and tastes differ, students need
access to a variety of topics, genres, and formats. And because we read for
many purposes, reference books, lists, written directions, menus, catalogs,
and the like are legitimate materials for the classroom. (See chapter 3 for
more information about classroom materials, including the setup and use of
classroom libraries.)

Harste (1989) says that effective literacy learning environments are
"littered with print." This is a useful visual image for thinking about both room
arrangements and availability of materials. Although organization is apparent,

classrooms are arranged and stocked with materials so that students naturally read and write in the process of completing tasks.

What Do Teachers Do?

The teacher has an essential role to play in developing and maintaining an effective instructional framework. This role is shaped by beliefs and attitudes as well as instructional skill. Teachers must (a) expect all their students to learn, (b) see the value of everything that students bring into the classroom, (c) believe that it's more important to focus on what students can do rather than on what they can't do, and (d) believe that learning is easiest when students have choices and their instructional opportunities are based on interest and relevance.

Moreover, teachers are models of literate behavior. Through what they do as well as what they say, teachers show students what it means to be a reader, how readers handle problems, what value reading can have in a person's life, and so on. This teacher-as-model role is critical to the development and maintenance of an effective instructional environment.

Other aspects of the instructional environment are equally important. Teachers who recognize the power of talk as a vehicle for learning invite collaboration and encourage children to share with one another and to talk through problems to be solved. In constructivist literacy classrooms, students focus on creating, comprehending, and communicating meaning. The teacher designs instructional activities and supports children's efforts at learning.

Teachers' attitudes toward mistakes are also important. Effective teachers look for what's right about students' work. They encourage students to take risks, try new ideas, learn new skills, and expand their learning horizons. Taking these risks will lead to student errors, but good teachers know that mistakes are an inevitable part of the learning process, part of the human condition. They communicate this attitude to their students through what they say and do.

Jackie taught developmental readers in college. Her reflections about that experience summarize key aspects of the instructional environment and the teacher's role:

> I think of my developmental reading students who were "conditionally admitted" because they weren't successful enough in their bottom-up, form-before-content schooling. Many blossomed in the nonthreatening environment I tried to offer. All were readers and writers, but more important, all were thinkers, and they repeatedly demonstrated this when invited to do so.
>
> I saw Brian again today. He was driving a campus bus and called to me as I walked across the parking lot. He's confident, majoring in English, and plans to be a secondary teacher. He's a junior, I think, but as a first-semester freshman when he read my comments about his fine

writing, he said, "No one ever said that to me before." How could his teachers of 12-plus years not see him as a writer? I think it's because they saw him as "at risk" rather than inviting him to take risks.

Jackie's comments concern a college-age student, whereas Betsy's, mentioned in the introduction to this chapter, depict first graders. Despite the significant differences in their students' ages, the two teachers share fundamental assumptions about literacy teaching and learning. More important, they believe that their students can learn, and they have developed instructional frameworks based on their assumptions and reflective of their beliefs.

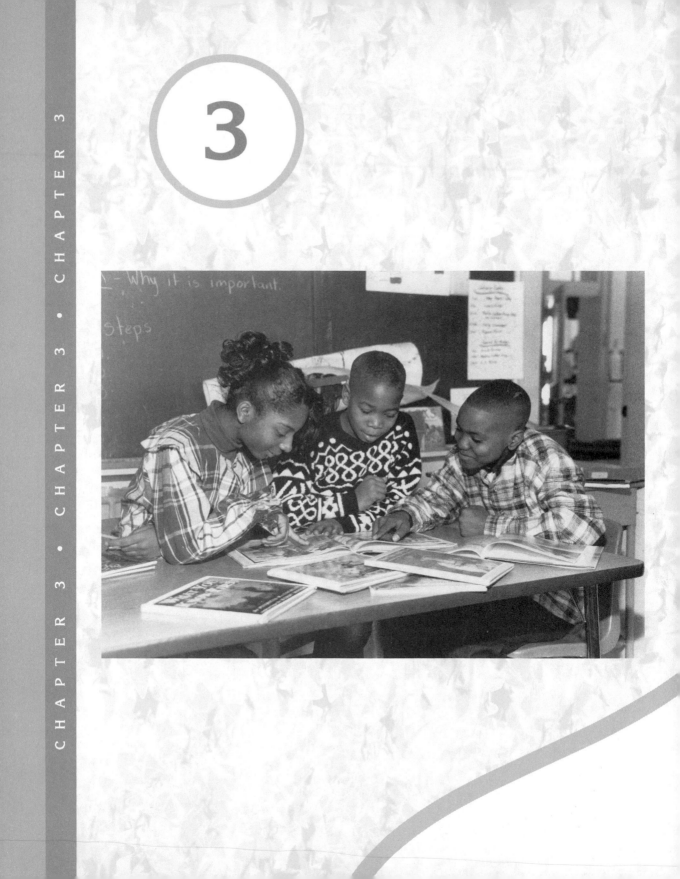

Developing Positive Attitudes About and Ambience for Reading

Children are born with the desire to learn. They are curious—interested in objects, people, and events in the world around them. Parents and others encourage this curiosity and, in general, support children's learning. Consequently, almost all children enter school wanting to learn, which includes learning to read, and expecting to do so successfully. Most *are* successful.

When children repeatedly experience difficulty learning to read (or any other kind of learning), however, they may become frustrated or tired of failing. They may lose their enthusiasm for reading. Often their desire or motivation to read is stifled. These negative attitudes can hamper both learning and the desire to learn.

"I learned about the importance of attitudes the hard way," said Barb, who recently left her third-grade classroom to teach a self-contained group of intermediate- grade students with learning disabilities. "I knew the curriculum, and I had studied ways to accommodate students' learning needs. I thought I was all set. The first few days of school were all right, but something was nagging at me. A week or two into the year, it struck me like a bolt of lightning: I was surrounded by kids who *absolutely hated* reading! As I think back on it now, I guess I should have expected that. But it really took me by surprise. I wasn't prepared for the intensity of their feelings. After all, they're just kids."

Instructional planning for students who find reading difficult must include systematic attention to promoting and maintaining positive attitudes toward reading. In this chapter, we present some principles for developing a literacy learning environment in which readers will succeed and want to read. First, however, we provide an overview of several issues related to attitudes and motivation, from both the perspective of young motivated readers and the perspective of psychologists who study human motivation. Then we suggest some ways to discover students' attitudes and interests in reading.

Throughout the chapter we refer to results of a five-year, federally funded research program, which included dozens of separate studies all conducted by scholars associated with the National Reading Research Center or NRRC (e.g., Baker, Afflerbach, & Reinking, 1996; Baumann & Duffy, 1997; Gambrell, 1996). This research was guided by the "*engagement perspective,* which specifies the goal of reading instruction as developing motivated and strategic readers who use literacy for pleasure and learning" (Baumann & Duffy, 1997, p. 5). Attitudes and motivation are critical, especially for children who struggle as readers. Moreover, NRRC researchers established a synergy between motivation and ability—the two are mutually reinforcing phenomena. The more motivated one is to read, the more strategic one becomes in reading. And greater strategy use results in greater satisfaction and motivation for reading.

Motivation to Read: A View from Children

What motivates children to read? In this section, we report the results of three large-scale research studies designed to help teachers find answers to this important question.

Palmer, Codling, and Gambrell (1994) used questionnaires and interviews to explore the reading preferences, habits, and behaviors of 330 third- and fifth-grade students. Their NRRC-sponsored research documented four powerful influences on children's motivation to read:

- *Prior experiences with books.* Children at both grade levels mentioned this category most often. Children reported reading books that their teachers or parents had previously read aloud to them or books based on television programs or movies they had seen. They also frequently mentioned rereading favorite books and reading series books, which may appeal because "the characters, setting, and general story structure remain consistent, but the plot provides new and challenging information" (p. 177).

- *Social interactions with books.* Children placed high priority on reading books that they had heard about from friends, parents, or teachers.

- *Book access.* Easy availability of books, both in the classroom and at home, was important. Most children reported selecting books to read from their classroom libraries, which underscores the importance of the quantity and quality of books available in the classroom.

- *Book choice.* Children were most motivated when they read books they had selected themselves. Often these were books that someone else had recommended, which suggests that choice and social interaction may be related in an important way.

These categories of responses point the way to classroom adaptations that can help struggling readers develop and maintain positive attitudes toward reading. Children need easy access to books and the freedom to choose their own reading material. Moreover, both teacher read-alouds (see chapter 2) and consistent opportunities to talk about books with others (see chapter 8) appear critical in developing children's motivations to read. We agree with the researchers that "teachers are in a position to have a positive influence on children's motivation to read through careful planning with respect to the classroom literacy environment" (Palmer et al., 1994, p. 178).

Ivey and Broaddus (2001) explored similar issues in a study of more than 1,700 sixth-grade students' motivations for reading. When asked about the activities they enjoyed most in their language arts classes, students indicated preference for free reading and reading in social contexts, including opportunities to discuss reading with peers and teacher read-alouds, above all other activities. Choice was also important to students; in fact, they complained about assigned reading and "pointed to difficulties in understanding as the main reason for not liking these texts despite the fact that so much time was spent on activities to help them understand" (p. 368). Students suggested that the classroom literacy environment would benefit from more nonfiction, which they reported reading regularly outside of school.

Sweet and Guthrie (1996), who also explored children's reasons, goals, and motivations for reading, believe that children's motivations are "multidimensional and diverse" and that teachers must learn to recognize the characteristics of these motivations to foster long-term literacy growth. Children in Sweet and Guthrie's NRRC-sponsored research reported both intrinsic and extrinsic motivations. *Intrinsic motivations,* which originate in personal interests and private experiences, include *involvement,* or the phenomenon of "getting lost in a book"; *curiosity,* reading to satisfy personal questions or hypotheses; *social interaction,* which is similar to the Palmer et al. (1994) finding; and *challenge,* such as the challenge involved in solving a mystery. Intrinsic motivations have both short- and long-term value. In classrooms, children need strong intrinsic motivations to learn complex strategies, such as summarizing, and to benefit completely from integrated, student-centered instruction. The long-term benefit of intrinsic motivation is that children develop lifelong, voluntary reading habits.

Children in the Sweet and Guthrie study also reported reading for *extrinsic reasons*—that is, for reasons that originate outside themselves, such as with their teachers or parents. Examples of these motivations include *compliance* ("because the teacher said to"), *recognition* ("to get as many points as I can"), *competition,* and *work avoidance* ("I am writing this story so I won't have to read my book"). Sweet and Guthrie believe that extrinsic motivations are powerful because they cause immediate attention and effort but are limited because motivation ceases when the particular task ends. Unlike intrinsic motivations, extrinsic motivations do not regenerate themselves.

We, of course, want students to develop and maintain intrinsic motivations for reading. Unfortunately, children who find reading difficult are not typically intrinsically motivated readers. Understanding motivation from a psychological perspective can provide helpful information in solving this problem.

What Affects Motivation?

Psychologists who study people's motivations to achieve recognize two crucial variables. The first is whether or not we expect success. We are more willing to engage in activities if we expect that we will do well. The second critical variable is the value we place on succeeding at the activity. If we care about doing well, we try harder. Both expectations and value affect persistence with any task, including the task of learning to read (Wigfield & Asher, 1984). Our challenge is to create an instructional environment in which students are continually successful so that they learn to expect success, and in which students come to value reading because it meets their needs and satisfies their interests.

Attribution theory attempts to explain how people think about why they succeed or fail at a task. Most of us think we succeed or fail for one of three reasons: *ability* ("I am/am not able to do this"), *effort* ("I tried/did not try to do this"), or *luck* ("My success/failure had nothing to do with me"). Research comparing ideas about attribution between students with high and low motivation has found differences that have instructional implications. Highly motivated students tend to believe that they succeed through ability and fail through lack of effort. Poorly motivated students, on the other hand, tend to attribute their success to luck but their failure to lack of ability (Weiner, 1979).

Attitudes affect motivation, and motivation affects our thinking about why we succeed or fail. Moreover, those who repeatedly fail may begin to believe that they are incapable of success. This syndrome is often called *learned helplessness* because the feeling of helplessness is learned through repeated negative experiences. People with an attitude of learned helplessness frequently quit trying; they don't see any point in trying because they are convinced that they will fail.

Fortunately, learned helplessness and other negative attitudes can be unlearned; that is, students who believe that they cannot learn to read successfully can begin to believe in themselves as readers. An environment in which students come to expect success and in which they value reading can help them overcome feelings of learned helplessness. To develop such an environment, we must first learn about our students' attitudes and interests in reading.

Finding Out About Attitudes and Interests

Children with reading difficulties often associate reading with failure, and this often leads to negative attitudes toward reading. Some may view reading as a chore, while others view it as a waste of time. Many may choose not to read

[handwritten marginal note: Poorly motivated students believe their successes are gain through luck not ability or their neart felt attempts]

to avoid frustration or failure. But this grim portrait can be altered—as this book will describe. Finding out about children's attitudes and interests is an important first step in this process.

The best ways to find out about attitudes and interests are to observe children's behaviors in the classroom and ask students to share their ideas in conversation or writing. Questionnaires or surveys can also assist (for example, Henk & Melnick, 1995; McKenna & Kear, 1990). Although surveys are efficient when dealing with groups of children, we cannot rely solely on their results. Children often see through to the purposes behind the questions and may respond with "right" answers rather than those that reflect their true feelings. Observations permit us to check survey responses against actual behavior, and interviews allow us to extend or clarify children's responses (Rhodes & Shanklin, 1993).

Careful observation may be the most effective way to learn about students' attitudes and interests. As we suggest in chapter 13, observations should be conducted objectively, over time, and in a variety of situations. Observation is easier when the teacher focuses on key questions. With regard to attitudes and interests, it is important to focus on both independent and organized reading in the classroom.

These questions about independent reading might provide focus for classroom observation:

How does the child react to independent reading?

Does she choose to read?

Does he appear to enjoy reading?

Does she appear to concentrate?

Does he use books as resources?

What types of reading material does she select?

Observation can also aim at discovering attitudes toward reading instruction, which may be different from attitudes toward independent reading. This sort of observation can be framed by questions like these (Padak, 1987):

Does the child participate willingly?

Does she stay actively involved and seem able to concentrate?

Does he interact freely with teacher and peers?

How does she react when asked to read orally? Silently?

See chapter 13 for further information about observation, including suggestions for recording information.

Informal discussion can be another way to learn about children's attitudes and interests. For discussion to yield useful information, however, children must feel comfortable sharing their thoughts honestly. If not, discussions can suffer

We can learn about interests by talking with children about hobbies, interests, and favorite books and authors.

the same "right answer" syndrome that often plagues written surveys or scales. Discussion can also confirm hypotheses generated through observation. More-over, we can learn about interests by talking informally with children about hobbies, leisure-time interests, favorite books or authors, and so forth.

Teacher-made surveys or checklists are yet another way to investigate students' attitudes and interests. To gather information about students' atti-tudes toward independent reading, for example, we might ask

Do you like to read at home? Why or why not?

Do you like to read at school? Why or why not?

Do you like to go to the library? Why or why not?

Survey questions can also yield information about students' attitudes toward reading instruction:

What's your favorite thing to do during reading instruction? Why?

If you could change one thing about our reading class, what would you change? Why?

Checklists and surveys are efficient ways to gather initial information about children's reading interests. A simple approach is to prepare a list of broad topics, such as animals, real people, mysteries, sports, make-believe, or humor. Then ask children to check topics of interest or rank the topics by preference. We can also examine lists of books that children have read to draw some conclusions about their reading interests. Figure 3.1 provides additional questions that teachers frequently use to explore children's interests in reading, what they enjoy reading, and their interest in reading and writing as activities.

Barb, whom we introduced at the beginning of this chapter, uses all these tools to find out about her students' attitudes and interests. "I usually give kids a couple of written surveys at the beginning of the year," she says. "It's a good way to start getting to know them and their interests, and I pick up a few clues about their attitudes, too, which are usually pretty negative." Next, Barb observes as children begin adjusting to her classroom. "I look for

---

Reading Interests

1. What sorts of books do you like to hear others read?
2. What's your favorite school subject?
3. If someone were going to buy a book for you, what would you want it to be about?
4. What kinds of stories do you like to write?
5. What kinds of magazines do you like to read?
6. What are your all-time favorite books?
7. Who are your favorite authors?
8. What section do you head for first in the library or a bookstore?

Interest in Reading

1. If you had a free day from school, what would you do?
2. Do your parents (or someone else at home) read to you? How often? Do you like this?
3. Do you read to your parents or someone else at home? How often? Do you like this?
4. Do you like to go to the library? How often do you go there? Do you usually find some books to take home?
5. Do you like reading by yourself? Do you like reading with others?
6. Where do you like to read at home? Is there a time of day when you like to read? How long do you usually read when you read at home? How often do you read at home?
7. What's the best way to become a better reader?

Figure 3.1

Reading Interests and Interest in Reading

the good times—instances where children are actively involved as readers and seem happy to be here. I use these to plan instruction. That is, after I have figured out what children enjoy, I try to plan more and more sessions like that." Barb saves conversations about attitudes and interests until she and the children know each other better. "It takes a while for the kids to trust me, and I know that they won't share the real in-depth stuff until then, especially if it's negative."

Helping her students develop and maintain positive attitudes is important to Barb. She also wants to know about their reading interests to better plan instruction, suggest books, and help children form interest groups for inquiry. She believes that although written surveys can provide some understanding of her students, observing and talking with them provides an even more complete and accurate view. Each year, Barb uses what she knows about attitudes, motivation, and interests and what she learns about her students to develop a classroom environment in which her students can learn to expect success and value reading.

Learning to Expect Success

Most of Barb's students, like others who find reading difficult, expect *not* to succeed as readers. They have developed these expectations based on previous reading experiences in school. Unfortunately, such expectations usually take time to change; this is especially true for older students who have experienced longer term feelings of failure. The good news is that students can and do change their expectations for success. Classroom environments in which this sort of change occurs share some common characteristics.

Exemplary Classrooms

Mike Rose (1995) spent five years searching for exemplary classrooms (preschool through high school) throughout the United States. He spent time with teachers and students in those classrooms identifying what the classrooms had in common. Rose summarizes these critical instructional characteristics eloquently:

> These classrooms, then, were places of expectation and responsibility. Teachers took students seriously as intellectual and social beings. Young people had to work hard, think things through, come to terms with each other—and there were times when such effort took a student to his or her limits. (p. 415)

Rose (1995) found four similarities among these diverse classrooms.

- ■ Students felt safe, both physically and psychologically. They knew their ideas were valued, that they wouldn't be insulted, that they could "push beyond what you can comfortably do at present" (p. 413).

■ Teachers demonstrated respect for students, and students demonstrated respect for the teacher and each other. This attitude of respect fostered feelings of psychological safety.

■ Authority and leadership were distributed in the classrooms. Students and the teacher shared responsibility for leading classroom activities. When appropriate, students had opportunities to be "experts." In other words, classrooms were characterized by community and cooperation (see chapter 2).

■ Students believed that classroom learning was vital. That is, they saw the importance of what they did as learners and believed that instruction was in their best interest.

We can use these four characteristics to develop a literacy learning environment in which students learn to expect success as readers. For example, consider the issue of psychological safety. Most of us feel safe psychologically if we believe that others are interested in our ideas—that we will not be ridiculed or put down based on what we say. If others are interested, we are more likely to share our ideas and share them more successfully.

This cycle can help students learn to expect success: Others' interest leads students to try, which leads to success. Over time, the accumulation of these successful experiences can alter expectations about the likelihood of future success. In other words, providing a psychologically safe learning environment can reverse the thinking that initially led students to expect failure.

Vital classrooms begin with vital teachers. Students will feel good about what they do when the teacher is excited and enthusiastic about their abilities and the topics studied. Such an enthusiastic teacher can transmit a love of learning to students as well as help them learn to believe that they can be successful. In contrast, a teacher will hardly excite someone else about an idea or activity when his language and actions demonstrate no real interest.

We have heard that the great anthropologist Margaret Mead was asked why children in some cultures find certain things easy to learn while those in other cultures find the same things difficult. Mead responded that children find it easy to learn those things valued by important adults in their lives and cultures. Teachers (and parents) need to communicate to children that reading is important and useful and that they expect children to learn to read successfully. Similarly, attention to the other features in Rose's exemplary classrooms, when applied to literacy learning environments, can help students learn to expect success as readers.

Conditions of Language Learning

Like Mike Rose, Brian Cambourne has attempted to understand "exemplary learning" and provide instructional suggestions based on his insights. Cambourne has studied the environmental factors and conditions that support children as they learn to speak their native languages. The findings of this research, conducted over 20 years, offer another way to think about creating classroom environments in which students learn to expect success as readers. Cambourne (1995) has identified eight conditions always present when language is learned. He believes that these conditions co-occur and are synergistic—that is, each affects and is affected by the others. The following paragraphs briefly describe each condition.

Immersion.   *Immersion* refers to being immersed in or engulfed by what is to be learned. For example, young children are typically surrounded by conversation and other forms of oral language. In terms of effective environments for literacy learning, immersion refers to the quality, quantity, and availability of reading (and writing) materials. As we noted in chapter 2, the classroom should be filled with interesting and attractive reading materials. Students should have ample opportunity to browse through materials and read them.

Although reading materials are usually dispersed throughout the classroom, the classroom library should house the majority. Every classroom should have a library stocked with a variety of books, at least 10 per child. To the extent possible, children should be involved in book selection for the classroom library; they should also be responsible for organizing and maintaining the library. (See Appendixes A–E for books you might include in a classroom library.) Children in the Palmer et al. (1994) study overwhelmingly reported selecting "most enjoyable" books from their classroom libraries. This finding points to both the quality of the classroom library and children's access to books as significant factors in motivating children to read. Dina Feitelson also experimented with factors related to book access and children's "ownership" of classroom libraries (Shimron, 1994). Both factors led to increased engagement with books and reading, which led her to conclude that literacy growth can best be supported in an environment "in which an individual can discover that reading is interesting and fun and in which it is considered a virtue to be a 'reader'" (p. 95).

Demonstrations.   *Demonstrations* provide the examples and raw data that enable learning. Demonstrations occur naturally as others in the environment use what children are learning. For example, listening to others talk helps young children decide about the functions and forms of language. Cambourne notes that demonstrations associated with oral language learning always take place in a meaningful context and serve relevant purposes.

Likewise, demonstrations that arise from peer discussions about books and reading help students find success as readers, which ultimately leads to their expecting to be successful readers. Classroom demonstrations of literate behavior are vitally important as well. This is one of many reasons why classroom reading activities should be as authentic as possible: Students need repeated opportunities to engage authentically and successfully as readers to develop expectations for success.

As teachers, the models of literate behavior we provide, whether reading aloud, talking about a favorite book, or participating in an authentic story discussion, are also demonstrations. Teacher-as-model is a common theme throughout this book, but here we wish to underscore the affective nature of modeling. Students cite their teachers' behaviors as motivators for their own behavior (Gambrell, 1996). They can learn to appreciate reading from teachers who genuinely love to read. Teachers who demonstrate their own real, personal affection for reading are much more likely to have students who share that enthusiasm.

Engagement. *Engagement* refers to active participation in reading. This is influenced, of course, by attention, perceived need or purpose for reading, and willingness to make attempts. Children learn to talk because they actively try to talk. And they try because they believe they are capable of succeeding, see the value of learning to talk, and feel no anxiety about attempting it.

So it is with learning to read. In fact, Cambourne believes that engagement is the single most important condition of learning. The feelings and attitudes associated with engagement—seeing value, being free from anxiety, and so forth—are remarkably similar to those Mike Rose found in his exemplary classrooms. The activities, strategies, and instructional routines included in this book are all designed to promote active participation or engagement—real reading.

Expectations. *Expectations* about the learner's ability and eventual success are communicated by others, both overtly and subtly. About learning to talk, Cambourne (1995) says, "Try asking the parents of very young children whether they expect their offspring to learn to talk. Pay attention to the kind of response you get" (p. 185).

We know that teachers' expectations have an enormous influence on children's learning. This has been a persistent finding from decades of research (for example, Good, 1987). At the root of this relationship are two facts: (a) teachers are "significant others" in their students' lives, and (b) expectations often translate into behaviors, which in turn influence learning. Thinking through the effect of teacher praise or criticism may help us understand how this cycle works.

Consistent verbal encouragement, such as "You can do this, Jeremy. I know you can!" or "Good thinking, Marie!", can lead students to believe that they *can* achieve and *are* good thinkers. Such beliefs may lead to positive learning gains. Unfortunately, the reverse is also true. Excessive criticism, for example, leads to anxiety, and anxious people have divided attention: part concentrates on doing the task, while the other part worries about how well they are doing. Thus, anxiety can contribute to some children's attention problems in school. In fact, Cooper (1977) found that children's behaviors changed when their teachers stopped criticizing them. Children began to interact more positively with the teacher and their peers; they were also more actively involved in their academic tasks. Differential praise and criticism—that is, expectations—influence children's motivation to achieve.

Responsibility.   *Responsibility* refers to decision making and choice. Children learning to talk decide what they will attempt to say and to whom. They also choose to pay attention to some noises and ignore others. Other people provide opportunities to learn, of course, but children decide the nature of the language interaction in which they will participate.

This condition also applies to the literacy learning classroom. Self-selection of reading materials, for example, which we address in this chapter and elsewhere in the book, fosters student responsibility for learning. Likewise, providing choice during instructional sessions (see chapter 2) and encouraging choice in responses to reading (see chapters 8 and 9) enable students to develop feelings of control and responsibility for their own reading.

Approximations.   Children don't wait to talk until they can enunciate fully formed sentences. Instead, they *approximate,* or say whatever they can, and their attempts are received enthusiastically. No one worries about approximations because we know that immature forms of talk will eventually be replaced by more conventional forms. No parent frets that a child will continue saying "da-da" into adulthood. Like learning to talk, learning to read and write are gradual, developmental processes in which first attempts are approximations of skilled, mature behavior. Beginning readers and writers, too, need support and encouragment for their efforts. Thus, positive attitudes toward and acceptance of approximations (or mistakes) are essential components of the classroom's psychological environment.

Employment.   *Employment* refers to opportunities to use and practice oral language. Most of these opportunities occur in interaction with others, especially parents or caregivers, but children also practice talking to themselves. Just as oral language opportunities are authentic—real and functional—for the language learner, reading and writing opportunities should be as authentic as possible, and plentiful and consistent, too. Children should have opportunities throughout each day to engage with the written word.

Response.   *Response* is the final condition of language learning. Children receive feedback and additional information as they attempt to talk. They use this feedback to support further learning. As in the reading classroom, some of this feedback comes from adults in the form of praise or scaffolding to foster further learning. Students also need opportunities to respond in personal ways to their own reading. Response journals, poetry, discussion groups, artistic responses, notes to the teacher, skits, and music are some ways students can respond to their reading. Opportunities to respond to peers are equally important, as are times for quiet reflection so that learners can respond for themselves.

When Tom, a sixth-grade classroom teacher, allowed students to give creative oral book reports on Friday afternoons, enthusiasm for reading swelled in his class. Some students who read books together did book talks that resembled television movie reviews (thumbs up—thumbs down!); others shared artwork and skits they had created, and still others brought in artifacts from home that represented special items and events from their stories. "I had expected the standard book report in oral form. I couldn't believe what they were coming up with, and they were selling the other kids on the books they had read. This was the start of a classroom book club for us," Tom said. By tapping into students' responsibility and choice, employment, and personal response, Tom unwittingly unleashed previously restrained potential for making reading come alive for his students. This led to greater enthusiasm and motivation for reading, which led to even more reading.

Excellent Literacy Educators

Recently, several groups of researchers have spent countless hours observing excellent literacy educators at work in order to identify common factors associated with effective instructional environments. In exemplary first-grade classrooms, for example, Pressley, Allington, Wharton-McDonald, Block, and Morrow (2001) found excellent classroom management and a positive, cooperative tone. Skills instruction was explicit; teachers provided support and scaffolded children's learning. Students spent abundant time reading, writing, and working independently in these academically "busy" classrooms. They had access to excellent literature. Their instruction was challenging but not frustrating.

Another study of primary-grade classrooms (Taylor, Pearson, Clark, & Walpole, 2000) compared effective teachers to less-effective teachers in low-income schools. Compared to their less-effective colleagues, accomplished teachers provided

- more small-group instruction
- more coaching/scaffolding
- more phonics teaching with emphasis on application in real reading
- more higher order questioning (e.g., inferences, integration, application)
- greater outreach to parents
- more independent reading
- more engagement (greater amounts of time spent reading and writing).

Based on long-term observation of exemplary literacy teachers at a variety of elementary levels, Dick Allington (2002) and his colleagues note that effective reading instruction is based on six constructs:

- *Time.* In effective classrooms, up to 50 percent of the day involves actual reading or writing.
- *Texts.* Effective teachers use authentic texts. Students have a large supply of reading material from which to choose. In exemplary teachers' classrooms, struggling readers (and all others) read many "easy" texts—those they can read accurately, fluently, and with good comprehension.

■ *Teaching.* Teaching in exemplary classrooms <u>is active; teachers model and demonstrate useful strategies that good readers employ.</u>

■ *Talk.* Exemplary teachers foster more talk—teacher–student and student–student. They encourage, model, and support purposeful talk across the school day. Teachers and students discuss ideas, concepts, hypotheses, strategies, and responses. Teachers pose open-ended questions. The classroom talk is more often conversational than the typical interrogational talk that dominates in many other classrooms.

■ *Tasks.* Children's work in exemplary classrooms is substantive, challenging, and requires more self-regulation than commonly observed in elementary classrooms.

■ *Testing.* Exemplary teachers evaluate student work and award grades based more on effort and improvement than achievement. Thus, all students can earn good grades, and they become responsible for earning their grades. Students cannot attribute bad grades to bad luck, because the evaluation scheme is rather transparent to them. Rubrics provide the information they need to improve their grades. Such classes spend almost no time in test preparation. None of the teachers rely on test-preparation materials or activities. Instead, they believe that good instruction leads to enhanced test performance; their students' achievement data bears out their beliefs.

A Success-Based Classroom

Can students who find reading difficult learn to expect success? We believe the answer is a resounding yes! Moreover, we believe that such expectations are critical to long-term reading growth and the development of lifelong reading habits. And we believe that teachers can create success-based reading classrooms by using researchers' descriptions of effective classrooms as a framework for making instructional decisions.

Barb applied this framework to her class, and here's what she says about it:

> When I realized how pervasively negative my students' attitudes were, I knew I had to do something. I did some reading, I talked to a few colleagues whose opinions I respect, and I did a lot of thinking and soul-searching. I finally decided that it all boiled down to several key factors. I wanted students to see reading as vital and to be active, frequent readers. For this to happen, I knew I needed to provide lots of good books, to set aside blocks of time for reading, and to encourage kids to try to read what interested them. I also knew that my own attitudes would be critical. I really *did* respect my students as learners and expect them to be successful, but I needed to find ways to communicate these feelings to my students.

Quite a bit of this fell into the "easier said than done" category for me. But I believe the goals are important, so I made a plan. I have separate sections of a small notebook for the goals I want to achieve. In each section, I have made some notes about the kinds of things I think I should do to help achieve the goals. And then every so often I look at the goals and the plans and ask myself, "Have I been doing what I planned to do? What else could I be doing?"

This is the way I work at implementing the goals consistently throughout the school year. Other people will probably have other ways of doing this, but for me it's important to keep the goals in mind and to make and evaluate concrete plans. And I think my plans are working. I have seen a difference in students' attitudes. I believe that they are beginning to believe that they *can do* it.

Learning to Value Reading

Learning to expect success is only one part of the equation for helping struggling readers develop and maintain positive attitudes toward reading. Learning to find value in reading is the other. It's easy to see how these two factors are related. For example, Barb's efforts to help her students begin to believe in themselves as readers have the added benefit of showing children that reading is a worthwhile activity, that it is fun and can help them learn and satisfy their curiosities.

How Do We Decide About the Value of Reading?

We value what we find desirable, useful, or important. Our students' attitudes about the value of reading are no doubt influenced by their families and reading practices in the home. Children who routinely watch their parents and others at home read for enjoyment, learning, and work come to see the value of reading for all these purposes. In this way, parents and others at home become powerful models for not only literate behavior but also positive attitudes toward reading.

Children's peers may also influence their attitudes about the value of reading. If peers view reading as a desirable and important activity, this collective attitude encourages all members of the peer group to value reading. This is one reason for the powerful influence of social interaction around literacy activity.

Children's interactions with parents and peers can influence reading outside of school. And reading outside of school is important. Research has consistently shown that reading ability is positively related to recreational reading. An analysis of results from the National Assessment of Educational Progress (NAEP), a standardized instrument administered to thousands of 9-, 13-, and 17-year-olds across the United States, showed just how powerful this relationship is. Students who reported reading for fun at least once a week had higher achievement scores than students who reported never or hardly ever reading for fun (U.S. Department of Education, 1996, 2000).

Of course, teachers and classroom activities also influence the value that children perceive in reading. Gambrell (1996) says that children value reading in classrooms that feature "choice and voice": choice in what to read, whether to read, and how to respond to reading; and voice in terms of the teacher's and peers' respect for children's ideas. Moreover, she has found that classrooms where children are motivated to read often feature an activity she calls "blessing books" (Gambrell, 1998). Several times a week, teachers select several books they think children will enjoy and do brief book-talks about them. Teachers add value to the books by holding them and making brief comments ("blessing"). Books are then displayed, and children quickly check them out to read. This guidance in choosing reading material is especially important for struggling readers who often select books on their own for the wrong reasons (e.g., number of pages, presence of illustrations, size of print).

Guthrie, Schafer, Wang, and Afflerbach (1995) provide another view of developing positive attitudes about the value of reading. They studied how classroom experiences influence children's interest in reading by analyzing NAEP results. They found several aspects of instruction associated with increased amounts of reading (which itself was associated with increased reading achievement) and high interest in reading:

- *Social interaction.* Students who said they read many books also reported spending lots of time talking with others about books, reading in general, and writing, both in and outside the classroom.

- *Cognitive strategies.* Guthrie et al. (1995) believe that teachers created interest in reading in part by helping students find and understand books that met their needs. That is, teachers taught reading strategies that helped students read to fulfill their own purposes. Moreover, interested and voracious student readers often reported that their teachers asked them to share their opinions about their reading, to think about how books were alike and different, and to support their ideas with reference to books they had read. Baumann, Hooten, and White (1999) explored this relationship between strategy instruction and increased motivation in a year-long study of teaching comprehension through literature in a fifth-grade classroom. They "sensed a kind of synergy between the reading strategies and literature appreciation. We saw the students becoming more strategic readers, which enhanced their aesthetic understanding, while their growing aesthetic appreciation facilitated their growth in reading ability" (p. 50).

- *Personal significance.* Interested and voracious readers reported that reading was personally significant for them. They also credited their teachers with supporting these feelings. They said their teachers gave them freedom of interpretation, choice in reading material, and time to discuss reading with peers.

Guthrie et al. (1995) conclude that these factors converge to help students see the value of reading, which in turn sustains long-term motivation for reading. Thus, they can provide a firm foundation for an instructional program that helps students view reading as valuable.

Special programs to promote positive attitudes can also help students view reading as valuable. In the following section we describe several programs that appear to work particularly well. Some are schoolwide efforts, and others involve single classrooms.

Schoolwide Programs

Reading Millionaires (Baumann, 1995; O'Masta & Wolf, 1991; Shanahan, Wojciechowski, & Rubik, 1998) is a schoolwide program with a single goal: Collectively, students and staff attempt to read independently for a million minutes over a specified period of time. Like other schoolwide programs, Reading Millionaires takes a bit of organizing. For example, it requires a plan for reporting the number of minutes read. In addition, someone, perhaps a group of students, must tally all those minutes.

Reading Millionaires can be simple or elaborate. A simple version might involve only advertising the start of the project, periodically announcing total minutes read, and celebrating the achievement of the goal. In some schools, the principal agrees to do something—usually silly—if children reach their goal. At one school, for example, the principal agreed to spend a whole day sitting on the roof; at another, the principal tried to milk a cow while the entire student body watched.

Baumann (1995) describes some additions that made Reading Millionaires successful in her school. For example, she occasionally held raffles for paperback books, with students' returned reading logs as the "ticket" for the raffle. She also created a "Reading Hall of Fame" bulletin board that spotlighted classes of especially voracious readers. And the parent organization in her school funded the purchase of small mementos for participating students, which were presented at a schoolwide celebration after the goal of 1 million minutes had been met. Shanahan et al. (1998) enhanced their program by adding reading posters throughout their school as well as by holding schoolwide gatherings or rallies to encourage the reading habit.

Some schools have annual *read-ins,* somewhat like slumber parties that focus on reading. Larger schools may organize read-ins by grade levels; smaller ones often combine primary grades for one read-in and intermediate grades for another. At some schools only students and staff participate; at others parents may attend.

All read-ins involve children and books. Here is how one might look: Early Friday evening, children (and parents) return to school with books, sleeping bags, and pillows. All assemble in the school gym or multipurpose room with teachers, the principal, and other volunteers. Activities for the evening focus on books and reading. Children and adults read silently. Some

Some schools organize read-ins, like slumber parties that focus on reading.

might enjoy oral reading to partners or larger groups by both children and adults. Participants listen to storytellers and reader's theater or watch puppet renditions of stories. Physical activities and snacks round out the night. On Saturday morning, everyone leaves, having spent a night sharing the fun of reading and enjoying the companionship of others.

Schoolwide reading projects can involve the *community,* too (Rasinski, 1992). Some schools form alliances with senior-citizen homes or centers, where children read aloud for their senior buddies or listen to stories the buddies read. Pen-pal relationships may develop. Able seniors sometimes visit the school.

Community connections can also form in more subtle ways. For example, children might create posters advertising the joys of reading and then ask local stores to display them. Some schools organize "Reading Days" at local malls. This usually involves some sort of visual display about reading, a few rocking chairs, and groups of children rocking and reading. Teachers and children can build floats for local parades that focus on books and reading. Some schools even have book parades that include children walking through the school neighborhood dressed as book characters or holding posters about their favorite books.

Classroom Programs

Most teachers are familiar with *Book It!,* a national reading incentive program sponsored by Pizza Hut. The rules for participating classrooms are relatively simple. The teacher specifies the number of books to be read each month, and children who achieve the goal receive coupons for small pizzas. Teachers in some communities have sought similar support from local businesses (for example, fast-food restaurants, amusement parks, or movie theaters) to reward their students for independent reading. The key here is a connection by which the extrinsic motivator promotes the intrinsic value of reading. Teachers must promote reading for the love of reading, not just for pizzas and prizes.

Classroom Choices is modeled after the annual *Children's Choices* project, which is jointly sponsored by the International Reading Association and the Children's Book Council. Children's Choices involves groups of children from all over the United States reading and rating new books. Their favorites are published each October in *The Reading Teacher*. Some states follow similar procedures to select favorite books among school children residing in the state. (These projects are usually sponsored by state reading or language arts groups. Teachers interested in participating should contact these groups for further information.)

Classroom Choices resembles national and state projects but runs on a much smaller scale: the classroom. For a school year (or a shorter specified period of time), children read and vote on their favorite books. In some classrooms, books are subdivided by genre, such as favorite make-believe book, favorite true story, and so on. Votes are tallied in various ways. For example, children can simply count up yes or no votes about whether or not they liked a book. This can result in some interesting "run-off" discussions at the end of the voting, for many titles may receive unanimous support. Another option is to allow weighted votes, such as a 3-2-1 scale, where 3 is "Terrific! You have to read this book!" and 1 is "I wouldn't bother if I were you." Tallying these weighted votes and determining averages for titles can be an interesting and functional math lesson for older students.

Cheryl has a Classroom Choices project in her second-grade classroom each year. "I started because I noticed that the children were sharing good books with each other naturally," she says. "And so I thought, 'Why not go farther with this?'" Her project begins in early fall each year and ends at the spring recess. "We always write a class letter to the winning author. We tell him or her about the project and explain what we liked so much about the winning book. If we write early enough in the spring, the author usually responds in some way before school is out. Boy, do the kids love that!" Cheryl has found that her Classroom Choices project encourages children to read and share good books with each other. "It *is* a competition, in a way," she says. "But the books are competing and not the kids. I like that aspect of it. I also like the opportunities that arise to talk about what makes good books good, if you know what I mean."

These special programs invite children to engage in authentic reading activities, encourage cooperation rather than competition, and feature celebration of children's abilities as readers. Although each program involves some external motivation, the programs are built on the assumption that internal motivation for reading will naturally develop when a spark for reading is ignited by the externally motivating activity. In other words, special programs alone cannot sustain long-term motivation for reading. Effective teachers also encourage social interaction around reading, provide necessary strategy instruction, and help students view reading as a personally significant and rewarding activity.

Learning to Value Reading

At the beginning of this chapter, we commented on the close relationship between achievement in reading and attitudes, including motivation. Instruction to support children who struggle as readers must focus simultaneously on both attitudes and achievement. Oldfather and Wigfield (1996), who looked at the research in both areas, offer concepts that can help teachers plan effective instruction. Students will be motivated for literacy learning when they see themselves as competent readers and writers and when they view literacy skill as personally valuable. These understandings and beliefs are most likely to develop in those instructional environments that allow students to pursue some of their own interests, to find resources (print and people) they need, and that assure students that others will be interested in and respectful of their ideas and their literate actions. These conditions can create and sustain positive attitudes.

We want students to develop and maintain positive attitudes about reading and themselves as readers for at least two critical reasons. First, these attitudes allow students to develop the motivation they need to sustain interest in reading and persist in their efforts to become better readers. Second, knowing how to read is not enough; it's equally important (some would say more important) to value reading. That is, our goal should be to help students become both competent and avid readers, or, as NRRC researchers put it, the "*skill* to read and learn is not sufficient; students must also ultimately acquire the intrinsic *will* to exercise their developing reading proficiencies" (Baumann & Duffy, 1997, pp. 10–11).

Accessibility and availability have major influences on children's choices to read. A classroom environment that nurtures an interest in reading has the following characteristics:

- The teacher is enthusiastic about books and consistently supportive of children as readers.
- Children have easy access to many well-selected books.
- Children have regular time to browse, choose books, and read them.
- Books are the subject of much comment and discussion.
- Appreciation for reading develops through cumulative personal experience and response.

Students who find reading difficult often have negative attitudes about reading and themselves as readers. These negative attitudes can shut down further learning. So teachers must consider sources of attitudes, how they may hamper learning, and what to do about them. In this chapter we have provided a few specific ideas and many more abstract principles that can help teachers think about the relationships among attitudes, motivation, and reading.

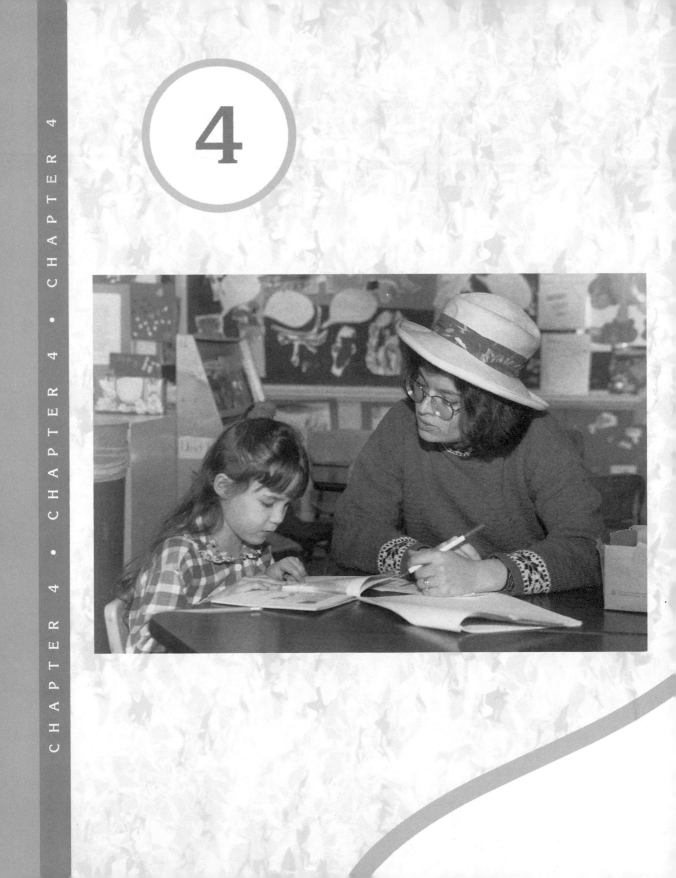

Early Intervention

This book is about helping children who struggle in learning to read. Its main thrust is to provide you—the teacher or clinician—with instructional strategies, routines, ideas, and activities to help students become proficient, efficient, and lifelong readers. When overcoming reading difficulties, the earlier we intervene with children who struggle, the more likely it is that our interventions will be successful and lasting. Indeed, the best way to overcome a reading problem is to not have one in the first place! Instruction and nurturance in reading are absolutely essential for developing early and successful readers.

In recent years, we have learned much about early reading—factors developed early in life that seem crucial to later success in reading; assessment of those factors; and instruction in those factors for preschool, kindergarten, and first grade. In this chapter, then, we present information on exemplary reading instruction in the early years and suggestions for those children who, even in their earliest experiences with literacy, may seem at-risk for failure.

Components of Exemplary Early Reading Instruction

How do teachers of young children (and we include parents in this notion of teachers) promote children's successful emergence into reading and writing? In this portion of the chapter we present instructional activities that seem most likely to produce successful and engaged readers.

Read to Students

An enduring research finding is that children who are read to regularly (daily) tend to succeed in literacy learning. Dolores Durkin (1966) found that children whose parents read to them regularly at home are more likely to find early success in reading than children who lack such opportunities. Moreover, the advantage early successful readers have over their nonearly reading classmates remains over the years. Indeed, early successful readers tend to extend their advantage over their classmates as they progress through the grades.

Why is reading to young children so important? First, it communicates that reading is an important part of life, both in the home and in the classroom. Stories are enjoyable, and sharing a story with an important adult makes it even more special. Thus students who are read to tend to have more positive attitudes toward reading. In addition, the story reading helps students develop their comprehension abilities and vocabulary, as well as a sense for the conventions (rules) for stories. These are crucial aspects of becoming fully literate. Being read to by a fluent adult also provides students with a model of what reading aloud should sound like. And finally, if parents and teachers read to students in such a way that the students can see the text, students can naturally develop basic concepts about print (what a word is, directionality in reading, and so on), letter knowledge, and early recognition of words. Need we say more? Reading to students is perhaps the most important literacy activity we can share with students in preschool, kindergarten, and beyond.

Language Experience

In language experience activities (see chapter 5), students dictate a text to the teacher, who then writes the students' words on a piece of chart paper. The text reflects some experience that the children have had, individually or as a group. A walk around the school grounds or a field trip are wonderful experiences to talk about and eventually turn into a text to be read. Because the text reflects children's own experiences and words, comprehension and readability are assured. Students can read the text because they created it. Here is an example of a dictated text students composed with their teacher after studying birds and visiting the bird exhibit at the zoo.

BIRDS

All birds have feathers. A lot of birds know how to fly. Some birds walk. Some birds swim. Birds are different colors. Some birds are small. Some birds are big. Some birds have crests. All birds have bills. All birds lay eggs. Birds eat different things.

Language experience (dictated) texts are wonderful vehicles for early reading. With the teacher's support, students can read their text chorally and alone, again and again. The teacher can begin to draw students' attention to individual words and letters, helping children make connections between the written text and the pronounced word or sound represented by the writing. From the example above, the words *birds* and *bird* would certainly be good candidates for learning as well as the connection between the letter *b* and /b/. Words drawn from several dictated texts can be turned into word banks and can be practiced, sorted, and made into games. The words can also be listed on the classroom word wall (see chapter 5) to draw children's attention to them throughout the school day. Dictated texts are a great bridge from oral to written language, from speech to reading. Moreover, informed teachers use these easy-to-read and understandable texts to provide sophisticated instruction in vocabulary and word recognition to students.

Predictable and Enlarged Texts

As students further immerse themselves into the written word, they need to move on to more conventional texts, texts written by others. Predictable texts work well here. Predictable texts are stories, poems, song lyrics, or other forms of written text that have easy-to-read features such as repetitive words, phrases, sentences, rhyme and/or rhythm. (We have included lists of predictable stories and poetry collections in Appendixes B and C.)

When presented in enlarged formats—big books or on chart paper—predictable texts work much the same as dictated texts. Students read and reread the texts. The predictable nature of the texts may allow students to reach the point at which they can "read the story without even looking at the print." Reading involves paying attention to the written words so teachers who use predictable texts with students need to *decontextualize* the reading—read the text without the pictures; read the text as a set of sentence strips and then reassemble the strips to create the text; read individual words from the text, first in context but later in isolation; and finally explore the letters and letter patterns within words. Words from the predictable text can be added to word banks and word walls for further study and exploration. As with dictated texts, these activities help students develop not only understanding of whole stories, but also understanding of how texts, words, and letters work in the reading process.

The patterned nature of predictable texts makes it easy for teachers and children to create their own versions. The cumulative story *This Is the House That Jack Built,* for example, can easily transform into *This Is the Trip Our Class Took* as a response to a class field trip. In addition to being an authentic and engaging writing activity, the familiar pattern of the new text makes it easy for students to read, but the new text forces students to closely examine and learn the words.

Stacy, a first-grade teacher took a cue from poet Bruce Lansky (1996) to write several of her own versions of "Yankee Doodle." "All I did was change what 'Yankee Doodle' came to town on and the rest just came." Here's one of her creations:

> Yankee Doodle went to town
> Riding on a ducky.
> Found a dollar on the ground
> And called himself real lucky.

Once students read and memorized the original "Yankee Doodle," I introduced the ones I had written, one every other day. I put them on chart paper and we read and reread them throughout the day. Because we had several versions of "Yankee Doodle" hanging from the walls, the children had to look at the words in order to know which one we were reading. Later, we studied the rhyming words for word families and we pulled words out from the poems, put them on our word wall, and practiced them there. What really surprised me was when students began to bring in their own versions of "Yankee Doodle" that they had written at home with their parents. Even some of the students I've been worried about brought in their own poems. We read all the poems the kids brought in. The kids loved it and I did too. What started as reading and reciting one simple text turned into a full blown words-and-writing activity.

Read Together—Choral Reading

A major aim of all schooling is to develop a sense of shared purpose—a classroom community. Community or *choral reading* can help to develop this goal (Rasinski, 2003). In choral reading the entire class or group participates in the reading experience. Younger students chorally read an enlarged predictable text or language experience story. The class reads and rereads the text together as the teacher points to the text. The practice in reading, combined with reading and hearing the words read at the same time, develop students' word recognition and fluency (Kuhn & Stahl, 2000). And, it is fun to read together.

Moreover, different forms of choral reading add a degree of variety to the choral reading experience (Rasinski, 2003). The teacher can divide students into smaller groups with each group handling a refrain or a portion of the text. In echo reading, the teacher reads a line and the students echo the teacher's reading. A cumulative form of choral reading begins with one student or group reading a line and, with each succeeding line, another student or group joins in. The reading begins softly but ends with gusto! No matter how you do it, choral reading is good reading and good fun.

Shared Book Experience

The *Shared Book Experience* (SBE) (Holdaway, 1979, 1981) combines elements of teacher read-aloud, choral reading, and independent reading with an enlarged text. It is a wonderful example of moving from teacher modeling to supported or scaffolded reading, to independent reading.

To begin, the teacher introduces and expressively reads a big book or chart story to students. Following a brief discussion and retelling of the story, the teacher rereads the text and invites students to join in chorally over either the entire passage or a shorter segment. Choral rereadings continue over several days as students master word recognition and fluency. Later, the teacher uses the text as the basis for teaching book and written-language

Community

Everyone is equal

low readers feel comfortable

lead & get used to followers

words they don't know

conventions (e.g., left to right progression of text on a line) and reading skills and strategies. Students may even read smaller versions of the book independently or with friends.

One study compared the effectiveness of two instructional practices with second-grade students: SBE with round-robin reading (the traditional oral reading turn-taking activity) (Eldredge, Reutzel, & Hollingsworth, 1996). Students receiving the SBE instruction demonstrated superior gains in word recognition, fluency, vocabulary, and comprehension over students doing round-robin reading.

Marcia, a seasoned first-grade teacher has used the shared book experience with her students for years. "What I really like about the Shared Book Experience is that students go from watching me read to reading on their own. But between my reading to them and their independent reading, we read together, myself and all the kids. For these early readers, the reading and rereading of stories orally is the perfect bridge between not reading but seeing me read, to students' individual reading."

Environmental Print

Another bridge between the children's lived-in world and the world of literacy can be built with *environmental print*. Environmental print is simply the print that children see in their daily lives—traffic signs; store, restaurant, and gas station signs; print on grocery bags; and so on. Informed teachers bring examples into the classroom for their students to read. When that same print is rewritten in a more conventional format, without the context of the sign, teachers focus children's attention on those features that communicate the meaning—the printed letters. These words, taken from children's own environments, can be added to their word banks and examined and played with in the same way as other word-bank words.

Daily Independent Reading

Young students need to develop the reading habit. This means giving students time every day to read on their own, even if they are not yet reading conventionally or independently. Students peruse books and the pictures in books or pretend to read during the 10 minutes (or so) of independent reading. They read silently alone or aloud with a partner. The important point is that students are honored with the opportunity to read books of their choosing, for their purposes, and with whomever they wish to read. Teachers need plenty of books and other reading material from which children can choose. In addition, teachers should read during this period so that children see reading as a lifelong avocation.

We know that the amount of reading one does at home and school predicts overall reading achievement. Accordingly, we need to nurture this habit early in children's lives.

Daily Writing

As with independent reading, many young students cannot write convention- ally. Nevertheless, we should write every day with students. One approach is for each student to keep a personal journal. During journal time, students write freely. Early writing may be scribbles or drawings, but as students learn more about reading and writing, they begin to apply this knowledge to their writing. Extended line scribbles may begin to resemble individual word scrib- bles. These scribbles later emerge into conventionally formed words, or words that, although not spelled correctly, can be read as students begin to apply their knowledge of sound-symbol correspondences. We will add to this notion of invented or phonemic spelling later in this chapter when we discuss phonemic awareness.

It is absolutely critical that the teacher also write and show students what she has written. This provides firsthand proof that those written symbols can be turned into real words that express the writer's thoughts. Students quickly begin to emulate the writing they see their teacher doing.

Terra, a first-grade teacher, makes sure that when her students write, she writes, too.

> And then I show the students what I have written. I read it to them and then they have lots of questions about how I turned my thoughts into writing. I leave my journal open for students to look at it whenever they like. Every day at least one or two students go up to the journal, examine it, read from it, or talk about how they are going to make their writing look like mine. Even though we often do a mini-lesson on some aspect of writing before we write, I think that my modeling is the best lesson I can give my students.

Parent Involvement

Preschool, kindergarten, and first-grade parents are most likely to work with their children on reading. Even low-literate parents can help their children read at these grades. The more reading practice children have, the more likely they are to become successful readers. The list of ways parents help their children is nearly endless. Teachers must urge parents to read to and with their children every day. Parents of children who are already reading conventionally can also listen to their children read and respond with heaps of praise and encouragement. Parents can write with their children, taking dictation, making lists, exchanging notes, or sharing a *dialogue journal* (a journal passed between parent and child in which parent and child converse in writing). Parents can make sure that their home is stocked with literacy materials such as books, magazines, paper, writing tools, and the like.

More formal activities also stimulate learning. See chapter 12 for a description of *Fast Start,* a parent-involvement program for young students, as well as other approaches for helping parents help their children.

I like that ask Parents if they will write notes for kids. List for Things to do etc.

Phonemic Awareness: A Necessity for Reading

The activities and concepts presented so far are absolutely essential to children's early development in literacy. Through read-aloud, language experience, predictable books, environmental print, daily independent reading and writing, and parent involvement, students learn about stories and written texts; they develop their comprehension skills and build their vocabularies; they learn how print works and the basic concepts or conventions related to print; and they begin to examine words to add them to their sight vocabulary and develop understandings of how letters and letter patterns represent language sounds. That's a lot to learn.

But we want to add one more piece to this puzzle—a piece that recent research suggests is a possible reason that many children struggle in reading. It's called *phonemic awareness.*

Lately, the issue of phonics instruction has received much attention. Parents, legislators, and the public have been captured by the notion that phonics instruction is the singular key to student reading success. We certainly recognize that proficiency in phonics is necessary for reading. We disagree with the view that phonics is the sole component to effective literacy instruction and the only competency required for proficient reading. This view is much too narrow. Certainly, readers can and do employ other approaches to decode words. Full development in reading and writing requires competencies in language, comprehension, and vocabulary, to name just a few. Moreover, other areas of instructional emphasis are equally important for student success in reading, such as parent involvement in children's reading, time for independent reading during the school day, and opportunities for students to discuss their reading with others. We fear that exclusive attention to phonics will skew the curriculum in such a way that many students lose the opportunity or instruction they need to become full-fledged members of the literacy community. We must recognize the importance of phonics, and also its proper place in a comprehensive reading program.

Although we discuss phonics in chapter 5, we introduce you to it here to place phonemic awareness in proper perspective. *Phonics* involves associating written letters with sounds in order to decode or sound out words in print. Phonics is the knowledge of letter-sound correspondences. Readers use phonics when they visually examine letters or letter combinations in words and produce a sound or sound combination that corresponds to the visual stimulus. Blending the separate sounds in a word should result in pronunciation of the word.

Phonics depends on one's abilities to visually examine words and to recognize, segment, and blend sounds of language. This latter ability is more commonly known as phonemic awareness. Recent research into phonemic awareness suggests that it is an important precondition for learning phonics as well as general progress in reading (Adams, 1990; Ball & Blachman, 1991; Bradley & Bryant, 1983, 1985; Fielding-Barnsley, 1997; Hiebert, Pearson,

Taylor, Richardson, & Paris, 1998; Perfetti, Beck, Bell, & Hughes, 1987; Stanovich, 1986; Yopp, 1992, 1995a) and writing (Eldredge & Baird, 1996). Students who lack phonemic awareness are among those most likely to experience difficulty in reading (Catts, 1991; Maclean, Bryant, & Bradley, 1987). So, even before we ask students to make connections between oral language sounds and written symbols (phonics), we must ensure their ability to deal with (recognize, segment, and blend) sounds (phonemic awareness). Phonemic awareness, then, is a necessary precondition to successful phonics learning as well as, for most readers, to successful reading.

How Students Develop Phonemic Awareness

Fortunately, most students develop phonemic awareness naturally through their everyday early childhood experience. Young children have many opportunities to play with language sounds. These opportunities range from reciting nursery rhymes and childhood poems with parents, family members, and friends, to chanting and creating jump-rope cadences and chants, to singing childhood songs (e.g., "Old MacDonald"), to simply conversing with family members and friends. As they manipulate the sounds of language, children begin to develop this awareness of sounds and how they work. By the time children enter kindergarten, they have developed enough awareness of language sounds to begin to profit from phonics instruction.

It works this way for most children, but not all. Some children enter school with insufficient awareness of the sounds of language. We do not fully understand how this fails to happen for them. Some children may have had chronic ear infections that inhibit their development of this awareness. Other children may have lacked opportunities to play with language through childhood rhymes and songs. Many of our kindergarten and first-grade teacher colleagues tell us that more children are entering school with less knowledge of common rhymes and songs than children in previous years have had. Other researchers suggest that some children have within them a less-developed ability to perceive, segment, and blend language sounds. Whatever the cause of this problem, children with insufficient phonemic awareness will not profit from phonics instruction to the same extent as children proficient in phonemic awareness. If certain children have difficulty perceiving sounds even when not associated with letters, how can we expect them to make the next step into phonics, which involves associating letters and sounds and then blending the sounds into words? For many young children, this will be one of their first frustrations in reading, and if not addressed early on, perhaps the first of many reading frustrations through the school years.

Assessing Phonemic Awareness

Phonemic awareness is important to reading success, and we need good tools for assessing it. Fortunately, a fairly simple assessment instrument can be administered to young children as well as to older students. Our adaptation of the Yopp–Singer Test of Phonemic Segmentation (Yopp, 1995a), in which we have removed difficult-to-perceive *r* sounds, is a set of 22 words that students segment into constituent sounds (see Figure 4.1). For example, the teacher says the word *bat* and the student says the three separate sounds that make up *bat:* /b/-/a/-/t/.

The 22-item test takes only minutes to administer, yet the results can give us some indication of students' later success in reading. Yopp (1992) has followed children to whom she administered the phonemic segmentation test

---

Test of Phonemic Segmentation

Student's name _____ Date _____

Student's age _____

Score (number correct) _____ Examiner _____

Directions: I'd like to play a sound game with you. I will say a word and I want you to break the word apart into its sounds. You need to tell me each sound in the word. For example, if I say "ham," you should say "/h/-/a/-/m/," *(Administrator: Be sure to say the sounds in the word distinctly. Do not say the letters.)* Let's try a few practice words.

Practice items: *(Assist the child in segmenting these items as necessary. You may wish to use blocks to help demonstrate the segmentation of sounds.)* kite, so, fat

Test items: *(Circle those items that the student correctly segments: incorrect responses may be recorded on the blank line following the item.)*

1. to _____
2. be _____
3. might _____
4. mow _____
5. he _____
6. vain _____
7. is _____
8. am _____
9. my _____
10. feet _____
11. jack _____

12. knock _____
13. lace _____
14. mop _____
15. this _____
16. jet _____
17. slow _____
18. nice _____
19. cot _____
20. shoe _____
21. bed _____
22. stay _____

Figure 4.1

Test of Phonemic Segmentation

Note: Adapted from Yopp, H. (1995a). "A test for assessing phonemic awareness in young children." *The Reading Teacher, 49,* 20–29.

in kindergarten through their later years in school. She found that students' scores are significantly correlated with reading and spelling achievement through Grade 6. Clearly, this and similar research results (Stanovich, 1994) suggest that we must consider phonemic awareness when assessing young children and students experiencing difficulty in reading and when designing instructional programs for students who appear to lack sufficient awareness of sounds.

Yopp has found that second semester kindergarten students obtained a mean score of 12 on the test. That suggests to us that kindergartners who fall significantly below this threshold, say a score of 5 or below, should have additional instruction in phonemic awareness. As we shall discuss later in this chapter, many children who appear deficient in the area of phonemic awareness can be taught successfully with methods that fit well within a normal kindergarten classroom.

However, this assessment instrument has implications well beyond kindergarten. We routinely administer the Test of Phonemic Segmentation to many students, ranging from second grade through high school, who are referred to our clinical reading programs. Although not all struggling readers perform poorly on the test, a surprising number do. By the beginning of second grade, students should be able to complete the test with little trouble. We expect all students at second grade or beyond to score 20 or better. And yet, it is not unusual to find fifth- and sixth-grade students, frustrated in reading, who score between 10 and 15.

We wonder if these children's struggles in reading might have begun in their early years when they were asked to master phonics, for which they were developmentally unready. Moreover, many of these older students, failing to learn to read through phonics, simply received more phonics, slower phonics, and intensive phonics. Rather than an alternative route to reading, many of these students were pushed down a road that already had too many obstacles to negotiate successfully. It is easy to imagine how they became turned off to reading. While their normally achieving classmates moved on to reading for pleasure and information, these students were stuck reading less and drilling more (Allington, 1977, 1983, 1994).

The Test of Phonemic Segmentation is a tool of enormous value. Identifying students at risk as early as possible may save many children from years of reading frustration. Insight into the problems of older readers allows us to either help these students overcome their problems in phonemic awareness or design an alternative instructional program that bypasses phonics.

Teaching and Nurturing Phonemic Awareness Through Text Play and Writing

Phonemic awareness, for most students, is more nurtured than taught. Children learn the nature of language sounds through their daily playful involvement with the world. That same playfulness about language and the sounds of language can easily extend itself into preschool and kindergarten classrooms. Informed teachers have many ways to nurture this ability.

Perhaps one of the most useful is simply bringing rhymes, chants, and songs that feature and play with language sounds into the classroom or clinic. Younger children may profit most from the reading and rereading of nursery rhymes, jump-rope chants, and children's poetry and songs. Playing with nursery rhyme lines such as

> Dickery dickery dare, the pig flew up in the air . . .
>
> Hey diddle diddle, the cat and the fiddle . . .
>
> Diddle diddle dumpling, my son John . . .

helps children grasp the concept of the sound of *d* (/d/). And the tongue-twisting rhyme, "Peter Piper picked a peck of pickled peppers . . ." will help children develop an awareness of /p/.

Jump-rope chants, poems, and songs can serve the same purpose. Griffith and Olson (1992) recommend that teachers read rhyming texts and other texts that play with sounds to students daily and help develop students' sensitivity to sounds. Moreover, these texts can be altered to feature different language sounds (Yopp, 1992). For example, the familiar refrain of "Ee-igh, ee-igh, oh" in "Old MacDonald" can be transformed into "Dee-igh, dee-igh, doh" to emphasize /d/. The "Camptown Races" exclamation can be changed from "dooh dah" to "booh bah" or "sooh sah," depending on the sound being emphasized.

Older students can approach the same task with more sophisticated texts. Rhymed poetry for older children, as well as tongue twisters, and lyrics to popular songs and raps lend themselves to being learned, altered, rewritten, and ultimately performed to emphasize particular language sounds.

Hinky Pinkies are another gamelike activity for developing sound awareness in a playful way. Hinky Pinkies are simply riddles for which the answer is two or more rhyming words. To make one, begin with the rhyming answer and then come up with the riddle that describes it. For example, if "sandy candy" is the answer, the question might be *What do you call sweet stuff that you drop on the beach?* Students love making as well as figuring out Hinky Pinkies. The Hinky Pinky idea could also be altered so that the answers are two or more words that begin with the same sound (alliterations). A large swine, then, is a *big pig* when the answer rhymes, but becomes a *huge hog* when you a change the game to alliterations.

These textual activities require students to attend to language sounds in order to perform the song or rap, or provide the correct response to the riddle. Inviting students to play with language in this way develops their sensitivity to sounds. In addition to songs and poems, many books deal with sounds. Yopp (1995b) provides an extensive list of books (reprinted at the end of this chapter) that help children develop phonemic awareness.

Although these books are most appropriate for younger children, older students needing help with phonemic awareness can pair with younger students and learn to read such books to their younger buddies. The books also lend themselves to many useful extensions, including having students write their own versions of the stories by changing the sounds emphasized.

Some literacy scholars suggest that reading and sharing alphabet books can help develop phonemic awareness in students (Brabham, Murray, & Hudson, 2001). Many of the letters of the alphabet have their sounds embedded in their names. Moreover, alphabet book texts often contain alliterative sentences and passages aligned with the target letters that focus readers' attention on distinct sounds associated with the letters.

Other scholars (Clay, 1985; Griffith & Klesius, 1990; Morris, 1998) argue that writing, in particular writing in which students are encouraged to use their knowledge of sound-symbol correspondences, also known as invented or phonemic spelling, is a powerful way to help students develop their phonemic awareness as well as basic phonics knowledge. When students attempt to write words using their knowledge of language sounds and corresponding letters, they segment sounds in words and order and blend the sounds to make real words. Even if the words are spelled unconventionally, this type of writing provides students with unequaled practice in employing their knowledge of sounds. When a child, for example, spells the word *truck* as *chruk,* that child is making a written and phonological representation of the word that is probably closer to the actual way that most people pronounce *truck* than the correct conventional spelling itself. Thus this child, although not spelling the word correctly, is still making wonderful use of sound and letter knowledge.

The research behind invented or phonemic spelling, by the way, makes clear that it is simply a developmental stage. Just as children move from babbling and incorrect pronunciation when learning to talk to full and correct pronunciation, children move rapidly toward correct spelling. By the late primary grades little if any difference in spelling proficiency appears between children taught to spell in a highly rigid and disciplined system and other children who receive encouragement and support to play with their knowledge of sounds and letters through invented spelling. In fact, one study of first graders showed that children encouraged to invent their spellings were more fluent writers and better word recognizers than children who experienced a traditional spelling curriculum (Clarke, 1988). Considering all the sound-symbol thinking that occurs when children invent their spelling, these results are no surprise.

Kevin works with older students having difficulty with reading. He also has a background in music.

After reading about the role that phonemic awareness plays in reading I began assessing my students on it. I was surprised to find that many of my fifth and sixth graders had trouble on their conceptualization of sounds that I thought they should have mastered years ago. I have a pretty good store of songs for children, and I found that they worked in very well to my instruction. The kids love the singing, not that we do it for the entire lesson. But we do usually sing a new song and an old song every day or so. I print the lyrics on chart paper so that they can also read them. But afterwards we also do some talking about the sounds they hear, how the sounds relate to sounds in other words, and how they might be substituted. I wondered if it would be successful, but all the kids like it and a few in particular have seemed to come to a new level of understanding about sounds just through this song activity.

Try it! maybe it works maybe not. But my job is to put myself out there

Teaching and Nurturing Phonemic Awareness Through More Focused Activities

For many children, playful reading, reciting, and performance of sound-oriented texts are enough to develop appropriate sound awareness for reading in kindergarten and primary grades (Ericson & Juliebo, 1998). Other children, younger children at risk, and older students who lack sufficient phonemic awareness skills and have profited little from phonics instruction need more specific instruction. Yopp (1992) has identified several conceptual levels of activity to develop phonemic awareness:

- ■ sound matching
- ■ sound isolation
- ■ sound blending
- ■ sound substitution
- ■ sound segmentation

These levels provide a framework for designing instruction that comprehensively treats phonemic awareness instruction in a sequence from easy to more complex and that eventually leads to learning the associations of sounds to written letters and letter combinations (phonics).

Sound matching.   As the name implies, *sound matching* simply requires students to match a word or words to a particular sound. A teacher who asks students to think of words that begin with /p/ challenges students to find words that match that sound. Having students think of the way they form their mouths to articulate individual sounds may help them match to other words and form a more lasting internal concept of the sound. Sound matching can extend to middle (vowel) sounds, ending sounds, and rhyming words. As students become familiar with the written form of words, the words can be placed on a word wall (see chapter 5) according to their beginning (middle, ending, or word family sounds).

Another sound-matching activity involves presenting students with three words, two of which have the same beginning sound, for example, *bat, cat, cane.* Students must determine which two words have the same initial sound. Again, this same sort of activity plays with middle and ending sounds as well as with rhyming words.

Sound isolation.   *Sound-isolation* activities challenge students to determine the beginning, middle, or ending sounds in a word or set of words. For example, the teacher may say three words that begin with the same sound (*this, that, them*) and ask students to tell what sound begins the words (Yopp, 1992). The same procedure works for middle and ending sounds as well as for word families or rimes. As students develop proficiency in determining individual sounds from similar words, they can analyze for individual sounds from single words. For example, the teacher may ask what beginning sound students hear in these words: *bake, swim, dog, pin, that.* Using the same set of words, students can work to determine (isolate) the middle and ending sounds.

Sound blending.   *Sound-blending* activities move students to the kind of synthesis we use to decode words using phonics. In a gamelike or sing-song format, the teacher simply presents students with individual sounds and asks them to blend the sounds together to form a word. The teacher might, for example, say to the class, "I am thinking of a kind of bird and here are the sounds in its name /d/, /u/, /k/" (Yopp, 1992). Of course, the children should say *duck* as the correct response. If this sort of task is too difficult, teachers can make it easier by presenting three pictures of birds and asking students to pick the correct one from the presentation of sounds. Students who are more adept at the activity can come up with their own questions and present their own sounds and riddles to classmates.

Sound substitution.   *Sound substitution* requires students to subtract, add, or substitute sounds from existing words. Questions such as "What word do you get when you take the /p/ off of *pin?*" require students to segment sounds from words and then reblend the sounds using the remaining sounds. Similarly, teachers can add sounds to existing words to make up new words: "Add /t/ to the beginning of *win,* and what do you get?"

If students can add and subtract sounds, they are ready to try substituting one sound for another in words. You might ask students to consider what the names of their classmates might be if all their names began with a particular sound, for example (Yopp, 1992). If /s/ were the new sound, Billy's name would become Silly, and Mary and Gary would have the same name— Sary. Middle and ending sounds can also be substituted as students develop proficiency with initial sound substitution.

Sound segmentation.   As the title implies, *sound-segmentation* activities require students to go beyond isolating one sound in a word to determining all the constituent sounds. This may begin with simply segmenting words into *onsets* (the sounds that precede the vowel in a syllable) and *rimes* (the vowel and consonants beyond the vowel in a syllable; another name for word family). So *stack* would be segmented into /st/ and /ak/. Later, students can segment words into their specific sounds. This time, *stack* would be segmented into /s/, /t/, /a/, /k/.

All the generic activities described here can easily turn into a variety of games, performances, and playful activities. Informed teachers make these activities engaging and enjoyable for students and also share them so that parents can participate in their children's development of phonemic awareness.

Making it concrete for students.   The notion of playing with sounds is somewhat abstract for many students. Think of it—sounds cannot be seen or held. You can't even make them stay, because as soon as you make a sound, it's gone. Children who learn tasks best in concrete ways often find sound awareness difficult. One way to make the task more concrete is to use physical objects to represent sounds—say, colored blocks. The teacher, for example, might have each block of a different color represent a particular sound. A blue block can represent /b/, the red block can be the /t/, the white block can be /a/, and the yellow block can represent /i/. Using these blocks, then, teachers can work with individuals and groups of students in learning to blend, substitute, and segment sounds in words.

In such activities, teachers put, for example, the blue, white, and red blocks in a row and ask students to blend the sounds into the word *bat*. Then, teachers remove the blue block to make the word *at*. If the red block is moved from the end of the word to the beginning, the sound produced becomes /ta/. Four or five blocks, each representing a sound, can provide many opportunities for students to make sense of how sounds work.

Older students already familiar with the alphabet can accomplish the same task with magnetic letters on a cake pan, with the added important feature of having the letters that represent the sounds in words.

Griffith and Olson (1992) also advocate the use of Elkonin boxes, popularized by Reading Recovery, to add a dimension of concreteness in hearing and segmenting sounds. An *Elkonin box* is simply a series of boxes drawn on a sheet of paper (see Figure 4.2). As students listen to words the teacher reads and hear discrete sounds, they push markers into the boxes, one marker for each sound. Later, as children become more familiar with written letters, they can write individual letters or letter combinations that represent individual sounds in the words.

Figure 4.2
An Elkonin Box

Creating Powerful Instructional Routines

Informed teachers put these and other texts and activities together to support children's early efforts at reading. Brief (5–10 minutes and throughout the day) instructional routines (see chapter 11) that combine several activities provide powerful and effective instruction for students.

We need to emphasize that phonemic awareness, while important for reading, is not the whole package. Teachers and children should develop student literacy skills in many other ways. For example, children need to be read to daily from the best children's literature available. They need to explore word meanings with the teacher daily, and daily language experience stories should be part and parcel of every elementary classroom. Predictable books, big books, poems, and stories should be read in a supportive environment. Although phonemic awareness is important for later success in reading, it is only one part of a comprehensive and effective program for young children and many older students who struggle in reading.

As the old saying goes, "An ounce of prevention is worth a pound of cure." In a way, the ideas presented in this chapter are both prevention and cure. That is, we have answered two related questions in this chapter: How can we prevent beginning readers from becoming at risk? When beginners struggle, what can the classroom teacher or specialist do to help them grow as readers? The answer to both questions is to plan instruction that is developmentally, theoretically, and empirically appropriate.

Books for Developing Phonemic Awareness

Brown, M. W. (1993). *Four fur feet.* New York: Doubleday. In this simple book, the reader is drawn to the /f/ sound as the phrase "four fur feet" is repeated in every sentence as a furry animal walks around the world. The same pattern is used throughout the story as we see four fur feet walk along the river, into the country, and so forth. The book must be turned around as the animal makes its way around the world.

Butler, J., & Schade, S. (1988). *I love you, good night.* New York: Simon & Schuster. A mother and child tell each other how much they love one another. When the child says she loves her mother as much as "blueberry pancakes," the mother responds that she loves her child as much as "milkshakes." The child says she loves the mother as much as "frogs love flies," to which the mother responds she loves her child as much as "pigs love pies." The two go back and forth in this manner until "good night" is said. The rhyme invites the listener to participate and continue the story.

Cameron, P. (1961). *"I can't,"* said the ant. New York: Coward-McCann. Household items discuss the fall of a teapot from the counter in a kitchen and the means by which to put it back. In a series of brief contributions to the conversation, each item says something that rhymes with its own name. "'Don't break her,' said the shaker" and "'I can't bear it,' said the carrot."

Carle, E. (1974). *All about Arthur (an absolutely absurd ape)*. New York: Franklin Watts. Arthur, an accordion-playing ape who lives in Atlanta, feels lonely and travels from Baltimore to Yonkers making friends. In each city, he makes a friend whose name matches the initial sound of the city, from a banjo-playing bear in Baltimore to a young yak in Yonkers.

Carter, D. (1990). *More bugs in boxes*. New York: Simon & Schuster. This pop-up book presents a series of questions and answers about make-believe bugs who are found inside a variety of boxes. Both the questions and answers make use of alliteration: "What kind of bug is in the rosy red rectangle box? A bright blue big-mouth bug." Following a similar pattern is the author's *Jingle bugs* (1992, Simon & Schuster), which has a Christmas theme and makes use of rhyme: "Who's in the chimney, warm and snug? Ho, ho, ho! It's Santa Bug!"

Deming, A.G. (1994). *Who is tapping at my window?* New York: Penguin. A young girl hears a tapping at her window and asks, "Who is there?" The farm animals each respond, "It's not I," and she discovers that it is the rain. The book is predictable in that each pair of animals rhymes. The loon responds, followed by the raccoon. The dog's response is followed by the frog's.

de Regniers, B., Moore, E., White, M., & Carr, J. (1988). *Sing a song of popcorn*. New York: Scholastic. A number of poems in this book draw attention to rhyme and encourage children to experiment. Also included are poems that play with sounds within words. In "Galoshes" the author describes the slippery slush "as it slooshes and sloshes and splishes and sploshes" around a child's galoshes. In "Eletelephony" sounds are mixed up and substituted for one another: "Once there was an elephant, /Who tried to use the telephant. . . . "

Ehlert, L. (1989). *Eating the alphabet: Fruits and vegetables from A to Z*. San Diego, CA: Harcourt Brace Jovanovich. Fruits and vegetables are offered in print and pictures for each letter of the alphabet in this book. The following are displayed for B, for instance: blueberry, brussels sprouts, bean, beet, broccoli, banana.

Emberley, B. (1992). *One wide river to cross*. Boston: Little, Brown. This Caldecott Honor Book is an adaptation of the traditional African American spiritual about Noah's ark. Through the use of rhyme, the author describes the animals gathering on board one by one (while "Japhelth played the big bass drum"), two by two ("The alligator lost his shoe"), and so on up to ten, when the rains begin.

Fortunata. (1968). *Catch a little fox*. New York: Scholastic. A group of children talk about going hunting, identifying animals they will catch and where they will keep each one. A frog will be put in a log, a cat will be put in a hat, and so forth. The story concludes with the animals in turn capturing the children, putting them in a ring and listening to them sing. All are then released. The music is included in this book. A different version of this story that includes a brontosaurus (who is put in a chorus) and armadillo (who is put in a pillow) is J. Langstaff's (1974) *Oh, a-hunting we will go,* published by Atheneum, New York.

Galdone, P. (1968). *Henny Penny*. New York: Scholastic. A hen becomes alarmed when an acorn hits her on the head. She believes the sky is falling, and on her way to inform the king she meets several animals who join her until they are all eaten by Foxy Loxy. This classic story is included here because of the amusing rhyming names of the animals. A recent release of this story is S. Kellogg's *Chicken Little* (1985), published by Mulberry Books, New York.

Geraghty, P. (1992). *Stop that noise!* New York: Crown. A mouse is annoyed with the many sounds of the forest and implores the cicada to stop its "zee-zee-zee-zee," the frog to stop its "woopoo," until it hears far more disturbing sounds—the "Brrrm" and "Crrrrr RACKA-DACKA-RACKA-SHOONG" of a bulldozer felling trees. The presentation of animal and machine sounds makes this book useful in drawing attention to the sounds in our language.

Gordon, J. (1991). *Six sleepy sheep*. New York: Puffin Books. Six sheep try to fall asleep by slurping celery soup, telling spooky stories, singing songs, sipping simmered milk, and so on. The use of the /s/ sound, prevalent throughout, amuses listeners as they anticipate the sheep's antics.

Hague, K. (1984). *Alphabears*. New York: Henry Holt. In this beautifully illustrated book, 26 teddy bears introduce the alphabet and make use of alliteration. Teddy bear John loves jam and jelly. Quimbly is a quilted bear, and Pam likes popcorn and pink lemonade.

Hawkins, C., & Hawkins, J. (1986). *Tog the dog*. New York: G. P. Putnam's Sons. This book tells the story of Tog the dog who likes to jog, gets lost in the fog, falls into a bog, and so forth. With the exception of the final page, where the letters *og* appear in large type, the pages in the book are not full width. As the reader turns the narrower pages throughout the text a new letter appears and lines up with the *og* so that when Tog falls into the bog, for example, a large letter *b* lines up with *og* to make the word *bog*. This is a great book for both developing phonemic awareness and pointing out a spelling pattern. Also by the authors are *Jen the hen* (1985), *Mig the pig* (1984), and *Pat the cat* (1993), all published by G. P. Putnam's Sons.

Hymes, L., & Hymes, J. (1964). *Oodles of noodles*. New York: Young Scott Books. Several of the poems in this collection make use of nonsense words in order to complete a rhyme. In "Oodles of Noodles," the speaker requests oodles of noodles because they are favorite foodles. In "Spinach," the authors list a series of words each beginning with the /sp/ sound until they finally end with the word "spinach." Words include "spin," "span," "spun," and "spoony." Many of the poems point out spelling patterns that will be entertaining with an older audience.

Krauss, R. (1985). *I can fly*. New York: Golden Press. In this simple book, a child imitates the actions of a variety of animals. "A cow can moo. I can too." "I can squirm like a worm." The rhyming element combined with the charm of the child's imaginative play makes the story engaging. On the final page, nonsense words that rhyme are used, encouraging listeners to experiment with sounds themselves: "Gubble gubble gubble I'm a mubble in a pubble."

Kuskin, K. (1990). *Roar and more*. New York: Harper Trophy. This book includes many poems and pictures that portray the sounds that animals make. Both the use of rhyme and presentation of animal sounds ("Ssnnaaaarrll" for the tiger, "Hsssssss . . . " for the snake) draw children's attention to sounds. An earlier edition of this book won the 1979 NCTE Award for Excellence in Poetry for Children.

Lewison, W. (1992). *Buzz said the bee*. New York: Scholastic. A series of animals sit on top of one another in this story. Before each animal climbs on top of the next, it does something that rhymes with the animal it approaches. For instance, the hen dances a jig before sitting on the pig. The pig takes a bow before sitting on the cow.

Martin, B. (1974). *Sounds of a powwow*. New York: Holt, Rinehart, & Winston. Included in this volume is the song "K-K-K-Katy" in which the first consonant of several words is isolated and repeated, as is the song title.

Marzollo, J. (1989). *The teddy bear book*. New York: Dial. Poems about teddy bears adapted from songs, jump-rope rhymes, ball-bouncing chants, cheers, and story poems are presented. Use of rhyme is considerable, from the well-known "Teddy bear, teddy bear, turn around, Teddy bear, teddy bear, touch the ground" to the less familiar, "Did you ever, ever, ever in your teddy bear life see a teddy bear dance with his wife?" and the response, "No I never, never, never.... " Play with sounds is obvious in the poem "Teddy Boo and Teddy Bear" where the author says, "Icabocker, icabocker, icabocker, boo! Icabocker, soda cracker, phooey on you!"

Obligado, L. (1983). *Faint frogs feeling feverish and other terrifically tantalizing tongue twisters*. New York: Viking. For each letter of the alphabet, one or more tongue twisters using alliteration is presented in print and with humorous illustrations. *S* has smiling snakes sipping strawberry sodas, a shy spider spinning, and a swordfish sawing. *T* presents two toucans tying ties, turtles tasting tea, and tigers tying trousers.

Ochs, C. P. (1991). *Moose on the loose*. Minneapolis, MN: Carolrhoda Books. A moose escapes from the zoo in the town of Zown and at the same time a chartreuse caboose disappears. The zookeeper runs throughout the town asking citizens if they've seen a "moose on the loose in a chartreuse caboose." No one has seen the moose, but each has seen a different animal. Included among the many citizens is Ms. Cook who saw a pig wearing a wig, Mr. Wu who saw a weasel paint at an easel, and Mrs. Case who saw a skunk filling a trunk. Each joins in the search.

Otto, C. (1991). *Dinosaur chase*. New York: Harper Trophy. A mother dinosaur reads her young one a story about dinosaurs in which: "dinosaur crawl, dinosaur creep, tiptoe dinosaur, dinosaur seek." Both alliteration and rhyme augment this simple, colorful book.

Parry, C. (1991). *Zoomerang-a-boomerang: Poems to make your belly laugh*. New York: Puffin Books. Nearly all of the poems in this collection play with language, particularly through the use of predictable and humorous rhyme patterns. In "Oh my, no more pie," the meat's too red, so the writer has some bread. When the bread is too brown, the writer goes to town, and so forth. In "What they said," each of 12 animals says something that rhymes with its name. For instance, a pup says, "Let's wake up," and a lark says, "It's still dark."

Patz, N. (1983). *Moses supposes his toeses are roses*. San Diego, CA: Harcourt Brace Jovanovich. Seven rhymes are presented here, each of which plays on language to engage the listener. Rhyme is predictable in "Sweetie Maguire" when she shouts, "Fire! Fire!" and Mrs. O'Hair says, "Where? Where?" Alliteration makes "Betty Botter" a tongue twister: "But a bit of better butter that will make my batter better!" Assonance adds humor to "The tooter" when the tooter tries to tutor two tooters to toot!

Pomerantz, C. (1993). *If I had a paka*. New York: Mulberry. Eleven languages are represented among the 12 poems included in this volume. The author manipulates words as in "You take the blueberry, I'll take the dewberry. You don't want the blueberry, OK take the bayberry. . . ." Many berries are mentioned, including a novel one, the "chuckleberry."

Attention is drawn to phonemes when languages other than English are introduced. The Vietnamese translation of the following draws attention to rhyme and repetition: I like fish, Toy tik ka; I like chicken, Toy tik ga; I like duck, Toy tik veet; I like meat, Toy tik teet.

Prelutsky, J. (1982). *The baby Uggs are hatching.* New York: Mulberry. Twelve poems describe unusual creatures such as the Sneepies, the Smasheroo, and the Numpy-numpy-numpity. Although some of the vocabulary is advanced (the Quossible has an irascible temper), most of the poems will be enjoyed by young children who will delight in the humorous use of words and sounds. For instance, "The Sneezysnoozer sneezes in a dozen sneezy sizes, it sneezes little breezes and it sneezes big surprises."

Prelutsky, J. (1989). *Poems of A. Nonny Mouse.* New York: Knopf. A. Nonny Mouse finally gets credit for all her works that were previously attributed to "Anonymous" in this humorous selection of poems that is appropriate for all ages. Of particular interest for developing phonemic awareness are poems such as "How much wood would a wood-chuck chuck" and "Betty Botter bought some butter."

Provenson, A., & Provenson, M. (1977). *Old Mother Hubbard.* New York: Random House. In this traditional rhyme, Old Mother Hubbard runs errand after errand for her dog. When she comes back from buying him a wig, she finds him dancing a jig. When she returns from buying him shoes, she finds him reading the news.

Raffi. (1987). *Down by the bay.* New York: Crown. Two young children try to outdo one another in making up rhymes with questions like, "Did you ever see a goose kissing a moose?" and "Did you ever see a bear combing his hair?" Music is included.

Raffi. (1989). *Tingalayo.* New York: Crown. Here the reader meets a man who calls for his donkey, Tingalayo, and describes its antics through the use of rhyme and rhythm. Phrases such as "Me donkey dance, me donkey sing, me donkey wearin' a diamond ring" will make children laugh, and they will easily contribute additional verses to this song/story.

Sendak, M. (1990). *Alligators all around: An alphabet.* New York: Harper Trophy. Using alliteration for each letter of the alphabet, Sendak introduces the reader to the alphabet with the help of alligators who have headaches (for *H*) and keep kangaroos (for *K*).

Seuss, Dr. (1963). *Dr. Seuss's ABC.* New York: Random House. Each letter of the alphabet is presented along with an amusing sentence in which nearly all of the words begin with the targeted letter. "Many mumbling mice are making midnight music in the moonlight . . . mighty nice."

Seuss, Dr. (1965). *Fox in socks.* New York: Random House. Before beginning this book, the reader is warned to take the book slowly because the fox will try to get the reader's tongue in trouble. Language play is the obvious focus of this book. Assonance patterns occur throughout, and the listener is exposed to vowel sound changes when beetles battle, ducks like lakes, and ticks and clocks get mixed up with chicks and tocks.

Seuss, Dr. (1974). *There's a wocket in my pocket.* New York: Random House. A child talks about the creatures he has found around the house. These include a "nooth grush on my tooth brush" and a "zamp in the lamp." The initial sounds of common household objects are substituted with other sounds to make the nonsense creatures in this wonderful example of play with language.

Shaw, N. (1989). *Sheep on a ship*. Boston: Houghton Mifflin. Sheep sailing on a ship run into trouble when facing a sudden storm. This entertaining story makes use of rhyme (waves lap and sails flap), alliteration (sheep on a ship), and assonance ("It rains and hails and shakes the sails").

Showers, P. (1991). *The listening walk*. New York: Harper Trophy. A little girl and her father go for a walk with their dog, and the listener is treated to the variety of sounds they hear while walking. These include "thhhh . . . ," the steady whisper sound of some sprinklers, and "whithh whithh," the sound of other sprinklers that turn around and around. Some phonemes are elongated as in "eeeeeeeyowwwoooo . . . ," the sound of a jet overhead. Some phonemes are substituted as in "bik bok bik bok," the sounds of high heels on the pavement.

Silverstein, S. (1964). *A giraffe and a half*. New York: HarperCollins. Using cumulative and rhyming patterns, Silverstein builds the story of a giraffe who has a rose on his nose, a bee on his knee, some glue on his shoe, and so on until he undoes the story by reversing the events.

Staines, B. (1989). *All God's critters got a place in the choir*. New York: Penguin. This lively book makes use of rhyme to tell of the places that numerous animals (an ox and a fox, a grizzly bear, a possum and a porcupine, bullfrogs) have in the world's choir. "Some sing low, some sing higher, some sing out loud on the telephone wire."

Tallon, R. (1979). *Zoophabets*. New York: Scholastic. Letter by letter the author names a fictional animal and, in list form, tells where it lives and what it eats. All, of course, begin with the targeted letter. "Runk" lives in "rain barrels" and eats "raindrops, rusty rainbows, ripped rubbers, raincoats, rhubarb."

Van Allsburg, C. *The Z was zapped*. Boston: Houghton Mifflin. A series of mishaps befall the letters of the alphabet. *A* is crushed by an avalanche, *B* is badly bitten, *C* is cut to ribbons, and so forth. Other alphabet books using alliteration include G. Base's *Animalia* (1987), published by Harry N. Abrams, K. Greenaway's (1993) *A apple pie*, published by Derrydale, and J. Patience's (1993) *An amazing alphabet*, published by Random House.

Winthrop, E. (1986). *Shoes*. New York: Harper Trophy. This rhyming book surveys familiar and some not-so-familiar types of shoes. The book begins, "There are shoes to buckle, shoes to tie, shoes too low, and shoes too high." Later we discover, "Shoes for fishing, shoes for wishing, rubber shoes for muddy squishing." The rhythm and rhyme invite participation and creative contributions.

Zemach, M. (1976). *Hush, little baby*. New York: Dutton. In this lullaby, parents attempt to console a crying baby by promising a number of outrageous things including a mockingbird, a diamond ring, a billy goat, and a cart and bull. The verse is set to rhyme, e.g., "If that cart and bull turn over, Poppa's gonna buy you a dog named Rover," and children can easily innovate on the rhyme and contribute to the list of items being promised.

Note: The preceding list is from "Read-aloud books for developing phonemic awareness: An annotated bibliography," by H. K. Yopp, 1995, *The Reading Teacher, 48*, pp. 538–543. Copyright 1995 by International Reading Association. Reprinted by permission.

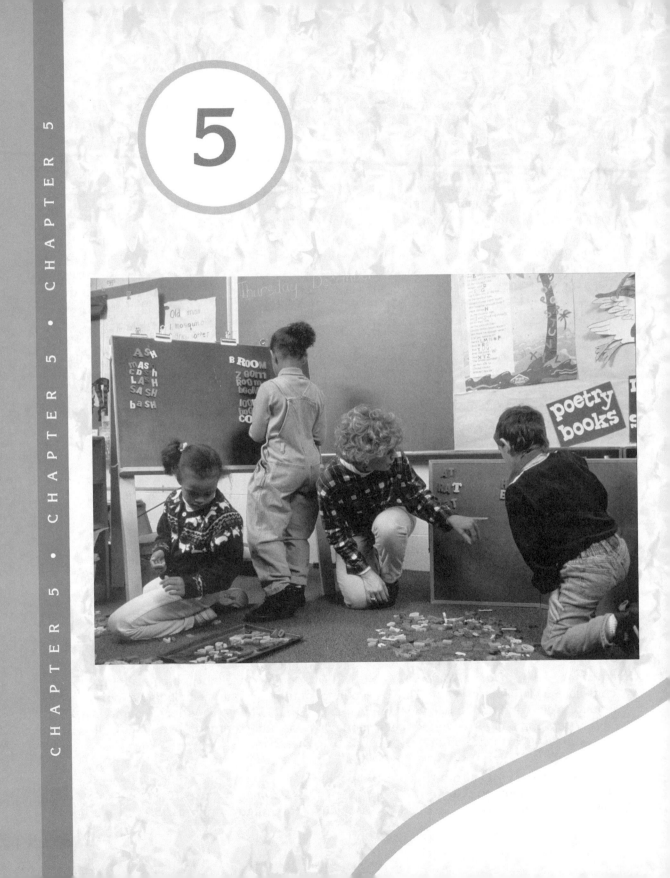

Word Recognition

Reading involves constructing meaning from written text. Clearly, unless readers have some understanding of the text, we can hardly say they are reading. To construct meaning, however, readers must recognize words quickly, accurately, and effortlessly. By *recognize* we mean the ability to translate written symbols grouped into words into their oral representation, even if that translation is done within the reader's head, as in silent reading.

The less efficient readers are at recognizing or decoding written words, the more mental energy they must devote to the task. Thus, they have less mental energy available for making sense of the text as a whole. We want readers to become so efficient at word recognition that they can decode words with minimal effort and focus all their attention on making sense of the author's message. When students encounter familiar words, they should recognize them instantly or automatically—that is, without the use of conscious attention. Unfamiliar words (often longer or content-specific words) should be recognized quickly and accurately by using effective word recognition strategies.

In our work with struggling readers, we have noticed many who demonstrate difficulty in word recognition and fluency. They labor over too many words, repeat many words several times before pronouncing them correctly, hesitate before attempting unfamiliar words, and seem to treat reading as a task of "getting the words right" rather than comprehending the text. We admire students who persevere and make any sense out of what they read when their reading is frustratingly slow and labored. Nevertheless, they find reading much more difficult and frustrating than it ought to be.

Less proficient readers—the children this book aims to support—are likely to experience even more frequent and debilitating problems with words. Because of the extra decoding time, children with word recognition difficulties read fewer words than more proficient readers. As a result, they make smaller gains in word recognition, comprehension, and overall reading proficiency. Without effective intervention they continue to fall behind and associate reading with frustration and failure.

Word recognition develops as a result of daily and sustained reading experience and through direct and systematic instructional interventions. Word recognition should be so well developed that it bcomes an unconscious part of the reading process. Listen to the good readers you know. They recognize words so effortlessly yet precisely that you hardly pay attention to their word recognition. What you do notice is their ability to process the text in a way that makes meaning easily accessible to the reader and listener.

We agree with some literacy scholars who criticize traditional teaching of word recognition. In the past, word recognition instruction has largely been divorced from meaningful and engaging reading. More often word recognition instruction and activities were designed to be completed independently. Students passively completed workbooks and worksheets, did incessant and meaningless drills on words or parts of words in isolation, and memorized phonics rules and generalizations. Such approaches are not the most efficient, effective, or meaningful ways to develop proficiency in word recognition.

Word recognition develops best when it is an integral part of meaningful and authentic reading experiences. Children learn to deal with words when they are actively involved in interesting and constructive experiences. The following principles help us create instructional experiences that keep students' attention focused on reading while allowing them to explore the nature and structure of written words.

- ■ Word recognition instruction should be an inherent part of real reading experiences. It should proceed from a whole text to examination of parts of the text and then back again to the whole. That is, word recognition instruction should begin with reading a text; move gradually to considering particular words and parts of words from that text; and end with a return to the text in the form of rereading, responding, or reading something else. Moreover, after instruction in a skill or strategy, students should have the opportunity to consider its usefulness or applicability to their reading.

- ■ Word recognition instruction should allow students some freedom to choose, explore, make, and play with words. This playfulness encourages the risk-taking behavior that leads to insight. By thinking about and acting on words they create for themselves, children develop a thorough understanding of how words work.

- ■ Instruction should include daily and extended times for group and independent reading of authentic texts that offer opportunities for students to put their word recognition competencies to use. Students need many chances to apply their decoding knowledge for the essential purpose of reading: making sense of printed discourse. Only in this way will students master word recognition strategies and, through exposure to a multitude of words in their reading, make their subsequent recognition of words more efficient and effortless.

■ Word learning requires students to see and read words repeatedly. In addition to reading words daily on lists or flash cards, students need to see words in a variety of texts. Multiple exposures are the result of seeing and reading the words in many texts that contain the target words. Sandy McCormick (1994, 1995) has called this principle of word recognition instruction *Multiple Contexts/Multiple Exposures*. Her own work with struggling readers demonstrates the power of this principle.

■ Materials used for word recognition instruction should manifest balance between decodability and predictability. Decodable texts contain numerous words or word parts that students have learned and can decode, and should be able to read in text. Students can also read predictable texts, with their easy-to-detect patterns of repeated phrases, sentences, or other language units (see Appendix C). Because they are so easy to read and memorize, however, repeated readings of such texts should include detailed and focused examination of individual words in the text as part of word recognition instruction. This process of going from a rich authentic text to the study of words and word parts is called *decontextualization*.

Any materials that repeat certain words, word parts, or phrases provide a natural context for repeated exposures. Verse poetry, chants, and lyrical songs also provide near-perfect textual environments for word recognition (see Appendix B). Often series books (see Appendix D) are excellent choices for reading and word recognition; many of the same words and concepts find their way from one book in a series to another. Moreover, familiar characters, plots, and author styles make series books highly predictable (and successful) reads for all readers.

Texts of students' own composition can produce powerful word recognition instruction. Because students express their own words and ideas in the compositions, familiarity is guaranteed. Creative teachers also generate texts—stories or poems—that highlight and use words students are studying. Adding a personal touch by including students' names or familiar settings and events can make such texts even more inviting and predictable. The excitement of knowing the author of a text is added incentive to read it well. A selection with too many unfamiliar words may overwhelm the reader, though, so short texts that contain fairly familiar words are optimal.

■ The teacher's role in word recognition instruction is to help students understand and use basic word recognition strategies and then immediately apply them to real reading. Teachers should never treat word recognition development as an end in itself but constantly and vigorously turn students' attention to applying the strategies in real reading. Be cautious about testing students' skills in applying various strategies when their actual reading indicates that they recognize the words they encounter. Never treat word recognition as a set of skills to be taught, mastered, and tested outside actual reading. In fact, word recognition skill is worth little unless it can be applied to the task of reading.

Old and New Ways of Word Recognition Instruction

Traditional word recognition instruction features lists of words in isolation, flash cards, learning phonics rules or generalizations (e.g., "When two vowels go walking the first one does the talking"), and repetitive drills with isolated words. We believe this approach to word recognition has serious problems. The number of children who have difficulty learning to recognize words suggests that they, too, have serious problems with the old way. Theodore Clymer (1963, 1996) examined phonics rules often taught to elementary students and found that a significant number apply less often than we might hope. The "two vowels go walking" rule, for example, applied to only 45 percent of the words with two adjacent vowels found in elementary reading books.

Many activities in this chapter can extend into flash cards and word-list reading activities, but we are cautious about recommending their extensive use. Although some evidence indicates that flash card work can aid students' word learning (Nicholson, 1998), we suggest it be only a small part of word-study instruction. Extended and dominant use of flash cards in a reading program tends to communicate the message that reading is simply a matter of getting the words right rather than making sense of the passages. It also suggests that word-by-word reading is the way to process text. Even more important, a set of isolated words contains little of inherent interest.

The best alternative to word-list or flash card reading is real contextual reading. In real reading students practice words and phrases, work to comprehend the author's message, and learn and enjoy the fruits of their efforts in ways that real readers do. It bears repeating that one of the most enduring findings in all reading research is that good readers read a lot and poor readers read little. We must learn to maximize students' contextual reading because it is the best practice for improving their reading.

Jane works with students who have significant difficulty learning words, yet she chooses not to engage in flash card activities with them:

> I don't use flash cards for a number of reasons. I know it sends a message to the kids about what's important about reading. It's also a very inefficient activity. As one student is looking at a flash card, the other students I'm working with are usually thinking about something else. I prefer to encourage my students to read. Through wide reading they will encounter the words on the flash cards. And they also deal with contextual clues,

phrasing, and making sense of the passage. Real reading makes a lot more sense than the humdrum flash cards.

Other teachers we know use flash cards for quick warm-up activities that foster automatic recognition of high-frequency words.

We advocate word recognition instruction that features a great deal of student choice about and ownership over words. Students will more easily and enduringly learn words meaningful to them and their friends. Word recognition should provide opportunities for students to think, talk about, act on, and use words and elements of words and consider how they work. To become good at recognizing words, students need to know how words work and how elements from known words can inform them about unknown ones. They accomplish this by discussing words with others, thinking about words, playing with and acting on words, and using words in the context of real reading and writing, not by mindless drill and memorization.

In the following sections we describe various effective word recognition strategies. We have used them with success in our classrooms and clinics. As with all instructional strategies, however, they should never be given to students in a mechanical or uniform way. Informed teachers design lesson formats that both meet students' needs and match their own styles of teaching.

Phonics

Phonics refers to the relationships between sound and spelling patterns within written language and the reader's use of this knowledge to decode unknown words. We believe, and research tends to confirm, that phonics knowledge is extremely useful to readers. Some readers develop and use phonics knowledge naturally. Others need guidance from knowledgeable teachers to understand and use phonics generalizations. We do not question whether phonics should be taught but rather to whom and how.

We disagree strenuously with the uninteresting, mindless, mechanical way in which phonics is taught in many classrooms today. Indeed, we are convinced that many children end up in remedial reading classes, permanently turned off from reading, because of the incessant skill-and-drill activities and worksheets foisted on them. In some classrooms first and second graders spend more time saying "buh, aah, tuh; baaaat; bat" than they do reading real, interesting books. As a result, we see many unmotivated children in remedial reading classes who think that reading is more about sounding out the letters than trying to make sense of the passage.

Steven Stahl (1992) has identified several principles that may help guide teachers in developing phonics instruction for their classrooms or clinics. These principles include the following:

1. Phonics learning should proceed from what children already know about reading. It should gradually move from an understanding of stories

toward an analysis of letter–sound relationships within stories students have read. Phonics, as part of a total word recognition program, should proceed from whole to part. Moreover, phonics and word recognition instruction is only one part of the total reading program, whether in a classroom or a remedial reading setting. Students, first and foremost, need to both read and talk about what they are reading.

2.   Phonics instruction should be clear, direct, brief, and focused on real words and text. Activities in which children circle pictures, color, cut and paste, and so on, do not help them learn the essentials of phonics.

3.   Phonics instruction should focus on reading words, not learning rules. It should lead directly to students using their new knowledge to read words and stories. When children encounter unknown words, teachers should model or explain how phonics knowledge can help unlock letter patterns and decode the words.

4.   Phonics instruction should focus on onsets and rimes within syllables, with the ultimate goal of students noticing letter patterns within words. *Onsets* are the part of a syllable before the vowel, and *rimes* are the part of the word from the vowel to the end of the syllable. Rather than focusing on individual letters, students who deal with onsets and rimes can attend to larger segments of words and syllables more easily recognized and more consistent in pronunciation.

5.   Children need opportunities to experiment with and manipulate letters and sounds in making words. Invented spelling, for example, helps students develop and apply phonics knowledge. Successful teachers encourage children to experiment with the writing and spelling system through their spellings of words. Although unconventional, these spellings allow children to apply their knowledge of sounds, letters, and letter patterns in their writing. Preliminary work in this area suggests that children who are encouraged to invent their spellings are better at decoding than those who learn to spell and read in more traditional programs.

Many of the instructional activities described in this section deal with elements of phonics. Children need to learn how to use phonics, but only within an environment of real and purposeful reading. Encourage other activities that guide students in letter and word manipulation and experimentation, too.

Based on our own work with struggling readers and recent research into effective instruction, we would add a few more principles to Steve's list.

6.   Students learn words by comparing and contrasting words as they learn. In a recent book on effective instructional strategies, Robert Marzano and his colleagues (Marzano et al., 2001) identified a set of teaching and learning strategies demonstrated as effective through instructional research. At the top of their list is analyzing items under study for similarities and differences, which we do through word sorts. In *word sort* activities, students

group words according to criteria established by the teacher or class member (e.g., "put all words that contain the long o sound in one pile and those that don't in another"). We describe word sorts in more detail later in this chapter.

7. We should teach only those generalizations students must learn. If a child demonstrates mastery over a phonics element, do not teach it. That student's time would be better spent practicing the knowledge in real reading. Of course, this requires teachers to be good observers of students' reading behavior—teasing out what they know from what they don't by watching students read, talking with them, and observing them in interactions with others.

Language Experience Approach

The *Language Experience Approach (LEA)* to reading is often associated with beginning reading instruction, but we have found it an excellent format for providing word recognition instruction at a variety of levels. In LEA, students use texts that they have composed; therefore, they have the important benefit of dealing with stories and words with which they are already familiar. Students own the text and words.

In the basic form of LEA, students dictate, either individually or in a group, their own brief text to the teacher. The teacher writes the students' text on a sheet of large chart paper or, for one child, on a sheet of notebook-size paper. After several readings over several days, students become familiar with many of the words and identify them more effectively in other reading settings. In fact, Russell Stauffer (1980), an LEA pioneer, suggests that students have copies of their dictations on which they underline the words they can recognize each time they read the texts.

Once children become adept at reading the whole text, we often begin the process of decontextualization: We begin to focus attention on parts of the text as we strip away parts of the context. Students' initial success in reading the story may reflect their use of context (such as pictures or familiar phrases) as well as familiarity with the whole passage. Decontextualization requires students to take a closer look at individual sentences, phrases, words, word parts, or even letters and letter combinations.

One way in which teachers decontextualize is by using sentence strips and word cards from the passage. Paula, a Title I teacher, has had great success using LEA with students. She tries to do at least two texts each week. For example, on Monday she might discuss an interesting experience from the previous week with her students. After the discussion, the group dictates a story related to the experience, which Paula writes on chart paper. At the end of the session the students and Paula read the dictation several times—chorally, individually, orally, silently, and with Paula reading while the children follow along.

On Tuesday, after a few rereadings of the story (as well as stories from previous lessons), Paula engages her students in decontextualization activities.

She creates a second copy of the text on chart paper and begins to cut this copy into sentence strips in front of the students. Together, the group practices reading the sentences and puts them in their original order to remake the story. They also experiment with reordering the sentences. After some work with sentence strips, Paula cuts the strips into phrase strips and word cards that are also practiced, sorted into various categories of the students' choosing, put together to form new sentences, and played with in other ways. Students and teacher experiment with changing word beginnings, middles, and ends to make new words. Paula also makes copies of the story for all students to read on their own in school and at home to their parents.

On Wednesday, Paula may continue reading the story and playing with its words and sentences, depending on how well the students have learned the story and its parts. She also will begin a new LEA story with her class about the interesting speaker who came to school on Tuesday. She will make it a point to return to Monday's story periodically over the next several weeks.

Key Words and Word Banks

Key words and word banks are forms of decontextualization that give students some personal control and investment in the words they learn. This personal ownership of words provides a powerful incentive for students' learning. A *key word* is simply one that the student chooses from a reading. Students choose particular words because they find them interesting—the way they sound, their length, or what they represent. Children will often choose words well beyond those typically found in materials for their age or grade level. Because the words are their own, however, students learn them easily and recognize them quickly in future reading. We have seen kindergartners and beginning first graders choose and learn words such as *microphone, carriage,* and *malevolent.*

When key words are written on index cards, they become part of a student's word bank. A *word bank* is a collection of words taken from students' reading and chosen by the students and the teacher. We have found that one or two story words chosen by the student and one chosen by the teacher are sufficient to maintain an active word bank. Students may choose any words they like, but teachers might choose those that can be generalized into other words by substituting letters or adding word parts. (For example, *dog* can be expanded into *doggy* or can be part of a word family that includes *log* and *jog.*) Children should control the size of their word bank as well as the words that go into it.

One idea is for students to keep two word banks: one in which they keep words they are learning, and another in which they keep words they can recognize on sight. Students choose the bank appropriate for each word and decide when a word moves from one bank to another. Words in both word banks can be practiced, sorted, used to make sentences, or used to play word games with other people. Moreover, teachers can use the contents of students' word banks to teach phonic principles. For example, students can sort their *a* words into groups according to the sounds that *a* makes in the words.

This immersion and practice with words develops students' word recognition proficiency. For every LEA story, Paula's students write their key words on cards and share them with the group, telling why they chose their particular words and making up sentences that include the words. Paula also chooses a word that students write on cards and add to their word banks. From the most recent LEA story, Paula chose *table,* which she will use to illustrate the words that can be made from the *-able* word part and discuss the "consonant plus *le*" generalization.

Several times a week Paula's students warm up for reading by reading their word bank words with a partner. Partners also use their word bank words to make sentences. At least once a week students sort their word bank words into categories that Paula provides or that students think of. Students also use their word banks for games such as *Word Match* (duplicate sets of word cards are laid face down and players find matching pairs) and *Word War* (the word played with the most letters and read correctly wins the war). In addition, Paula uses word banks to practice alphabetizing and other word-related concepts such as word families and phonics generalizations.

Weekly Word Bank

Most word banks are year-long affairs. Students begin their banks early in the year and add and remove words throughout the year. The sense of continuity and accomplishment garnered as words are mastered and removed from the bank is a positive characteristic of such banks. However, teachers and students may wish to add a bit of variety to their word bank activities; moreover, teachers may want banks that contain the same words for all students. We accomplish this through an alternative we call the *weekly word bank.*

One major positive of a weekly word bank is its connection to real literature read by or to students. The weekly word bank begins with the students reading a selection or the teacher reading a selection to them, usually near the end of the week. Students are asked to identify words from the selection they find interesting. Between 10 and 20 words are identified and discussed after the reading. Students explain their reasons for choosing their words. This helps them understand the power that comes from an unusual word, a word that has a peculiar sound, or a word that fits the context of a selection perfectly. Students will become better wordsmiths in their own writing after they think about words chosen by authors whom they read.

The chosen words are written on the chalkboard or a piece of chart paper. Students (and teacher) use the words in their writing and conversation throughout the next week. Students also make word cards and store them in individual envelopes. Students may practice the words with a partner, use the words in their writing, play games with the words, put them in alphabetical order, or try to make up sentences using two or more words for each sentence. But the most important part of the weekly word bank is the daily word-sort activities students engage in during the week.

Word Sorts

Word sorts invite small groups of students to categorize words according to some dimension identified by the teacher or a student. Students use their knowledge and learn from and with each other. Teachers can focus on particular word elements, depending on student need, or the activity can be totally student-centered. Moreover, word sorts work particularly well when students in small groups sort the words from their individual word banks. Here are some categories we have seen teachers use in their word-sort activities with students:

- Words sorted into three piles: words with one syllable, words with two syllables, and words with three or more syllables.
- Words that contain consonant blends (anywhere in the word) and words that don't.
- Words with long vowel sounds, words with short vowel sounds, and words with both.
- Words with other words spelled within them.
- Words sorted into nouns, verbs, adjectives, and all others.
- Words that describe a person's feelings and words that don't.
- Words you really like and want to use in your speaking and writing and words you don't particularly like.
- Words with more than one meaning and words with only one meaning.

As you can see, students may enjoy an almost limitless number of sorts.

Paula uses word sorts with her students several times each week. After a mini-lesson on syllabication, Paula's students work in groups of three to sort their word-bank cards into words containing one, two, three, and more than three syllables. On other occasions, she asks students to sort words by initial consonants, vowels sounds, long and short vowels, prefixes and suffixes, and other word characteristics with which she wants her students to become familiar. She says,

> I think it's important for students to put into practice the strategies we are exploring. Word sorts give students the opportunity to test their knowledge with words they are already familiar with, and the sorts allow me to observe how well students have grasped and can use the strategies. I think it's also important to note that when groups of students use word sorts they actually teach and reinforce each other as they go.

Word sorts work because they are a two-barreled approach to word recognition. On the one hand, several word sorts with a set of words give students repeated exposure to those words. This is a critical element of successful word recognition learning. Second, every word sort requires students to examine each word from a particular perspective. During one sort students may look at a set of words for the number of syllables they contain. A second sort may require students to examine the same words for consonant blends or vowel digraphs. A third sort focuses on word meanings. With each new exposure to the words, students examine them from different perspectives. This helps students develop fully analyzed, in-depth knowledge of words, an essential word recognition skill, especially for those students who struggle in reading (Gaskins et al., 1997). Students can also sort their words into their own creative categories, an approach that Paula sometimes uses with her class. After a few minutes of sorting, groups of students try to guess (infer) the categories created by other groups. Sometimes Paula simply asks each group to explain its way of categorizing. "But they really prefer the guessing," she says. "It's like a game to them, but I'm constantly amazed at the high level of thinking."

Word Families (Phonograms)

Many words that children encounter in their reading are made up of common word parts, or rimes. Recognizing the *an* word part can help students decode words such as *can, pan, ant, pant, fantasy,* and so on. Edward Fry (1998) has identified 38 of the most common *word families.* See Appendix F for a list of common word families and letter patterns. Knowledge of word families can help students figure out unknown words.

Word families or phonograms have had wide appeal to teachers for many years. The big question, though, is how they can be taught in a thorough manner that leads students to reading real text. We believe the following routine does just that. This three- or four-day sequence requires about 30 minutes per day, in which students go from brainstorming words belonging to a particular word family to actual reading and writing text that contains the word-family words. The routine goes as follows:

On the first day, the teacher introduces students to a particular word family. Let us say that word family is *old,* as in *gold* and *fold.* The teacher begins by introducing students to the three-letter *phonogram* along with the distinct sound associated with the combination of the letters. Students examine the phonogram and its sound. Then, with the teacher, they brainstorm words that contain the phonogram, or that rhyme with it. The teacher writes words such as *gold, fold, mold, bold, sold, scold, cold, hold,* and *told* on chart paper as students pronounce them. Relatively rare or unfamiliar words are discussed as presented. In addition, the teacher and students contribute longer words, such as *golden, unfolded,* and *scaffold,* to illustrate that even longer words can be at least partially unlocked with their knowledge of the *old* phonogram. These words are then read a couple of times and discussed further.

The second day of this instructional routine begins with students again chanting and talking about the words they had brainstormed during the earlier session. The teacher introduces the students to short texts that contain several instances of the phonogram in question. In this case, students see the nursery rhyme *Old King Cole* written on another piece of chart paper. They listen to the teacher read it to them once or twice, then try it themselves, chorally, in groups, and individually if they like. Students may then point out words that contain the *old* phonogram. After this rhyme is read and discussed, a second poem is introduced and students read and examine it just as they did the first one.

When teachers cannot find a suitable poem, they can easily concoct their own or rewrite familiar song lyrics to feature the targeted phonogram. For example, *Mary Had a Little Lamb* could be rewritten as "Mary had a little gold" (that she liked to hold). These texts carry an important message to students. Students need to see their teachers as readers and writers if they are going to become readers and writers themselves.

At the end of the second day's session, teachers ask students to use the phonogram being studied to write their own 4–6 line poems. If younger students or others struggle with the task, older more experienced students may act as coaches and aids to the budding poets. Some students may want to write their poem in pairs or groups in order to make the task less daunting. Teachers may also ask parents to assist their children in developing these simple rhymes. Students write their poems down on a piece of paper and practice them in anticipation of the third day's session.

On the third day, students use chart paper to write enlarged versions of their poems. The chart poems are then hung around the room. Reading instruction, then, for this third day, consists of a poetry festival in which the entire class, or small groups therein, go around the room and read each poem several times, making sure to focus on words that belong to the targeted word family. If the author of a particular poem is in the group of students, that student author may begin by reading his or her poem aloud and explaining why and how it was produced. Following is the poem made up by one first-grade student, with his parents, after the class had studied the *et* phonogram and were now engaged in work on the *ick* phonogram.

> Icky sticky prickly pet
> Porcupines for dinner
> Have you had yours yet?

This may not be a prize-winning poem, but the child who wrote it was proud of his composition as well as his fluent performance of the poem for classmates.

Students love to perform, and they love to write when they know that their work will be honored and celebrated. Moreover, when students learn about decoding words at the same time, we'd say you were onto big and powerful instruction.

Once students have written several poems, they can be easily published. The teacher simply collects the poems, types them, adds appropriate student artwork, and has students create a cover. Then the typed poetry collection is copied and bound for each student and the classroom. The pride students take in seeing their poetry published will lead them to reading the poems again and again and writing new ones.

Making Words

Making Words is another activity to include in a comprehensive reading program (Cunningham & Cunningham, 1992). The activity has several key features. Students make up their own increasingly complex words by concretely manipulating a limited set of letters. Those who find word recognition difficult are often overwhelmed by the seemingly endless number of letters and letter-sound patterns they must encounter. Limiting the number of letters helps students focus on the essential characteristics of a few letters at a time. As with most activities, we recommend that students work in pairs or small groups so that they can learn more thoroughly by talking with and teaching each other.

Making Words begins when the teacher selects a "magic" word of between five and eight letters from students' previous reading and determines a set of words that can be made from the letters of the "magic" word. Anagram Web sites (e.g., www.wordsmith.org/anagram) are a good source for words.

The teacher hands out one 1-inch square of paper for each letter to each group, and calls out the letters of the "secret" word. Students write one letter on each slip. Then the fun begins.

Mel makes words with several of his primary Title I classes. He begins by asking student pairs to arrange the letters into two-letter words. Next, students call out their constructions and Mel writes a few of the words on the board. Mel also tells students words and observes their efforts to produce them with their letters. Next, students work through three-, four-, five-, and six-letter words. Mel writes many of these on the board as well. The activity ends with Mel challenging his students to determine the "secret" word, the word that uses all the letters from the day's lesson.

Mel and his students explore some of the words on the board, noticing word families and moving from one word to another through letter changes. "What would I have to do to change *part* to *art* to *par*? To change *art* to *arch*? To change *par* to *parka*?" Mel often cuts up a transparency into squares and does the activity with his students on an overhead projector so that students can see the manipulations. He may do the same with large index cards and a pocket chart. Making Words is fast-paced. Students learn, in a concrete way, that words and the letters that form them can be manipulated in a variety of ways. Mel's students like the fast pace of the activity and being actively involved throughout the 10- to 15-minute session.

Making and Writing Words

Making Words is a powerful way to help students understand how words are composed of letters. Its use of letter cards or squares can be a bit messy as cards fall to the floor or become lost during the lesson. *Making and Writing Words (MWW)* (Rasinski, 1999), a variation, involves students making words by writing them rather than manipulating letter cards. The act of writing the words may facilitate, even more, students' memory for the words that they make. Because MWW requires facility in writing, it may be more appropriate for slightly older students, Grade 2 and above.

Just like Making Words, MWW begins with selecting a set of consonants and vowels to use in the lesson. Students write the letters in the appropriate boxes on a blank form. Then, as with Making Words, students are guided through a series of words using the given letters, from short words to longer words. The final word in the set is always a "secret" word that uses all the letters in the vowel and consonant boxes. Following is a scenario for the MWW activity.

Vowels: a, o

Consonants: d, g, n, r

- In box 1, write this two-letter word /or/ as in "I would like either a bicycle *or* a basketball for my birthday."
- In box 2, write a two-letter word that means the opposite of *off.* *(on)*
- Box 3 needs a two-letter word that means the opposite of *stop.* *(go)*
- In boxes 4 and 5, write two words that belong to the /on/ word family and that are boys' names; remember what special thing you have to do to names of people. *(Ron* and *Don)*
- For box 6, write a three-letter word that is a name of an animal that people like to have for pets. *(dog)*
- In box 7, write the word *rag.* Who can tell the class what a rag is? *(rag)*
- Box 8 is a word that rhymes with *rag* and that describes what a child says a parent does when asking the child several times to do something the child doesn't want to do. *(nag)*
- In box 9, write the word *drag;* it has four letters. *(drag)*
- Okay, in box 10 write the word that describes what you might have done with a bell; four letters. *(rang)*
- Great. Now, box 11 is the mystery word. See if you can figure out what word uses all the letters we have used. *(dragon)*

Vowels		Consonants
1	6	11
2	7	12
3	8	13
4	9	14
5	10	15
T1	T2	T3

This secret word then becomes a segue into a story about dragons or a discussion or study of dragons. In addition, MWW forms include boxes marked T1, T2, and T3 for transfer activities. Here students write new words that rely on some of the patterns or letters found in the first 11 words, but also require application of new letters. The transfer activities allow students to generalize some of the letters and letter patterns they had been working with to new words. Here are some transfer words students may be asked to write:

- In box T1, write the word *stagger.* Look at some of the words you have written earlier to help you figure this word out.
- In box T2, write *drank.*
- And in box T3, write the word *wagon.*

In the final part of the MWW activity, students cut out the words they have just made and sort them into structural, pattern, and semantic categories.

Terri, a third-grade teacher, is a firm believer in Making Words. However, she finds that MWW makes the process easier for her and more engaging for all her students:

It's easy to do; all I do is choose the secret word, determine the words and their sequence to be made from the letters of the secret word, make copies of the Making and Writing Words sheet for each student, and we're ready to go. I like the idea that students actually write the words. Sometimes I ask them to write some of the more difficult words two or three times in the appropriate box so that they get a good mental and kinesthetic image for how the word is written. When I do Making and Writing Words with students, I usually have a transparency of the form and I do it with the students. If they have trouble, they only need to look up at what I have written on the overhead projector. Of course, sometimes I make purposeful mistakes to make sure they check my work, too. We often take two or three days with one set of letters. I try not to take more than 15 minutes on this activity. I want to do other word and reading activities with my students. So, on the first day, we might do the making and transferring part of the activity. On the second and third days we usually do a quick review, especially of word families, do a few more transfer words, and then do some quick word sorts. Students like the fast pace to the activity. And they also like the fact that they can be successful at it themselves.

Word Ladders

Like Making Words and Making and Writing Words, *word ladders* allow students to build and examine words with support throughout the process. In word ladders, each new word students make is based on the previous word. Thus, students gain support from their previously made words.

Word ladders begin with the teacher asking the students to create a numbered list and write the first word of the ladder next to number 1. Then, the teacher guides students in making a new word for each number. The word ladder below demonstrates the process.

1. *trick*
2. *track* Change a letter in *trick* to make a word that describes what trains ride on.
3. *trace* Change a letter in *track* to make a word that describes the process of copying of a picture by placing a transparent sheet of paper atop the picture and drawing the copy.
4. *Grace* Change the first letter to make a girl's name.
5. *grate* Change a letter to make a word that describes what you do to shred a hunk of cheese into smaller pieces.
6. *great* Rearrange the last three letters in *grate* to make a homophone word that means big or wonderful.
7. *treat* Change a letter in *great* to make a word that goes with the word next to number 1.

In word ladders, the last word should somehow be associated with the first word. This simple feature often invites students to develop their own word ladders. Teachers can challenge students to go from *first* to *last* or *girl* to *boy* by adding, subtracting, or changing one letter at a time, or rearranging the letters already in a word.

Word Walls

One of our goals in word recognition instruction is to create a physical classroom environment that encourages word exploration and play. One step toward creating such an environment is through *word walls*. Pat Cunningham describes word walls as one aspect of a four-part instructional strategy in reading (Cunningham & Cunningham, 1992; Cunningham, Hall, & Defee, 1998). We like to think of word walls as part community word bank, part graffiti wall, a place where students feel free to write their own words and commentaries.

A teacher may choose from several types of word walls and may have more than one word wall in her class. One might focus on words belonging to particular word families and be organized by word families. You might add

Word walls help create an enviroment that says "words are important here."

selected words built during Making Words or Making and Writing Words activities to your word wall. Another word wall may direct students' attention to high-frequency sight words, such as those found in Appendix O. These words may be introduced at a rate of 3 to 5 per week (over the course of grades 1 through 3) and arranged alphabetically on this second word wall. A third wall, which we like to call the graffiti wall, contains words that teachers and students find interesting and provocative in their own reading. These may be placed alphabetically on the word wall, or randomly, as graffiti is often arranged. Finally, words that students encounter in other content areas may become the content of a fourth word wall. Of course, some teachers may want to integrate different types of words onto one word wall, but distinguish them by color or code (e.g., all words that have an asterisk next to them belong to a particular word family).

One of the great appeals of word walls is the implicit message they send to students and any other visitors to the room. Just imagine walking into a classroom in which you are greeted with words, words, and more words. Word walls tell students that words matter, that words are interesting, and that words are worth exploring and knowing. We can think of no other way to make this powerful message more apparent than through classroom word walls.

A word wall begins when the teacher places a large piece of butcher or chart paper on a classroom wall. Every day the class adds a word or two to the wall. The words may relate to a current world or community event. Teacher and students explore other words related to the chosen words for the day and write them on the wall, often connecting them with lines like an idea web. Teacher and students also look for letter patterns in the chosen words and brainstorm other words that contain the pattern. Students practice and refer to the words on the wall often. In some classrooms, students may use the word wall to jot down their own words or ideas to be read by all students and to spur lively oral and written discussion.

Sherrie is a fifth-grade teacher. A visitor to her class can't miss the word wall; it takes up an entire bulletin board. One day the word *portage* was selected for the wall because a student came upon it in his reading. (The school, incidently, is located in Portage County.) After talking about the meaning of the word, Sherrie and her students added and discussed other related words (either by meaning or structure). Among them were *canoe, river, port, porter, portable, sort, porous,* and *sage.* Sherrie reports that each word wall fills up in less than two weeks. She leaves it up for a few days after it is filled because her students often refer to the words in their own writing or discussion and continue to add words that connect to the ones on the wall. Even though the wall may look a bit messy after several days of student contributions, Sherrie notes that it is important to the class as a whole because the words are meaningful for students, and the wall itself is a joint venture to which all students want to contribute.

Contextual Analysis

In addition to analyzing letters and letter combinations to decode or recognize words, proficient readers use *context.* In other words, readers use passage and sentence meaning as well as their own knowledge about the world to predict unknown words. For example, consider the following sentence:

The mail carrier was bitten by a _____.

Readers figure out the unknown word by combining sentence information with what they know about the stereotypical predicament of postal carriers on their rounds. Combining this information leads to the prediction or inference that the missing word is most likely *dog.* Thus, a reasonable prediction can be made without using any letter or phonic information from the word itself.

We can help readers use context by asking them to think about what an unknown word might be based on the meaning of the passage rather than always advising them to "sound it out." Similarly, teachers occasionally explain to their students how they figure out unknown words in their own reading. Some experts call this explanation of one's problem-solving process "think alouds." Teaching is about making such subtleties clear and apparent to students.

Another activity that helps develop readers' use of context is the *cloze procedure.* Cloze may seem like an odd name, but it is based on the psychological understanding that human beings attempt to provide closure or completeness to incomplete illustrations or objects. In the cloze procedure the reader attempts to impose closure on incomplete linguistic data by using the available contextual information. The teacher deletes certain words from a passage by marking over them with a marker or retyping the passage with blanks for the deleted words. Cloze texts for younger readers may be big books or chart stories in which the teacher simply covers selected words or word parts with sticky notes. Here is an example of a cloze activity taken from *Strega Nona's Magic Lesson* by Tomie dePaola, 1982:

> Bambolona, the baker's daughter, was angry. Every day, summer, fall, _____, and _____, she had to get up before the sun to bake the _____. Then, piling the _____ on her head, she went to deliver them.

When creating a cloze passage, it is a good idea to leave the first sentence intact so that readers can establish a mental framework for the text.

The reader's job is to use the context before and after the deleted words to identify the deletions. After completing a passage with 20 to 30 deletions, students share their guesses with one another and discuss the clues they used to make their predictions. The teacher may also provide the author's actual words. Cloze activities work well in groups as students verbalize their own strategies for predicting words with their partners.

The cloze procedure has several variations. Students unfamiliar with the procedure or who are dealing with a difficult text may be overwhelmed by a passage containing many deleted words. The task can be made easier by placing possible answers next to each blank or listing all the deleted words at the end of the passage. The activity is then called a *maze* or *multiple-choice cloze*.

> One day Bambolona said, "Papa, there is too much _____ (work, noise, money) to do. I need some _____ (fun, work, help)."
>
> "Get up earlier," her father said.
>
> "But I get up now before the _____!" said _____. "And I'm the last one in town to _____ to bed."
>
> "That's the way things are," _____ father said as he went out the _____ on his way to the _____.
>
> (Bambolona, square, her, go, door, sun)

Good readers simultaneously employ both context and letter information to decode difficult words. Cloze activities can be designed so that students integrate both sources of information about words. Here's an example from Gary Paulsen's *Hatchet,* 1999:

> Somehow the plane was still flying. Seconds had passed, nearly a m_____, and the plane f_____ on as if nothing had happened, and he had to do something, had to do something but did n_____ know what. . . .
>
> He st_____ one h_____ toward the p_____, saw that his fingers were trembling, and touched the pilot on the chest. . . .

> The pl_____ lurched again, hit more t_____, and Brian felt the nose dr_____. It did not d_____, but the n_____ went down slightly and the down-angle i_____ the speed, and he knew that at this angle, this slight angle d_____, he would ultimately f_____ into the tr_____.

In this passage readers employ both context and the beginning letter or letter combination, which are the most salient graphic cues for trying to recognize missing words.

Key elements in succeeding with the cloze procedure include choosing texts that challenge but do not overwhelm, giving students time and assistance in predicting the missing words, and encouraging students to share strategies and clues in identifying the unknown words. Other examples of cloze passages are found in Appendix G.

Karen, a Title I teacher who works with primary-grade children, finds that many students become so hung up on sounding out words that they fail to attend to the meaning of the passage. They often come up with responses that are nonwords or words that fail to fit the meaning of the passage. Karen designs cloze passages for these children. She chooses stories that students have read a few days previously and found interesting. "This ensures that the students have a familiarity with the content and that they have a motivation for reading," she says. As students become more adept at using context she may choose unfamiliar passages from a sequel or written by a familiar author.

She may also add challenge by increasing the number of blanks within a given passage but always ensuring that enough context remains for making good predictions. As a rule of thumb, Karen provides at least four words of actual text for every word she deletes when developing her most challenging cloze passages.

Karen believes that student talk really counts in cloze activities. "I think that the most important part of the cloze activity is when we talk after the groups have had a chance to fill in the blanks. Students talk about the various strategies they used to figure out the blanks. This is where you see the lights go on in students' heads as they say to themselves, 'Oh yeah! I didn't think about doing it that way.'"

Dealing With Longer Words

Long words can daunt young and struggling readers, and initially these unfamiliar words are often difficult to handle as whole units. When proficient readers come to longer words, they tend to break the word into manageable chunks and apply basic word recognition strategies to the chunks until they become familiar with the word. Struggling readers should be guided to use the same type of approach. Readers can choose among several strategies to break down longer words into more manageable units.

Syllabication rules. Longer words can often be broken into vowel-dominated sound units called *syllables*. Two basic syllabication rules can be quite helpful for students.

> VCCV When two vowels are separated by two consonants (each repre-
> senting a consonant sound), try separating the word into syllables
> between the two consonants (e.g., *center, bottom, winter, cancel,
> mentor, chapter*).
>
> VCV When two vowels are separated by one consonant, try separating
> the word into syllables before the consonant (e.g., *open, basic, pilot,
> laser, final).*

Compound words. *Compound words* are combinations of two whole words. For example, *everybody* divides into *every* and *body,* and either can be identified as a whole word or analyzed in smaller units.

Meaningful word patterns. Earlier in this chapter we mentioned the importance of recognizing patterns of letters within words in decoding words. Those patterns, called phonograms, word families, or rimes, are sound-based patterns. The combination of vowel and consonant produces a consistent sound that is helpful when attempting to decode an unknown word.

These are just a few kinds of patterns students should learn. Many worthwhile meaning-bearing patterns are found in prefixes, suffixes, and word parts derived from Greek and Latin. These are often called *morphemes.* Longer words are often divided into smaller parts by morphemes (prefixes, suffixes, base words) (e.g., *microscope, uniform, interplanetary, bicycle, submarine*).

Because these patterns bear meaning, knowledge of morphemes helps students decode and determine the meaning of words. For example, knowing that the following word patterns are derived from Greek and are meaningful, *acro* meaning high place, *polis* meaning city, and *phobia* meaning fear, will help readers decode and understand the words *acrophobia* and *Acropolis.* Indeed, creative minds can even invent new words such as *poliphobia* (fear of cities) and challenge classmates to determine the meaning of the new words.

Appendix J contains a list of meaning-bearing word parts useful with elementary students. Chapter 7 provides more information on the use of Latin and Greek derivations to develop vocabulary.

Teaching these meaningful word patterns may resemble the routine used with phonograms. Day 1 might be a mini-lesson to introduce one or two patterns and invite students to identify words that contain them. Subsequent days could be spent writing, reading, and having fun with texts that contain the targeted patterns. With regular use, students will begin to make good use of their knowledge of meaningful patterns in their reading.

Reading and Games

The best way for students to put their word recognition strategies to use is through plenty of contextual reading. Through actual reading, readers become adept at using helpful word recognition strategies. Moreover, through repeated exposure to many words, they add to their sight vocabularies—words that can be recognized instantly at sight without having to rely on any recognition strategy. Thus, reading actually reduces the number of words readers must decode.

Occasional games can add a different dimension to reading instruction while giving students enjoyable practice at recognizing words. Most are simple, and many are variations of popular television game shows. Here are a few of our favorites.

Scrabble. This classic board game challenges players to construct words from a limited set of letters that fit within an array of letters already on the board.

Hangman and Wheel of Fortune. Players guess unknown words and phrases by calling out possible letters within the words and having the letters entered into the word frame. Players have limited opportunities to call out letters that might fit into the unknown word or phrase.

Wordo. This game is a variation of Bingo. In Wordo, blank bingo cards are randomly filled with words that students have been practicing (see Figure 5.1). Using no particular order, the teacher or game leader calls out the words, their definitions, or sentences containing the words in which the target word is left blank. Players find and cover up their word squares as the words are

Games can provide enjoyable practice in word recognition.

Figure 5.1

A blank Wordo card

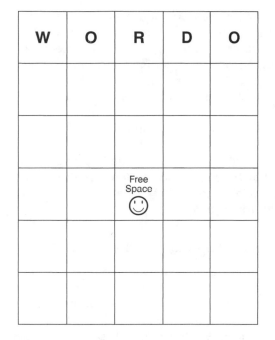

W	O	R	D	O
		Free Space ☺		

called or identified. (Dried lima beans are excellent inexpensive markers for covering words.) The first player with a complete line of words running across, down, or diagonally is the winner.

The traditional 5 × 5 Wordo matrix works well with upper elementary grades. Teachers may wish to give younger students a 4 × 4 or 3 × 3 matrix so as not to overwhelm them with too many words. Wordo is a good game for practicing and reviewing words under instruction, words that need extra practice to develop automaticity, and key words from other subject areas such as science and social studies.

Match. Match is a variation of Concentration, a memory game popular with young children. Match is played with 15 or 20 matching pairs of word cards. The cards are randomly laid in a grid on a flat surface. Players uncover two cards at a time, saying each word as it is turned over. If the two word cards contain the same word, the player keeps the cards and is allowed to uncover two more cards. Play continues until all cards have been matched and removed from the playing grid. Players count their cards, and the player with the most cards is declared the winner.

Word War. In Word War, a variation of the popular card game War, each player has a deck of cards. (One child can use the word-bank deck and deal it out evenly to all players.) Each player plays one card at a time by uncovering the card at the top of his deck, saying the word, and laying it on the table. She who plays the word with the most letters and says the word correctly wins the round and takes the other players' cards. In a tie, each player involved uncovers a second card and says the word. In this tie-breaking round, the player with the most letters wins all the cards played in the entire round. Another tie results in another tie-breaking round.

Gary teaches remedial math and reading to intermediate-grade students. In his class, word games create an added sense of playfulness and spontaneity. He reserves one day every two weeks for word games and uses quick games whenever a few extra minutes remain at the end of class. "Students respond well to the games and the games make our word study more like playing around with words, which is how I want them to think of it."

Although many commercially prepared reading games exist, we think games that teachers and students make or adapt are best. Teachers and students have ownership of these games, and students' own study words integrate better into the game.

Multisensory Approaches to Word Recognition

Some children still struggle with word recognition even with effective and varied instruction. They seem unable to perceive common familiar words and have tremendous difficulty seeing patterns in longer unfamiliar words. One approach for helping these children involves the use of several sensory modalities. This is often referred to as the *visual-auditory-kinesthetic-tactile approach (VAKT)*. *Kinesthetic* refers to the position and movement of body parts, hand, and mouth in recognizing words. *Tactile* refers to touch. An early version of this approach was described by Grace Fernald (1943), who developed a multisensory approach that she used successfully with children having extreme difficulty in learning to recognize words.

In VAKT approaches, students initially learn words of their own choosing by seeing, saying, tracing, and touching printed versions of the word until they can trace or write the words without looking at them. Thus students perceive words visually and aurally as they say and see them. Kinesthetic perception develops through the body movement involved in saying and tracing the word, and tactile perception happens when the student touches the written word as she says or traces it. The learned words become a word bank used in language experience stories created by the student and teacher.

Often children with severe reading difficulties need two or more months of instruction before beginning to recognize words without having to trace them. As students become more adept at perceiving words and word patterns, the teacher begins to reduce some of the modality support. Students might trace the words in the air while looking at a printed copy or move to the point of recognizing and writing words just from seeing and saying them. Students also move from reading their own stories to reading books, beginning with easy texts and progressing to more challenging ones. Eventually, students should learn to recognize new words by recognizing familiar patterns in them, as most proficient readers do.

The VAKT approach is labor intensive. It usually requires considerable time and is most effective in individual instruction. Thus, we consider it a method of last resort for children experiencing severe difficulty in word recognition. Nevertheless, teachers do use variations and portions of multimodal approaches within their regular classroom or clinical instruction.

Kim, a Title I teacher, had one group of second graders facing considerable difficulty recognizing and remembering the words they encountered in their reading. When these children added words to their word banks by writing the words on blank cards, Kim had them trace each word several times while slowly saying the word. Then she asked them to turn over the word card and write the word on a piece of scratch paper. Similarly, she encouraged students to trace with their fingers words added to the group's word wall when they were at the wall practicing the words or making an entry. "I really find that for these students the added practice of touching and tracing the words makes them easier to remember. And I found that I only had to do this for about eight weeks. Students quickly began to pick up key patterns in words. When they hit unfamiliar words, they began to trace them on their own. They saw the value of the tracing and touching without my even having to tell them."

Fluency Building and Wide Reading

Learning how to decode words accurately is only part of how proficient readers deal with text. They also read with fluency. That is, they read effortlessly and expressively in phrases and other large chunks of text, not word by word.

In chapter 6 we discuss instructional strategies that help students become more fluent in their reading. Fortunately, these strategies for building fluency also help students with word recognition. Studies have found that students who engage in fluency-building activities such as repeated readings or paired reading also make substantial improvement in their ability to recognize words accurately and quickly. As you read chapter 6, keep in mind that these strategies can also help children who experience difficulty in decoding written text.

Once again, we repeat this critical point: Wide and authentic reading must be at the heart of all successful reading and word recognition instruction. All readers, whether proficient or struggling, need to read real texts of their own choosing. Through wide, in-depth reading, children practice their word recognition strategies. Moreover, by encountering new words and becoming exposed to words and word parts that appear frequently, students begin to recognize many words automatically.

Reading programs that successfully help children learn to read, overcome difficulties in learning to read, and develop a genuine love of reading seem to have one thing in common: Students read plenty of connected discourse. They read daily in their regular classrooms; for a large portion of their corrective or remedial reading time; and at home, encouraged and supported by parents. The more children read, the better they become in all aspects of reading—word recognition, fluency, attitude, vocabulary, and comprehension. As Gary has told us, "You can't expect children to *learn* to read if they don't get the *chance* to read. . . . You have to read!"

Making It Work Through Instructional Routines

Knowledge of instructional strategies is only one part of developmental, corrective, or remedial reading instruction. The other part is designing coherent instructional packages or routines that use selected strategies in informed ways. Sensible instructional routines begin and end with students who are reading real texts. Word recognition should be a small but consistent part of instruction if students experience difficulty in this area. Don't try to use every instructional activity presented here. Rather, choose a few that make sense for your students and apply them consistently from one day to the next. Thus, instruction becomes predictable for students, and teaching time is used efficiently in actual instruction rather than in explaining a new activity or managing behavior.

That's how Mary designs instruction for her students with word recognition difficulties. She works with groups of five students for 30 minutes a day, 5 days a week. She begins the instructional period by reading a short story or poem to the students. Next, the group chorally reads and rereads the same text but presented in an enlarged format (perhaps on chart paper). Previously introduced stories are also read. Next, students choose a word or two from the text to add to their word banks. For 5 or 10 minutes students work in pairs on various word-bank activities including word sorts and games. Three days a week, Mary works with students on word-family exploration, and on the other 2 days the group works through cloze texts taken from passages the students have recently read in Mary's class or their regular class. In addition, Making and Writing Words word games are regular parts of the instructional period.

Mary's instructional periods are all business. Because students are familiar with the routine, they are highly engaged in reading throughout the lesson and benefit well from instruction. Progress is increasing and sustained where once it was painfully slow.

Word recognition is only one part of learning to read proficiently. It is an important and necessary part, however, and many struggling readers cannot recognize words accurately and quickly. Word recognition instruction should have two major aims: to help children learn to decode unknown words, and to help them recognize familiar words quickly or automatically. The best way to accomplish both goals is to provide a little direct instruction in word recognition and a lot of guided authentic reading experiences. Thus, children can apply the instruction immediately and repeatedly in real reading situations.

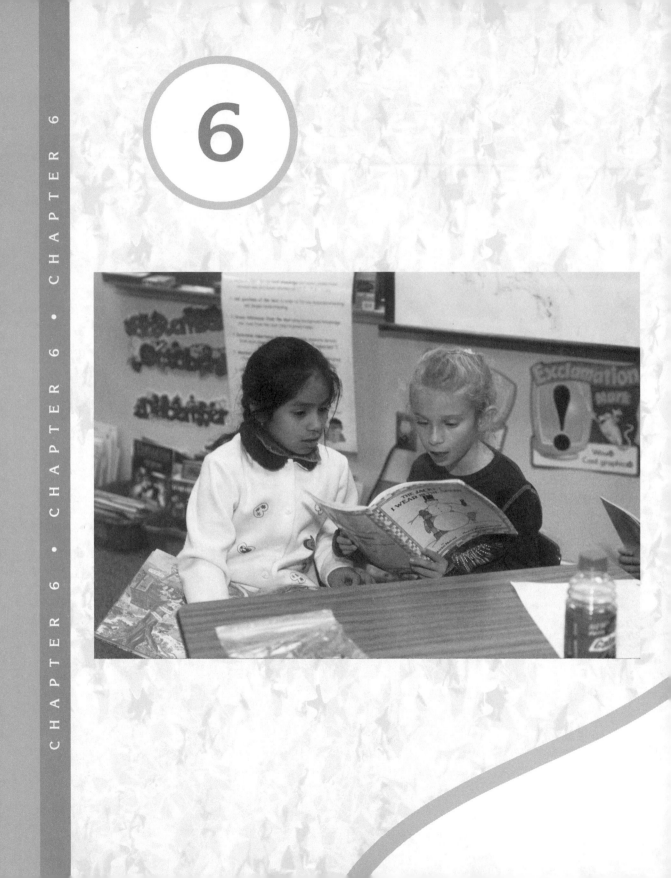

Nurturing Fluent Reading

Accuracy in word recognition does not ensure proficient reading. On the surface, students often exhibit good word recognition skills, reading with few noticeable errors. A slightly deeper analysis, however, may show that they read with excessive slowness and choppiness; their oral reading seems dull and expressionless, almost labored, as if they gain no satisfaction or enjoyment from reading. Most likely, these readers have significant trouble in achieving fluency.

Most people can tell when they are listening to a fluent reader or speaker. Words and phrases such as "quick," "with expression," "good phrasing," or "reads in a meaningful way" indicate fluent reading. We agree that these terms, and others, are valid indicators of reading fluency.

One of the best ways to think about fluency is to consider that it deals with larger, multiple-word units of texts. Disfluent readers read so slowly that they appear to deal individually with each word they encounter. Fluent readers, on the other hand, read quickly enough and with appropriate phrasing and expression to make clear they are working with larger units of text. Phrases, clauses, and sentences are more important units of text and meaning for fluent readers.

Why is the ability to read quickly and in appropriate textual units so important? We like to use the analogy of fluent and disfluent speaking when discussing the importance of reading fluency. Fluent speakers actually help listeners understand their message. They speak fast enough that the listener can quickly process the message. They speak in meaningful phrases and embed expression and pauses into their speech to help the listener make sense of the speech as easily as possible. Disfluent speakers, on the other hand, speak in a slow, labored, word-by-word fashion that makes it difficult for the listener to discern the intended message.

In the same way, a fluent reader efficiently processes the text's surface-level information to make it as easy as possible to comprehend. Word-by-word, expressionless, slow reading diminishes the reader's ability to understand the text. Those listening to disfluent oral reading often have similar comprehension problems. We believe that problems in fluency are a major contributor to reading difficulties among elementary and middle-school students.

The National Assessment of Educational Progress (NAEP)(Pinnell et al., 1995) study of students' reading fluency development showed that 45 percent of all U.S. fourth graders read below minimally acceptable levels of fluency. Indeed, only 13 percent of fourth graders were found to be reading at the highest level of fluency. According to NAEP, then, nearly one out of every two elementary readers fails to read with acceptable fluency. Recently, we studied elementary-grade children from a large urban school district who were referred for special tutoring in reading in the Title I program (Rasinski & Padak, 1998). As part of their initial diagnostic assessment, children read and answered questions about two passages that were near their grade placement. From this reading we could measure students' word recognition, reading fluency, and comprehension. Fluency was measured by rate of reading. We found that students' performance tended to be below grade level in all three areas. Word recognition and comprehension, however, were not drastically below grade level, but fluency was. These students' reading performance was dramatically and consistently marked by excessively slow and labored oral reading. Anyone listening to these children read knew that they were struggling.

We believe that reading fluency is a significant obstacle to proficient reading for elementary students and many older struggling readers. Indeed, a large majority of the students referred to our university reading center for corrective reading tutoring manifest significant problems in achieving fluency.

Although important, fluency has been an ignored instructional goal for reading. In 1983, Richard Allington called reading fluency the neglected goal of the reading program. Fluency suggestions were largely absent from reading instructional materials. More recently, Rasinski and Zutell (1996) looked at published instructional materials for reading. Thirteen years after Allington's claims about fluency, Rasinski and Zutell found that much the same conditions existed. If fluency is not nurtured through published instructional materials, then informed and dedicated elementary teachers must see that students receive adequate and appropriate instruction in this absolutely essential aspect of reading.

Despite its relative neglect, recent reviews of research on reading fluency (Kuhn & Stahl, 2000; National Reading Panel, 2000) have determined that fluency is an important and necessary component of successful reading instruction. Moreover, our own work with struggling readers indicates that it is an area of concern. Fortunately, the research also indicates that reading fluency can be effectively taught. In the following sections we address how teachers assess and provide effective instruction in this critical area.

Assessing Reading Fluency

We assess readers' level of fluency in several ways. When teachers desire a quantifiable method for assessing fluency, reading rate offers a relatively simple and direct approach. An easy way to calculate rate is to ask a reader to read a text orally in his normal manner. The chosen text should be at the reader's grade level in difficulty. Time the reader, and at the end of 60 seconds tell him to stop or mark the point in the text the reader has reached in 60 seconds. Then count the number of words read correctly (or corrected if they were initially read incorrectly). This is the reader's rate in words correct per minute (wcpm). Do this procedure a few times and determine an average rate. Compare the student's oral reading rate against the following norms for grade level and time of year (adapted from Hasbrouck & Tindal, 1992; and Howe & Shinn, 2001):

Grade	Fall	Winter	Spring
1			60 wcpm
2	53	78	94
3	79	93	114
4	99	112	118
5	105	118	128
6	115	132	145
7	147	158	167
8	156	167	171

If the reader's rate is consistently and substantially below the appropriate grade-level rate, you can assume the student has fluency difficulties.

Another approach to assessing fluency is simply to listen to students read orally. By paying attention to students' expression, phrasing, and pace, teachers build a good idea of each student's reading fluency. Choose a text at or below each student's instructional level. Usually a text one or two grade levels below grade placement will ensure this. Allow the child to read through the passage silently and answer any questions about the pronunciation or meaning of specific words in the passage. After this preview, ask the student to read the same passage orally for you. Tape record the passage and simply observe the student during the reading. Look for signs of frustration or strain during the student's oral reading.

Later, when you are alone, listen to the student's tape-recorded reading. Without looking for word recognition errors, rate the reading in terms of expression, rate, and phrasing. You must develop an "ear" for reading to do this sort of assessment. This information, combined with the reading rate, provides a good assessment of fluency.

Teaching Fluency

Fortunately, several holistic approaches for improving reading fluency (Rasinski, 1989; 2003) also boost word recognition proficiency and students' feelings of success as readers.

Model Fluent Reading

Struggling readers often do not know what fluent reading should sound like. They lack good self-awareness of fluent reading. They are often segregated into groups of children with similar difficulties. The readers they hear are usually like them—disfluent and frustrated. Most of us would agree that learning something is difficult if we don't understand what it should look or sound like. That is why modeling fluent reading, commonly called reading aloud to and with children, is especially important for less able readers.

When these children learn what fluent reading sounds like, they can develop their own models of what fluent reading is. Reading to children helps accomplish this goal, which can be further reinforced by talking with children about fluency after read-aloud sessions. Before the read-aloud begins, a teacher might ask students to listen for variations in voice, phrasing, rate, expression, or volume. After reading, a teacher might ask students, "How did I communicate love or hate or fear or excitement with my voice during the reading?" Asking students to listen for various aspects of fluent reading and talk about them is a first step toward helping students read fluently on their own.

Another appropriate practice is for the teacher to read a text aloud to students before asking them to read it on their own. This preview reading helps students develop a sense of how the text should sound; it also conveniently and unobtrusively introduces students to words they may not have encountered before in print.

Terri knows about modeling fluent reading for her third-grade class. She recognized early in the school year that several of her lower-achieving students were disfluent readers. She has developed a program that involves her students in paired and repeated reading, which we describe later in the chapter. But an equally important part of her fluency instruction involves reading to her class every day:

> About once or twice a week I try to talk with the class about fluency after my reading. At first I had to ask them specific questions about my reading. After a few weeks I only had to ask, "What did you think about my reading?" They began talking about my voicing, phrasing, rate, emphasis on words, and how I used these elements to help convey meaning. Now, when I ask my students to read orally, I remind them to think about

fluency. Not only do they think about it, they read with greater ease and expression. Even the lower kids have gotten into this. I think I've noticed them more because they've made the greatest gains of all.

Terri frequently reads a passage to students and then asks them to read the passage to themselves or aloud to a partner. She believes that preview reading is a good alternative to asking students to read the text silently or introducing the text through a discussion or other activity not directly related to the text reading itself. "This way students get a good introduction to the passage itself because they hear and understand it before they actually read it themselves."

Repeated Readings

Repeated readings is a simple instructional procedure in which students are asked to practice reading one passage several times until they achieve a predetermined degree of fluency, usually defined in terms of rate or word recognition accuracy. Like musicians or athletes, readers must practice certain passages to achieve fluency. Although the activity itself may be simple, the effects of repeated reading are quite powerful. In an early study of this method, Jay Samuels (1979) asked students diagnosed as learning disabled in reading to practice reading short texts until they could read a passage fluently (85 wpm). Samuels found that his students exhibited progress on the passages they were practicing and on new passages. In other words, the benefits of repeated readings were internalized and transferred. Other studies (Dowhower, 1987, 1994; Herman, 1985; Kuhn & Stahl, 2000) have validated Samuels's original finding that repeated readings can help improve students' fluency, word recognition, and comprehension.

Teachers often ask, "How can we persuade students to read a passage more than once?" The best answer to this dilemma is to create situations in which students have a real reason to do so.

In writing classrooms the desired outcome for most writing is some form of publication. In a similar fashion, the natural outcome for practiced reading should be some form of performance. Teachers must think of ways and reasons for students to read for others. Poems are meant to be shared orally, as are play scripts. Informed teachers use poetry, scripts, and dramatic reading as vehicles for repeated reading. Students also practice reading short stories to share with reading buddies in another class or grade. Some students are motivated by the opportunity to work with a friend. Pat Koskinen and Irene Blum (1984, 1986) found that repeated reading is successful in group situations called *paired repeated reading,* in which students read a passage to a partner several times. The partner provides positive feedback and assistance. After several readings, the roles are reversed. Koskinen and Blum found that students enjoyed the alternative format and demonstrated strong gains in fluency, word recognition, and reading for meaning in as little as 15 minutes a day, three times a week, for five weeks.

When fluency difficulties are so severe that performance is not a reasonable option, easier texts may serve. After all, everyone can become disfluent when reading material is difficult. After students develop the fluency habit by practicing with easy, predictable texts, they can return to more challenging material.

Some children in our university tutoring program enjoy reading their texts into recording equipment. They then listen to their oral reading and, with the tutor, decide how to make the next reading more fluent. This process may be repeated several times until the children are satisfied with the sound of their reading. At that point a more public performance may be planned. Recording and analyzing repeated readings helps children develop fluency and an awareness of their own progress in becoming fluent readers. Another suggestion is to track students' performance as they practice reading texts. Then, using a simple graph of reading performance, teachers can show students their progress in increasing their reading rate or decreasing the number of word recognition miscues over several readings of the same text.

Sheila noticed that several of her sixth graders exhibited fluency difficulties—their oral reading was excessively slow with little attention to meaningful phrasing and expression. Sheila believed that these students had developed negative attitudes about reading and themselves. They balked at any opportunity to read aloud and began to cause disruptions during any type of in-class reading. Sheila decided that these students needed opportunities to engage in repeated readings with relatively easy texts so they could experience success in reading. She made arrangements with Tim, a first-grade teacher in her building, to pair each of her sixth-grade students with a first grader. The reading buddies would meet once a week, and during each visit the buddies would read a book to one another. The sixth graders were encouraged to choose books appropriate for first graders. (These were also ideal for her disfluent sixth-grade readers.) Sixth graders practiced these books diligently throughout the week. By Friday they had them down pat, and when they shared them with their buddies, they glowed about their reading success and the awe they inspired in the first graders.

After a few months, Sheila was delighted with her students' progress. "These students have begun to believe in themselves again as readers. They see that they can read fluently and that their reading can have an impact on other children. When I provide instruction for these students they can relate it to their work as tutors and buddies."

Her students have thrived on their weekly sessions. Nonetheless, Sheila has begun to think of other ways for her students to have authentic purposes for reading to others. These include reading at home to parents and developing partnerships with residents of a nearby retirement center. "It really doesn't take a lot for something like this to work," Sheila says, "just someone willing to honestly listen to these children read and give them encouragement. After experiencing so much failure in reading, these kids need to practice to get good, and they need people to tell them that they are good."

Performance.   Students will eagerly practice a passage several times if they know that somewhere down the road they will be asked to perform it. Think of times in your own life when you may have been asked to read a passage or a prayer orally at a friend's wedding or family function. Chances are you practiced that text several times through so that you could read it without error and with good and meaningful expression. We have found that the same is absolutely true for elementary students. The key questions we consider in this notion of performance address just what kinds of performances and texts we want students to engage in. Actually several types of wonderful performance opportunities work well in elementary classrooms and clinics.

Poetry is almost perfect for performance. By its very nature, poetry is meant to be read aloud. The meaning of a poem comes not only from the words, but from the way in which the words are spoken—fluency! Poems feature rhyme, a sense of rhythm, and repetition, which make them highly predictable, easy, and enjoyable to learn to read. Finally, poems are generally short, and students can practice a poem several times through in a short period of time.

Poems should not be a sort of practice text. Rather, we think that poetry study, performance, composition, and appreciation should be a natural part of any elementary classroom. Students and teachers should learn to love poems. Poetry can add unique and valuable benefits to the classroom community. Just one great byproduct of poetry study and performance is the opportunity to foster fluency.

We recommend strongly that teachers develop a space in their professional bookshelves for poetry anthologies. (See Appendix B for a list of poetry resources.) Find poems that match a mood, a time of year, or a special event and share those poems with students. Read and reread poems to students regularly and encourage them to do the same. If you make books of poetry available to students, if you read poetry to your students and enjoy it and invite your students to do the same, you will find your students choosing their own poems, practicing them, and performing them for their classmates. The result is a love affair with poetry and a natural way to nurture fluency in students.

One of our colleagues, Maureen, loves to share poetry with her third-grade students. Indeed, she has taken her love of poetry to new heights. About once or twice a month, students will walk into her classroom and find books of poetry as well as individual poems scattered throughout the room. Students know that this is the signal that they will be having "poetry club" that Friday.

After a brief browsing period, students choose a poem. Some students work in pairs, trios, or quartets for their poems. Other students decide to write and perform their own original poems. Then, throughout the week, when students have an opportunity, they practice their selected poems, making sure that they will be ready to read them during "poetry club."

When Friday afternoon rolls around, the last hour or so of the day is given over to poetry performance. The room is rearranged to resemble a coffeehouse atmosphere. A stage area is created in the front of the room with a stool and microphone (a karaoki machine can fill this purpose nicely). Overhead lights are dimmed, a few desk lamps are lit, and appropriate music plays in the background to create just the right ambience. Maureen usually brings in popcorn and makes hot cider or hot chocolate to complete the coffeehouse. Of course, parents, the school principal, and other school staff are invited to the poetry club.

After everyone has their refreshments, the poetry begins! Students come to the stage and perform their poems. Usually students will talk about why they chose a particular poem or share information they discovered about the poet. Initially, each performance was greeted with applause until a grandparent attending the poetry club, a child of the '50s, suggested that audience members snap their fingers as a way of demonstrating their approval of a poem while not making so much noise that other classrooms were disturbed. Students thought this was really cool.

Maureen thinks her poetry club is cool, too. "My students love it. They ask for it all the time. It just goes to show that when we create real-life environments for students, and when we trust students to do their best, they will. Maybe I can't give all the credit to the poetry club, but I have seen some really significant gains in several students' reading since we started the club. And, I have even seen some student writing that has bowled me over!"

Another type of performance activity to consider is *reader's theater*, in which a group of students performs a script. However, the performance has no costumes, props, movement, scenery, or memorization of lines. Performers simply stand in front of the audience in their normal attire and read the script to the audience. Of course, for the script to have any effect on the audience it needs to be read with expression—hence reader's theater is a superb fluency activity. Performers must practice their lines to eventually perform for their audience in a convincing and entertaining way.

Scripts are found in many places. Collections of short plays are available for elementary readers. Occasionally, the basal reading series or the weekly news magazine for students will have a topical script for performance. Make sure each script can be successfully performed in a reader's theater format. Some books for children are written in a reader's theater format. Books such as Angela Johnson's *Tell Me a Story, Mama* and Donald Hall and Barry Moser's *I Am the Dog; I Am the Cat* have delineated parts that make them a natural for reader's theater performance.

Of course, the best reader's theater scripts are those written by students themselves. This often means simply recasting a picture book or a segment or chapter from a longer book into script form. If you want to try this with your students, direct them at first to short books with a clear plot and lots of dialogue. This is a highly scaffolded experience for students, as they have the original text written to support their writing. Students choose the main characters and number of narrators, making sure that all students in a group have a part. They can simply rewrite the original text as a script without any changes, or they can make additions to the script and delete characters and portions of the text from the original to make it more their own. In all cases, the original text supports, guides, and models their own writing. (If you're thinking this may be an unauthentic writing activity, simply cast your eyes to Hollywood, where an entire industry is devoted to taking books and rewriting them into screenplays!)

Once the script is found or written, a group of students chooses parts within the script and practices the text. The text's interactive nature helps students develop a sense for creating meaning through a shared text. When students feel comfortable with the text and believe they can read it and convey the appropriate meaning, a performance should follow. Usually the performance is for one's own classmates. However, really well-done scripts often "go on the road" to other classes or groups such as PTAs, school boards, retirement centers, and so on.

Fourth-grade teacher Lorraine has been using reader's theater for the past 2 years (Prescott, 2003). She had read an account of reader's theater in a second-grade classroom where students experienced a year's growth in reading in just 10 weeks (Martinez, Roser, & Strecker, 1999) and decided to try it in her own classroom. Students were assigned scripts each Monday, practiced throughout the week, and performed their scripts for the class on Fridays in a reader's theater festival. During the two years in which reader's theater has been an integral part of Lorraine's reading program, her Title I students have averaged more than three year's growth in reading per year.

A final type of performance is through great speeches (and documents) from history. You may be thinking, memorize and perform speeches, yuck! Yet, great oratory from U.S. history is a superb way to integrate reading and fluency into the social studies curriculum. Many great events from history are marked by speeches. Study of the Civil War is not complete without a rendition of Lincoln's *Gettysburg Address*. The history of the women's rights movement needs students to hear Sojourner Truth's *Ain't I a Woman* speech. How can the American Revolution be studied without a performance of Patrick Henry's *Give Me Liberty or Give Me Death* oration? And wouldn't an exploration of the Great Depression miss something important if at least a portion of Franklin Delano Roosevelt's first inaugural speech, *We Have Nothing to Fear*, were not presented by someone in the class taking on the role of FDR?

Memorizing and presenting speeches in a monotone voice is deadly. However, when students know some background for the speech and are asked to go back in history and become part of the audience for the speech, and when the speaker presents the speech with verve and expression, a classroom study of the Civil War or women's rights can come alive. Again, for students to perform the speech with appropriate meaning and expression, they must practice and, for even a few minutes, take on the role of the person who originally delivered it. Interestingly, speeches and documents of U.S. and world history are easy to find. Many printed versions of famous speeches are readily available on the Internet.

David teaches fifth-grade social studies and reading. He has found that exploring U.S. history by combining textbooks, trade books, and students' performance of speeches is an unbeatable combination.

> I start by reading the *Gettysburg Address* to them, usually in November near the anniversary of the speech. But beforehand, I tell them some of the background to the speech: The Battle of Gettysburg that occurred in the middle of the previous summer, the invasion of the North by Lee's Confederate army, the unbelievable number of deaths in such a small town, the need to create a cemetery and bury all these dead soldiers, the dedication of the cemetery and the three-hour speech given by the featured speaker. And then I tell them to place themselves in Gettysburg, as citizens who have seen the tragedy of war over the past several months. "You have listened to a man speak for hours at this dedication, and now you see President Lincoln heading to the podium. What are you thinking? How do you feel about all that has happened? Now listen to President Lincoln's words." I read the speech with all the expression I can muster. And you know, the students listen with such intensity that you can hear a pin drop. After they see what I can do with a speech, they want to do the same. That's when I give them their own speeches to study and perform.

Reading While Listening

Paired reading. In the 1960s the professional literature began describing a new approach to corrective reading (Heckelman, 1969), the *Neurological Impress Method (NIM),* which is much simpler than its name implies. Basically, NIM involves pairing good and poor readers. The readers sit side by side and read one text aloud and together.

Early research about the approach was impressive. Pairs read together for relatively short periods of time, usually no more than 15 minutes per session. Heckelman (1969) found that poor readers made substantial progress relatively quickly. One student, for example, made gains of 5.9 grade levels after doing NIM for a total of 7.25 hours over 6 weeks. The average gain was 1.9 grade levels for 24 students over the same time period.

For whatever reason, NIM never fully caught on in the United States. Few teachers seemed to use it with their less able readers. But this was not the case in England, where researchers developed an activity similar to NIM, called paired reading. Perhaps the more easily understood name has helped its popularity.

Paired reading was originally intended as an at-home supplement to children's reading at school. The approach calls for parent and child to read one text aloud and together. Normally, the parent reads in a moderately loud voice at a pace that tends to pull the child along. When the child wants to read alone, he signals the parent who then stops reading aloud or reads in a whisper at a rate that slightly trails the child's voice. As soon as the child begins to experience difficulty, the parent returns to her original role as leader.

Keith Topping (1987), who has led the paired reading movement in England, reports that students can make remarkable progress in a short period of time. With sessions of only 5 minutes per night, he reported struggling readers made three to five times their normal progress in word recognition and comprehension. Because children and parents read connected texts together fluently, it is easy to expect that fluency would improve as well. Paired reading also works well if peers or other adults take on the role of parent (Topping, 1989).

Katherine has been a Title I reading teacher for 15 years in an inner-city school. She takes seriously the Title I mandate to involve parents in her programs to improve her students' reading. Until a few years ago, however, she had difficulty with parental involvement. "We had all kinds of problems," Katherine says. "Either the parents didn't show up for the training program, or they didn't follow through and I didn't have the time to follow up with every child, or the program was more fun and games and really didn't involve sustained reading on the part of the child."

After hearing about paired reading at an in-service workshop, she decided to try it out with her students and their parents. She arranged for one-hour training sessions at various times throughout the day and advertised it furiously. Most parents came and were enthusiastic about paired reading. "This was something they could do with their children pretty much on their own," Katherine recalled.

On Fridays, students bring in record sheets that document the previous week's paired reading. Children select a book to read for the upcoming week and receive a new record sheet. Parents have stayed with the program. Katherine notes, "They see that it works, and I do, too. Children who do paired reading with a parent make significantly more progress during the year than those who don't. Paired reading is one of the best strategies for helping our less able readers that I have ever seen or tried."

Recorded passages.   Paired reading may be impossible for some students. They may not have anybody at home who can read with them. One alternative is to provide students with a recording of the reading text that they can listen to while reading the written version. Marie Carbo (1978) calls this approach "talking books." Carbo studied this approach for readers with learning disabilities. After only a few weeks, Carbo reported that students made reading gains significantly beyond expectations. They learned to read fluently what they were previously unable to read at all. In another study, students listening to high-interest recorded stories at their instructional levels for 15 to 25

Support from a reading
buddy or a recorded version
of a story builds fluency.

minutes daily for about 27 weeks made average gains of 2.2 years in their
reading achievement (Smith & Elley, 1997).

Although a variety of commercially prepared recorded texts is available for purchase, we believe that recorded passages prepared by the teacher
or someone else in the school may be more effective. The commercial
recordings often have distracting sound effects. They also may not provide a
word-for-word rendition of the passage, may be read at an inappropriate rate
for students, or have unconventional or inadequate signals for page turns.
These potential difficulties disappear if the teacher, aide, student, or parent
helper prepares the recording. In addition, students may find the voice of the
teacher or some other familiar person comforting and encouraging.

Ted uses recorded books in his elementary Title I reading program. Students who struggle with reading fluency choose a book and recording from the
extensive library he has collected and made over the years. Students read the
book over several days on their own and come to class on a designated day
and read the book (or a portion of it) to him. Ted believes this activity gives
students some control over and responsibility for their own learning; at the
same time, they learn to read and enjoy a good book. "Most of my students
really like learning to read these books on their own," he says. "It's an accomplishment they can feel proud of." Once students have become familiar with
Ted's format for the recorded versions of the books and developed some
degree of fluency, he invites them to make their own recorded books to add to
his library. Students like listening to books recorded by their classmates.

Recorded books also work well with students for whom English is a
second language (ESL). Koskinen et al. (1999) found that having ESL students use books and recordings for reading practice resulted in increased
reading achievement and interest as well as greater self-confidence. Students, parents, and teachers noted significant improvements in students'
reading. Least proficient readers reported practicing their reading more often
than more proficient classmates. In their use of recorded books, Koskinen et

al. (1999) recorded two readings per story. The first reading was a slower, more deliberate presentation, and the second was a faster, more fluent rendition. This allowed students to move from an initial focus on individual words and phrases to a more fluent reading of the stories.

Choral reading.   *Choral reading*—reading orally in groups—is similar to paired reading in that less able readers receive simultaneous support while reading. Choral reading has become something of a lost art in elementary schools. In past generations, students learned and chorally recited poems, songs, famous speeches, interesting passages from stories, and other selections. Even the least able readers could join in without risk of failure or ridicule. After several readings they were able to read the passage on their own with considerable fluency. Today, however, with so much emphasis on silent reading, children have few opportunities to engage in this community form of reading.

Choral reading captures readers' interest through antiphonal reading and other variations. In *antiphonal reading* the class is divided into groups (girls and boys, January to June birthdays and July to December birthdays, and so on). Different parts of the text are assigned to each group. The entire group may read some parts, and individuals may read others. Thus, the choral reading becomes a complex and orchestrated arrangement. Students enjoy deciding on parts for antiphonal reading. To do so, of course, they must read the text several times, which is good fluency practice, and think about how different groups of voices can convey meaning. In addition, assigning parts and directing practice with the texts helps students develop ownership of their reading and fosters a sense of a reading community. Choral reading activities let less able readers benefit from group support, the camaraderie and joy of participating in a group activity with peers who have a variety of abilities, and the valuable practice of reading one text in a variety of ways.

Choral reading is a way of life in Elizabeth's second-grade classroom. Each morning she uses choral reading to warm up the class to reading and language. She usually finds a short, suitable poem for the class to read together. She either writes the poem on chart paper or puts it on an overhead transparency so that all the children can see it. Her routine is to read the poem to the class first, talk about it with the children, then invite them to read it chorally several times and respond to it through discussion.

> I really like doing this at the beginning of each day because it helps create a sense of togetherness and community in the class. After reading it a couple of times I might ask four or five individual students of varying reading ability to read it to the class. Choral reading really lets those less able readers shine with their peers! Later in the day, when I'm working with those struggling readers, we will usually go back and practice the poem together some more and do some word-analysis activities with it. Really, you can create a whole lesson that's fun and interesting from this initial group choral reading.

Not every day means a new poem. Sometimes Elizabeth reintroduces students to an old favorite, and about halfway through the school year, students begin to read the poem to the class each morning. The day before, she gives a selected student a copy of the poem for the next day. She asks the child to practice reading it at home and to lead the class in reading it the next day. For some less fluent readers, she will supply a recorded version of the poem to aid their practice.

Marking Phrase Boundaries

Phrasing is important to fluency because meaning is embedded in multiple-word chunks of text or phrases, not in individual words. Peter Schreiber (1980, 1991) has theorized that many readers characterized as disfluent suffer from a poor ability to phrase text appropriately while reading. This may reflect lack of sensitivity to semantic and syntactic cues that mark phrase boundaries in the text, or disfluent readers may have routinized their word-by-word reading and not have automatic recognition of most words. Regardless of the cause, the result is continued difficulty in fully understanding the text.

Consider the following sentence:

The young man the playground equipment.

At first reading, the sentence may sound like nonsense. That is because you probably chunked or phrased the text as most readers would: after the noun *man.* However, in this contrived sentence, if you chunked the text this way, your comprehension suffered—the text has no verb phrase. Rephrase the text (hint: *young* can be a noun and *man* a verb). Rephrased, the sentence is easily understood. When readers have difficulty determining appropriate text boundaries, many sentences can give them similar comprehension problems.

Repeated reading can help students overcome this difficulty. Schreiber has noted that repeated reading activities give the reader practice in discovering text cues that mark phrase boundaries. Another approach is to mark or highlight phrase boundaries in the text itself, using a pencil slash or vertical line to specify the boundary (see Figure 6.1). A review of research shows that marking phrase boundaries has considerable potential for improving reading performance and comprehension, especially with less able readers (Rasinski, 1990).

Ted has found that marking phrase boundaries for them helps his less fluent Title I students:

If we are studying a short passage or poem that I want students to read orally, I will lightly mark phrase boundaries in the passage with a pencil and run enough copies of the text for each student. I use single slash marks for within-sentence phrase boundaries and double slashes for the ends of sentences. After talking about the role of the marks, we might read the passage chorally and attend to the phrase and sentence breaks.

Grant was not a military genius/who took brilliant gambles/and made flashing strikes.//
His position/as one of America's premier field commanders/was the result/of more
solid qualities:/ a wide vision of the war/and what had to be done to win,/balanced
judgment,/dogged courage,/common sense,/and good luck/at the right time.//[1]

Today/Kevin and I turned out/for track. //Mr. Kurtz,/the coach,/gave us a pep
talk/about the importance/of taking part/and doing the best we can.// He said/it's
not the winning,/it's the competing that's important.// He stressed/looking for
improvement/within ourselves.//[2]

Figure 6.1

Phrased Text

1 From Robertson, J. I. (1992). *Civil War! America becomes one nation* (p. 79). New York:
Knopf.
2 From Cleary, B. (1991). *Strider* (p. 126). New York: Morrow.

Later, as students become fluent and phrase-sensitive to the text, Ted
gives them the same text without the slash marks. He believes this is a good
way for students to transfer their newly learned sensitivity to phrase boundaries
to passages in a conventional format. He occasionally gives students new passages as well and asks them to mark their own phrase boundaries. This is followed by a discussion of the marks and the need to read in chunks or phrases.
Ted notes that his students appear to make real progress in their ability and
desire to read in appropriate phrases when reading both orally and silently.

Choice of Texts

The texts chosen for reading can aggravate or ameliorate fluency problems.
More often than not, aggravation is the result. Students with fluency difficulties often face texts too difficult for their current reading level. Such texts
ensure disfluent reading and perpetuate students' evaluations of themselves
as poor readers. In dealing with fluency problems, choose texts relatively
easy in terms of word recognition and syntactic complexity. If the text is challenging, provide students with sufficient support before and during reading to
ensure success. Reading relatively easy texts helps students develop power
and self-confidence in their reading.

Easier texts that ensure fluency are the best choice for independent
reading. Allington (2002) found that highly effective teachers were more
likely to guide their students into easier materials than less effective teachers.
Predictable or patterned texts are particularly well suited to helping students
develop fluency when reading independently. These texts are written in a distinct and easily detected pattern that makes them not only easy to read but
also require readers to attend to the pattern through phrasing and expression.
A bibliography of predictable pattern books can be found in Appendix C.

Patterned texts can also be found in poetry and song lyrics for children. Verses have the particular advantage of being short (thus lending themselves to repeated readings) and appealing to a variety of grade levels. Children's verse is also written in rhyme, which makes the poems even more appealing and predictable. (Poetry collections that we have found useful are listed in Appendix B.) For example, Shel Silverstein's *Where the Sidewalk Ends* and *A Light in the Attic* contain poems sure to delight children of all ages. Many poets write verse for children, and several published poetry collections can be read for both sheer enjoyment and to build fluency. Teachers and children can also compose their own original verse or verse modeled after favorite poems and put them together into class collections for reading.

Jean's students are in transitional second grade because they did not successfully complete the first-grade curriculum during the previous year. They have particular trouble emerging into conventional forms of reading. Jean has found that predictable books and poems are great ways to capture the reading interest of students who previously spent most of their reading time doing worksheets and unsuccessfully manipulating letters and sounds. Each day she introduces one or two new predictable stories written in the form of big books or poems written on chart paper. She explains, "The large texts allow the reading to be a community and choral reading experience."

As the lesson begins, students read several patterned stories and poems from previous lessons—perhaps Joy Cowley's *Mrs. Wishy Washy,* or Sue Williams's *I Went Walking.* Jean points to the words and lines in many of the stories. After reading them several times as a group and asking individuals and pairs of students to read them, Jean helps students detect individual letters, word parts, and words. She makes word and letter cards, which students match with words and letters in the stories. Children work in groups to find words from the stories that begin or end with particular sounds, letters, or letter combinations.

After several minutes spent looking at various aspects of the familiar texts, Jean introduces her students to a new book. Her routine includes showing students the cover or telling them the title and asking what the story may be about. She asks students to brainstorm various possible plots and select the most plausible. After this discussion, she reads the text to her students, pointing to individual words as she reads. Students then talk about the story. Were their predictions correct? What did they like about the story? Were any words particularly interesting? After a brief discussion Jean rereads and points to the words again. Then she invites the class to join her in a third reading. After a few more choral readings she moves on to other activities. But she makes sure that the text is available for her students so they can read and explore it on their own during free time. In upcoming days, the class continues to read the patterned story and explores in more detail the sentences, words, letters, and sounds in the text.

When students have the opportunity to practice a text to fluency (i.e., texts used to teach fluency), they may be ready for more challenging texts. In their review of the research, Kuhn and Stahl (2000) found that students who engaged in fluency instruction with more challenging texts were likely to achieve the greatest gains in reading. Although such texts may be challenging for students, the opportunity to read and reread them with teacher support or with other fluent readers will eventually lead the reader to also read them and similar texts with fluency and comprehension.

Instructional Routines

Fluency Development Lesson

So far we have been discussing individual aspects of successful fluency instruction, but lessons, or instructional routines, that employ more than one aspect will increase the effectiveness of instruction. One example of this principle is the *fluency development lesson (FDL)* (Rasinski, Padak, Linek, & Sturtevant, 1994). We devised the FDL for teachers who work with primary-grade children experiencing difficulty in achieving even initial stages of fluent reading. The FDL combines several principles of effective fluency instruction in a way that maximizes students' engagement in authentic reading in a relatively short period of time and requires cooperation between two or more students. The FDL has been used as a supplement to the regular reading curriculum. Implemented at the beginning of each day, it took 10 to 15 minutes to complete. Teachers made copies of brief passages (50–150 words) for each child. Often the passages were in verse form.

A typical fluency development lesson looks like this:

1. The teacher distributes copies of the text to each student.
2. The teacher reads the text to the class while students follow along silently with their own copies. This step can be repeated several times.
3. The teacher discusses the text content as well as the quality of her reading of it with the class.
4. The entire class, along with the teacher, reads the text chorally several times. The teacher creates variety by having students read in antiphonal and echo styles.
5. The class divides into pairs. Each pair finds a quiet spot, and one student practices reading the text to her partner three times. The partner's job is to follow along in the text, provide help when needed, and give positive feedback to the reader. After the first three readings, the roles are switched. The partner becomes the reader and reads the text three times as well.
6. Students regroup, and the teacher asks for volunteers to perform the text. Individuals, pairs, and groups of up to four perform the reading for the class. Sometimes students perform the text for the school principal, secretary, custodian, and other teachers and classes. The performing students are lavished with praise.

7. Students take the passage home and read it to their parents and other relatives. Parents are asked to listen to their child read as many times as they would like and to praise their child's efforts.

During our work with the FDL, teachers implemented it three to four times a week from October to June. We found that nearly all children benefited from the lesson: They experienced greater improvement in their overall reading achievement, word recognition, and fluency than did a comparable group of children who received more traditional supplemental instruction using the same passages. The poorest readers made the greatest gains. Teachers and students who used the FDL liked reading and talking about the enjoyable passages, the opportunity to read chorally and with friends, and the noticeable improvement the approach offered students.

Maria has used the FDL in her class for more than two years. As a result, several of her second graders have made extraordinary progress. "The main thing about this lesson is that it allows children to be successful in reading. Even though this is second grade, several of my students essentially begin the school year not reading. These kids need intensive help in word recognition and developing fluent reading habits. I honestly think that FDL is one answer to helping these youngsters."

At the beginning of the year she asks parents to purchase a particular collection of poems for children. Each day, whenever possible, Maria and her students explore one or more poems from the collection using the FDL format. She has made one significant modification that she believes (and we agree) helps reinforce students' word recognition learning. After each FDL she asks students to choose a favorite or interesting word (or two) from the poem, write it on an index card, and add it to their personal word banks. These banks are then used in word practice and word sort activities. (See chapter 5 for a complete description of these activities.) Students like the opportunity to work with others when practicing their reading and enjoy performing their readings for others. Indeed, Jean (whom you met earlier in this chapter) has recently worked with a first-grade teacher to develop a program where second- and first-grade readers are paired for reading practice in much the same way as in the FDL.

Oral Recitation Lesson

Hoffman's *Oral Recitation Lesson (ORL)* is another fluency-instruction routine that integrates several key characteristics of effective fluency instruction (Hoffman, 1987; Hoffman & Crone, 1985). The ORL consists of two components. The first, the direct instruction component, begins with comprehension. The teacher reads a story to students and guides them in discussing and analyzing the content. This analysis results in a story map that identifies basic story elements such as characters, setting, major episodes and events, and resolution. Students use the story map as a guide in writing a story summary.

Next is a practice phase in which the teacher models reading story segments. Students practice the segments individually and chorally. In addition to the modeled reading, the teacher talks about fluent reading and leads students in practicing elements of effective expression during oral reading. Finally, students read self-selected segments of the story for others. Students reap positive comments from their classmates after the performance.

In the second component of the ORL, indirect instruction, students work for 10 minutes every day on passage segments from the direct-instruction component of the lesson. Each student practices reading in a barely audible voice, a method called soft reading. During this time, the teacher checks the progress of individual students. The ORL is meant to cover several days, normally two to four instructional periods. The format has been found to lead to improvements in fluency and reading comprehension (Aslett, 1990; Reutzel & Hollingsworth, 1993).

Shared Book Experience

The *Shared Book Experience (SBE),* another integrated lesson format for developing fluency, particularly with younger readers, is based on the assumptions that learning to read is a social experience and that children need positive guidance and support in group reading experiences (Holdaway, 1979).

In the SBE the teacher faces the students with an enlarged text (this is usually a big book; but for older students the text could also be written on chart paper or the chalk board). After introducing the text the teacher reads it with good expression and engages students in a discussion of the text. The text is then reread several times, with the teacher offering support and encouraging students to join in the reading, especially during any repetitive parts. Throughout these rereadings the teacher draws students' attention to words, word patterns, letters, and other language elements in the text, often using a word window to isolate individual words and letters.

As students become proficient in reading the enlarged text, they often receive conventional-size versions of the same text for individual practice at school and home. Although students may read several stories during a lesson, their work with a particular story may stretch over several lessons and days. Thus, students develop a repertoire of big books that they may request, revisit, and reread. See chapter 4 for more on the SBE.

Support-Reading Strategy

The *Support-Reading Strategy (SRS)* was developed by Morris and Nelson (1992) in response to the needs of low-achieving second-grade students. SRS contains several fluency instruction elements and is meant to integrate into a traditional class using basal materials. It follows a three-day instructional cycle that lasts 20 to 25 minutes at a time.

- ■ *Day 1.* The teacher reads a story to a small group of students in a fluent, expressive voice. Throughout the reading, the teacher asks students to clarify text information and predict upcoming events. Teacher and students then echo-read the story, with the students reading from their own books. The teacher monitors individuals' reading and provides assistance, support, and encouragement as necessary.

- ■ *Day 2.* Students are divided into pairs that include a good reader and a less proficient one. The pairs reread the story, alternating pages as they go. The children are then assigned a short segment (100 words) from the story. In pairs, the students read to their partners, who provide help as needed. Finally, if enough time remains, the pairs reread the entire story, alternating pages so that each child reads the text read by the partner in the initial partner reading.

- ■ *Day 3.* During a seatwork period, individual children read their assigned parts to the teacher, and the teacher checks the reading for word recognition accuracy.

Many students in this program had made virtually no progress in reading during the 11 months preceding it and were still at the initial stages of reading development when they began SRS. After 6 months of SRS, their reading ability had increased substantially (Morris & Nelson, 1992).

Fluency-Oriented Reading Instruction

Fluency-Oriented Reading Instruction (FORI) integrates fluency instruction into the regular basal reading program (Stahl & Heuback, in press). The lesson begins with the teacher reading the assigned story to the students and engaging students in a discussion of the story and other comprehension activities. The teacher also leads the students in rereading or echo reading portions of the story. The story then goes home with the students for additional practice with parents. (Children who are struggling in reading take the story home over several days.) The next day, students orally read the assigned story with a partner, alternating pages as they work through the text, while the silent partner monitors the reading.

Testing FORI over two years in second-grade classrooms, Stahl and Heubach (in press) found that students made an average gain of two years in reading during their second-grade year. Moreover, they found that only 2 of a total of 105 students were reading below grade level at the end of their second-grade year.

We Cannot Neglect Reading Fluency

The activities we have described in this chapter share a common purpose: to help students develop the ability to read fluently. This goal is important because fluent readers can better identify unknown words and comprehend text. For example, the repeated readings embedded in fluency activities allow readers to develop their sight vocabularies naturally and without special emphasis or instruction. Moreover, knowing that one's reading sounds good boosts self-esteem. Students enjoy these activities, and their successes

Repeated Reading
- Students practice reading texts until they achieve fluency.
- Students perform texts for interested audiences—peers, younger students, family members, and so on.

Paired Reading
- Student selects book.
- Student and parent (or other good reader) read book aloud together.
- Parent's reading slightly leads or follows, depending on student's need and desire.
- Student logs paired-reading activities.

Choral Reading
- Teacher or students select text and determine or assign parts (if it is antiphonal reading).
- Teacher reads text aloud; students listen and read along silently. Discussion may follow.
- Teacher and students read text together.
- Choral or antiphonal choral reading is performed.

Recorded Passages
- Teacher or other competent reader prepares recordings of texts.
- Individual students select books and recordings. They read and simultaneously listen to books several times.
- Individual students perform books or a portion of them for an audience.

Fluency Development Lesson
- Teacher selects short text and prepares copies for students.
- Teacher reads text; students listen and critique reading. Discussion may follow.
- Teacher and students read text together.
- Student pairs take turns reading the text to each other. Listeners provide assistance and positive feedback.
- Students perform the text for interested audiences.
- Students add words from text to their word banks.
- Students read text at home for parents.

Oral Recitation Lesson
- Teacher reads story to class.
- Story discussion is followed by the development of a story map.
- Students write story summary.
- Teacher models reading of story and discusses fluency.
- Students practice segments of story.

Figure 6.2
Procedures for Fluency Routines

- Students read or perform texts for others.
- Students "soft-read" (practice) segments of story on their own for 10 minutes per day.

Shared Book Experience
- Teacher discusses and reads a big book to the class.
- Teacher and students reread book several times over several days.
- Teacher draws students' attention to segments of text (words, word parts, letters).
- Students read smaller versions of the book on their own at school and home.

Support-Reading Strategy
- Teacher reads story; students predict upcoming events.
- Teacher and students echo-read story.
- Student pairs reread story, alternating pages once or twice.
- Students practice 100-word segments with partners.
- Students read assigned segments to the teacher, who checks reading accuracy.

Fluency-Oriented Reading Instruction
- Teacher reads story to students.
- Teacher and students discuss story and do comprehension activities.
- Teacher and students reread portions of the story.
- Students reread story at home.
- Next day, students orally reread the story with a partner.

Figure 6.2, *Continued*

engender positive attitudes toward reading and about themselves as readers. Finally, these fluency activities frequently involve joint decision making and cooperative activity and performance, all of which develop a sense of community among students.

Each of the fluency activities highlighted in this chapter has been proved and endorsed by teacher practice and professional research. They all work with many types of texts but may be most appropriate with short, predictable pieces such as poetry or patterned books. Figure 6.2 summarizes the steps involved in each of the activities we described in this chapter.

Richard Allington (1983) and others (Anderson, 1981) argued long ago that fluency is a neglected goal of the reading curriculum. Subsequent research has found that fluency is indeed important, especially for struggling readers. The source of difficulty for many readers who struggle lies in fluency. We are certain that focused, intensive, engaging, and authentic activity in this essential area of reading will help turn many struggling readers into succeeding students.

7

Building Vocabulary

The association between vocabulary knowledge and reading proficiency is an early finding from reading research (Davis, 1944). Good readers tend to know many words and understand many concepts, and people who know many words tend to be good readers. That finding makes sense to us. To comprehend, you must understand the words that make up the text. Moreover, as you read, you encounter new ideas, concepts, and words, and you see existing ideas, concepts, and words in new ways. As a result, your knowledge of words grows. Indeed, word knowledge is one of the most potent predictors of reading comprehension (Anderson & Freebody, 1981).

That's the good news, but here is also some bad news: If reading frustrates you or gives you little enjoyment, you may choose to read less or to avoid reading altogether. This decision leads to fewer encounters with new and interesting words; and as a result, your growth in reading slows, and reading becomes even more difficult and frustrating. The cycle continues—but in the wrong direction.

Many struggling readers have limited word knowledge. Particularly when they read instructional texts, they may be overloaded with the vocabulary and overwhelmed by the conceptual load of the text. Reading is slow, laborious, and frustrating; learning is impeded. In fact, when any reader confronts text that contains many unfamiliar words, comprehension suffers. Thus all teachers must engage students in regular vocabulary exploration, particularly teachers in specialized subject areas and those who work with struggling readers.

We like to think of vocabulary exploration as word play or having fun with words, but this does not characterize traditional forms of vocabulary instruction. Before we present our instructional suggestions, let's take a look at how vocabulary is currently taught around the world.

Traditional Vocabulary Instruction

Nearly every person who has attended school in the United States can remember being regularly assigned lists of words to learn. More often than not, the words had little or no connection to curricular areas; they might even have been words that students had never encountered. The weekly assignment usually went something like this: "Find and write a definition for each word," or "Use each word in a sentence." At the end of the week came a test, and within a short time the words were probably forgotten and never thought of again!

When Mike (son of author Tim Rasinski) was in seventh grade, he received a list of 75 words to define for an upcoming vocabulary test (See Figure 7.1). Reluctantly and with great frustration, Mike spent the better part of a weekend completing the task. He looked the words up in a dictionary; he did reasonably well on the examination. However, it had a cost: Mike found the assignment "stupid." This was his way of saying that the words had little or no connection to his world or any content he was studying. The words were too difficult for a middle-school student. He saw simply too many words to work on at one time, and he was overwhelmed.

Tim recently asked Mike, now an adult, if he remembered any of the words from the list and, if so, what they meant. His memory of the assignment was burned painfully into his memory. However, his memory of the words or their meanings was vague at best! Indeed, we recently asked a group of graduate students to define a set of words from this list. Most were unable to define more than half of the words.

Unfortunately, this type of vocabulary instruction continues in some classrooms. Yet most teachers, not to mention students, would agree that such an approach rarely increases vocabulary. It only adds to many students' frustration with words and reading, magnifies their negative attitudes toward reading, and contributes to lack of growth in reading. Moreover, students may come to believe that words and concepts are not important, at least not beyond the test on Friday.

Such approaches are exercises in futility for at least three reasons. First, the words have little connection to students' existing knowledge or what they are studying in other subjects. Learning new ideas, concepts, and words involves connecting or integrating the new information into what learners already know. If students have little background knowledge about the new words and concepts or cannot see the connections, then the process of integration drags. Learning will occur neither efficiently nor effectively.

Second, finding definitions or using words in sentences does not ensure understanding. Official definitions can be just as confusing as the words they are supposed to clarify, and sentences that students compose often demonstrate a remarkable lack of understanding. Take, for example, the following sentences from student compositions, compiled by Richard Lederer in his book *Anguished English:*

②   Part of Speech & Definition   Mike Rasinski

Antonyms   Due Next Fri   Read per 1

Sent   March 1

VOCABULARY LIST

Do First 5

1. adroit - adj. skillfull & clever
2. apprise - v. to notify
3. aromatic - adj. having an aroma
4. ascetic - adj. self denying, austere n. one who leads a life of self denial
5. bayou - n. in Southern U.S. A marshy inlet or outlet of lake, river, etc.
6. bellicose - adj. quarrelsome, warlike
7. choleric - adj. easily angered
8. cloister - n. a monestary or convent
9. conjecture - n. guess, inferring without complete evidence
10. copious - adj. copious abundant
11. coquetry - n. a girl or woman flirt
12. cornice - n. a horizontal molding projecting along the top of a wall, etc.
13. courageous - n. brave
14. debris - n. bits & pieces of stone, rubbish, etc.
15. decorum - n. whatever is suitable or proper
16. diadem - n. crown, ornamental headband
17. docile - adj. easy to discipline   ☐ not on test
18. dogmatic - adj. asserted w/o proof positive or arrogant in stating opinion
19. doleful - adj. sad, mournful
20. efface - v. keep from being noticed, blot out

21. garrulous - adj. talking too much about inconsequential things.
22. grapple - n. hand to hand struggle, a grip
23. guidon -
24. impose - v. to place a burden on to force onto others
25. interpose - v. to intervine, interrupt
26. knell - v. to ring slowly, ominously - ommen of death
27. languor - n. lack of vigor, weakness
28. ludicrous - adj. causing laughter because absurd or ridiculous
29. malevolence -
30. maudlin - adj. foolishly, often tearfully sentimental
31. melee - n. confused general hand to hand fight
32. molten - adj. melted by heat
33. myriad - n. adj. very many persons or things
34. orb - n. globe or sphere
35. ostracism - n. practicing banishing one
36. pantaloons - n. trousers
37. pariah - n. any outcast person formly in India any oppressed class
38. pathos - n. quality of something arousing pity
39. perilous - adj. dangerous, involving peril
40. plaintive - adj. expressing sorrow

41. restive - adj. restless, uneasy hard to manage, refusing to go ahead
42. reverie - n. dreamy thinking of pleasant things
43. roseate - adj. roseate color, cheerful optimistic
44. rueful - adj. sorrowful unhappy causing sorrow
45. sallow - adj. having a sickly yellow complexion
46. sardonic - adj. bitterly sarcastic, scornful or mocking
47. savant - n. a learned person
48. sententious - adj. saying much in few words
49. sexton - n. person who takes care of a church, rings bells, arranges burials
50. sinuous - adj. having many curves or turns. ② indirect, untrustworthy
51. suffuse - v. overspread (with liquid, dye, etc.)
52. surmount - adj. rise above ② overcome
53. surplice - n. broad sleeved white gown worn by members of clergy or choir
54. sylvan - adj. characteristic of woods. wooded.
55. tableau - n. presentation of a scene by costumed person or group
56. tedious - adj. tiresome boring hackneyed
57. travail - n. hard work or severe pain
58. undulate - v. to cause to move by waves
59. vanquish - v. to defeat
60. venerable - adj. worthy of respect because of one's dignity etc.

Figure 7.1
Traditional Vocabulary List and Assignment

Socrates died from an overdose of wedlock.
Solomon, one of David's sons, had 500 wives and 500 porcupines.
The inhabitants of ancient Egypt were called mummies.

What command do the students who wrote these sentences have over the major concepts in the sentences?

Finally, this age-old method of vocabulary instruction is no fun at all. It is drudgery, and students treat it as such. The unfortunate consequence is that students may learn that any type of word exploration is boring.

Vocabulary instruction need not be boring. Indeed, it can be a delightful and insightful experience for many students. To be truly effective, word play must be based on words that students need to know or have some interest in. Therefore, we must help them see connections between unknown words and familiar words and concepts. We must also make sure that vocabulary activities are interesting and playful. When students become interested in and knowledgeable about words, reading fluency and comprehension take a major leap forward.

Two Important Dimensions of Vocabulary

Normally when we think of vocabulary learning, we think of adding new words, ideas, or concepts to our mental dictionary or lexicon. Although this is certainly one aspect of vocabulary learning, there is another.

If adding new words can be thought of as increasing the breadth of one's vocabulary, the other part of vocabulary learning involves adding depth to the existing understandings one has of words already in one's lexicon. Words can have connotative as well as denotative meanings. *Denotative* meanings are explicit. For example, the word *right* denotes something correct or acceptable. However, *right* also has a *connotative* or implied meaning of skepticism. When a person utters "right" after hearing a friend argue a point, that "right" can either denote that the person agrees with the argument or it can connote that the person is skeptical of it. Additionally, words can have several denotative meanings. *Right* can also mean good or a particular side or direction (as opposed to *left*), among other meanings.

Exemplary vocabulary instruction, then, is multidimensional. Just as it focuses on developing students' breadth of word knowledge, it also works to increase students' depth of word knowledge as well. A student may understand a word one way or in one context and yet lack a full understanding of the word. Good vocabulary instruction both develops the richness of already known words and also introduces new words.

Good Ways to Learn New Words

Before we share specific instructional activities, we want to describe two of the best ways for students (and all of us, for that matter) to learn new words and concepts. Learning words and concepts is not exclusively a school activity.

Children learn new words through direct experiences.

Children learn thousands of words and word meanings before they ever set foot in a school. How? They learn most words and concepts through life experiences that they later discuss with their parents and other important people in their lives. A child going to McDonald's will learn about hamburgers, cheeseburgers, french fries, and McNuggets. A visit to the dentist can help someone learn about dentists, X-rays, cavities, and Novocaine. Our life experiences, no matter our age, give us wonderful opportunities for learning new words and concepts, especially if we discuss our experiences with others. A summer vacation to Europe or the Black Hills of South Dakota will lead a child or an adult to discover new words in a rich and concrete context. All experiences are important. Successful teachers remember the great opportunities available to expand student vocabularies through direct experience—everything from school field trips to investigations within and around the school itself. The conversations that surround these experiences can provide fertile ground for vocabulary development.

We also learn words through secondhand or vicarious experience. Movies, television shows, and reading are examples of ways in which we share experiences we do not actually have. Reading, in particular, is a superb way to increase vocabulary. We mentioned previously that reading is associated with vocabulary growth. The reason should be clear. As we read, we encounter words unfamiliar or only partly familiar. The story context (its meaning, synonymous words, and illustrations) helps us understand more about these words.

We believe that reading is far superior to other forms of vicarious experience for learning vocabulary. Movies and television often deal with familiar situations and incorporate known words. Such events are often directed toward a lowest common denominator—those viewers with the smallest conceptual and vocabulary backgrounds—so that everyone can understand the story. In reading, however, authors often take readers to new experiences, even within familiar situations. And authors choose vocabulary that is rich and interesting—words that create a particular mood, feel, or texture. In other words, reading gives readers many opportunities to learn new words (Cunningham & Stanovich, 1998).

This is another reason to encourage reading in and out of school: Reading expands readers' vocabularies, which makes further reading easier. Listening to stories can have much the same effect. Indeed, because elementary-grade students have limited word recognition abilities, they usually comprehend stories at a higher level of sophistication when they listen than when they read. Reading to students can have an even more powerful effect on students' vocabulary development than their own reading, and its facilitative effect is well established in the research (Cohen, 1968). Now you have one more reason to read every day to your students, no matter their grade or age. To expand this effect, take a few minutes after a read-aloud and talk with students about the interesting words they heard as well as their meanings and use.

Principles of Effective Vocabulary Instruction

Students can also learn and explore words through direct instruction or word-play activities. Students must learn many words for success in school—it has been estimated that from elementary through high school, students learn 7 words per day, or 2,700 to 3,000 per year (Snow et al., 1998). Teachers must do everything possible to expand and enrich students' vocabulary. We recommend regular direct instruction and focused activity on vocabulary, especially for struggling readers. Five minutes of word play every day can go a long way toward expanding vocabulary and improving comprehension. As we have already seen, traditional vocabulary instruction can be deadly to students' interest and growth and is largely ineffective. Nevertheless, alternatives exist to word lists and memorization. Vocabulary researchers William Nagy (1988) and Steven Stahl (1986) offer several principles for effective vocabulary instruction; to this list we add one final and, we believe, essential principle.

1. *Vocabulary instruction should be integrative* (Nagy, 1988). That is, it should help students connect new words with their existing knowledge of words. Students must learn, for example, that *bullpen* is a word connected to baseball in general and pitchers in particular. That sort of connection

makes words memorable. A dry, abstract, or out-of-context definition may not stick with the student. Vocabulary instruction, like all instruction, should move from what students already know to what is new. Their existing knowledge serves as an anchor for their learning.

2. *Vocabulary should be learned deeply through active processing and discussion.* Stahl (1986) calls the process of making connections between new and known information and between contexts *deep processing.* Making such connections involves deep thinking; the result is a better understood concept. Class or group discussion is one of the best ways to encourage deep processing. As students talk about new words and concepts, they make connections to other knowledge domains and share these connections with classmates.

Stahl suggests that deep processing consists of three levels:

- The first level is *associative.* This occurs when students make a simple connection between a word and another word or a specific context. For example, providing a synonym for an unknown word is a form of association.

- The second level is called *comprehension.* This happens when students demonstrate understanding of the word through application, such as categorizing a set of words, or filling in a word deleted from a sentence.

- The final and deepest level of word learning is *generational,* or using a word in new ways. Examples are defining a word using one's own words, using the word in authentic writing or conversation, or using the word in new ways (Stahl, 1986).

3. *Vocabulary instruction needs to include repetition* (Nagy, 1988; Stahl, 1986). Students must see, hear, and use words many times in many contexts to learn them. Few people can see a word once and know it. Most of us require multiple exposures to cement a new word and its meaning in our memories. The repetition needs to be within meaningful contexts, and not simple or drill-like repetition with word lists or flash cards.

4. *Words and concepts are best learned when presented in meaningful ways* (Nagy, 1988) *with attention to definitional knowledge* (Stahl, 1986). Meaningful repetition might simply involve connecting a read-aloud, student reading, and a direct experience concerning the same topic. These meaningful contexts provide the repetition that helps to ensure thorough word learning. Meaningful repetition makes thematic units of study inviting. Such units expose students to words and concepts numerous times and in several meaningful contexts over the course of the unit study. Meaningful use entails not only seeing the words in meaningful contexts but also thinking about and using them in meaningful ways. When students use new words meaningfully, their understanding is enhanced, and they develop more flexible control over their use.

Stahl (1986) adds, however, that contextual presentation along with definition may be the most powerful way to learn new words. Effective vocabulary instruction combines definitions and various contextual presentations or examples of how the words are actually used.

5.   *The teacher's own attitude toward words and word learning plays a critical role in vocabulary instruction.* In our earlier example involving the author's son, Mike, vocabulary was primarily taught as a set of difficult and exotic words to be looked up in the dictionary, memorized along with the definition, and responded to mechanically in a weekly test. This sort of instruction not only is ineffective but also is likely to stifle any interest in words students may have.

Words can be a fascinating area of study. However, students' attitudes depend on teachers' attitudes. If teachers find word study fascinating, many of their students may also become interested in words. This means escaping the vocabulary workbooks and developing a playful attitude toward words.

Many words have interesting stories behind them. Words and word combinations can make uninteresting sentences and paragraphs come to life, and words can be the fodder for enjoyable classroom activities and games. Students and teachers can even invent words. Word learning is most effective when teachers have a playful, inquisitive, and inventive attitude toward words. That attitude can be highly contagious! Figure 7.2 provides a list of some of our favorite books about words—books that contain interesting and engaging stories about words.

In the remainder of this chapter we present specific instructional strategies that share these characteristics. We recommend that you be flexible in your use of them. Apply them before reading to acquaint students with specific words they will encounter. Use them within a regular classroom framework of general word exploration or play. Whether you broaden students'

John Ayto. *Dictionary of Word Origins.* New York: Arcade Publishing, 1993.

Charles Funk. *Thereby Hangs a Tale: Stories of Curious Word Origins.* New York: Harper & Row, 2002.

Paul M. Levitt & Elissa Guralnick. *The Weighty Word Book.* Boulder, Co: Court Wayne Press, 1999.

The Merriam-Webster New Book of Word Histories. Springfield, MA: Merriam-Webster, 1991.

Marvin Terban. *Guppies in Tuxedos: Funny Eponyms.* New York: Houghton Mifflin, 1988. (one of a series of books on words by the author)

Figure 7.2
Books That Tell the Stories of Words

vocabulary for a specific topic or the more general purpose of fascination with words, their overall reading will improve as well.

List Group Label

List Group Label (LGL) fits within almost any curriculum area and can be used at any age level. The instructional heart of the activity involves drawing out students' own knowledge of a topic and inviting them to organize that information (Marzano et al., 2001). Because the students supply most of the material for the activity, they control its difficulty. Here's how LGL works:

1.   The teacher or students choose a topic for study. It may come from a subject area, an upcoming reading, a theme to be explored by the class, a holiday, and so on.

2.   Groups of students brainstorm all the words they can think of related to the topic. Words are listed on the chalkboard or a sheet of paper that everyone can see. The teacher may also participate in this activity and call out a word or two to be entered into the mix. After brainstorming, students may be asked to explain unfamiliar words.

3.   Once students exhaust their store of words, they organize their list by choosing two or more words that share a common characteristic, listing them together, and supplying a title or label that describes the category. This new organization is also recorded on the chalkboard if the whole group is working together, or on sheets of paper if the students are working in small groups. Students categorize and label the categories until the list is exhausted.

4.   Next, students add words to the categories on their organized lists. When a meaningful organization is imposed on a list of concepts, students usually find they can more easily recall related concepts from memory. Students might discuss the reason—meaningful organization assists memory.

5.   If students are working in groups, each group shares with the entire class its method of categorization and the added words. Lively discussion takes place as students analyze words and concepts for shared and defining features.

6.   Students can extend the activity by transforming their list of organized concepts into a semantic web (see Figure 7.3) or prototypical informational outline. The final product as well as the related discussion introduces students to new concepts and can act as a guide and background for further study.

Karen, a Title I teacher, likes to use LGL when she introduces students to a new set of readings. She finds that students like to brainstorm their own words and mention and explain words unfamiliar to others. "The part I like best about this activity," she explains, "is the student control. They're not

Figure 7.3
Semantic Web for "Baseball"

working with words I chose or the text provided. My students love to do this, and all students, even the brightest, learn new words or new ways for thinking about words they already know. If you think about it, LGL requires kids to do some pretty sophisticated and creative analysis of words and concepts."

Other Categorization Activities

As students put similar concepts together, the process of categorization helps make their world more manageable. It also gives students the chance to meet new words and think about familiar words in new ways. Like List Group Label, word sorts, which we have mentioned in several chapters in this book, also challenge students to categorize words. If your students maintain a word bank in the form of a deck of word cards, you can ask them to sort their words into categories that you name. For example, when teaching word-recognition skills, we ask students to sort their word bank words by number of syllables, sounds, affixes, and so on (see chapter 5) to give them practice and to focus their attention on certain aspects of words. Later, we might ask students to sort their cards into more semantic categories such as words mostly used at home and words mostly used at school, indoor words and out-door words, words related to fun and words related to work, and so on.

Categorizing words allows students to explore their meanings.

Word sorts can also be related to a topic under study. For example, if the class is studying animal life, the teacher might present words such as *bear, dog, elephant, mouse, horse, tiger, giraffe, wolf, rabbit,* and *coyote.* Word-sort categories could include North American and non–North American animals, predatory and nonpredatory animals, domestic and wild animals, and so on. Sorting the same set of words in a variety of ways helps students think about word features. In the animal-life sorts, for example, students can think about bears as North American *and* predatory *and* wild.

If the teacher provides the categories, the activity is called a *closed sort. Open sorts,* on the other hand, encourage divergent thinking among students. The teacher presents words, often derived from past of current readings, and asks students to work in pairs or small groups to arrange the words into meaningful groups. When they have finished, students share their reasoning with the rest of the class.

Another categorization activity we call *Pair 'Em Up.* It requires students to justify their thinking as they pair up words. The teacher (or a student) presents three words to the group. Students determine which two go together and provide a justification for the pairing. Recently, we observed a second-grade class that had a few extra minutes before heading off to lunch. After introducing the activity, the teacher called out, "Trees, sky, and dirt."

One student said, "Trees and dirt go together because they both are on the ground."

"Okay," said the teacher. "Anyone else have other ideas?"

Another child responded, "Sky and dirt because they're not alive."

A third child answered, "I think it's trees and the sky because trees grow into the sky."

Then, a fourth said, "Hey, how about this? Trees and sky go together because they have long vowel sounds."

After a brief discussion on the merits of each response, students continued the activity in pairs. The idea behind Pair 'Em Up is not so much to elicit the correct answer as to challenge students to think about the many ways that words can be connected to one another. This flexible categorizing helps students create depth and breadth in their vocabulary.

Concept Map

When a List Group Label activity is converted into a semantic map, students see the connection between words and higher order or categorical concepts. The visual display helps many students develop the notion that words connect to one another through meaning.

A refinement of this notion, sometimes known as a concept-of-definition map, we call a concept map (Schwartz & Raphael, 1985). A *concept map* is a visual representation of the definition of a concept or word. Besides defining particular words, concept maps help students understand the variety of ways to define words and concepts. One can define words by contrasting words or concepts (using opposites) or identifying the hierarchical category to which they belong. Subordinate categories or examples can also help clarify the meaning. Finally, words or concepts can be defined by their essential characteristics or properties. Figure 7.4 is an example of a completed concept map.

The teacher usually begins a concept map lesson by presenting only the word to be defined, which is written in the center of the map. As a class or in several smaller groups, students define the word by filling in the various elements of the map. Small-group work can demonstrate divergent thinking: Some groups are conventional in their definitions while others are more creative. All maps are acceptable, however, as long as students can defend their decisions.

Wayne, a fourth-grade teacher, has used concept maps for several years.

We do a word a day—I choose from current events or what we are studying in a thematic unit, or I'll ask a student to think of a word to share with the class. You need to choose words for which higher order concepts as well as examples or subordinate concepts exist. We usually do it at the beginning of each day as a sort of warm-up for the class. Most of the time the students work in small groups or pairs and then share their work with the class. What I really like about concept maps is that they help students understand how words are defined and that they don't need to rely totally on a dictionary to provide meaning for a word.

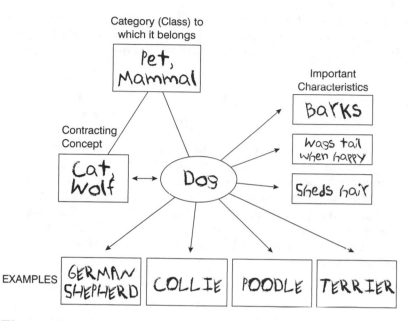

Figure 7.4
Concept Map for "Dog"

Once the maps are done I'll put them on display in the hallway or we'll create our own classroom dictionary that consists of a set of maps put in alphabetical order and bound into a book or three-ring binder. It's interesting to see how students will look over the maps on display or actually leaf through the class concept-map dictionary. I know I'm touching some of the kids' interest in words through this and some of the other word activities we do.

Possible Sentences

A simple method for teaching vocabulary in content area reading is *Possible Sentences* (Moore & Moore, 1986). In this activity, the teacher previews an upcoming reading and selects six to eight challenging words from the text. These are usually key concepts for the reading. Then, the teacher chooses an additional four to six words that are a bit more familiar.

The teacher lists the words on the chalkboard and introduces them to students, providing brief definitions as needed. Then students are then challenged to devise sentences that contain two or more list words they think they may encounter in the reading. The sentences students come up with, both accurate and inaccurate (but all possible), are listed and discussed by the class. After students talk about the possible veracity of the sentences, they read the passage.

Following the reading, teacher and students return to the possible sentences and discuss whether each sentence could be true based on the passage. If a sentence could not be true, students talk about how it could be modified to make it true.

Possible Sentences and similar activities generate considerable discussion. Stahl and his colleagues (Stahl & Vancil, 1986; Stahl & Clark, 1987) have found that talk is an important aspect of vocabulary learning. Stahl and Kapinus (1991) found that the Possible Sentences strategy was more effective than semantic mapping in helping intermediate-grade students learn the targeted words and comprehend the texts. Thus Possible Sentences not only enhances vocabulary, it also is an effective comprehension strategy. Stahl and Kapinus note that "the group discussion appears to improve learning by having students more actively process the information about the to-be-learned words . . . students think more deeply about the relations between the new words and the words they already know. These links lead to learning" (p. 43).

Analogies

Analogies are formal statements of the relationship between several words or concepts. Research by Robert Marzano and colleagues (Marzano, 2003; Marzano et al., 2001) indicates that solving analogies is a powerful learning and teaching tool that promotes vocabulary learning and complex thinking. Analogies are usually in the form *A is to B as C is to D* (sometimes written as *A : B :: C : D*). Here's an example of an analogy problem that Wayne has used:

Abraham Lincoln is to the Civil War as William McKinley is to what?

To solve the problem, we must determine the relationship between the first pair of words or concepts (i.e., "president" to "war during his term") and then apply that relationship to the next pair. When we determine that McKinley was president during the Spanish-American War, we find the answer.

As you see, analogies easily apply to nearly any topic or subject area. Moreover, students engage in sophisticated reasoning as they determine or infer the relationship between word pairs and extend the relationship to a second pair. Again, this activity focuses on helping students make connections between words and concepts to create greater depth of understanding.

Wayne's students enjoy doing analogies, but he adds the following:

I always present them as a type of play or as riddles to solve. I think kids get a kick out of trying to figure these out and then explain their reasoning to the rest of the class. What's really neat is asking students to create a few analogies as a response to their reading, using words or ideas they encountered. Once they get the idea, the best analogies come from the students. We have a ball playing around with them. I find that through analogy play my students are more able to think flexibly about words and think about various ways that words might be related.

Because the analogies are developed from students' own interests and areas of study, difficulty level is self-controlled. Analogies work well with both primary-grade children and older students.

EXAMPLES OF ANALOGY PROBLEMS

Steering wheel is to car as handlebar is to _____. (part to whole)

Night is to day as win is to _____. (opposites)

Storm is to rain as blizzard is to _____. (cause and effect)

Mt. Everest is to the Himalayas as the Matterhorn is to _____. (geography)

Boat is to ship as firearm is to _____. (synonym)

Word Stories and Classical Roots

Words often have interesting histories. Exploring word origins with students helps them develop indelible memories as they link specific words to stories of their origins. In addition, they learn to appreciate the historical context of certain words and concepts. For example, a teacher might mention that *tank,* a heavily armored military vehicle, was originally used as a code word among the Allied powers to help conceal the vehicle's development and existence from the Axis powers during World War I. That interesting story not only describes the word and concept but also helps students understand an aspect of world history.

Learning the origin of place names, particularly those within their own community, is a great way for students to link history with vocabulary play and development. In a local elementary school, Jeanine, an intermediate-grade teacher of students with learning disabilities, interests children in words by relating the stories and rationales for place names in nearby communities. Jeanine works in Summit County, in which Akron, Ohio, is located. She invites students to speculate on the origin of the county's name. A few students know that *summit* refers to a high place and suggest that Summit County contains the highest point in the state. Jeanine compliments her students for a good guess and then shares the real story of Summit County: It was the highest point on the Ohio and Erie Canal, which ran from Lake Erie to the Ohio River. Her story leads to a discussion about the numerous canal locks in the county, their purpose, how they worked, and their relation to the type of land where that part of the canal was built.

Jeanine notes that the origin of the name *Akron* is also related to summits. She points out that the city's name is derived from the Greek word *akros,* which means "topmost." Then she challenges her students to find other words that include the *akro* or *acro* word part and determine how they relate to a high place. Within minutes, students find *acrobat, Acropolis,* and *acrophobia.* After everyone discusses the meanings of these words, Jeanine ends her mini-lesson with "akros = summit or high place" written on the chalkboard. Students have

Edward Fry, Jacqueline Kress, & Dona Lee Fountoukidis. *The New Reading Teacher's Book of Lists* (4th ed.). San Francisco: Jossey-Bass, 2000.

Ida Ehrlich. *Instant Vocabulary.* New York: Pocket Books, 1988.

John Kennedy. *Word Stems.* New York: Soho Publishing, 1996.

Figure 7.5
Source Books for Classical (Latin and Greek) Vocabulary Study

a clear idea of what these words mean and how they fit into the texture of their own communities. Familiar place names such as Pittsburgh, Pennsylvania, Florida, Baton Rouge, Vermont, Montana, Los Angeles, Palo Alto, and many others have interesting and important word histories.

Many English words are derived from other languages such as Greek, Latin, French, and Spanish. Indeed, it has been estimated that nearly 75 percent of the words in English are derived from Greek or Latin. Gaining insight into words and word parts from other languages will give students strategies for understanding many new words. Appendix J lists some common word parts derived from Greek and Latin that will help students unlock the meanings of many other words they encounter.

Teaching one derivation per week can go a long way to developing students' vocabulary. Tanya introduces her fourth graders to a new derivation each week. She spells the word on the chalkboard, circles it, describes the meaning of the root, and asks students to find English words connected to it. After introducing *terra* (meaning land or earth) she was surprised to find that students came to class the next day with *terrace, territory, terra cotta, extraterrestrial, terrarium,* and *Terra Haute* ready to connect to the root word on the board. But even so, Tanya dazzled her students with a few additional words for the chart: *Mediterranean, terrapin,* and *terrier.* She invited students to speculate on how each new word had the concept of land or earth locked within it.

According to Tanya, her students love the opportunity to expand their vocabulary in this way. It makes them feel smarter. Learning one Latin or Greek root can expand students' knowledge of many English words.

Exploring word histories with students is fun, but when we share these ideas with teachers, the first question they ask is often, "But how do we find out about words and where they come from? We can't be expected to have all these words and their histories at our fingertips." The solution to this problem is as close as the public library. Just ask the librarian where you might find a few of the many books written about word histories. For a start, look over our list of favorite books on Latin and Greek derivations in Figure 7.5. Then, design your own captivating entrée into the world of word origins for your own students.

Words for the Day

Students learn on average seven words every day (Snow et al., 1998)—that is a lot of words. One way to keep students thinking about words is to begin each day with "Words for the Day." As students (and teacher) come across new, interesting, or important words from the news or their own reading and interests, they take note and contribute them to the class's daily word list. Because students choose most of the words, they are more likely to know and use them in their own language.

List the words on the chalkboard or a sheet of chart paper. Students tell why they chose the word, how they found it, and what they think it means. Notes are made on the chart, and students (and teacher) make efforts to use the words throughout the day in their speech and writing. Most students take it a step further by looking for the words in their own reading.

Jane, a sixth-grade teacher, makes a list of 5 to 10 words every day with her students. "Sometimes I have them make concept maps with the words. Mostly, though, we just encourage each other to use the words throughout the day. It's a challenge for all of us, and we take note when one of us uses a particularly unusual word, like *recession,* which has been in the news lately. I can't believe how sensitive students become to interesting words in their world after a few weeks of doing this simple activity." At the end of the day, Jane posts the list of words on her word wall so that students continue to see the words from previous days. "When they are writing, I often see them gazing at the word wall to find interesting words."

Games and Puzzles

Vocabulary learning should be fun, and one way to accomplish this is through games and similar activities. It is easy to create variations of well-known games that students find engaging and entertaining. Here are just a few that we have found to be student pleasers.

Wordo

This form of bingo uses Wordo cards almost identical to bingo cards. (See chapter 5 for an example of a *Wordo* card.) Choose 24 words to review and play with. Students randomly write one word in each square, leaving the center square as a free spot. The teacher then randomly selects one word at a time and presents the definition, an antonym, a sentence with the target word missing, or some other clue to the meaning of the word. Players must figure out the word and cover it with a marker. As in bingo, a player wins when a vertical, horizontal, or diagonal line is covered. Then a new game starts. Individual games can last 5 to 10 minutes.

John has used Wordo with his Title I students as well as his fifth graders:

At the beginning of the year, I run off a hundred or so of the Wordo sheets. . . . Then we're ready to play whenever we have the time, and the students and I want to play. They really like it. I think they'd play it every day if they could. Sometimes I give out cheap prizes to the winners. I have three empty coffee cans, two with prizes and one with a slip of paper that says "Zonk." The kids think this is fun.

I've found that after a while, rather than my saying the clues or giving the antonyms, a student can do that job, too. It gives them extra practice in playing with word meanings. Of course, a student will want to play emcee for only one or two games. Then, they'll want to get back and play the game!

Concentration (or Match)

In *Concentration* two decks of cards are laid out in a grid. One set of cards contains words to be learned and practiced; and the other set contains definitions, synonyms, or antonyms or some other way of matching the first set. As in the television version of the game, players (or teams of players) uncover pairs of cards seeking matches. When a match is made, the player takes the cards and keeps playing. If no match is produced, then the cards are turned back over, and the next player takes a turn. Players who find the most matches win the game.

Scattergories

Scattergories can be played with the commercial version or one adapted for instructional use. In the adapted version a set of 5 to 10 letters or blends is determined and listed vertically on each player's paper. Then categories are determined—for example, vegetables, countries, presidents' last names, or rivers. (See Figure 7.6 for an example of an adapted playing sheet.) The categories can also be developed from themes and content areas. For example, a unit on state geography can include categories of cities, manufacturing products, agricultural products, rivers, boundary states, and so on. Working with a time limit of several minutes, individuals or groups of players think of words that begin with the given letters and fit the category. Players with the greatest number of unique words (words chosen by only one individual or team) win that round.

Balderdash

This game also is available in both commercial and adapted forms. An adapted version of *Balderdash* goes like this: Each player chooses an uncommon word from the dictionary. One player presents a word and a definition—either the real definition or a made-up one. The other players individually guess whether the definition is correct. Presenting players earn a point each time they fool another player.

CATEGORIES				
Initial Consonants & Blends ⬇				

Figure 7.6

Adapted Scattergories Sheet

Hinky Pinkies

Hinky Pinkies are word riddles. Students love to apply their word knowledge to solve them and make their own. The answer to a Hinky Pinky is two or more rhyming words. For example, a cold place of learning is a *cool school;* an obese feline is a *fat cat.* A variation of Hinky Pinkies uses alliterative combinations of words instead of rhymes. Thus, a sleepy flower might be a *lazy lily,* and a 4,000-pound farm vehicle would be a *two-ton tractor.*

Hinky Pinkies are fun, easy, and quick. Many teachers save them for when they have a few extra minutes in the school day. Other teachers use them as alternative assignments in various content areas. After studying the states, students in one class were asked to describe states using Hinky Pinkies. California was described as *west, warm, and wild,* whereas Florida was *fun in the sun.*

Regular, but not exclusive, use of games and puzzles adds another dimension to vocabulary learning. Students appreciate the variety that these games can bring to the study of words and concepts. Sometimes, they exercise their creative talents by developing their own vocabulary games and puzzles.

Integrating Vocabulary Routines Throughout the Curriculum

The strategies and activities we have outlined in this chapter have the potential to increase students' interest in and knowledge of words, which in turn will have a positive effect on their reading. Informed teachers modify and use these approaches to fit their own curricula, teaching situations, and styles of teaching to meet their students' needs and learning characteristics. These teachers integrate and mass their approaches in planned and purposeful ways. They do not use them hit-or-miss once or twice a week for a few minutes or during a lull in the instructional day. Instead, they incorporate these strategies into their own framework of teaching.

Most teachers, especially at the elementary level, teach a variety of subject areas. Even those who specialize in one area teach a variety of topics within the subject. Each topic or subject area brings new words and concepts for students to understand, use, and learn successfully and efficiently. The strategies and activities from this chapter can become an essential element of subject-area reading and learning.

However, just as we think of science or social studies as specific and separate areas of the curriculum, word play and word study need "spotlighted" time during the school day. Teachers promote vocabulary learning by massing the activities, by putting together 10- to 15-minute vocabulary lessons three to five times per week for students to explore and play with words. They may tie the words to a particular subject, or not. They may extract words from interests, hobbies, current or upcoming events, anniversaries, holidays—almost anywhere. Then, they play with them. Thus, students develop an interest in, improved knowledge of, and greater flexibility in learning and using words they encounter in their lives.

In addition to content area integration and word play, teachers can dedicate specific times of the day to instructional routines devoted to vocabulary development. Rich, a third-grade teacher, does "*Wordshop*" three times a week:

> I like to play with and learn new words, and I try to share my enjoyment with my students. . . . For about 15 minutes on Mondays, Wednesdays,

and Fridays right before lunch, we play with words. We might do three or four activities during this time such as a couple of analogy problems, introduce the origins of two or three words, or learn about some Latin or Greek roots, and play a game like word Concentration or Wordo. It's really fast-paced, and the kids like it. Best of all, I see many of them playing with words on their own!

Word knowledge or vocabulary may be only one part of reading, but it is an important part. And it challenges many of our struggling readers. Many students think of word learning as drudgery; as a result, they avoid it or make inefficient use of their time and efforts for learning words.

Word learning need not be that way. Tapping into students' own interests and knowledge; employing interesting, effective, and challenging learning activities; allowing students to collaborate with others in shared learning experiences; and creating a playful environment in which words are played with, played on, manipulated, and used in a variety of ways can make the difference between vocabulary instruction that hinders reading and vocabulary instruction that nurtures reading.

8

Comprehension Development with Narrative Text

Comprehension is what reading is all about. Reading is the "process of constructing meaning from written texts . . . a holistic act" that depends on "the background of the reader, the purpose for reading, and the context in which reading occurs" (Anderson, Hiebert, Scott, & Wilkinson, 1985, p. 7). Whether we're reading a novel, a technical manual, or a number from the telephone directory, comprehension is involved. Thus, a primary goal for literacy instruction, regardless of age, grade level, or achievement level, is to help students become purposeful, independent comprehenders.

Yet, most struggling readers we have encountered are neither purposeful nor independent readers. Instead they try, usually in vain, to guess at desired responses. Or, even sadder, they simply choose not to participate at all. Effective comprehension instruction can make all the difference for these children.

What makes comprehension instruction effective? What kinds of discussions or activities help students construct meaning from print? How can we foster students' thoughtful interaction with text? These are critical questions effective teachers consider as they plan instruction. In the mid-1980s, the Commission on Reading (Anderson et al., 1985) suggested that comprehension instruction should help students focus on relevant information, synthesize the information, and integrate it with what they already know. Discussions should provoke thought and motivate higher level thinking. More recently, research reviewed by the National Reading Panel (2000; Armbruster, Lehr, & Osborn, 2001) has underscored the same issues—comprehension is purposeful and active; students' comprehension is enhanced through strategy instruction.

These guidelines raise another question: What kinds of strategies are worth teaching? Robert

Marzano and his colleagues (2001), researchers at Mid-Continent Regional Educational Laboratory, conducted a study to help answer this question. They gathered research studies of instructional strategies, grouped the studies by type of strategy, and applied a research technique called meta-analysis to determine the relative power of the particular strategies. Categories of strategies that made a significant difference in student learning included those that focused on

- identifying similarities and differences
- summarizing and note taking
- nonlinguistic representation (nonword responses)
- cooperative learning
- generating and testing hypotheses

In both this chapter and the next we discuss many strategies that encompass one or more of these characteristics.

To help struggling readers become purposeful, active, and strategic comprehenders, several other guidelines are worth noting:

- Comprehension instruction must involve students in real reading situations. Instruction must keep the process whole and real rather than focus on artificial bits and pieces that draw attention away from authentic purposes for reading. In other words, completing exercises about specific skills enhances comprehension less effectively than reading interesting material and talking about it with others.

- Strategy instruction should help students focus on meaning as thoughtful readers. In other words, children should develop their own understanding of what they read, not try to guess the teacher's. Thinking is at the center of all reading. The meaning that individuals actively construct while reading depends at least in part on their own knowledge, experiences, and purposes for reading. Two readers may comprehend the same piece of material in different ways without one being right and the other wrong. Comprehension is relative, not absolute.

- The instructional environment must promote risk taking. Proficient readers are active and strategic; they speculate. They think about what they know and what they are likely to encounter while they read. If their reading fails to confirm their predictions, they may continue to read, looking for clues that help them alter their ideas and make sense of the material, or they may reread for missed clues and make alternative predictions. Making predictions, or educated guesses, and evaluating them are essential aspects of reading. Making a guess means taking a chance, and readers are unlikely to take chances in an environment that stresses being "right" or that exposes their ideas to ridicule or dismissal. Rather, we must show students that we care about their reactions to what they read, that their thoughts are important.

■ In classrooms, learning is a social process. Students must interact with text to enhance their abilities as comprehenders. Interacting with others is equally important. The instructional environment should foster group inquiry and problem solving by giving students opportunities to clarify their thinking and understand the thinking of others. Instructionally, two or three heads working together are almost always better than one.

■ Readers need opportunities to respond to what they have read. Moreover, children need choice of options for responding to reading. Students may wish to talk with others, write down their thoughts or feelings, develop written or oral narratives that explore or extend various aspects of their reading, engage in creative drama or art activities, or participate in reader's theater. The list can go on and on. By making time for response, sharing a variety of response activities with children, and encouraging students to respond to reading in personally meaningful ways, we show students that "reading/thinking continues after the book is closed" (Goodman & Watson, 1977, p. 869). Equally important, we show children that their personal responses to reading are important and that others value their thinking.

These instructional priorities reflect our current understanding of the reading process. We know that reading is the process of constructing meaning and that readers accomplish this by using what's in their heads as well as what's on the page. We also know that children learn best when we give them opportunities to learn. Struggling readers develop proficiency more readily with consistent and plentiful opportunities to behave as successful readers.

Each instructional activity described in this chapter and chapter 9 reflects these instructional priorities. This chapter focuses on activities that work especially well with literary materials, especially narratives. By *narrative* we mean story, whether imaginary, such as fiction, fables or tales, and many poems, or true, such as biographies, autobiographies, or memoirs.

Supporting Comprehension Before Reading

To understand what they read, readers need some knowledge of the topic. This can be as true for narrative as it is for informational material. Knowledge of concepts in the reading and familiarity with the author and his or her writing style as well as characters, settings, and problems presented in the text can help any reader make meaning while reading. Many struggling readers have limited knowledge of the topics they encounter in their reading. A few minutes spent to develop interest and background before reading can greatly benefit students' understanding of the text.

Of course, one way to ensure that students have some background about a topic is for them to choose their own reading materials, but free choice is not always possible or desirable. Brief before-reading activities can generate interest and help students develop some initial understanding of the topic. Here are several easy ways to support comprehension before reading.

Jackdaws

Teachers are notorious collectors. One person's junk is often a teacher's treasure. *Jackdaws* are collections of artifacts built around a particular book topic or theme. By bringing in real or facsimile artifacts connected to a book and talking about them with students, teachers help create interest and background that carry students through texts they may otherwise find difficult. Figure 8.1 lists the types of items that may go into a jackdaw.

As students become familiar with the concept, they can add to the teacher's jackdaw, which is then displayed in a mini-museum for all students to see, touch, and ponder. Students can also create and share their own jackdaws as an after-reading response activity. What a creative and interesting way for students to demonstrate understanding of a text!

For the past several years, Tim's sixth-grade class has explored the Great Depression in the United States. One of the core books is Irene Hunt's *No Promises in the Wind*. Tim says:

> I found that this can be a difficult book for many students, as they don't have a very good understanding of what it was like to live through such desperate times. Several years ago, my mother-in-law was going through some of her old things. I noticed she had many items from the Depression— an old camera, some clothing made from sackcloth, old records, an iron that was heated by sitting on the stove, some letters from her brothers who had to leave home to look for work, and many other things. I thought to myself, "What a wonderful way to introduce my students to the Depression!"
>
> With her permission I took the items in and shared them with my students prior to reading the book. I was amazed at how just touching and talking about these items created instant interest and gave students enough background to read the book successfully. Even our discussions of the book seemed livelier as a result of the jackdaw. It wasn't long before students were talking with their parents and grandparents and bringing in their own items related to the Depression.

Tim has used jackdaws with various books and themes concerning U.S. history, including the Civil War and the Vietnam era. In addition, he frequently uses jackdaws for stories that take place in different parts of the country and the world. "I guess Show and Tell has a place in the upper grades," he says.

A *jackdaw* is a collection of interesting artifacts that provides information about a particular subject, period, or idea. The term comes from the British name for a bird, similar to the American grackle, that picks up brightly colored, interesting, and attractive objects and carries them off to its nest. For children, jackdaws are particularly useful for building background and interest in books, stories, and other texts.

Artifacts can be collected from a variety of sources in a variety of ways to aid the understanding of particular portions of books. The elements of a jackdaw are synergistic. Each individual artifact may add only a little to a student's background or understanding. Yet when taken as a whole, the jackdaw can create a comprehensive background and make a book come alive.

When making jackdaws, teachers may wish to consider what artifacts might add to a deeper understanding of a text. The number and types of items are limited only by one's imagination and creativity. They might include the following:

1. Clothes of the type worn by particular characters in a book—catalog pictures, paper dolls, collages, old photos, and so on.
2. Songs or music from a period or event depicted in a book—sheet music, recordings, demonstrations, titles, or musical instruments.
3. A news article from the period, real or a facsimile.
4. Photographs from the time period or geographical area depicted in the book.
5. Household items from the period depicted in the book.
6. A time line depicting the occurrence of events in a book (may also include real-world events not mentioned in the book).
7. A map showing any journey that the main characters make.
8. Recipes and food dishes typical of the time period in the book.
9. Selected poems that reflect the theme of the book.
10. A glossary of interesting or peculiar words in the book.
11. Dioramas that illustrate particular scenes from the story.
12. A biographical sketch of the book's author.
13. A list of other related books (by story, theme, characters, and so on) that students can read to extend their literacy experience.

After the teacher introduces jackdaws, students may wish to add to existing collections or create their own jackdaws in response to their reading.

Figure 8.1

Jackdaws

Note: The term "Jackdaw," when used for a collection of artifacts assembled for educational purposes, is copyrighted by Jackdaw Publications of Amawalk, New York.

Related Readings

Just reading one story or text about a topic can often create sufficient interest and background for further reading. This is why thematic readings and units of study are such a powerful approach to learning. As students' understanding of a topic deepens through reading, their expanded background allows them to read more complex and sophisticated texts successfully.

When selecting texts for theme study, the issue of what "counts" as text is worth initial thought. Douglas and Jeannette Hartman (1993) advise that we foster student exploration of selected themes by selecting both linguistic texts—stories, chapters, articles, and poems—and nonlinguistic ones—art, music, video or film, and speakers. Access to as many different types of texts as possible promotes understanding of the concepts or themes under study and also helps students realize that many "ways of knowing" are valuable resources for their learning.

Students can read the texts themselves, or the teacher can read aloud to establish background for further reading. Kathy, a primary-grade teacher of struggling readers, has developed a reading unit that includes Cinderella stories from various cultures. She has found that one story sets the stage for the next. She even includes Judith Viorst's poem "And then the prince knelt down and tried to put the glass slipper on Cinderella's foot" (from *If I Were in Charge of the World and Other Worries*). "This really gets the talk started," she says.

Reading books by a particular author is also a great way to familiarize students with a writer's style. Books by William Steig, for example, contain many common elements, such as magic, animals that assume human roles, rich vocabulary, a subtle sense of humor, and much alliteration. Developing these understandings about Steig can help any reader tackle his next book. Moreover, this sort of "companion" reading helps students learn that authors explore ideas in many ways and that texts read together can lead to different insights than those read separately (Hartman & Hartman, 1993).

Series books are particularly potent because they combine one author's style with common characters, settings, and similar story lines. Reading one book in a series creates a rich background for reading, understanding, and enjoying other stories in the same series. Readers need not become familiar with general author and content variables and can devote their thoughts to making sense of the story at hand. Richek and McTague (1988) developed a sensible reading program for struggling readers built around the notion of series books. (See chapter 11 for a description of this program. In Appendix D we list some popular series books.)

Prevoke

Jackdaws are collections of artifacts, and related readings are collections of texts. *Prevoke* is an instructional activity based on collections of words—words children will encounter in their reading. (Variations of this activity, which is a type of word sort, are also called Prereading Predictions, Probable

Passages, and Predict-o-Gram; see Billmeyer & Barton, 1998.) To prepare a Prevoke activity, the teacher selects 12 to 20 words or short phrases from a text that students will read. The words may be written on the chalkboard or chart paper; some teachers have students write the words on small slips of scrap paper.

The teacher also prepares a two- or three-column chart that students will use for sorting the words. Good sorts for younger children may be "people," "places," or "things that happen." Older students may work with columns called "characters," "setting," "plot," "problem," "solution," "theme," and so forth. Prevoke involves pairs or small groups of students deciding which words might fit into which columns and (of course) why they think so. Students often share their ideas with others before reading, and the teacher sometimes asks students to speculate about the story based on the ways they have sorted the words. Students can even be asked to write a possible summary based on their predictions. After they read, they may return to the chart to reorganize the words and phrases.

Charlie, a school librarian who sponsors a book club, selected these words and phrases from the first two chapters of Christopher Paul Curtis's *Bud, not Buddy,* for example: *case workers, Bud, blue flyer, Herman E. Calloway, suitcase, Rules and Things, Toddy, home, street urchin, depression, Momma died, Flint, giant fiddle, best liar, Mrs. Amos, beastly little brute,* and *padlock.* "Eavesdropping on students' conversations was fascinating," she says. "Most groups thought *depression* and *Momma died* would be related— that the kid would be depressed because his mother died. I heard a few gasps when students encountered *depression* in the text—that's one of the things I really like about Prevoke. Students are so engaged in their reading!"

Story Mapping

A map is helpful when driving in an unfamiliar city. Studying the map before driving helps you familiarize yourself with important intersections, street names, and landmarks to help you negotiate your way through unfamiliar streets and neighborhoods. Similarly, introducing students to a story by sharing a map of the text can help familiarize them with the major characters and events they will encounter in their reading. A *story map* (or story board) is simply a visual display of the major characters, settings, and events arranged in story order (see Figure 8.2). It can depict the complete story or provide only enough information to start readers into a text. Students can also create their own maps or complete partial maps as a postreading activity. Some teachers ask students to make notes on maps as they read, as well.

Bob, a teacher who works with upper-elementary students who have difficulty reading, puts it this way:

> Sometimes I ask students to read stories that are quite complex. I know that the story can be confusing for them. For these times I will often sketch out a map for them to show them how the story develops and

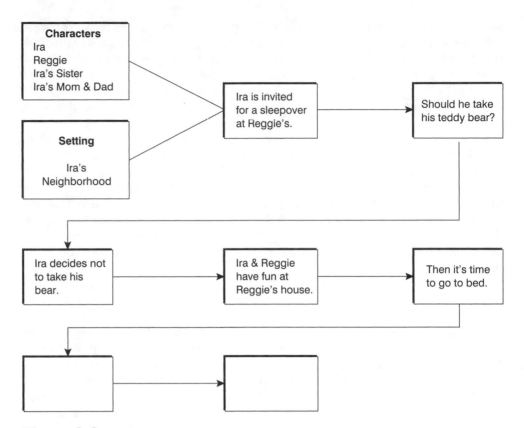

Figure 8.2

Story Map for Bernard Waber's *Ira Sleeps Over*

point out some of the diversions that may get them off track. I think many of my kids are helped a lot by the maps. Often, they go up to the map that's on a wall chart and study it as they read. It helps them make sense out of the story.

Other Media and Activities

Another way to build background and interest is to role play some aspect of a story before reading it. This often allows students inside the issues and characters that form the story. Before Jane read *Say It* by Charlotte Zolotow to her students, her second graders went out to the playground. She asked students to walk in pairs pretending to be mother and daughter or father and son. Then she challenged them to think of ways to say that they loved or were angry with the other person without using the words *love, angry, mad,* or other words that directly expressed those feelings. Later, the students talked about how they did. Jane recalls, "It was a challenging task and many students had difficulty with it. But it got all of us thinking about the subtle ways we can communicate with each other, it made our reading of *Say It* that much more personal and meaningful, and it led to an excellent discussion when I finished reading the story."

Guest speakers from the local community (perhaps parents who are experts in particular areas) can excite students about a topic that they will later explore in reading. Before his students read Jane Yolen's *The Devil's Arithmetic,* James, a fifth-grade teacher, invited a Holocaust survivor to speak with the class. Her moving story created an interest that sped many students through the book and into several other books about the Holocaust.

Field trips and movies or videotapes (commercially produced or developed by the teacher or others) can develop interest and background for reading. In his class's study of slavery and the Civil War, Tim arranged for a field trip to a preserved station on the Underground Railroad. Before reading Paul Fleischman's *Bull Run* and performing it later as a reader's theater, Tim showed the class selected segments from the PBS television series *The Civil War.* He says, "I think sometimes we assume that students have a good background on a topic when they really don't. Then we're disappointed when they have a poor understanding and don't enjoy a story we thought would knock their socks off. I really think that a key to successful reading experiences, including comprehension and enjoyment, is making sure that students have a solid background in the topic they are to encounter."

Even illustrations can generate conversation about and interest in a story. Many primary teachers invite children on "picture walks" before they read or listen to a new book. By showing several illustrations and asking children what they see and what they think might be happening in the story, teachers help students discover much that will aid their comprehension. In fact, all of these activities are about aiding comprehension. Whether students learn something new or are reminded of what they already know, whether they make predictions or simply become curious, their minds are engaged and they're ready to read.

Supporting Comprehension During Reading

To plan comprehension instruction, we must first understand how comprehension happens. Meaning construction (comprehension) depends on several types of prior knowledge as well as on active thought. To read we must understand the features of written language as a form of communication. We make use of our underlying knowledge of *grapho-phonology* (sound–symbol relationships), *syntax* (word order), and *semantics* (vocabulary and meaning). Furthermore, reading involves thinking and predicting, which are based in part on experiential and conceptual background. In other words, reading is an active thinking process dependent on the reader's thoughts, language, and experiences as well as the text.

Situational pragmatics, or the context in which we read, also influences comprehension. External contextual influences such as lighting or distractions

Instructional support should provide students with a framework for thinking about text and sharing ideas with others.

can affect comprehension, as can other, more subtle contextual factors. One of these is *purpose,* which we use to determine if we have comprehended adequately. Students' perceptions of the classroom instructional environment, including the kinds of interactions encouraged, are equally important. To support meaning construction, communication should be open during text discussions. Free and voluntary exchange of ideas allows students to try out their ideas and modify them after they hear what others have to say. As Lehman and Scharer (1996) note, "Children's primary personal responses are valuable and form the basis for literary conversations. However, left unexamined they can also be limiting" (p. 33). Teachers can expand children's personal understanding through activities that encourage them to express their thoughts, explore new possibilities, and even challenge others' opinions. In other words, instructional support during reading should provide students with a framework for thinking about the text and sharing ideas with others.

Directed Reading–Thinking Activity (DR–TA)

The Directed Reading–Thinking Activity (DR–TA) (Stauffer, 1980) is a problem-solving discussion strategy designed to support comprehension. Lessons evolve through cycles in which students generate hypotheses and subsequently validate, reject, or modify them.

First, students make predictions about story content based on the selection title (and, if appropriate, initial illustrations) and prior knowledge.

Students read silently to predetermined stopping points. Discussions follow, which the teacher facilitates by asking students to indicate whether or not their predictions were confirmed and encouraging them to support their ideas. Next, students refine their original predictions and/or make new ones. This cycle of predicting; reading to confirm, modify, or reject; providing support from the text; and making further predictions continues until the entire selection has been read.

To prepare for a DR–TA, the teacher decides where students will stop for discussion. Divisions between episodes in a story often work well. Preparation may also involve becoming comfortable with DR–TA questions, which are different from more traditional comprehension questions. For example, the teacher initiates discussion by asking, "What do you think this will be about?" The teacher then may ask for elaboration or clarification, asking, "Why?" or "What makes you say that?" After students have read, the teacher may ask, "Did anything surprise you?" or "Did things happen like you thought they would?" to encourage students to evaluate their earlier ideas in light of information in the text. Finally, the teacher asks students to think ahead: "What will happen next? Why?" Students then read, and the discussion cycle begins again.

Bonnie conducted a DR–TA with a group of eighth graders, and we reproduce several excerpts here. The students were reading and discussing the short story "All the Years of Her Life" (Callaghan, 1935), which tells what happens when a mother learns that her son has been caught shoplifting.

Bonnie:	What do you think this story's going to be about?
Lucy:	Somebody's life. . . .
Joseph:	A diary. It'll be a diary about her life. . . .
Lucy:	She's going to be older.
Bonnie:	Why do you say that?
Lucy:	Well it's a story about her life.
Heather:	It says, "All the Years." . . .
Lucy:	So, that means she's going to be, like, older. . . .
Bonnie:	Some other predictions? . . .
Joseph:	Someone's problems.
Bonnie:	Why do you say that?
Joseph:	I don't know. You can just tell by her life. And usually people have problems.
	[Students read. Later in the lesson the conversation continues.]
Bonnie:	Well, what do you think will happen next?
Joseph:	I don't think they're going to go get a cop.
Bonnie:	No? Why not?

Joseph: Why not? I just don't think that. Uh, with the mother's attitude, the way she came in, I think that it might have changed the owner's mind.

Lucy: Yeah, you know, with a mother like this maybe the kid'll turn out okay.

Bonnie: Is there any sign of that in the story?

Lucy: Yeah. Well, he couldn't believe the attitude that his mom came in with. Maybe that might change his opinion about her.

Heather: I think that he's more likely to get a cop if she came in nice like that. That's what I would do.

Andrew: Yeah, because he thinks that she's probably not going to do anything to him, or punish him for what he did. . . .

Heather: The store manager thinks that the mother sort of planned for him to take something. . . .

Bonnie: What do the rest of you think?

Joseph: Well, maybe the store manager let him off the hook because he'll probably punish himself enough. . . .

Bonnie: Tell some more about that.

Joseph: Guilt.

Heather: Yeah, the way he'll feel about himself from now on.

Lucy: And he probably won't do it again.

Bonnie: Okay.

Andrew: Well, the kid's already scared as it is.

Did you notice how little Bonnie said? In a DR–TA, students do most of the talking. Did you notice that she did not provide important ideas or generalizations for students? Her goals were to encourage thinking and facilitate group interaction rather than manipulate students' thinking or test their recall. The instructional context signaled that students' ideas were valued—that they should explain their ideas so others could understand their reasoning and listen to and talk with each other. In short, students were intellectually involved with text concepts.

The DR–TA is a staple in Bonnie's classroom. She says:

We probably do DR–TAs more often than any other "while-they-read" strategy. The kids love it. They enjoy telling us all what they think, and they seem to find others' ideas fascinating. These discussions really support kids' reading, especially when we have different hypotheses going as they read. Maybe it's because we stop to talk while they read, maybe it's the personal commitment they make or the curiosity that develops so naturally, or maybe it's because kids know we'll want to know where their ideas are coming from—for whatever reason, the DR–TA is really a powerful reading strategy!

Think–Pair–Share

Like the DR–TA, *Think–Pair–Share* provides students opportunities to talk about a story as they read it. To prepare for the activity, students find partners. The teacher identifies stopping points for discussion and shares these with students, who can make light pencil marks in their texts to remember where to stop.

Students read to the first stopping point and then pause to think about the reading. They might consider such issues as what they found interesting or puzzling; they often make brief notes about their thoughts. After each partner has completed this thinking, the pairs talk with one another using their notes to remind them of the points they wish to make. Finally, the larger group shares, focusing on interesting issues that arose during the partner discussions. Depending on students' interest and need, these discussions may be brief or lengthy. When the first Think–Pair–Share cycle is complete, students read the next portion of the story and begin the cycle again.

Think–Pair–Share is an extremely adaptable organizational structure for conducting classroom discussions. For example, it can also be used as an after-reading activity and works well with expository text. Harold, who uses the strategy frequently in his work with students with disabilities, sees two major benefits:

> My students often need support as they are reading a story. If we use Think-Pair-Share a couple of times while they read, the thinking and talking allows everyone to be successful. I also like the fact that individuals think things through for themselves (and often write their ideas down) before discussing them with partners. They don't "shoot from the hip." This activity encourages individual response to reading, which I believe is important to helping kids learn, and the writing beforehand makes the partner discussions more lively.

Character Sketches

In *Character Sketches,* students use the Think–Pair–Share structure to focus their attention on character development. At the first stopping point in their reading (or listening), students jot down words and phrases to describe one or two major characters. This becomes information that they share, first with their partners and then with the larger group. At each successive stop, students return to their notes about the characters, modifying them based on the new insights they have developed through reading. A character who initially seemed selfish or unfeeling, for example, may be revealed as shy or grieving. After modifying their lists, students again talk with partners and the entire group. The Think–Pair–Share cycle continues until students have completed the story.

At the conclusion of the activity, students have notes that reflect their descriptions of major characters. These can be used for a discussion of how authors develop characters or a variety of other follow-up activities. Students also have an increased understanding of the story because characters typically reveal their personalities through what they say and do.

Linguistic Roulette

This small-group discussion technique was developed by Jerry Harste. After reading a portion of a story, each student skims through it again looking for a single sentence that she finds interesting, important, puzzling, or special in some other way. This sentence is written on paper.

Discussion begins when all members of the group have read and selected their sentences. Each student reads a sentence aloud and invites group response. Students often explain why they selected their sentences, which can give rise to interesting comprehension discussions. After all group members have shared, students read the next portion of the story, and the cycle is repeated.

Linguistic Roulette fosters comprehension in several ways. First, stopping periodically to talk with peers supports comprehension. Moreover, students must think again about the story to select their sentences for discussion. Hearing others' sentences and participating in the small-group discussions sometimes encourages consideration of alternate perspectives.

Karen provides resource-room support for intermediate-grade children with learning disabilities. "To tell the truth," she says, "I was pretty suspicious about Linguistic Roulette at first. I wondered how anything that *easy* could really work." But Karen was curious, so she tried it.

> And, let me tell you, I eavesdropped on those first discussions. What a surprise! I found that my students were perfectly capable of discussing a story independently and that they were really proud that they could do so without me. In fact, the Linguistic Roulette discussions are usually freer and more wide-ranging than they are when I'm part of the group. I like the way it provides a framework for kids—because they know what they need to do, they can manage the discussion on their own.

Imagery

Narratives lend themselves to rich images that readers create as they read. The text is rather like a blueprint that readers flesh out by adding their own background, understandings, and experiences. The result is a mental image that is unique yet gives the reader a clearer picture or understanding of the story. The images that individuals create reflect their own interpretations, which may explain why people usually like the book version of a story better than the movie version in which a director imposes images on the audience.

Good readers may take for granted this ability to create internal images as they read. It seems so easy and natural. But many struggling readers fail to spontaneously create text-related images. Some scholars have argued that the dominance of television and now video games in our society has inhibited children's ability to create mental images. As a result, many readers have difficulty using this strategy for comprehending stories.

To nurture this ability in most children, teachers simply remind them to form images as they read and invite them to talk about their images after reading. Quick sketches can be effective as well. (See Sketch to Stretch in the next section.) Title I teacher Janet told us that many of her students seem to have difficulty creating images of texts:

> I found it helpful to begin with stories and poems that lend themselves to images. We always talk about students' "mind pictures," too. This seems to help their retention of the stories. Also, after reading a story I'll sometimes bring a videotaped version and we'll watch part of it. Then we'll talk about how our own images compare with the tape. It makes for a lively discussion.

Text discussions during reading can enhance comprehension if the instructional environment fosters sharing, group inquiry, and problem solving. All the activities we have described encourage students to read actively and thoughtfully. Over time, such instruction will help them learn that they can (indeed, must) construct meaning as they read.

Extending Comprehension After Reading

Discussions during reading should promote thoughtful consideration of the text and individual and group efforts at understanding. Instruction after reading should encourage continued interaction with text content. The activities in this section are all effective techniques for encouraging students to continue thinking widely and deeply about what they have read and to integrate the text information into their own cognitive structures. The teacher's role in all these activities is to promote sharing, encourage and model critical thought, and moderate discussions. The students' roles require reading, thinking, solving problems, making decisions, and interacting with the text and each other.

Group Mapping Activity

The *Group Mapping Activity* (Davidson, 1982) promotes individual response to reading and provides a framework for discussion. After reading, students create maps, which they share with and explain to others. Classmates may ask questions or make comments, which generally prompts continued discussion.

A map is a diagram or symbolic representation of the reader's personal response to text. Young readers often make pictures when asked to map; older readers tend to use lines, arrows, or other symbols to represent their response. Students may use a few words to label portions of a map, but mapping is primarily a nonverbal activity. The first time students map, the teacher can help them understand the concept by offering directions: "Put your ideas about the story in a diagram. You can sketch if you want to, or use circles, boxes, or arrows. Try to show your ideas without using too many words. Don't worry about a 'right' way to map; there isn't one." This detailed explanation is necessary only for students' initial encounter with mapping. When they see the variety of responses, their concern about being right quickly diminishes.

Students' maps need not be detailed; in fact, making one should take only a few minutes. Mapping allows readers to synthesize their responses to the text. Its real purpose, however, is to provide a framework for the discussion that follows, which typically allows students to develop further insights about the text. The Group Mapping Activity helps readers recall and retain text information while providing them with a means to respond personally to what they have read.

Sketch to Stretch

Sketch to Stretch, another nonverbal response activity, is an interesting elaboration of imaging. Individual students draw a quick sketch of a favorite or memorable event or scene from a story they have read and show it to a small group. Rather than describing and explaining the picture, however, each student invites classmates to provide their own interpretation of the drawing: "What is this a picture of?" and "What did the illustrator think was important about the story? Why?" After others give their interpretations, the illustrator is free to explain the drawing.

Sketch to Stretch encourages students to create images on paper and use them as the basis for interpretive discussion of the story. Thus, all students participate in high-level thinking and discussion.

Anna began using both the Group Mapping Activity and Sketch to Stretch some time ago. When she learned about them, she said, "I knew they were *made* for my second graders. They love to draw, and many are still beginning writers, so they often have more to say than they have patience to write." Anna has been pleased with children's responses: "The diversity of responses is truly amazing! Children show genuine interest in each other's maps and sketches, and the discussions that accompany sharing are fascinating. I feel certain that the kids' understanding is enhanced."

Tableau(x)

A third type of nonlinguistic representation involves "illustrations" that students create with their bodies instead of pencil and paper. We learned about *tableaux* from our colleague Mary, who used them in her high-school English and drama classes. The activity, every bit as effective with younger students, begins with a text students have read or listened to. Next, groups of students select some aspect of the text to represent by means of a tableau, which is a "living picture" or a depiction of a scene by silent and motionless people. Students prepare and share their tableaux with the rest of the class, who then attempt to determine what is being portrayed and what roles individual members of the tableau play. To manage this aspect, we ordinarily encourage the audience to whisper their ideas with others and then to raise their hands when they think they know what the tableau is. If the audience cannot decide what they're looking at, we tap the shoulder of one person in the tableau, who then provides a clue.

"The energy and excitement is amazing," says Jocelyn, who works with intermediate-level struggling readers. "At least once or twice a week, kids request tableaux, and I usually relent because I quickly noticed how much learning goes into this activity. The kids like it because it seems like a game, but I like it because the groups dig deeply into meaning as they decide on their tableaux and then the audience does the same—it's like two or three comprehension activities all rolled up into one!" Jocelyn has expanded her use of tableaux into content areas. Children may, for example, depict events from history. She has used tableaux in science as well: "You should have seen their simple machines in science. Amazing!"

(Write and Share)[2]

Responses to literature may vary among readers, and comprehension is enhanced by considering others' ideas as well as developing one's own. *(Write and Share)*[2] fosters response by incorporating both these opportunities (Davidson, 1987). Students write twice and share twice (thus the name) in response to text they have read.

In small groups, children first read the same text. Then students write, quickly jotting down words and phrases that represent their responses to the text. Teachers often tell students not to worry about putting their ideas into sentences but rather to make quick notes. This helps students attend to their ideas rather than the mechanics of writing. The first small-group discussion follows, with each student sharing notes and all students reacting to the ideas presented.

When the first sharing session ends, students again write, this time developing their thoughts into prose, using the text, their own initial notes, and the shared responses as the basis for this second writing. Finally, students share this writing with each other and discuss both the text and their reactions to it. To encourage further response, the teacher may ask volunteers to read their final pieces to the whole group. Another alternative is to ask each small group to select one piece to be shared with the larger group.

As in Think–Pair–Share, the initial note taking allows students to capture their individual responses before sharing them with others. With the first discussion, the note taking serves as a kind of prewriting activity as students generate and organize their ideas. Of course, hearing and discussing others' ideas during both sharing sessions often help students see and appreciate different interpretations and responses to the same text as well as deepen their own understanding. In short, this easy-to-implement activity has a variety of powerful effects on students as comprehenders.

Agree or Disagree? Why?

In this small-group discussion activity, students talk about statements related to what they have read or heard. To prepare for the activity, the teacher writes several statements that reflect issues and may yield differences of opinion. For example, the following statements might accompany the first chapter of E. B. White's *Charlotte's Web:*

- Fern's parents showed that they loved her.
- Animals should be treated like people.
- Sometimes adults have to do cruel things.
- Mr. Arable should have killed the runt.

Small groups assemble after students have read or listened to the story or a chapter. Group members discuss each statement to decide if they agree or disagree with it and make notes about their reasons. When the small groups have completed their discussions, the teacher may wish to convene the larger group to facilitate further discussion of the story.

Carol frequently uses Agree or Disagree? Why?, especially when she reads aloud to her primary Title I students. "Sometimes the books kids read independently are rather straightforward," she says, "but those I read aloud hardly ever are. I tend to select read-alouds that encourage children to think about life's complexities. Agree or Disagree? Why? provides a framework for them to share their thinking about some of these ideas. It's also a perfect way to extend the read-aloud experience for kids."

Bleich's Heuristic

David Bleich (1978) has long argued that individual, subjective responses to literature have worth and power. His heuristic, or framework, provides a structure within which students develop individual responses and see how they may connect to both the text and their own knowledge and experiences.

Bleich's Heuristic asks students to think about their response in two ways—affectively and associatively. Affective response is prompted by questions such as, "How did you feel about this story?" and "What's your reaction/response to this reading?" Questions can also promote associative thinking, in which students consider connections among their responses, their own experiences, and the text: "How did you come up with this reaction?" "What did the author do to create your response?" "Why did you respond like that?" "Have you ever had an experience like the one the author describes?" and "What's the most important word in this piece? Why?"

Students respond to these questions by talking or writing; both writing and talking, as in Think–Pair–Share, also works well. Wayne, who has tried all these variations, advises flexibility but cautions that sharing is essential.

> I first learned about this as a writing activity, so that's the way I introduced it to the kids. It was okay, I guess, but I noticed that students were naturally talking with each other about what they had written. So then I tried just tossing the questions out as discussion starters. We all talked about our responses, even me. And that was okay, too, but it seemed like some of my more hesitant students got kind of bowled over by others who had firm ideas. So, I have also asked kids to write their answers to the questions or at least jot some ideas down before the group convenes to share. That, too, is okay. I guess my advice to others would be to try it all three ways and evaluate students' responses. For me, and my students, the sharing is really important. It's a powerful activity, though, so it's hard to go wrong.

Compare-and-Contrast Charts

An important aspect of comprehension is the ability to make thoughtful comparisons across texts, between events within stories, and across other aspects of stories that students read. For many students making comparisons can be daunting, and neither textbooks nor teachers always explain the process sufficiently. *Compare-and-Contrast Charts (CCC)* help students make good comparisons. The foundation for this activity is rather generic. We've seen versions of it before in many other activities, including distinctive-features activities or charts (described in chapter 9).

Teachers begin the CCC activity by creating a grid, either on a large sheet of chart paper to be displayed for the entire class or on individual sheets of paper. Along one axis of the chart are listed the items to be compared (for example, books by Tomie DePaola, Cinderella stories, biographies, or characters in William Steig stories). On the other axis students brainstorm key characteristics that distinguish at least one item from another (see Figure 8.3). Students then work in pairs or groups to fill out the remainder of the chart. Completed charts provide the information from which students compare and contrast the items listed. Students can use their charts in further discussion or as a way to organize their writing.

"These really do work," says Toni, an elementary reading specialist.

> I use this with children from first through sixth grade. With the younger ones we make the charts simpler—fewer things to be compared and fewer characteristics against which to compare them. And in some cases students dictate their thoughts to me and I write them in the appropriate boxes. But over time I see really noticeable gains in my students' ability to analyze and compare two or more stories or other items.

Books	Country or Setting	Main Characters: How Are They Special?	Our Feelings
Fin M'Coul	Ireland	Fin-he's a giant	It's a funny story. Fin acts like a baby.
Strega Nona	Italy	Strega Nona-Grandma witch. She has magic powers	Funny. Big Anthony makes a mess with Strega Nona's magic
Now One Foot, Now the Other	U.S.?	Bob-his grandfather	Kind of happy. The boy has to help his grandpa.
Nana Upstairs and Nana Downstairs	U.S.?	Nanas—they are grandmothers	It's sad. Nana Upstairs dies.

Figure 8.3
Compare-and-Contrast Chart: Tomie DePaola Books

Reader's Theater

Reader's theater, which we describe in chapter 6 as a fluency development activity, is also an enjoyable and beneficial way for students to respond to their reading. Because performers in reader's theater use only their voices and facial expressions to convey meaning, the action is left to audience imagination. Thus reader's theater can be a powerful comprehension activity for the performers, who must comprehend to convey meaning to others, and the audience, who must comprehend to understand the script. We agree with Jo Worthy and Kathryn Prater (2002) that reader's theater is an "instructional activity that not only combines several effective research-based practices but also leads to increased comprehension even in very resistant readers" (p. 294).

Response Journals

The reading–writing combination is powerful. In fact, opportunities to respond to reading in writing are associated with higher comprehension scores on standardized tests (e.g., NAEP, 2000). Response journals provide a special place for capturing reactions and thoughts related to reading. Journal entries can be either open or closed. An *open entry* is just that: Students can write whatever they want about what they have read. *Closed entries* focus students' thinking in particular ways. A teacher who wants to encourage summarization, for example, might ask students to write brief plot summaries. Similarly, a prompt such as "Write about your favorite part of the book so far. Tell us why you like that part so much" encourages evaluative response. Both open and closed entries support students' efforts to construct meaning as they read.

Kate's fourth graders are active journal writers. "Children's ideas provide us with an unending supply of topics for small-group or whole-class instruction," she says. Kate also uses response journals as a way to link reading and writing. "If we're working on great details or ways to 'show, not tell,' I frequently ask children to use their response journals to jot down snippets of language that grab them from the books they are reading. We collect all of these, put them on the board, and talk about what makes them so special so that we can use them in our own writing."

As you might guess from Kate's comments, response journal entries find several uses. That's what makes them so powerful. The teacher may read and respond to entries, or students may trade journals among themselves to read and respond to a peer who is reading (or has read) the same book. Sometimes teachers invite discussion by encouraging students to read journal entries aloud so that classmates can talk further about the issues or ideas raised. Closed journal entries can become that basis for mini-lessons on particular areas of focus. For example, students can share their summaries and talk about what makes a good summary. Students can also keep response journals for their own purposes, a record of their thinking during reading rather than a product to share with others.

Readers' Workshop and Literature Circles

Readers' Workshop and *Literature Circles* are student-centered instructional routines that support individual comprehension development within the collaborative context of classrooms. Although more teacher-centered versions of these routines exist, they are most effective when students control decisions about what to read and how and when to share their responses with others (Heald–Taylor, 1996).

Readers' Workshop was originally designed for middle-school students (Atwell, 1987), but its effectiveness has led to widespread use in elementary and high schools as well. To initiate Readers' Workshop, teachers need a block of time—daily or several times each week—and lots of books. Teachers often begin each workshop session by asking students to plan their activities for the session. Brief mini-lessons are often part of Readers' Workshop as well. Early in the school year, these may focus on book selection or response options; later mini-lessons may address comprehension fix-up strategies, literary features such as character development, or authors' stylistic features. The mini-lessons are focused, brief, and related to children's current needs as readers.

The biggest chunk of Readers' Workshop time belongs to students. They read; share with peers; respond individually; and occasionally prepare more public responses, perhaps using art, drama, or writing. The teacher circulates to ensure that students are engaged but may also confer with individuals, conduct small-group response discussions, or even facilitate book selection. The teacher may also set expectations for activity completion by requiring a certain number of response log entries or interpretive activities over the course of a week or month.

Literature Circles (Daniels, 2002; McMahon & Raphael, 1997; Noe & Johnson, 1999) may be part of Readers' Workshop or conducted as a separate instructional routine. In either event, small groups of readers discuss their books. Students can self-select groups (the teacher may want to "book talk" the titles or provide time for students to peruse books), or the teacher can assign them. Possible models for organizing texts and readers are as follows (adapted from Fountas & Pinnell, 2001):

- Whole group, same text: Students read or listen to the same text. The whole group formulates questions for discussion. Small groups meet to discuss, make notes, and report back to the whole group.
- Small group, same text: Teacher "book talks" several titles. Students select titles of interest, and groups are formed. Groups may plan a culminating activity (reader's theater, drama, technology) to share with whole group.
- Small group, different texts: Students choose from a variety of different texts that have something in common (e.g., strong characters; genre, such as biography; same author; issues, such as coming-of-age or race relations; content area study, such as Civil War books or books about hurricanes). Group may be formed somewhat randomly. Students read their individual titles. Group discussions focus on the common element (e.g., characterization, qualities of a biography, etc.). A culminating activity summarizes and synthesizes all group discussions.

Group discussions should be held at least two to three times per week. Students read or listen to text before the discussion group assembles and may want to prepare for the discussions by making notes, writing in response journals, using sticky notes to mark places in the text for discussion, and such. As students become accustomed to Literature Circle discussions, which are largely student-directed, it's often helpful for them to assume roles. Students select roles before reading or listening to the text. Many teachers have found assigned roles unnecessary as students become more comfortable with Literature Circle discussions. Possible roles include

- Group Leader: leads discussion, encourages participation, keeps track of time.
- Summarizer: begins discussion with summary of text.

- Comparer: compares text to other text(s).
- Connector: compares text to other non-text people, events.
- Sentence Finder/Word Finder: finds and shares interesting sentences or words.
- Questioner: finds and shares unresolved issues.
- Predictor: leads discussion about upcoming portions of the text.

With appropriate preparation and support, even primary-level students can participate in effective discussions (Jewell & Pratt, 1999). Literature Circle discussions aim to be entirely student-led, although teachers may want to lead occasional mini-lessons about the qualities of effective discussions or remind students of response options. Activities such as Linguistic Roulette, Group Mapping, or Sketch to Stretch, all described earlier in this chapter, provide excellent preparation for Literature Circle discussions.

Readers' Workshop and Literature Circles provide frameworks within which students have time to read and opportunities to respond. Both routines promote reflection, interpretation, and inquiry, all of which support comprehension growth.

Instruction to Promote Comprehension

Comprehension is like model building. Readers construct text interpretation or their own models of the text by relying on many raw materials: content and linguistic information provided by the author, their own knowledge and experiences, and their understanding of how written language works. All this happens in a social, environmental, and instructional context that is critical in determining both what and how students comprehend. The overall environment for instruction and the activities and techniques employed should reflect knowledge of these factors and influences. Moffett and Wagner (1992) synthesize them quite well:

> People read for diverse reasons and in diverse ways—casually to sift, studiedly to recall, raptly to become spellbound. The more schools open up the repertory of authentic discourse, the more apparent this becomes. Thus reader response is a factor of reader purpose and the kind of discourse. But response and purpose go back to choice. (p. 142)

Response and reflection (Rosenblatt, 1938, 1978) are hallmarks of literary comprehension and therefore worthy instructional goals. Within this overall framework, teachers can focus students' attention on *literacy* development, basic learning-to-read issues like constructing main ideas or developing vocabulary knowledge. But too heavy an emphasis in this domain may not serve students well: "Unfortunately . . . literature [may be] treated more like information to be memorized and tested than an experience to be enjoyed and appreciated" (Dugan, 1997, p. 87). Providing opportunities for *literary* development can help us avoid this situation. Barbara Lehman and Pat Scharer (1996) urge us to plan instruction that also focuses on the "understanding of literature and how it acts as a work of art to generate readers' responses" (p. 26). Fortunately, strategy instruction and the development of appreciation for literature can coexist in classrooms. A combination of strategy teaching and plentiful opportunities for students to read independently appears to provide the balance that makes this possible (Baumann, Hooten, & White, 1999).

We began this chapter by raising several vital questions about how to encourage students to integrate text information with prior knowledge and interact thoughtfully with the text and each other. When students enter real reading situations in environments that promote thinking, taking risks, and sharing, these questions answer themselves.

9

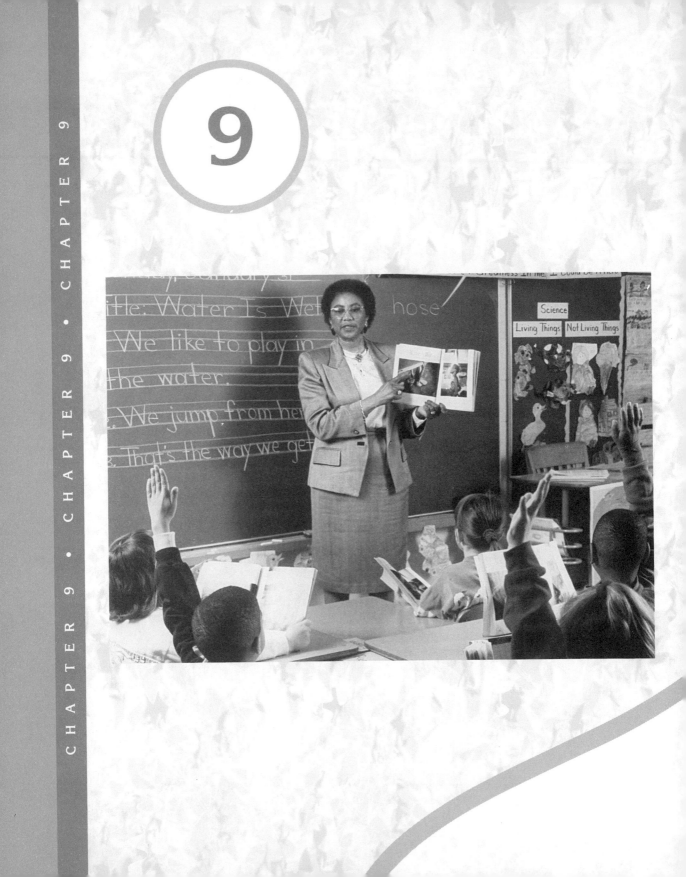

Comprehension Development with Nonfiction Text

Our goal is for all students to enhance their growth as independent, purposeful readers and learners. In chapter 8 we presented ideas for fostering students' comprehension of narrative or storylike materials. In this chapter we raise questions, offer information, and describe strategies that will help students make sense of nonfiction, including textbook material and Internet resources.

Twenty or more years ago, the distinction between fiction and nonfiction was easy to see in classrooms. In elementary schools, children read fiction, often from their basal readers, during "reading time"; nonfiction reading, usually from content area textbooks, was reserved for "social studies time," "science time," and so forth. Drawing these distinctions in today's classrooms is not so easy because teachers are designing more integrated curricular themes, and

> . . . both fiction and nonfiction texts are needed to fully develop the goals. For instance, a primary theme on rain involves the science of the water cycle, the social studies of how rain affects daily life around the world, the mathematics of measuring rainfall, and the aesthetic components reflected in poetry, songs, and stories associated with rain. (Doiron, 1994, p. 618)

When is it appropriate to use the strategies described in this chapter? That choice has more to do with purpose than with classroom schedules. Nonfiction teaching strategies are appropriate when students' and teachers' main interest is in learning something new or more thoroughly or acquiring information. Although instruction designed to help students learn new information has always been a major goal of schooling, the information explosion sparked by technological advances makes it even more critical. To be lifelong learners, students must learn how to learn. This demands more of them than acquiring facts. Students will need "to recognize when information is needed and have the ability to locate, evaluate, and use effectively the needed information" (American Library Association Presidential Committee on Information Literacy, 1989, p. 1). Well-crafted instruction can help students develop these skills.

Like those best suited for fiction, instructional strategies for ensuring students' comprehension of nonfiction text must incorporate understandings about readers' interactions with text and students' interactions with the teacher and each other. Toward that end, we offer several guidelines for developing effective instruction:

- Activating and engaging readers' background knowledge about a topic before reading enhances learning. That is, students need opportunities to become aware of what they already know about text content and to think about it before they begin reading. They also need opportunities to consider what they don't know but want to learn about a topic.

- Predictions about text content must be encouraged. Good readers think backward and forward when reading; they draw conclusions about what they have read and make predictions about what they are likely to encounter. Like scientists, proficient readers constantly entertain and test hypotheses about the content in the text.

- The instructional environment should help students learn to comprehend actively and purposefully and evaluate their own efforts as readers and learners. This critical stance is particularly significant as students learn how to read the Internet: "Even more than with traditional texts, then, we need to help students develop the skills that they need to determine the accuracy, authenticity, and point of view of Internet materials" (Burke, 2002, p. 38). Teachers support this learning by providing frameworks for sharing, discussion, and exploration and modeling literate, inquiring, and learned behavior themselves.

- Activities that foster cooperative involvement and joint problem solving enhance learning. The instructional environment must foster taking risks and sharing ideas, and students must know that their thinking is valued.

Instruction based on these criteria helps readers grow in their ability to comprehend and learn from nonfiction text. The strategies described in this chapter work with readers of all ages and abilities. Although most of the strategies work with individuals, they work best when small groups of students share their ideas with one another.

Prereading Activities

Too often, students are simply told to read or are given an artificial reason for reading, such as "read to see how tornadoes are formed." We believe that this sort of guidance neither prepares students effectively for reading nor motivates them to read. Effective prereading activities should invite students to do the following:

- Consider what they already know about the reading and share these ideas with others.
- Anticipate and make predictions about what they are likely to encounter as they read.
- Develop their own purposes for reading.
- Build curiosity and motivation for reading.

Several prereading activities meet these criteria.

Word Sorts

Open word sorts (see chapters 5 and 7) can be an effective prereading activity to prime students for comprehending a text (Bear, Invernizzi, Templeton, & Johnston, 2000; Gillet & Kita, 1979). The teacher selects about 20 words or phrases from the text students will read. For example, Becky, an intermediate-grade Title I teacher, selected these words and phrases from an article about spiders:

liquid silk	tiny claws	egg sac
four pairs of legs	poison fangs	mandibles
spinnerets	water	trap door
wolf balloon	tarantula	
orb weaver		

After Becky prepared and distributed sets of word cards to pairs of students, she directed the children to "put these into groups that make sense to you. Be ready to explain your reasons." Students examined the words, looking for relationships between and among them. To establish and agree on categories, students discussed the chosen concepts, shared knowledge with each other, and engaged in hypothesis testing.

When the small groups completed sorting the words, Becky invited groups to share both the categories and their reasoning. Here's how one group of fourth graders sorted the words:

Things Spiders Have	*Where Spiders Live*
liquid silk	trap door
tiny claws	water
four pairs of legs	egg sac
poison fangs	
	We Don't Know
Kinds of Spiders	mandibles
tarantula	spinnerets
wolf	balloon
	orb weaver

These students know something about spiders, but they also recognize what they can learn from the article. Whole-group sharing encouraged further exploration of key concepts. Finally, Becky asked them what they expected to be reading about and why. This summarized the word-sort portion of the lesson and encouraged students to make and share predictions. Then, the students read, armed with their own relevant knowledge.

Possible Sentences, described in chapter 7, another variety of word sort, is an excellent prereading activity, particularly with challenging text. Research has shown that it fosters both word and concept learning and text information recall (Stahl & Kapinus, 1991). Whatever their format, word sorts help students activate and share their prior knowledge about concepts and predict text content. They enhance curiosity and provide natural, meaningful purposes for reading: Students are eager to see if their ideas are accurate.

Brainstorming

Brainstorming activities are identical to word sorts except that students, rather than the teacher, generate the words and phrases. The brainstorming we describe here is similar to the List Group Label vocabulary activity presented in chapter 7. Students can brainstorm in small groups with a selected recorder, or the teacher can serve as recorder for the entire group. In either case, the teacher provides a key word or phrase and asks students for any words that come to mind when they think about the key word. Students should generate words quickly rather than stop for analysis or evaluation. Another group of Becky's students produced this list of words in response to the key word *spider: black widow, web, flies, bees, insects, ants, silk, haunted house, gross, neat, plants, basement, desert, round, furry, tarantula, jumping spider, eight legs.*

After 2 or 3 minutes of brainstorming, small groups categorize the words and provide titles for the categories, much like an open word sort. Students use chart paper and markers or an overhead transparency to record their categories so that others can easily see their decisions during the discussion and sharing that follows. Figure 9.1 shows a web that one group of children made with the words they had brainstormed. After discussion and sharing, students read.

Like word sorts, brainstorming is a cooperative activity where students learn from and with each other. Such cooperation fosters successful, purposeful reading among all students, but may be particularly helpful for struggling readers.

Anticipation Guides

A third prereading activity that activates prior knowledge and promotes purposeful reading is the *anticipation guide* (Herber, 1978; Vacca & Vacca, 2001). The teacher prepares written statements for students to think about

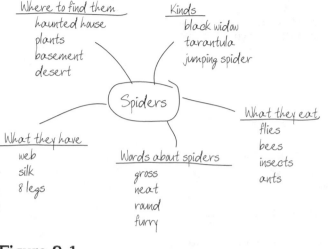

Figure 9.1
"Spiders" Web

and discuss before (and often after) they read. The statements are intended to activate prior knowledge and arouse curiosity. A sample anticipation guide, developed for a science article about spiders, appears in Figure 9.2. Note that the directions ask students to indicate those statements with which they agree and be ready to explain their thinking. This process of justifying or explaining their thinking allows students to sharpen and organize what they know about a topic and become aware of what they don't know.

After individuals make decisions about the statements, the teacher leads a discussion in which students share their ideas and knowledge with each other. The anticipation guide shown in Figure 9.2 directs students to return to the statements after reading the article, again indicating the statements they agree with but now supporting their ideas by referring to pages from the text.

Don provides resource assistance for intermediate-grade students with learning disabilities. He relies frequently on anticipation guides because, he says, "the kids really enjoy them, and I think they help kids' learning. It reassures them to know that they already know something about what they will be reading. Talking about specific issues seems to help them develop a purpose for reading, too." Although Don varies the way he uses anticipation guides, he typically asks pairs of students to complete the guides together. Before the group reads the text selection, he asks students to indicate whether they agreed or disagreed with each statement and give reasons for their decisions. Sometimes, this discussion proceeds quickly because students arrive at the same decisions for the same reasons. At other times, more lengthy discussions ensue because students' opinions differ or they raise complex issues. After reading, Don generally directs discussion to focus on those areas where students have changed

---

Directions: Read each statement about spiders. In the "Before" column, check the ones you agree with. Be ready to explain your thinking.

Before		After	Page(s)
_____	1. Spiders are insects.	_____	_____
_____	2. Spiders can move in any direction.	_____	_____
_____	3. Spiders have eight eyes and eight legs.	_____	_____
_____	4. Spiders are helpful.	_____	_____
_____	5. Some spiders can float through the air.	_____	_____
_____	6. Spiders use the same webs over and over.	_____	_____
_____	7. The silk in spider webs is stronger than iron.	_____	_____
_____	8. The silk in spider webs has been used in microscopes and telescopes.	_____	_____
_____	9. Spiders won't bite unless they are disturbed.	_____	_____

Directions: Now that you've read about spiders, read the statements again. This time check the statements you agree with in the "After" column. In the "Pages" column, write down the page or pages in the book that helped you decide. Again, be ready to explain your thinking.

Figure 9.2
"Spiders" Anticipation Guide

their minds or have additional information to share based on their reading. He says that this postreading discussion allows students to share what they have learned and raise issues for further exploration.

K-W-L

Students complete two portions of the *K-W-L* chart before reading (Ogle, 1986). This activity derives its name from the column labels on the chart: what we *know* about the topic, what we *want* to know from reading about the topic, and what we *learned* from reading. Pairs or small groups of students can work independently to complete the K-W-L activity; or the group can work together as a whole, with the teacher serving as recorder.

As with a brainstorming activity, the teacher begins a K-W-L discussion by providing a topic, key word, or phrase related to what students are about to read. They share what they already know about the topic and pose questions they want answered or issues they hope to learn more about. Notes are made in the *K* and *W* columns of the chart. After students read the text, they complete the third column by recording what they have learned. This may include answers to questions, information related to issues, or other information students find important or interesting. Students can use information from their K-W-L charts for writing, such as writing a summary, or to guide additional inquiry.

Betsy frequently uses K-W-L charts with her Title I students. She says the children enjoy sharing their knowledge before they read, and these discussions often offer her some effective incidental teaching opportunities: "Sometimes the ideas really come pouring out! After everyone has shared, we need to decide how to record children's ideas on the chart. So I say, 'Okay, how should I write this down?' and the students have to think back through the discussion and summarize and synthesize it so that we can decide what to record." Betsy also notes that sometimes children's questions about the topic (from the *W* column) aren't answered by the text selection. "This is good, in a way," she says. "If the kids are really curious, we find other resource books—a great reason for a trip to the library!"

Building Background Knowledge

Word sorts, Possible Sentences, brainstorming, anticipation guides, and K-W-L charts all invite students to think about general topics related to their reading and to recall and organize what they already know about those topics. In other words, these activities help students activate their background knowledge. Because students talk to and share with each other, they may also add background knowledge, make new discoveries, and learn more about the topic. In many cases, these prereading activities provide plenty of support for subsequent reading.

Sometimes, however, students need additional support. In cases where content is new, important, abstract in nature, or loaded with unfamiliar terms, the teacher may wish to help students *build* background knowledge—that is, learn new things about the topic before they read—rather than simply *activate* what they already know.

Activities to build background knowledge can involve reading or listening to additional texts—trade books, newspaper or magazine articles, speeches, or Web pages. Two characteristics of these texts make them especially effective for helping students build background knowledge: They tend to offer more elaboration or detail than textbook selections and are often storylike. These features can heighten interest and make information easy to remember, thus allowing students to learn new information that can, in turn, support their textbook reading.

Nonfiction is a great source for read-alouds. Calling high-quality non-fiction "the literature of fact," former teacher and librarian Ray Doiron (1994) offers this guidance for selecting and using books:

- Choose nonfiction that ignites the imagination rather than stuffs in facts.
- Look for authors who write with clarity, authority, and in a vivid style.
- Begin with books you enjoy. As with any other read-aloud, practice beforehand.
- Talk with children about the author, illustrator, publication date, and authority with which the text was written. Encourage them to think about the author's language and point of view.
- Sometimes use excerpts and invite children to "read more about it."

We agree with Doiron's conclusion that reading for information can be fun. Children are naturally curious, with a great thirst to know about the world around them. This "need to know" is a powerful motivator for reading nonfiction (Moss & Hendershot, 2002). Students are not bored by facts, data, or information; they are only bored by how such information is presented or what they are expected to do with it.

Nonreading activities are equally effective ways to build background knowledge. Jackdaws, described in chapter 8, can provide vehicles for exploring background and learning. As students examine and talk about the items included in the jackdaws, teachers have natural opportunities to share relevant information. Experiments and demonstrations also work well, as do media or audiovisual presentations, whether viewed on the World Wide Web or through more traditional means.

Increasingly, teachers use Internet resources to build students' background knowledge. They search for relevant information on the Web, evaluate the content of Web sites, and bookmark a few especially good ones for students to explore. (See Appendix H for a starter list of Web sites.)

Activities to build background knowledge take time—a precious commodity in most classrooms. Although we have no magic rule for deciding when such time is well spent, when information is important or abstract, or students need extra support to read successfully, it probably makes sense to include some background-building activities.

These prereading activities share common elements that make them successful. Each provides a framework and reason for students to consider what they already know (and don't know) about text content. Each also promotes sharing so that students learn from and with each other. Finally, each activity encourages students to hypothesize about the reading selection based on what they know, what others have said, and (in the case of open word sorts, anticipation guides, and Web browsing) the information provided or selected by the teacher. These factors combine to create readers ready to read actively, purposefully, and enthusiastically.

Activities to Support Students During Reading

Text discussions during and after reading have long been recognized as effective means of enhancing students' comprehension and learning. We certainly agree, but offer a caution: Discussions must reflect and enhance the comprehension process. If teachers were to ask predominantly low-level, literal questions during discussions, students might only collect individual and unrelated facts as they read rather than think about ideas.

Good questions are certainly a key to effective discussions about text. What makes a question good? First, good discussion questions are *authentic*—that is, they are asked because the asker doesn't know and wants to know the answer. "What do you think about . . . ?" is usually an authentic question because the teacher doesn't know the student's thoughts. In contrast, literal questions are usually nonauthentic because the teacher already knows the answers and is simply testing to see if the student does, too. This is not to say that literal information is unimportant in text discussions, for it certainly is. Rather, the issues are how and why students use literal information. Providing literal or factual support for one's ideas enhances text discussions, as does sharing appropriate prior knowledge. Questions that encourage this type of thinking will yield more effective discussions than those intended to test what students remember.

Authentic questions often provoke thought and motivate higher level reasoning. These, too, are qualities of good discussions. Students should be encouraged to focus on relevant, important information; to synthesize; and to integrate text information with what they already know. In short, good discussions should foster thoughtful consideration of text and promote group and individual efforts at understanding.

Discussions differ from conversations because they are planned, but in many respects a good discussion should be like a conversation: a social exchange of ideas, information, and opinions. A good environment for discussions should invite (but not demand) verbal participation; in other words, students should feel free to speak or not, as they choose. Furthermore, students should be encouraged to talk with each other rather than filter everything through the teacher. The result of effective text discussions is more than a collection of students' individual meanings and verbal reports; new meaning is constructed as students listen to and talk with each other and make new connections between ideas.

Effective discussions provide a framework for thinking and sharing about text. The strategies described below provide this sort of framework, as do several introduced in chapter 8 (e.g., Linguistic Roulette, Think–Pair–Share).

Directed Reading–Thinking Activity

The *Directed Reading–Thinking Activity (DR–TA)*, described in chapter 8, also works effectively with nonfiction text selections (Nelson & Linek, 1999;

Stauffer, 1980). As with fiction DR–TAs, discussions evolve through cycles in which students generate hypotheses and subsequently validate, reject, or modify them. Preparation for an expository DR–TA involves selecting readings for students and deciding where they will stop for discussion. Subheads in articles or textbooks provide natural stopping points.

Here is an excerpt from an expository DR–TA. Jane's eighth-grade students are reading a chapter in their history books that describes social reforms of the 19th century.

Jane:	What do you think this passage is going to be about from just looking at the heading?
Katy:	What's a reformer?
Karen:	Yeah.
Jane:	Who can tell us?
Matt:	A person who likes to reshape or something.
Jane:	What would a person be doing if he were trying to reshape?
Matt:	Change it.
Katy:	Make it better.
Mike:	Try to make it better for people.
Jane:	Can you give us an example of what you think they wanted to change back at that point?
Matt:	Slavery.
Mike:	Government.
Jane:	All right. What else?
Tony:	Laws.
Jane:	Read the first two paragraphs only.
	[Students read.]
Jane:	Were you right about anything?
Tony:	Yeah.
Matt:	Slavery.
Jane:	Anything else?
Karen:	Trying to help people defend themselves and that.
Katy:	What *reformers* meant.
Jane:	What do you think it means now?
Katy:	The same thing. Helping people. . . .
Karen:	A person who makes change.
Matt:	Try to do something better.
Mike:	Try to improve something.

As you can see from the excerpt, the questioning cycle for expository DR–TAs resembles the cycle for narrative. Jane encouraged prediction, reflection, and integrating text and prior knowledge. Good prediction questions for an expository DR–TA include "What do you think this will be about?" "What issues will the author address?" "What will we read about next?" and "Where is the author going with this?"

After students have read a portion of the text, the teacher can ask these types of questions: "Were your predictions on target?" "Did anything surprise you?" "Have you changed your mind about anything based on what you've read?" or "Now what do you think?" Either before or after reading, questions and comments can invite elaboration or clarification: "Why?" "What makes you say that?" "Tell us some more about that," and "Anything else?"

The teacher's talk is not intended to manipulate student thinking or test students' recall; rather, the purpose is to activate student thought, encourage the use of prior knowledge, and facilitate group interaction. Students learn that their ideas are valued, that they should justify their opinions so that others can understand their reasoning, that they should listen to and talk with each other, and that the responsibility for learning is theirs.

Students' writing can be celebrated through performance.

Important Ideas and Words

Because nonfiction text often contains a great deal of new information, students may struggle to decide what is important enough to remember. The Dialectic Journal and Important Words strategies offer students support as they learn to make these decisions.

The *Dialectic Journal* (Watson, 1987), a during-reading strategy, helps students identify important information from informational text, share these ideas with others, and develop their own opinions about what they have read. The strategy involves several stages:

- *Stage 1:* As students read a portion of an article, chapter, or other piece of expository text, they make notes about what they think is important. Notes can be made on separate paper or in a journal, as the title for the strategy suggests; or students can write on sticky notes or use pencils to write on the text itself.

- *Stage 2:* Small groups share what they have identified as important. As students listen to others' ideas, they may revise their own notes, add or erase underlines, and so on. Stages 1 and 2 continue as students complete the text.

- *Stage 3:* Having decided on important information from the text, students now make notes on their own opinions about what they have read. They consider issues such as what they agree or disagree with, how the information might be useful, and how new information fits in with what they already knew.

- *Stage 4:* Students share their individual opinions with others in their small groups. Groups discuss individual opinions, synthesize discussion, and may prepare written or oral summaries or lists to share with the entire class.

Important Words is similar to the dialectic journal, except that students identify words rather than ideas as they read. Then, in small groups, they share their individual choices, create a master set of important words, and categorize or organize the words in some way that shows the relationships among the words and the text. Carly, who teaches third grade, has found Important Words an effective way to introduce her students to note taking. "I recycle office paper by making little word cards for the children," she says. "This makes it easier for them to combine their words and move them around so they can test out possible organizations." Carly even uses the activity to provide a framework for units of instruction. "We began our simple machines unit with columns on the chalkboard labeled with types of simple machines. The children brainstormed important words related to each type. Then, they read from the science text and added more important words that they had found in their reading. Finally, pairs of children did copy change [see chapter 10] writing using *The Important*

[handwritten margin note: Too much encourages the lazy students]

Book [Brown, 1949/1999]. I was amazed at how much more the children remembered!"

Save the Last Word for Me

This activity, developed by Carolyn Burke, is also designed to provide support for students as they read challenging material (Watson, 1987). As with the dialectic journal, students first read a portion of a text and write individually. Then, they discuss the reading in small groups.

Here's how *Save the Last Word for Me* works: Students make notes on separate paper, in their journals, or on sticky notes as they read each portion of a text. They might note important information, copy a critical sentence, record what they don't understand, or jot down unfamiliar vocabulary; each student decides what to write. Discussion begins after all small-group members have completed reading the portion of the text. One by one, students introduce an idea from their notes for group discussion. Others in the group may respond to the idea, answer the question, or provide their own definitions for vocabulary words. Conversations take many directions. After all others have offered their thoughts, the student who introduced the topic has the "last word" and may offer an opinion or summarize the discussion. The next student in the group offers another topic, and the discussion begins again. After each group member has started a discussion, students read and make notes about the next portion of the text.

Ted teaches middle-school students who find reading difficult. He relies on all four of these during-reading strategies because "the kids need the support that the strategies can provide." Ted uses several criteria to decide which activity to use.

> Probably the most important factor in my planning is the difficulty of the text. I think the DR–TA is the most supportive strategy, so that's the one we use if I think the reading might be tough for the kids. I also think about variety, though. It's more fun for all of us if we vary the routine. And after we've done these things a few times, I sometimes ask students which strategy they want to use. I really don't worry about students' choices because I know all three help them understand what they read.

Ted finds that his students "read for their own purposes or for purposes that arise as part of the discussions. Either way, they care about what they read, and that's half the battle, as far as I'm concerned. Besides that, the discussions themselves foster learning." Students must think carefully while they read and listen carefully during discussions. As a result, according to Ted, "they learn content information. But they also learn that reading is an active, problem-solving process." Text discussions during reading can enhance comprehension and learning if the instructional environment fosters group inquiry, risk taking, and problem solving.

[handwritten marginal note: Like better · really forces each to work & think]

Postreading Activities

Good postreading activities give students continued opportunities for dynamic interaction with the text and among themselves. Sometimes students revisit prereading activities after they read. For example, open word sorts work well for refining and extending concepts after reading. Students can reorganize the words and phrases based on their reading and discuss the changes they made. Brainstorming, too, can follow reading, this time as a means of integrating new information with prior knowledge. And students can record what they learned as a result of reading and discussion in the *L* (what we learned) column of their K-W-L charts. Several other postreading activities that foster continued interaction with text follows.

Distinctive Features

Nonfiction reading often helps students think about similarities and differences between and among related concepts. In such instances, *Distinctive-Features* activities make effective postreading lessons. Figure 9.3 shows a distinctive features chart that Becky and her students developed for their science lesson about spiders.

After students read, Becky asked, "What kinds of spiders did we read about?" The children's answers, recorded on the chalkboard, ultimately became one dimension of the chart. Becky asked for the features of spiders described in the text: "What were some things that we learned about all of these spiders?" This information became the other dimension of the chart. Students returned to the text to verify their recollections and make any necessary changes before the final version of the chart was constructed.

Students then worked in pairs to complete the chart. They talked with their partners, reread if necessary, and decided what to write in each cell of

FEATURES	SPIDERS			
	Tarantulas	Trap-door Spiders	Wolf Spiders	Water Spiders
Size				
General areas where found				
Habitat				
Prey				
How prey is captured				

Figure 9.3
"Spiders" Distinctive Features Chart

the chart. After pairs had completed their charts, Becky reconvened the whole group and asked some questions to focus on similarities and differences: "How are all these spiders alike?" and "How are trap-door spiders and wolf spiders alike? How are they different?" Later, the charts were put on display for all to see and examine.

Distinctive features activities provide frameworks for organizing and categorizing concept information as well as synthesizing and making notes about what students have read. In addition, the completed charts are useful for later review and study.

Herringbone

The *Herringbone* activity also uses a chart to help students summarize and synthesize what they have read (see Figure 9.4). Students read and then work with partners to complete the chart. Together, they must decide on answers to each detail question on the chart. This frequently involves rereading but always involves discussion as students identify a variety of potential answers to each question and settle on the most important. Finally, they combine these details to develop a main-idea summary statement for the entire passage.

Like several other activities described in this chapter, the Herringbone chart provides a supportive framework for students to sort through the information provided in expository text and make their own decisions about what is important. Completing these charts also helps students think about the main idea, significant details, and the relationships among them.

Guided Reading Procedure

An adaptation of Manzo's (1975) *Guided Reading Procedure (GRP)* is yet another effective postreading activity. It is particularly effective when instruction

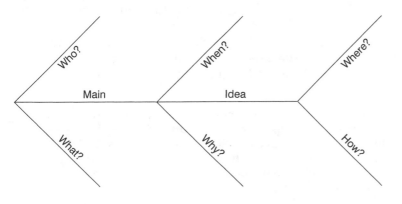

Figure 9.4
Herringbone Chart

seeks to promote recall or help students decide on and organize important information. The strategy involves reading, brainstorming, and making decisions about key information.

After students read a text selection, the teacher asks them to recall everything they can remember from the text in brainstorming fashion. The teacher records this information on the chalkboard. Next, the teacher provides a purpose for further work with the ideas. For example, he might ask students to write a summary or prepare an outline of the text using only information on the chalkboard.

With this purpose in mind, students return to the text selection, this time thinking about what to add, correct, or delete from the information they recalled. After a few minutes, the teacher reconvenes the discussion, asking for changes to the information on the chalkboard and reasons for such changes. The teacher might say, "Okay, you think we should erase _____ from our list. Why? What do the rest of you think? Should we erase _____ from our list? Why?"

This discussion is usually quite lively. To convince others of their ideas, students must rely on information from the text and their own reasoning ability. The purpose for the final list often enters into the discussion, too. For example, a student might say, "Yes, well, I think that *is* important, but we're supposed to be writing a summary. I think that's too detailed to go into a summary paragraph." Majority opinion should be the criterion for making changes. Finally, students write the summary paragraph or prepare the outline using the revised information from the selection.

Note that the teacher never makes recommendations about the information on the chalkboard. Doing so would undermine one of the major benefits of the activity: helping students learn to make decisions for themselves about what is important in their reading.

A similar procedure can be useful for helping students prepare written summaries of nonreading experiences in the classroom, such as conducting a science experiment, viewing a movie, or listening to a guest speaker. Students' outlines can be valuable additions to the content area study, particularly for readers who have difficulty reading their textbooks successfully.

Maria occasionally uses this adaptation of the Guided Reading Procedure in her work with intermediate-grade students.

> It seems like the older they get, the more important summarizing and synthesizing becomes. Years ago, I tried to help by giving kids outlines. Then, I tried to teach them to outline. Nothing worked. This GRP takes some time, but it really helps my students learn how to find what's important in their reading. They soon learn that what's "important" depends on why they're reading and what they need to do with the information. What's important for preparing an outline, for example, may not be the same as what's important for writing a short summary.

Maria also notes that this adaptation of the Guided Reading Procedure helps students learn the text content. "I bet that's because they read and reread. I like that aspect of the activity, too." Both the recall and decision-making tasks allow students to develop and extend their thinking about the information in the text.

Discussion Web

This activity, developed by Donna Alvermann (1991), is especially useful when students read about a complex problem, issue, or situation, one that generates controversy or has no simple solution. After students read (or listen), they work in pairs to complete a *Discussion Web* (see Figure 9.5) that contains a question developed by the teacher. Pairs generate as many reasons as possible for answering "yes" to the question; they do the same for "no." Next, each pair joins with another; the group of four considers all the "yes" and "no" responses and tries to agree on a conclusion. During this discussion, students make notes on the Discussion Web. Finally, groups share their conclusions with the entire class.

Belinda teaches in a multi-age primary classroom in a community where a controversy arose over cats. At issue was whether the current situation, allowing cats to run free, should be changed.

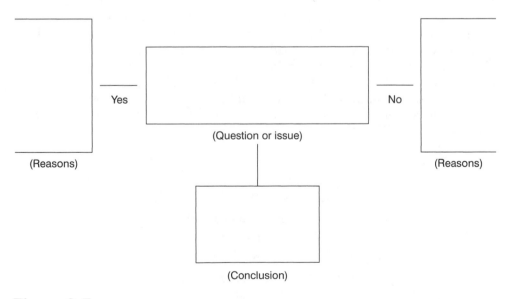

Figure 9.5
Discussion Web

I wasn't planning to address this issue, but the children were eager to discuss it. Predictably, kids who had "free-range" cats thought the status quo was just fine, and those who had others' cats in their yards didn't. I thought the Discussion Web might provide a way for the children to see both sides of the issue. So, I put this question on a large piece of chart paper: Should cats be allowed to run free in [city]? I tried to pair older students with younger ones, and I asked the older students to be the note takers. The children recorded their own thinking, but I also read newspaper articles and letters to the editor to them, after which they added more "yes" or "no" reasons based on what they heard. We never reached consensus, and I don't think too many children changed their minds. But I could tell that the children thought deeply about how others might think. And when the city resolved the situation by requiring people to register their cats and put ID tags on their collars, we had the chance to talk about compromise. What a civics lesson!

Response Activities

Response activities (see chapter 8) are effective ways for students to summarize, synthesize, and react to nonfiction texts. For example, many of the writing activities described in chapter 10 help students extend their thinking about text concepts. These can be as brief and informal as writing in a learning log or as extended and formal as preparing a class newspaper or magazine.

Poetry writing is often an effective response activity. In addition to "Name" poems or acrostics (see chapter 10), biopoems, diamantes, and other form poems work well. A *biopoem* (Gere, 1985) offers a framework for synthesizing what students have learned about a person, group, event, concept—almost anything they study. The lines for the biopoem can include name; location in time or place; relatives (or related concepts); and lists of needs, wants, fears, hopes, important contributions—whatever the teacher decides would provide a useful framework. Here, for example, is a biopoem based on *Bud, Not Buddy* (Curtis, 1999):

Bud

Thoughtful, persistent, funny, lonely

Relative of Mama and Herman

Who feels alone

Who needs a family

Who fears foster homes, the dark, and monsters

Resident of Michigan in the 1930s

Not Buddy

Diamantes, named for their diamond-shaped form, are also effective response frameworks. The form for a diamante is based on parts of speech:

noun

adj.   adj.   adj.

—ing verb   —ing verb   —ing verb

adj.   adj.   adj.

noun

Artistic representations such as murals, pictures, sculpture, or diora-mas may be appropriate response activities in some instances. Skits, reader's theater, or role-playing activities can also be useful. Amber and Dana, who use integrated thematic units in their classes, frequently encourage this sort of response as a culminating activity. "It's always an option," Dana says. "Some students are naturally drawn to these more creative ways of respond-ing, and others have the opportunity to look at things somewhat differently. Trying to role-play characters or situations from history, for example, really gives you a different slant on what you've learned."

Reader's theater has a place in their classrooms as well. "It really solved a problem for us," Amber notes. "We study Ohio history and have struggled for years with the section about the Amish, Quakers, Mormons, and Zoarites. The text is very dry, and library books are too hard for the children to read independently. Reader's theater to the rescue! We found information in the library and on the Web. The children were delighted with the four scripts we wrote, and we were delighted with their learning."

Amber, Dana, and their students occasionally enjoy a day of celebra-tion after they have spent some time exploring a theme or issue.

> We take part of a day to sort of sit back and reflect on what we've learned. We invite parents and grandparents to join us. The kids present their skits, explain their newspapers, or whatever. The children enjoy these days, and they're a great way to involve the folks from home in what we do in school. There's value to the sort of summary-thinking that leads students to their culminating projects, too, I think. And it sure makes a natural transition for us in our curriculum.

Principles for Effective Comprehension Instruction

Did aspects of these strategies seem similar? We hope so. They share assumptions about how teachers create effective comprehension instruction in which students read, think, solve problems, make decisions, and interact with the text and with each other. Teachers facilitate the process of compre-hension attainment rather than direct it or test whether students can remem-ber what they've read.

This instructional framework, the *Teacher–Student Generated Lesson* (Davidson, 1986), takes "into account the social nature of reading and its rela-tionship to comprehension, thinking, and learning" (p. 89). Teacher–Student Generated Lessons are based on four premises:

Artistic and meaningful representation may be an appropriate response activity.

- Learning is a social process.
- Students need maximum opportunities to use the language associated with the content area.
- Learners need to be actively involved.
- Students and the teacher construct meaning through interaction with each other and the text.

Lessons based on these principles benefit all students, of course, but they are especially helpful for struggling readers. These students need support, but they also need to maintain control over the thinking and learning processes. Teacher–Student Generated Lessons provide both.

Comprehension is the goal of reading. Before reading, readers must activate their prior knowledge, make predictions, and formulate purposes for reading. Discussions during reading should provoke thoughtful consideration of ideas in the text and promote individual and group efforts at understanding and learning. Finally, postreading instruction should encourage continued interaction with text content and among students. The teacher's role in all these activities is to promote sharing, encourage critical thought, and moderate discussions. The students' roles, on the other hand, require reading, thinking, solving problems, making decisions, interacting with the text and each other, and learning.

10

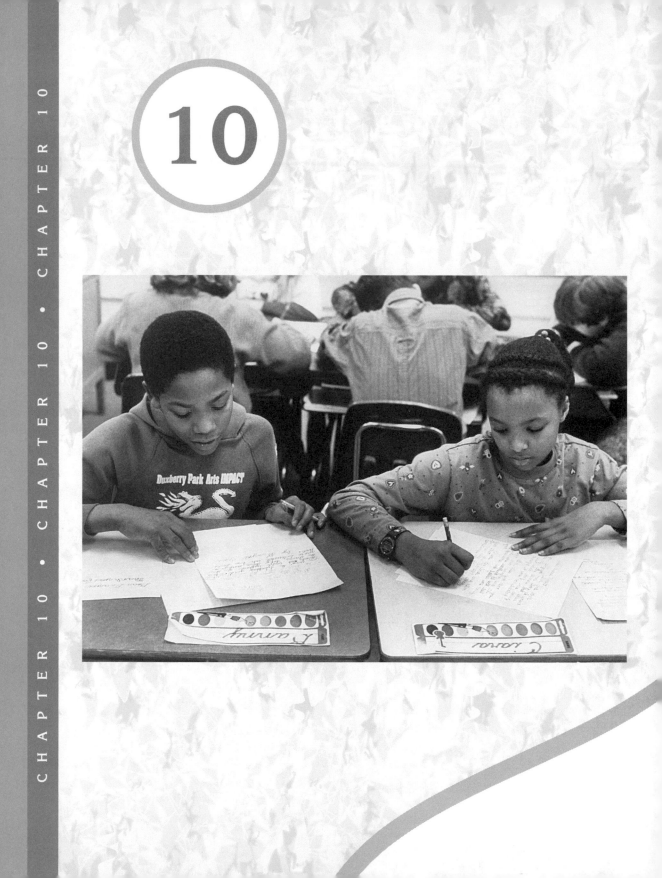

Writing Development

Jason and Amy were playing house. Amy, the mom, was getting ready for work and leaving instructions for Jason, the dad, who was going to watch the baby. She scribbled on a tablet, then tore up the page and began again. When asked what she was doing, she replied, "I have to put more down. I forgot that Jason doesn't know how to make eggs." Both Amy and Jason were three years old.

What does Amy know about written language? Quite a bit, actually. She knows that writing serves a purpose, in this case to communicate information about caring for the baby. She also knows that we write for an audience, that writing is meant to be read. She revised her note because "Jason doesn't know how to make eggs." Like many other children, three-year-old Amy has learned a great deal about written language. Yet she has had no instruction, and she is neither a reader nor a writer in the conventional sense. As with other aspects of language learning, some children learn about concepts of print earlier or more easily than others. Youngsters who have not yet developed notions about the form of written language need opportunities to do so. Until they do, they will find reading and writing instruction frustrating and confusing. In short, they will struggle.

We have written this book to help teachers help these children. In other chapters, we describe instructional strategies for reading that focus children's attention on important aspects of written language. Although critical, reading instruction is not enough. Frequent opportunities to write are also essential to support the development of understandings about written language.

Writers learn about both writing and reading. Young writers learn about the conventions of print. Writers of all ages learn how to think like authors, which helps them as they read what other authors have written. Moreover, writers learn the importance of using just the right word or sentence to communicate their intended meaning. This way of thinking about words and sentences also applies to reading. Writing is also a powerful means of response to reading. Indeed, the National Assessment of Educational Progress (2000) reports that high achievers in reading are more likely to write in response to their reading than low achievers in reading. Thus, a strong focus on writing is an important component in programs for struggling readers.

A comprehensive discussion of writing programs would provide enough material for another book. In this chapter, we address why and how writing can inform reading as well as provide suggestions about supporting writers and describe classroom activities that seem to enhance the reading–writing connection. First, however, we look at what children learn about written language, why readers should write, and how teachers can discover what writers know about the way that written language works.

Learning About Written Language

As young children learn to read and write, they begin to think about written language as a system and hypothesize about how it works. They learn how to use books, for example, and they learn that lines of print run from left to right and lines on a page run from top to bottom.

Children also develop concepts about units of written language. One critical understanding is that print carries meaning. An eager toddler may grab for a book being read to him, cover up the print, and look puzzled when the reader has to stop. Within a year or two, the same child may ask, "What does it say on this page?" or "Where does it say that?" Such comments demonstrate that the child has discovered that reading involves print. Related to this is the understanding that the print stays the same from one reading to the next.

In addition, children learn about the conventions of print—how written language represents meaning. Developing a concept of *word* as a unit of written language is particularly important, and this is no small task. First, children must be able to think about language as a system, to separate the form of language from its function. Then, they must be able to impose psychological segmentation on a steady stream of oral speech. In other words, children must learn to separate, think about, and become aware of individual words within spoken language. Finally, they must use their knowledge of oral speech to discover that words are also units of written language. In addition to the basic concept of the written word, children must learn about the convention of unmarked space before and after words and that the beginning of the word is on the left and the end is on the right. Further, they must develop similar understandings of concepts such as *sentence, line,* and other features related to written language.

As children write (not copy), they reinforce their own understandings about how letters and letter combinations represent sounds in language.

Thus, writing supports students' phonics and word recognition development. Learning about written language continues as students age. They may explore the common characteristics of a particular form of writing, such as mysteries or newspaper articles, or become interested in different types of poems, perhaps haiku or sonnets. Students of all ages may become fascinated by the way in which authors use language to communicate with others. In fact, readers and writers continue learning about written language throughout their lives.

Children learn about written language, as with other aspects of language learning, gradually and informally through many opportunities to hear, think about, and talk about written language. All children, especially those who find reading and writing difficult, need time and exposure to writing to develop these understandings. The learning process for developing concepts about written language is the same as for any other language learning: hypothesis generation and testing. For example, simply telling a child that words have spaces around them cannot guarantee understanding of the concept. In essence, children must invent their own understandings about written language and then test them as they interact with print and other readers and writers.

Certainly, children can learn a great deal about written language conventions through reading instruction. Accordingly, most teachers focus some instruction for beginning readers on the physical aspects of print. Much of this instruction is informal. When children watch something being read, such as a language-experience text or a big book, they gain knowledge about print conventions. Likewise, saying words while writing them during dictation is helpful. Some teachers even provide running commentary about the conventions of print as they take dictation. For instance, while they write, they may say, "That's the end of the sentence, so I'll put a period here. This new sentence will need a capital letter." Over time, such informal and incidental learning pays dividends in terms of children's understandings.

As children become readers, they must learn how written language works. To mature as readers, they need opportunities to explore the complexities of written language. Much of this learning can occur through reading instruction described elsewhere in this book, but a strong writing component can and should complement reading instruction.

Why Should Readers Write?

Children learn a great deal through writing that applies to their reading. Children who write frequently learn how writing works and come to understand what authors do and why. Through their own writing, children learn about the writing cycle (what writers do) and the writing process (how writers think). These understandings help children "see" the authors behind what they read and perhaps understand their purposes and processes. In two studies, teachers noticed connections between reading and writing (Menon & Mirabito,

1999; Silvers, 1986). Children read more and differently as they grew to believe in themselves as writers. The amount of free reading increased, and children's comments about books were more frequent and more critical. In other words, they read as authors to see how other authors had written. Graves and Stuart (1985) said it well: "Just as children who grew up on a farm know where milk comes from, children who write know where writing comes from" (p. 119).

As children write, they learn about the physical and mechanical aspects of written language; this, too, applies to their reading. Writing can help children crystallize their concepts of *word* and *sentence*. In addition, temporary or phonemic spelling provides valuable practice with the sound-to-letter system. Moreover, young writers learn that the beginning-to-ending sequences of sounds in words relate, although not exactly, to the left-to-right sequences of letters in words. Writers must attend to other aspects of directionality as well, such as words in a line and lines on a page. Children must solve all these problems to develop as literate persons, and they solve them most easily and naturally when they read and write often and purposefully.

A final answer to the question "Why should readers write?" is more practical: Lots of writing yields lots of reading material. Like all authors, young authors read and reread drafts in progress. They also read their finished products, both for their own pleasure and to share with others. And, of course, children like to read what their classmates have written. An active writing program, then, complements a reading program by providing a wealth of reading material in addition to helping children develop concepts about authorship and writing that form a foundation for reading development.

Discovering What Children Know About Writing

Planning an effective writing program is easier if we know a bit about children's current understandings of how writing works. In this section we describe several ways to gain these insights. We can learn about children's concepts of print and current hypotheses about the writing system by examining their unaided writing. Talking with children about their writing is also important, and simple surveys can help determine children's attitudes about writing. Finally, we can explore children's *grapho-phonic* knowledge (what they know about sound–symbol relationships) by examining their invented spellings. Look at Figures 10.1, 10.2, and 10.3, for example—pages from Mary's first-grade journal. Mary struggled with reading during much of that year. As you analyze her journal entries, examine how her concepts of print are revealed her writing, what she knows about the sound–symbol system, and how these understandings changed during the year.

Figure 10.1 accompanied a picture of two people sitting on a couch. Mary wrote to explain and elaborate on the picture she had drawn, showing that she knows the difference between drawing and writing. She knows that writing can communicate meaning, and she knows how lines of print are

Figure 10.1

Entry from Mary's September Journal

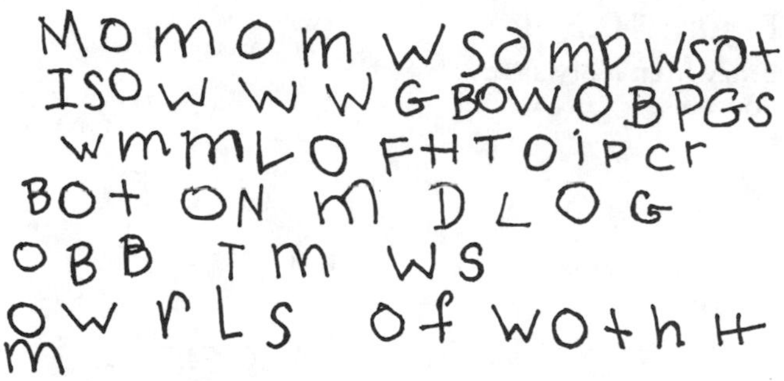

MOMOM WSOMPWSOt
ISOW W WGBOWOBPGS
wmmLOFHTOIPcr
BOtONMDLOG
OBBTMWS
OWrLSofWOthH
m

Me and my mom were sitting on the couch talking about birthday presents because my brother is going to have a birthday in two more weeks.

arranged on the page. Mary's teacher watched as she wrote and noticed that she wrote in left-to-right and top-to-bottom fashion. Although some concepts about print are evident in her writing, her writing also reveals concepts still developing. She knows how to make letters, but not how to make them work for her. Further, her writing lacks word boundaries, which suggests that her concept of word is still developing.

Mary's January journal entry (Figure 10.2) demonstrates growth in her understanding of print concepts. Her writing is fairly easy to read, and she has begun to leave spaces between words. By May (Figure 10.3), this concept of word is even stronger; space boundaries around words are clearly evident. Thus, we can see that Mary has developed important concepts about print during her first-grade year. What she knows is visible in her writing.

Children's unaided writing also reveals their graphophonic knowledge. Examining Mary's journal entries from this perspective reveals her growing understanding of sound–symbol relationships. Many of the words she spells are invented, but these inventions are not random. They are governed by her current hypotheses about how oral language and written language relate, which demonstrates her ability to use phonics as an aid to identifying words.

Scholars have been exploring the characteristics of young children's spelling since the early 1970s, when Charles Read's (1971) landmark work established the predictability of young children's spelling errors and the

Figure 10.2

Entry from Mary's January Journal

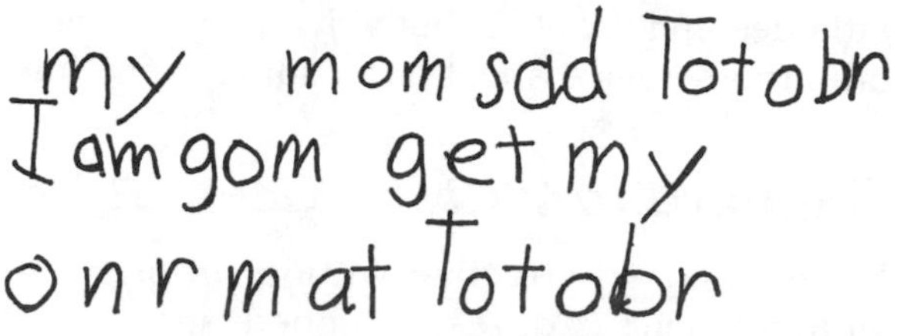

my mom sad Totobr
I am gom get my
onrm at Totobr

My mom said October. I am gonna get my own room at October.

Figure 10.3

Entry from Mary's May Journal

I want to go to the young Authors Conference because I write a lot of stories [and] because I publish a book.

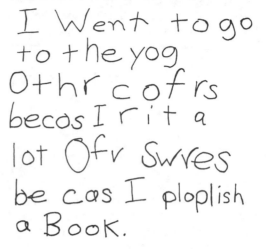

developmental progression of growth in spelling. In brief, this research has helped us understand how spelling develops: from random, incomprehensible strings of letters (and sometimes other symbols) to spellings that exhibit some understanding of sound–symbol relationships to conventional spelling. Thus, important word knowledge is revealed through invented spellings.

Looking at children's writing in this way underscores the hard work that goes on when they write. Their writing, including their temporary spellings, reflects their ideas about how written language works.

Talking with children about their writing and listening in as they talk to each other about writing are also valuable ways to develop insights into children as writers. Talk is often necessary to discover what beginning writers mean to say. For example, had Mary's teacher not asked her to read her early journal entry (Figure 10.1), we could not have figured out what Mary had written. Other kinds of conversations are equally informative. In general, questions should be open ended and aimed at discovering what the writer is doing, why, and how a teacher (or someone else) can support the writer's continuing development. Published surveys (e.g., Bottomley, Henk, & Melnick, 1997/98; Kear, Coffman, McKenna, & Ambrosio, 2000) also offer insights into students' attitudes and beliefs about writing and themselves as writers. In chapter 13 we offer more advice about using surveys and interviewing children.

Supporting Writers: General Principles

Developing an effective writing program depends on insights about how written language develops, understanding the role of writing in a program for struggling readers, and discovering what children know about written language. In this section we consider some general principles that apply across writing programs and specific writing activities. The best writing teachers we know use these principles to support active and involved writers in their classrooms.

Classroom Atmosphere: Lots of Writing

Perhaps the most important aspect of support for student writers is the classroom atmosphere itself. Children must learn to believe in themselves as writers, to believe that they can write and that what they have to say is worthwhile. One way to help these beliefs develop is simply to invite children to write every day, from their first day in your classroom or program.

Young children usually come to school expecting to learn to read and write. For them, invitations generally lead them to try. Older children, however, may hesitate when invited to write. Previous experiences in school may have convinced them that they cannot write, that they are not writers, that writing is difficult or boring. The teacher's patience and persistence are critical to unlearning these negative lessons. You must continue to invite, to praise attempts, and to establish the expectations that everyone can and will write.

First efforts from all writers, especially young ones, may be drawings rather than writing; but letters and words soon appear. Those who study young children's writing have explored the relationship between drawing and writing (e.g., Clay, 1986; Sidelnick & Svoboda, 2000; Sowers, 1985). Drawing may help some children think up ideas. In other cases, drawing helps children remember what they want to write—a bit like outlines or webs for older students. Drawing can even serve as a bridge to written language, as it did for young Hannah, whose success story is documented by teachers Mark Sidelnick and Marti Svoboda (2000). Whatever its purpose, drawing seems to facilitate writing for many children. Persistent teacher invitations to write, along with patience as children draw or develop the courage to try again, are essential features of effective classroom atmosphere.

Talk About Writing

Opportunities to talk and listen are equally important. Children talk for several reasons when they write (Graves, 1983). They sometimes plan their writing by talking to themselves or others. They may also read parts of drafts to themselves, as if to take a running start at what should come next. Some children compose aloud and translate their speech into writing rather than use the thought-to-writing process most adult writers employ. Others play with *prosodics* such as rhythm or intonation. Children may also talk themselves through writing by making procedural comments such as "There! Now I need to write 'The End.'"

Of course, children read drafts of their work to others, either to help solve problems or for more general feedback. This use of oral language may be particularly important for struggling readers and writers. Reading drafts

Talk is often necessary to discover what young writers mean to say.

aloud to an interested audience shows children that their writing has value and demonstrates the communicative power of writing and the link between reading and writing. Talking about revision possibilities also helps children understand and examine their options, which aids them in critically analyzing their own writing (Hanser, 1986). Those who respond to children's writing learn to listen carefully and ask pertinent questions. Of course, all this learning relates to reading as well. In fact, the concepts and procedures used in writing conferences easily apply to discussions about books written by authors outside the classroom.

Support, Encouragement, and Acceptance

Children need teacher support to develop as writers. Some of this support is mundane, such as having necessary supplies readily available. But other aspects of support, such as encouraging spelling efforts, may require a bit more thought. Accepting invented or temporary spelling allows children to be true to their own meanings and precise in their language because they can write what they want to say, not just what they know how to spell. In addition, children need opportunities to manipulate words and discover spelling principles so that phonological relationships become clear to them. In essence, children test their hypotheses about the way the alphabet works by contrasting the words they spell with the same words used in others' books (Templeton & Morris, 1999).

Teachers' responses to early efforts are crucial to children's continued experimentation with print. Anne Haas Dyson (1984) suggests the following:

> The most helpful response to early writing efforts [is] to accept whatever writing the child produces, respond to any written message, answer the child's emerging questions, and through sensitive questioning, focus the

child's attention on specific print features, thus promoting the development of more sophisticated encoding strategies. (p. 270)

Teachers can foster growth in spelling by encouraging independence and accepting the inventions that independence produces. Rather than directly answering a child's question about how to spell a word, the teacher can encourage the child to say the word. The teacher may then ask, "What sound do you hear at the beginning? What letter would that be? Good. Write it down. Now, say the word again. What sound do you hear at the end?" and so on. This strategy encourages children to develop independence as spellers. Listening for sounds and representing them with letters supports children's efforts at phonemic segmentation, or separating words into their component sounds. Children also learn phonics as they think about how to write the sounds in the words they want to use. In fact, one year-long study of phonics instruction in eight exemplary first-grade classrooms showed that nearly half of the phonics instruction occurred in the writing program. Researchers Karen Dahl and Pat Scharer (2000) note,

> Although discussions of phonics often center on reading, an important finding of this research was the linkage between reading and writing in these classrooms and the contribution that the linkage with writing made to the children's understanding of letter–sound relationships. As children used their reading experiences in their own writing, their need for knowledge about letters, sounds, and words became both immediate and purposeful. (p. 593)

Sometimes writing is for personal expression.

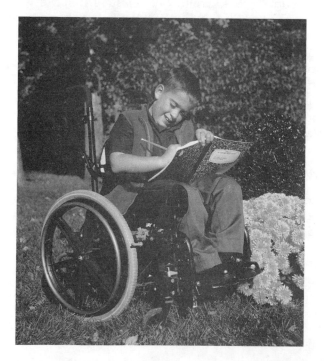

Children's first recognizable efforts at spelling will bear strong resemblance to the sounds they hear as they articulate words. Later, as children become readers, visual memory also plays a role in spelling; that is, children may inspect their efforts to see if they "look right." This is when standard spelling becomes an issue, particularly if the child's written work will be read by others. Like our colleague Jane Davidson, we suggest that teachers reply to students' queries of "Is it right?" with a statement like this: "It's good enough for now. You can read it, and I can read it. We both know what you're saying here. Later, we can make a few changes, if you'd like, to make your words look like they do in other books." This sort of discussion helps lessen concern about spelling at the idea-generation stage, yet assures writers that their efforts will receive the polish they deserve.

Modeling and Corrections

Two other general principles are important to consider as writing programs are planned: teacher as model and opportunities to connect reading and writing. In a way, these two principles are related, for both provide children with opportunities to learn from more sophisticated writers. Teachers who write when their students do, keep journals, and share their writing with students demonstrate why writing is important and how writers work. Likewise, writers benefit from opportunities to make the reading–writing connection—to use others' writing as a model (see the copy-change activity later in this chapter) or conclude a read-aloud session with a discussion of how the author used language. Frank Smith (1992) says that we learn to write by reading and learn to read by writing. We think he's right on both counts.

The atmosphere and attitude that best foster writing (and reading) development are characterized by support and encouragement. We can support children's writing efforts by nurturing their beliefs in themselves as writers. Belief leads to feelings of control and ownership, which in turn allow children to make their own decisions about the content and form of their writing. Having made these decisions, children are in a better position to understand the decisions other authors make.

Writing Activities

Most children are eager to express themselves in writing, particularly if they believe that others will read and enjoy their writing. Children should have daily opportunities for individual and shared writing. Classroom writing activities should also allow them to explore all the ways in which writing can be used, including as response to reading.

Those interested in developing a repertoire of writing activities will find many to choose from in other chapters of this book. For example, chapters 8 and 9, which address comprehension instruction, include descriptions of many reading–writing activities, such as Think–Pair–Share, character sketches, Bleich's Heuristic, (Write and Share)[2], Agree or Disagree? Why?, response journals, webbing or mapping, K-W-L, dialectic journals, distinctive-features activities, and Herringbone charts. All help students develop as writers in addition to fostering their understanding of what they have read. In this section, we describe several other writing activities. In combination with activities described elsewhere, these approaches will help students develop as writers and see connections between their reading and writing.

Personal Journals

Sometimes we write for personal expression. Children can express their thoughts and feelings in personal journals. Many teachers ask children to write in journals daily, either as an independent activity or during a specified period when the teacher also writes in a journal. Children should be free to write whatever they wish in their personal journals. Some children, particularly beginning writers, may decide to draw or write single words or lists of words. Others may recount important events or write stories. One enthusiastic first grader used her journal to write a letter to her father about school (see Figure 10.4). In fact, many teachers we know encourage students to write weekly letters to their parents in which they recount the week's learning.

Gay and Tina work as Title I teachers in the same school. Gay works with primary children, and Tina works with older ones. Both provide several times each week for students to write in their personal journals. Both also write while their students write. "It's fun," Gay says. "We all write at the same time. Often, children choose to write in their journals at other times or ask to take them home. That's okay, too, of course."

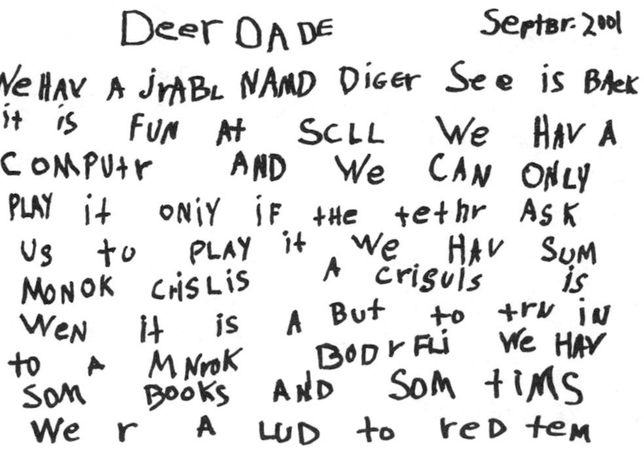

Figure 10.4
Entry in Elizabeth's Personal Journal

Gay and Tina write while their students write because they know the power of teacher-as-model. They see other benefits, as well. "We've noticed a dramatic drop in requests for assistance since we started writing with the children," Tina says. "It's almost as if they don't want to interrupt us. So, what happens is that the children become more independent, more willing to guess and try. That surprised us, but we're delighted because so many of our students *need* to learn to try."

Dialogue Journals

Sometimes we write to share information with a reader, as Elizabeth did in her journal entry (Figure 10.4). *Dialogue journals,* essentially notes written back and forth between two writers, let children sustain written conversation with others. Most teachers initiate dialogue journals by responding themselves to children's journal entries. This is a good way to get to know children at the beginning of the year, help them understand how dialogue journals work, and encourage fluent written expression without undue concern for mechanical perfection. Moreover, dialogue journals offer important vehicles for encouraging children to write in response to the books they read. Teachers can ask about characters or plot, for example, in their responses to children. In some classrooms, children use dialogue journals to write notes to friends. E-mail dialogue journals, either for general correspondence or for sharing responses to reading (e.g., McKeon, 1999; Sullivan, 1998) are becoming common in classrooms. Children are generally eager to read what another student or the teacher has written to them and to write responses.

Jeff provides resource assistance to middle-school students with learning disabilities. He and his students rely heavily on both personal and dialogue journals. "The choice is theirs," Jeff says. "They can use their journals in either way. My only rule is that everyone writes." Jeff has noticed that students frequently want feedback from him, especially early in the school year. He likes this because through journals he comes to know his students and establish a trusting relationship with them. "Sometimes what starts out as a personal entry, with a response from me, sort of mutates into a dialogue journal. I have a tendency to ask questions in my written responses to students, and that sometimes encourages them to do the same." As a new group of students becomes comfortable with one another, "they start writing for people besides me. It's kind of funny, in a way. I think it's like teacher-authorized note writing to some of them. And I guess that's exactly what it is! They're so eager to read what someone else has written to them and then to write back."

Learning Logs or Content-Area Journals

Sometimes we write to remember—to record thoughts, ideas, or facts for later use. Effective teachers encourage young writers to use writing for this purpose. Gloria, who teaches first grade, introduces new units of study in science or social studies by asking small groups of children to talk about what they would like to learn. One child in each group serves as a secretary to record group members' ideas. Figure 10.5 shows one group's report from a discussion that preceded a new science unit about space.

As each group read the report of its conversation about space to the rest of the class, Gloria prepared a large chart, titled "What We Want to Learn About Space," with enough room beneath each child's contribution to record information discovered during the course of the science unit. Every few days, Gloria and the children reread the chart, discussed what children had learned, and recorded new information where possible.

Children also write individual accounts of content-area lessons, record results of science observations or experiments, or write their own definitions of new concepts or descriptions of new procedures. This sort of writing resembles response journals (see chapter 8). *Learning logs, or content-area journals,* can be helpful for storing and organizing these writing efforts.

Learning log entries may be open or closed (Davidson, 1987). Open entries encourage personal response or reaction because students decide what to write for themselves. Closed entries provide for more structured response, such as note taking, outlining, charting, synthesizing, or comparing. For example, students may summarize a class demonstration or movie, record their observations about something they are studying, or make notes to remind themselves about a new procedure. Or they may simply write to remind themselves of what they have learned.

Fifth-grade teacher Christine Evans (1984) asked her students to make three types of log entries during two units of math instruction: definitions of new math concepts; explanations of new procedures, such as how to multiply

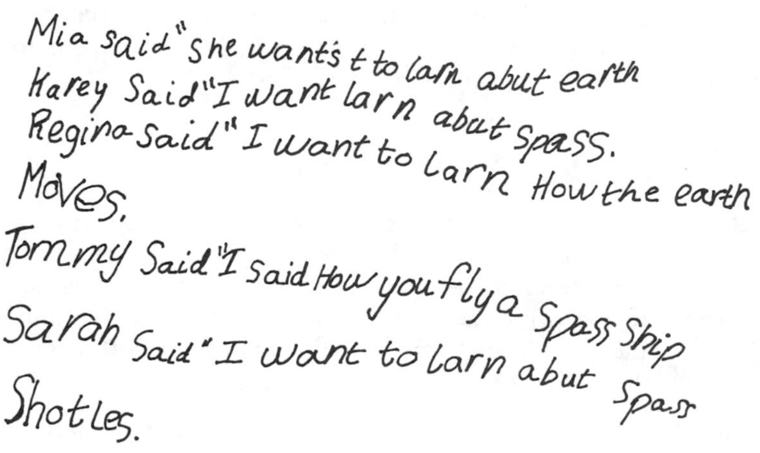

Mia said "she wants t to larn abut earth
Karey Said "I want larn abut Spass.
Regina Said " I want to Larn How the earth
Moves.
Tommy Said "I said How you fly a Spass Ship
Sarah Said " I want to larn abut Spass
Shotles.

Figure 10.5
Group Report about Space

decimals or draw a geometric figure; and troubleshooting, where students analyzed their errors and wrote about how and why they had made mistakes. Another fifth-grade teacher taught the two math units in the traditional manner. Both classes took publisher-prepared tests before and after each unit. Test results indicated that Evans's students began each unit with less math knowledge. After instruction, however, her students' test scores matched the other group's for one unit and exceeded them by 10 percent for the other. Evans attributes this growth to writing: Learning logs "get students to 'own' knowledge rather than just 'rent' it" (p. 835).

Learning logs also provide places for students to experiment with different discourse forms as they write about content-area learning. For example, they might write newspaper accounts of historical happenings and scientific discoveries or letters to the editor about past and current events. They might write first-person accounts of life in other places or at other times. They might write poetry as a means of reacting to or summarizing what they have learned. "Name poems" or acrostics, which use letters of a name or word to begin lines of a poem, can easily suit content-area concepts, as can "I used to think . . . but now I know" form poems (Koch, 2000). All learning log entries should be dated so that students can easily refer back to them. Children who forget how to perform particular tasks, such as subtracting three-digit numbers, for example, can simply look them up in their learning logs. Likewise, the teacher may use previous log entries as the basis for new ones: "Use your entries from September 18 and September 24 to analyze the . . ."

Learning logs give children a place to record their thoughts about and reactions to content area instruction. Keeping a log also introduces children to note taking in a natural and functional way. Moreover, the logs become valuable learning resources for students as the school year progresses and thus enhance content learning.

How journals look is not as important as what they do. Personal journals, dialogue journals, and learning logs give children authentic reasons for writing and for reading what they and others have written.

A Closer Look at Spelling

Spelling is a hotly debated aspect of language arts instruction. Indeed, although scholars have focused on spelling development for decades, much remains unknown about how children develop as spellers. Fortunately, certain widely accepted guiding principles help teachers integrate spelling instruction into their reading and writing programs (Bear et al., 2000; Fresch & Wheaton, 1997; Heald-Taylor, 1998; Templeton & Morris, 1999):

■ Learning to spell is a complex, developmental process dependent on both maturation and experience. Knowledge about spelling begins globally and develops gradually as children learn to differentiate and integrate insights about relationships between letters and sounds.

■ Spelling instruction should be a functional component of a writing program. Four principles help teachers accomplish this well: (a) accept children's approximations, especially initially; (b) use approximations diagnostically. By determining what children know about letter–sound relationships, teachers can determine appropriate emphases for instruction; (c) encourage children to work on only a few misspelled words at a time; and (d) help children learn to edit for spelling, especially prior to publication or sharing their written work in other ways.

Fresch and Wheaton (1997) describe a 5-day routine for spelling instruction that also addresses modifications for children with special needs. Each week, the teacher selects a spelling pattern for focus and three sets of words that follow the pattern, some easy, some of medium difficulty, and some challenging. Children take a traditional pretest over the words at the beginning of every week; the teacher uses the test results to determine which set of words each child will study. Each student may select a few additional words to study as well, which may not be associated with the spelling pattern. At the end of each week, pairs of students give spelling tests to each other.

During the rest of each week, students learn their spelling words and the spelling pattern that unites them by completing word sorts (see chapter 5) and other word games, locating the words in material they have read or written, looking for ways to use the words in their writing, exploring word origins and derivatives, and so forth. They even prepare the dictation sentences for their own spelling tests. Fresch and Wheaton (1997) summarize this innovative and workable program this way: "English is both logical and fascinating. Words are learned through using and manipulating language, not memorizing it" (p. 23).

In a review of research about spelling development, Templeton and Morris (1999) comment,

> Of the few methodological studies that have been conducted, none answers to everyone's satisfaction the question of whether spelling is learned primarily through reading and writing or primarily through the systematic examination of words. . . . What does emerge from the research is the suggestion that some examination of words is necessary for most students. (p. 108)

A successful spelling program, therefore, offers active opportunities to play with language and to organize and categorize words in ways that allow writers to discover generalizations about written language and the relationships between letters and sounds. Most important, however, may be the motivation to spell well that develops in classrooms where children write for interested audiences.

Copy Change

Children often create their own stories based on actual or fanciful happenings. Children's literature can be an effective springboard and scaffold for this type of writing. If children read or hear tall tales or fairy tales, discussion and subsequent dictation and a class text can focus on key elements or characteristics. Then, using the dictation as a guide, children can write their own tall tales or fairy tales.

Individuals or groups can write their own versions of books, too. This activity is sometimes called *copy change* because children use the author's copy as a framework for writing but change it to reflect their own ideas. Hesitant writers often need extra support or scaffolding to compose on their own, and the framework or ideas supplied by an exemplary author can provide this support.

Simple poetry works well as the impetus for copy-change activities. Children often find success with short poems in particular, which tend to be less overwhelming than longer pieces or stories. But predictable pattern books (see Appendix C) also work well for introducing children to copy change. For example, the pattern that Bill Martin, Jr. used to develop *Brown Bear, Brown Bear* is easy to discern and use to dictate or write new versions:

> Mr. Jones, Mr. Jones, what do you see?
>
> I see some first graders looking at me.

Copy changes can also be more complex. Figure 10.6 presents an example written by a group of fifth graders who applied the pattern in *If You Give a Mouse a Cookie* to their learning in social studies. Alphabet books also offer wonderful possibilities for copy change. One teacher we know assigns a letter of the alphabet to each child who attends a field trip, for example. During the trip, the child notes all the words that begin with his or her letter. When the class returns, children make an ABC book to record and remember what they learned.

Our favorite copy change book is Margaret Wise Brown's (1949/1999) *The Important Book*. This book offers observations about simple objects such as a spoon, an apple, shoes, the wind, and so forth. Each description follows a pattern: The important thing about _____ is _____. [Other details follow.] But the important thing about _____ is _____. Children quickly learn this pattern and use it to write *Important Book* pages about themselves, their classmates or family members, or what they are learning in science or social studies. The students in Alicia's Title I classes use *The Important Book* as a frame for writing reports in science and social studies. Figure 10.7 shows what Hannah learned about crayfish. "The children are so proud of their reports," Alicia says. "This book has helped children see alternatives to copying information from a Web site or the CD encyclopedia. It saves me from reading all that, too. I much prefer the creativity of these *Important Book* pages!"

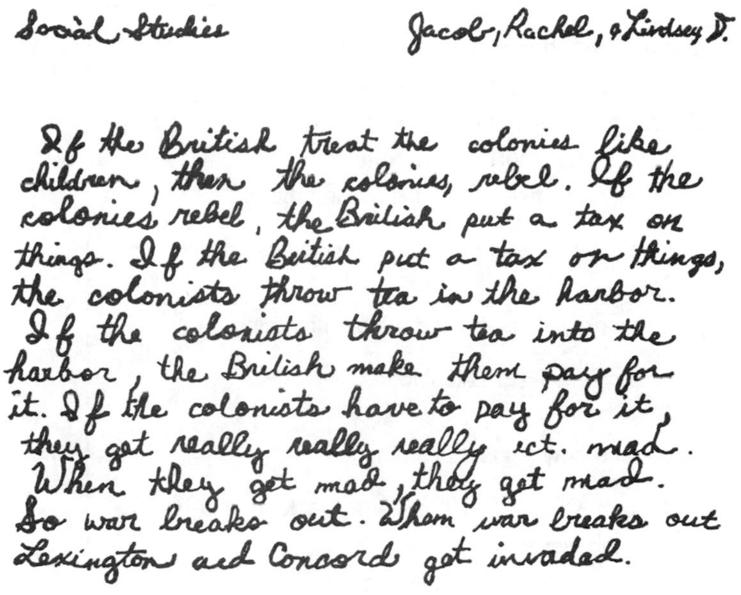

Social Studies   Jacob, Rachel, & Lindsey D.

If the British treat the colonies like
children, then the colonies, rebel. If the
colonies rebel, the British put a tax on
things. If the British put a tax on things,
the colonists throw tea in the harbor.
If the colonists throw tea into the
harbor, the British make them pay for
it. If the colonists have to pay for it,
they get really really really ect. mad.
When they get mad, they get mad.
So war breaks out. When war breaks out
Lexington and Concord get invaded.

Figure 10.6
Example of a Copy Change Activity

Students can recast a story as a script to perform as reader's theater (see chapter 6). This, too, is a form of copy change because students rewrite a favorite story in a different form.

Copy change, or what second-grade teacher Peter Lancia (1997) calls "literary borrowing," appears to come naturally in classrooms where lots of reading and writing is encouraged. Lancia noticed that some of his students "wrote new stories about familiar characters, such as George and Martha, Frog and Toad, Lyle Crocodile, Arthur, and Miss Frizzle. Others retold the original plot in their own words or modified the same events to fit a new setting. And occasionally some attempted to imitate the writing style of a particular author, book, or genre" (p. 470). One year, he decided to look more carefully at this natural copy change. He found it pervasive—all but one student "borrowed," and more than half (57 percent) of students' completed pieces of writing showed evidence of borrowing. Peter believes that if students "have the opportunity to interact with books and authors every day and to practice writing in an environment built on support and encouragement, authorship becomes real as they imitate their role models and write their own stories" (p. 475). We agree!

Whether they're simple or complex, copy-change activities encourage careful reading or listening so that students can discover and use the author's pattern. Thus, the pattern itself may provide a supportive framework for

The Important Thing About Crayfish

By Hannah

The important thing about crayfish is that it is a living thing.

A crayfish is short, and active, and smart, and harmful.

But the important thing about a crayfish is that it is a living thing.

The exciting thing about a crayfish is that it can do many things.

It can crawl, pinch, and walk.

But the exciting thing about a crayfish is that it can do many things.

The regrettable fact about a crayfish is that it pinches.

It will hurt and sting.

But the regrettable fact about a crayfish is that it pinches.

The incredible news about a crayfish is that it can grow back body parts.

It is called molting, and it is unbelievable.

But the incredible news about a crayfish is that it can grow back body parts.

The terrible truth about a crayfish is that they can kill each other.

It is scary, and incredible, and gross.

But the terrible truth about a crayfish is that they can kill each other.

Figure 10.7

Hannah's Copy Change of *The Important Book*

young authors, in much the same way as a poet might use a haiku or sonnet framework. Indeed, copy change and creating scripts from stories are authentic types of writing. Professional writers often emulate the work of writers they admire, and Hollywood is filled with professional screenplay or script writers.

Writing Is Meant to Be Read

Children need to write both for their own purposes and for others in and beyond the classroom, including the teacher. In fact, sharing writing can be one of the most gratifying aspects of the writing cycle. Figure 10.8 offers several ways for students to share their writing with others. All these activities make the connection between reading and writing strong and explicit for students.

Some schools sponsor student publishing companies to encourage authorship (See Appendix L for bookmaking ideas.) One such effort, at Central Elementary School in Morgantown, W. Va., was a collaboration among several classroom teachers and the Title I reading teacher (Barksdale-Ladd & Nedeff, 1997). All children were invited to write books, either singly, in pairs, or in

- Students can make individual books for the classroom library or the school library. Children's books from one classroom can be loaned for children in another classroom to read.

- Students can make class magazines, newspapers, or books. These can be collaborations, where children work together on one cohesive product, or collections, where children contribute their favorite story or poem to a class book. Children can also make class books related to content-area study.

- Students can create bulletin boards or corridor displays of their writing. These, like all other writing for children to read, should be displayed at children's eye level.

- Students can make posters of poetry, jokes, riddles, and so on.

- Photocopies of students' writing can be shared with families and friends.

- Students can write notes or memos to classmates or the teacher. These can be "mailed" and delivered daily.

- Students can enact or present their writing through drama, puppetry, and so on.

- Students can read their writing aloud to classmates during writing conferences, to classmates during daily sharing time, to students in other classrooms, or to the school community via the intercom.

Figure 10.8
Sharing Writing

author–illustrator teams. The Title I teacher, older students, and parent volunteers helped when needed. The upper-grade children even handled the business end of the publishing company by pricing materials, contacting vendors, recording sales, and so on. The student publishing company had a positive influence on children's self-esteem and attitudes about reading and writing. "In the library we hear statements like, 'Oh, I've read that book. It's an adventure story. We read adventure stories last year, and I wrote one'" (p. 573).

From informal notes or lists to published books, writing is meant to be read. This, of course, is a strong motivation for writing and a solid rationale for including writing activities in a program designed to strengthen children's reading. Through writing, children learn how written language works; they develop and deepen understandings about the conventions of print, the ways in which stories and other text forms work, and graphophonic knowledge. Moreover, by becoming authors, students learn to think like authors. They learn to think about purpose and audience and to analyze the author's craft. They discover that authors have options. All of this helps students understand that both reading and writing involve the manipulation of language and the construction of meaning.

11

Putting It All Together: Instructional Routines That Work

In the preceding chapters we presented sets of instructional strategies aimed at overcoming difficulties that children often encounter in their reading development. These strategies assist students just beginning to experience difficulty and children whose reading development has been significantly disrupted.

Authentic, engaging, and effective corrective or remedial instruction is more than just the sum of these various strategies. It is not enough to use them as separate instructional activities. Effective teachers develop a synergy in which the thoughtful combination and regular implementation of a logical set of instructional activities results in an effect that is larger than the sum effect of the activities implemented in a willy-nilly manner. Teachers must consider how the instructional pieces fit together to form a coherent and effective instructional package or routine. Effective corrective instruction means looking at the big picture and designing complete programs that make the best use of students' time in helping them achieve the goal of proficient reading.

By now you know that we believe firmly that teachers are in the best position to make instructional decisions for students who find reading difficult. Many reasons exist for this belief, but perhaps one is most important: We must teach in ways that reflect our beliefs about literacy learning. Students should also be actively involved in setting the direction of instruction. Packaged curricula, teacher's manuals, and other instructional resources can be good for finding ideas or provoking thought (indeed, that's why we wrote this book), but teachers and students together create curriculum and instruction in classrooms.

Teachers' instructional styles differ, as do students' needs and preferences. Moreover, aspects of the instructional environment vary from classroom to classroom. Imagine, for example, 10 Title I teachers teaching the same lesson to 10 groups of children in 10 different classrooms in 10 different schools in 10 different communities. What do you think would be the same about all these lessons? Beyond the general instructional focus, probably little. Such pragmatic realities also support teachers in developing their own curricula: No one knows you, your students, and the specifics of your teaching situation as well as you.

In this chapter we deal with a critical but too often ignored issue: developing instructional systems that work. In essence, we discuss putting the strategies in this book into systems designed for children's specific needs and teachers' styles of instruction. We suggest principles or guidelines for designing corrective instruction and provide examples of existing instructional packages based on these principles. We also discuss how individual teachers design such systems for themselves and their students.

Guidelines for Program Development

This section offers several guidelines for developing a program that will successfully meet the needs of struggling readers. We recommend that you think about these guidelines (and others that may be important to you) within an overall, four-step framework for developing curriculum and planning instruction:

1.   *Formulate an instructional philosophy.* We all have philosophies or sets of beliefs about literacy learning, but sometimes we fail to articulate them or consider the relationship between our beliefs and our instructional practices. The first step in the curriculum-development framework is to decide what you believe about the reading process, children as language learners, the role of the teacher, the classroom atmosphere, and appropriate materials and activities. We recommend that you write down these statements because you will need them in all other steps of planning and reading instruction. Also, you may want to consider the extent to which your beliefs are research- or theory-based.

2.   *Develop a few broad instructional goals.* The goals serve as a foundation for planning instruction. As such, they should reflect your philosophy, describe the general areas within which literacy instruction will occur, and be based on broad notions of children's needs. We have found that too many goals are hard to manage and tend to fragment instruction, so limit the number—perhaps no more than five. The National Reading Panel (2000) has identified phonemic awareness, phonics (decoding), fluency, vocabulary, and comprehension as essential elements of effective reading instruction. This framework developed by the Panel, along with the addition of writing,

provides us with a solid set of goals or foci for our instruction and instructional planning.

3. *Based on your instructional goals, plan instructional routines that consist of effective instructional practices.* Routines (described in chapter 2) offer children consistent opportunities to achieve the goals you establish. Moreover, because routines are predictable, they foster children's security and independence in the classroom. When you have made preliminary decisions about routines, look again at your goals. Make sure that the routines, as a whole, will help children achieve the goals.

4. *Develop a plan to evaluate the curriculum and students.* You might ask questions such as "How can I determine the extent to which instruction reflects my philosophy?" "How will I know that instruction really is providing students with opportunities to achieve the goals?" "How can I find areas that need fine-tuning?" Many of the ideas in chapter 13 can be use for evaluating both curriculum and children.

Instructional planning is part of teachers' professional responsibility. Many teachers with whom we have worked find the four-step framework helpful for thinking about the planning process and ensuring that what happens in the classroom reflects their best thinking about children and literacy learning. The framework is rather general; it is even useful for planning "regular" classroom instruction. Now let us consider several guidelines for program development that apply more specifically to the issue of helping struggling readers.

Focusing the Program

Reading programs for struggling readers should aim to help them overcome difficulties in specific areas of reading. They thereby improve their overall reading performance and become lifelong, engaged readers. Thus, to be truly effective, programs should address readers' specific problems and promote purposeful, authentic, engaging, and satisfying reading experiences.

If the reader manifests difficulty in reading fluency, providing experiences in vocabulary development will not ameliorate the problem at hand. Indeed, the child may have a superior vocabulary, in which case providing supplemental instruction in vocabulary may have minimal positive results. If fluency is the problem, we must design activities aimed at strengthening that essential aspect of reading.

The same is true for every difficulty—attitude toward reading, comprehension, vocabulary, word recognition. Please note that we define the area of difficulty rather broadly. We do not mean specific skill areas such as "fluency in multiple-phrase sentences" or "recognition of the *ed* ending in words." Difficulties in specific skills generalize to difficulties throughout that particular aspect of reading. Thus, corrective instruction should be aimed at the more generalized area of concern.

Effective instructional programs rely on a good understanding of children and their reading.

Developing a focused program also requires some attention to what students do as readers, observing behaviors and attitudes that can facilitate their literacy growth and those likely to impede progress. In other words, teachers must determine what strategies nonproductive readers use so that they can plan instruction to meet their needs. Here are three suggestions to guide this process:

1. *Watch for patterns of behavior across situations and times.* During any day, children read lots of materials for lots of reasons in lots of instructional situations. Drawing conclusions based on one type of reading situation ignores the complexity and diversity of reading demands.

2. *Rely on information from informal assessments, observations, and conversations as well as formal assessments.* To develop an instructional plan to support children, we need to understand how they operate within instructional settings. Therefore, standardized test results are only partially helpful in this type of instructional planning. For example, children who score poorly on the comprehension subtest of a standardized reading test may indeed have difficulties. To help them, however, we need to understand how they approach typical reading tasks and situations. We may know *that* they have problems in reading; we also need to understand the *whys* and *hows*.

3. *Focus on the total reader.* Especially with struggling readers, we tend to look for problems. These are important, to be sure, but we must look equally carefully at what children *can* do as readers. This focus on strengths is important psychologically for both teacher and students; moreover, instruction can frequently be planned to use strengths as a platform or scaffold for addressing weaknesses. *example 2.*

Children's attitudes about reading and perceptions about reading and their roles as readers also deserve attention. We know that people who enjoy reading usually read more and consequently have many opportunities to grow as readers. Moreover, children use their perceptions of the reading process to guide their actions while reading and evaluate the success of their efforts.

Massed and Spaced Practice or Activity

Whatever the reader's difficulty, overcoming it usually requires practice within that area, and plenty of it. Significant chunks of time devoted to the area of difficulty will help achieve significant and lasting progress. We must direct the reader's attention to the difficulty using a variety of activities, texts, and contexts. If, for example, a student is having difficulty with word recognition, an effective instructional routine will provide the reader with a variety of activities, strategies, and practice in learning to recognize or decode words quickly and efficiently; the reader also needs opportunities to apply that knowledge in real reading situations.

A more traditional and limited approach might isolate specific areas of difficulty or skills needed for word recognition, such as the *pl* consonant blend or vowel diphthongs or the *ing* ending. Such instruction would focus almost entirely on these skill areas and be in the form of worksheets that isolate the skill at the expense of applying it in real reading situations. These limited approaches fail to give the reader broad enough experience to practice the full range of skills and strategies needed to recognize all words efficiently. Moreover, they provide insufficient breadth to allow the reader to apply the practiced skill or strategy in the larger context of authentic reading.

This leads us to a related issue: the nature of material used for instruction and practice. Throughout this book, we have pointed to the value of using authentic reading material that children find interesting. Additionally, the reading material should be rather easy for children, especially as we begin to focus their attention on an aspect of the reading process that is new or difficult for them. Allington (2002) reports that highly effective teachers found ways to maximize the amount of easy reading their students did throughout the school day. We advise selecting material carefully to increase the likelihood of success and decrease the possibility of frustration.

If teachers are locked into using material that challenges students, they must find and implement ways to make that reading easier. This can be done

looking for words w/in words

through the teacher reading orally while the students point and follow along in their textbooks silently, echo reading and paired reading with reading buddies, providing prereading background knowledge and postreading summaries for students, and other strategies presented throughout the book.

Consistency Over Time

Readers need consistent instruction over the long term. Massed and long-term instruction and practice are the best assurance that the reader will permanently overcome the difficulty. Moreover, developing a consistent instructional routine that includes authentic reading experiences as well as instructional activity in the area of difficulty makes lessons predictable for students and the teacher. This results in a degree of student independence, more efficient use of time, and greater on-task behavior.

Developing a consistent routine need not result in lessons that students find uninteresting. Within the general lesson framework that includes work on the specific area of difficulty and authentic reading experiences, teachers have the freedom to vary the instructional activities (several activities can be devoted to any one difficulty area, as preceding chapters show), texts to be read and who makes the choices, how the text reading might occur (silent, oral, choral, paired), and the surrounding context for the instruction (such as where the instructional activity takes place: individually, in pairs, or with a group). So many variables ensure that all lessons can be fresh, engaging, and interesting.

Proficient, Professional Instructors

We firmly believe that highly qualified instructors provide the best instruction, especially with students who have difficulty reading. Indeed, studies show that excellent reading instruction and high student reading achievement are positively associated with the level of teacher training (Elley, 1992; National Reading Panel, 2000; Postlethwaite & Ross, 1992).

Staying professionally current is every teacher's responsibility, but we think it is particularly critical for those who work with struggling readers. We learn more about readers and reading each year, and much of this new knowledge has direct instructional application. By maintaining memberships in professional organizations, reading and discussing literacy-related journals, attending professional meetings, and interacting informally with colleagues, we can plan instruction based on best practice and state-of-the-art knowledge.

Moreover, those who select a particular program for reading instruction, such as the ones described later in this chapter, must understand the philosophy, purposes, and procedures of the program and be proficient in its implementation. This may involve initial professional development through reading or in-service education, frequent opportunities to talk with colleagues who also use the program, and ongoing in-service education on the program.

Staying professionally current is every teacher's responsibility.

Effective Instructional Programs

Reading Recovery

One of the best-known corrective reading instructional programs is *Reading Recovery* (Clay, 1993; Pinnell, 1989; Pinnell, Fried, & Estice, 1990). Reading Recovery is an individual tutoring program in which a highly trained tutor works for 30 minutes daily with a first-grade child experiencing difficulty in reading. This work takes place in addition to the child's regular classroom reading instruction.

Limited to first graders, the program operates under the assumption that the best way to correct reading problems is to treat them early and intensively. The older a student becomes, the more entrenched reading problems become; instruction, then, becomes more time-consuming and less effective.

Each Reading Recovery lesson uses a series of brief activities aimed primarily at improving word recognition and reading fluency. The activities are consistent from day to day; the routine is predictable. Students know what they will do in every session. With such consistency the tutoring sessions are intensive and involve little wasted time.

In the first part of the lesson, students read familiar stories they have read previously. The teacher performs a diagnostic check by keeping a running record of the child's oral reading of a newer text, one introduced in the previous day's lesson. Next, the child and teacher engage in letter recognition

I like it

and manipulation activities. The child dictates a sentence that the teacher records and rereads aloud, after which the child is guided in writing it. After practicing reading and writing the sentence, the teacher rewrites it on a strip of paper, cuts it into individual words, and asks the child to reconstruct the message. The words are taken home for further practice and play. Finally, the teacher introduces a new book that the child can learn to read successfully. The child and teacher explore the book; the teacher introduces new concepts, language patterns, or words to the child as necessary. After the introduction, the child attempts the book with the teacher guiding appropriate strategy use when the text becomes too difficult.

First graders remain in Reading Recovery until they read at about the average level of other first graders in their school. This usually requires several weeks of instruction. Research on Reading Recovery suggests that it is a highly effective program in advancing students to more normal levels of reading and that, compared with other corrective reading programs, Reading Recovery graduates are less likely to need continued reading assistance throughout their elementary years.

Tutors who specialize in Reading Recovery are certified teachers who engage in a year-long program of intensive education in Reading Recovery. The education program consists of studying the reading process of young children and methods of instruction and practicing, observing, and critiquing Reading Recovery instruction throughout the training period.

Literacy Lesson Framework

Based on her work as a classroom teacher, a Reading Recovery teacher, and a supervisor of a university reading clinic, Susan Tancock (1994) has developed a straightforward *Literacy Lesson Framework* (or routine) for struggling readers that is rooted in literature-based reading instruction. She notes that students who come to her clinic can be characterized by five areas of difficulty: (a) over-reliance on the sound–symbol system (labored sounding out of unknown words), (b) a perception that reading is chiefly accurate word recognition, not meaning making, (c) lack of fluency in reading, (d) minimal self-monitoring, and (e) few writing strategies. Tancock's framework has worked well to address these concerns and move students to more successful reading. The 5-step framework is described below:

1. Reading of familiar material (5–10 minutes)
2. Guided reading of authentic literature (30 minutes)
3. Writing (5–10 minutes)
4. Word sorting (5–10 minutes)
5. Book sharing (5–10 minutes)

In the familiar reading component students read easy materials they have read previously either silently or with a partner using a fluency technique such as repeated, echo, or paired reading.

In the guided reading section, the heart of the framework, the student reads a slightly more challenging and authentic text with the tutor's guidance. Before reading, student and tutor focus on relevant background knowledge and entertain predictions or questions about the text. During the actual reading, the tutor supports and monitors the student's reading and encourages the student to monitor her own reading. In particular, the tutor encourages the student to employ syntactic and semantic strategies ("Does what you just read make sense?") as well as phonics strategies in decoding unknown words. The actual reading is followed by students returning to and addressing their prereading questions or predictions and clarifying, refining, and extending their thinking about the text.

Writing activities range from students writing a sentence, cutting it up into words, and reassembling it to more extended story, journal, or other authentic writing. During word sorting, students analyze words for a variety of common features from structural (e.g., number of syllables, spelling patterns) to semantic (e.g., living things, nonliving things). In the final portion of the lesson, the tutor reads an engaging and interesting story to the student. Reading to students is more than entertaining; it develops positive attitudes for reading, comprehension and vocabulary, and provides students with a model for fluent reading.

The Four Blocks

The *Four Blocks* (Cunningham, Hall, & Defee, 1991, 1998), a primary-grade program, adapts easily to a variety of instructional settings. Students engage in daily literacy instruction through four 30-minute time blocks, each featuring a distinct aspect of literacy.

The *writing* block consists of a 5-minute mini-lesson in which the teacher demonstrates and talks about a piece of her own writing with the students. Writing conventions and strategies are modeled and discussed daily. Next, the child writes independently, receiving assistance and feedback from others and eventually publishing the work. At the end of the block, the group discusses its progress and shares completed work.

In the *guided-reading* block the teacher engages students in comprehension-focused instruction. During part of this period students read the stories from the text with a partner.

In the *independent-reading* block the teacher reads a book to students. Students read self-selected books on their own (including books published by fellow students in the writing block). Students also talk about their reading with other students.

The final time block, *working with words,* includes word wall and word-making activities. This period develops students' word recognition or decoding abilities. Students and teacher add about five words each week to the word wall. These common words are written on cards so that they can be arranged in alphabetical order. Students practice the words each day. Making Words is a word-building activity in which students manipulate a limited set of letters to make a variety of words. Both activities are described in detail in chapter 5.

The Four Blocks helps develop students' facility with word recognition while allowing them to apply their newfound knowledge to real reading and writing situations. Cunningham et al. (1998) report that with this approach, nearly 90 percent of first-grade students made exceptional or acceptable progress during a year's instruction.

Although we do not advocate a simple copied application of this or any approach for students encountering problems in reading, we appreciate the general sense of balance engendered by this approach. Several aspects of Four Blocks are worthy of notice and adaptation by teachers who face similar circumstances. First, children receive specific and extended instruction in the area requiring attention. Further, they immediately apply the learning to real and guided reading and writing situations. In addition, the consistent and pre-dictable daily blocks of instruction enable students to know what they will be doing. They do not waste instructional time learning new routines. We also like the active engagement of readers in choosing books, writing on their own, and making their own words.

A program like this works because students are engaged in real read-ing, real writing, and real problem solving through effective word recognition activities. Moreover, this good instruction is massed in a significant time period and is consistently applied on a daily basis.

Beth Ann, a fourth-grade teacher, has adapted the Four Blocks approach for her own class. She believes the framework has guided her to develop a reading curriculum that meets the needs of her students, especially those who struggle in reading.

> During the working-with-words block I have incorporated more fluency activities—paired reading, repeated readings, and vocabulary activities in addition to the word-decoding activities. My students need to move beyond decoding. Their problems are not so much with sounding out words, but in reading efficiently, putting those words together into mean-ingful chunks, and having a fuller understanding of what the words mean.

Literacy Teaching Framework

Taking a cue from Cunningham, Hall, and Defee's Four Blocks approach, Timothy Shanahan (2000) developed his own version of the four blocks that he calls the *Literacy Teaching Framework*. Shanahan keeps the word study, writing, and comprehension (guided reading) components from Cunningham, Hall, and Defee's approach. However, recognizing the importance of reading fluency, especially among struggling readers, he substitutes reading fluency instruction for the self-selected reading block of time. Implementing his approach in the Chicago area, Shanahan (2000) reports strong improve-ments in reading achievement where previously achievement was poor.

Success for All

The *Success for All* program is aimed at children in Grades pre-K through 3 (Slavin, Madden, Karweit, Dolan, & Wasik, 1992). It has been implemented in an inner-city elementary school with great success, bringing all children up to grade-level achievement In reading and other basic skills. The program is designed for use with special tutors who are certified teachers with experience in Title I, special education, or primary-grade reading instruction. Tutors work individually for 20-minute sessions each day during a 60-minute social studies period. Instruction focuses on what the students encounter in their regular reading curriculum. Each tutor works individually with 11 students per day.

During the 90-minute regular reading period, the tutors work within the classroom and serve as additional reading teachers. Thus, tutors provide additional on-line support to regular reading instruction and learn about the regular curriculum content in order to coordinate and reinforce their individual tutoring with the regular classroom instruction.

In regular instruction, students in Grades 1 to 3 are regrouped according to reading achievement across grades so that each class has about 15 students, all reading at the same level. This arrangement allows teachers to teach the whole class; increases time available for direct instruction; and largely eliminates the need for workbooks, photocopies, and other independent, "make-work," follow-up activities.

The reading instruction for beginning readers includes time for sharing and discussing children's literature to develop comprehension and vocabulary, oral reading of big books, letter and sound instruction, repeated oral reading of phonetically regular minibooks, composing, and instruction in specific comprehension skills including story structure. Older children (Grades 2–3) also hear and discuss literature and engage in cooperative learning of story structure through prediction, summarization, vocabulary, decoding, and story-related writing using a basal textbook series. Students are expected to read material of their own choosing for 20 minutes each night at home. This reading is discussed in regular "book club" sessions in school. Every eight weeks, students' reading progress is assessed. These results determine which students will receive tutoring in the upcoming weeks.

A family-support team made up of social workers and a parental liaison provides parenting education services and encourages home support of children's school learning. The team also intervenes when students are working below potential. Teachers and tutors receive two days of in-service training at the beginning of the school year to learn about implementing the program. Throughout the school year they receive regular in-service instruction on relevant topics.

Several aspects of Success for All seem worthy of mention. These include tutors' consistent and massed instruction for students most in need of instruction, ongoing student assessment, coordination with the regular reading curriculum to ensure consistency and maximize practice within a particular content or skill area, maximizing teacher–student contact through the efficient use of tutors and the regrouping process, connection between home and school, and attempts to increase students' voluntary reading. Together, these elements ensure intensive and meaningful instruction that leads to strong gains in reading achievement.

The Curious George Strategy

The *Curious George Strategy* (Richek & McTague, 1988) helps primary-grade students develop fluency and comprehension in their reading. It is based on the use of a particular type of children's book—series books—with the idea that authentic literature is more interesting to students than the dull, dry materials struggling readers often must read. Moreover, series books (see Appendix D), such as *Curious George* (H. A. and Margaret Rey), *Clifford the Big Red Dog* (Norman Bridwell), and *Harry the Dirty Dog* (Gene Zion), allow students to gain background knowledge about characters, setting, plot, and author's style, which can set the stage for comprehension and fluent reading.

The Curious George Strategy is implemented as a weekly cycle in which one book is covered per week during 30-minute group sessions. On the first day the teacher introduces a series book and reads it to the students. The teacher and students reread the first third of the book chorally or in some other joint way. Next, each child chooses five favorite words from the story for future study and reference. Students take copies of the book home to read and practice their words.

On the second day of the weekly cycle students begin by sharing their word cards with each other. Next, they read the second third of the book together. Finally, students choose five new words to practice on their own and are asked to read the book at home. Day 3 repeats the Day 2 session using the final third of the book.

Day 4 culminates the cycle. Children dictate their own version of the Curious George story to the teacher, who writes it in a large blank book. This language-experience activity sets the stage for other writing activities that follow. On Day 5, students can engage in other group and individual literacy-expansion activities.

In the following weeks students read other Curious George books with their teacher and later move on to other series books. Fluency and comprehension continue to improve as students' familiarity with the author, plot, characters, and words increase.

Evaluation of this strategy showed that students' comprehension and oral reading fluency improved significantly over a comparison group receiving more traditional corrective instruction. In addition, teachers and parents noted improvements in students' attitudes toward reading and their writing ability.

Often students, especially younger ones, are asked to read material in which they have little interest or background. As a result, they struggle in their reading as they attempt to make sense of the text. That struggle often leads to further difficulty and frustration. In addition to the consistency and focus of this program, the Curious George Strategy acknowledges students' need to become familiar with what they are reading in order to experience reading success.

Fluency Development Lesson

Although we detailed the *Fluency Development Lesson (FDL)* in chapter 6, we mention it again as an example of a lesson format that meets students' needs systematically and consistently. Rasinski, Padak, Linek, and Sturtevant (1994) created the FDL to address the needs of primary-grade students who lack the fluency skills to read texts easily, effectively, and efficiently. We combined important aspects of fluency instruction in an instructional package teachers quickly and easily implemented and students quickly accomplished. FDL relies on highly predictable texts; the notions of modeling, support, and assistance during initial readings of the passage; multiple readings of the text; focus on individual words of choice and word patterns; and opportunities for students to respond meaningfully to the passage and perform it for a wider audience.

First, teachers read a short, predictable text to students. Then, students read and reread the text, with initially high levels of support that gradually diminish as children become more familiar and fluent with the passage. At the end of each lesson students read the passage to the class or other groups of children or adults in the school.

The FDL was developed as a daily instructional routine that supplemented students' regular instruction. We found that over the course of a year, students receiving the FDL instruction made significant gains in reading compared with a group of children who also received supplemental instruction but in a more traditional manner (Rasinski et al., 1994).

Make It Work for You

The programs we described in this chapter are only a few of the many effective programs. Furthermore, although these programs work, you should refrain from following them blindly. We describe them only to demonstrate the wide variety that exists and point out their many common characteristics, such as focus and consistency.

In a review of programs for first graders who experience difficulty in learning to read, Pikulski (1994) identifies several critical instructional elements:

- Extra or supplemental reading instruction should coordinate closely with regular classroom instruction.
- Children benefit from additional instructional time.
- Simple texts, especially those employing predictable and natural language patterns, ensure success.

- Meaningful opportunities to reread foster fluency development.
- Instruction should focus where children need help.
- Writing activities foster reading growth.
- Close cooperation between school and home is beneficial.

Pikulski also urges careful monitoring of children's progress and encourages teachers to find professional support.

We believe that most of these suggestions apply to reading instruction for children of any age. By employing these guidelines and the principles we outline in this chapter and incorporating many of the instructional strategies we describe throughout this book, teachers can develop effective programs that respond to their own situations.

If you are a new teacher, you may find yourself overwhelmed by all the demands on your time. In addition to organizing your classroom, you must decide the instructional approach you will use with your students, what kinds of parent involvement activities you intend to employ, what materials you will need for your lessons, and so on. We advise you to take it slowly when designing instructional routines. Learn about yourself as a teacher and your students as learners. Acquaint yourself with new ideas about teaching through professional reading, graduate coursework and workshops, and conversations with your professional colleagues. Slowly develop a program that works for you and your students. Begin with a core set of activities or lessons and expand from there. Be willing to make changes if certain initiatives you take seem unsuccessful. But never stop working to design instruction that will improve your students' learning. Authentic and engaged teaching demands constant monitoring and work for improvement.

Ownership is one of the concepts that characterizes effective literacy instruction. Student achievement increases when students have ownership over their own learning, as when they choose what they need and want to read, how they respond to their reading, and with whom they read. The same notion applies to instructional design. When teachers have ownership over their instruction, when they determine their own methods and procedures, they invest more of themselves and their ideas in the program and see greater reason to make instruction work. Thus, we urge you to identify for yourself the principles of instruction key to successful intervention, develop a realistic and workable program, and make it work for you and your students.

12

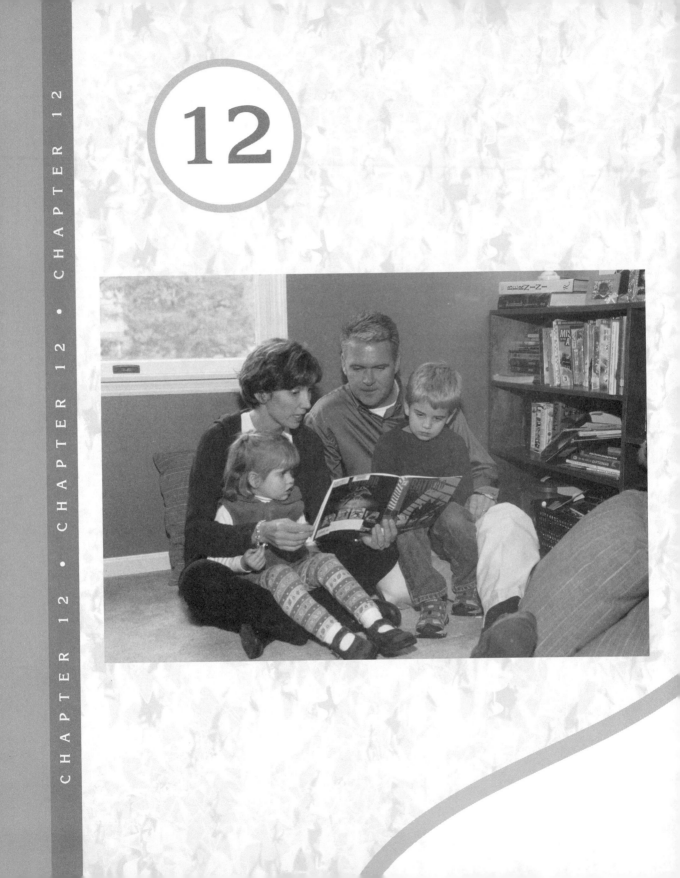

Involving Parents in Children's Reading

A central part of any reading program, and especially those aimed at helping struggling readers, is maximizing the amount of time that students engage in reading authentic text. We have emphasized the strong association between students' progress in reading and the amount of real reading they do. Yet, the unfortunate truth is that most students read little either in or out of school. One study reported that, on average, fifth-grade students in a Midwestern school read books less than five minutes per day when they were out of school (Anderson, Wilson, & Fielding, 1988). Other research has reported similar results at different grade levels.

Given the relative absence of children's authentic reading experiences, we wonder why more children don't have difficulty reading. We also wonder just how much better all readers, especially less proficient ones, might become if their volume of contextual reading could be increased. Because students currently engage in so little real reading, even a small increase would double or perhaps triple the amount of time they devote to reading. This is certainly a worthy goal for any school reading program.

The home can help in this. Elementary students spend most of their time at home, yet they do little reading there. Thus, home and parental involvement in reading are truly untapped sources for increasing the sheer amount that students read, which in turn will increase their proficiency in reading.

Parental involvement can significantly influence children's learning. Several extensive reviews of research suggest that parent involvement has a positive effect on children's academic achievement in general and reading achievement in particular. These reviews have found that parents can play a major role in children's academic success. Ann Henderson (1988), for example, concluded that parent involvement leads to improvements in student achievement, grades, test scores, and overall academic performance. Moreover, she concluded that parent involvement has the secondary but significant effect of improving community perception of school effectiveness and positively influencing the attitudes that families and educators have about one another. Results from nearly every National Assessment of Educational Progress have indicated that students who regularly participate in literacy-related activities with their families have higher levels of reading achievement than students whose parents are not actively involved in their reading. Similarly, an international study of reading instruction found that the "degree of parental cooperation" was the most potent of 56 significant characteristics of schools most successful in teaching reading (Postlethwaite & Ross, 1992).

Unfortunately, few schools or teachers make ongoing or consistent efforts to involve parents in children's reading. Many teachers have unsuccessful and unrewarding experiences when working with parents. Others believe they don't have time or energy for such a program when they seldom receive release time, remuneration, or recognition. Still other teachers feel uncomfortable around parents, who may question methods of instruction and assessment. Most parent involvement programs in reading tend to be one-shot affairs such as talks by local experts in reading, "make it and take it" workshops, prepackaged commercial programs, or short-term incentive programs. These approaches have little effect on students' reading achievement or attitudes. Still, when parental involvement receives active support from teachers and schools, takes place over the long term, promotes simple yet enjoyable activity, and offers parents ongoing communication and support from teachers, significant and positive results are possible. In fact, parent involvement can become a superb complement to school reading instruction.

In this chapter we discuss several important characteristics of successful parent involvement in reading programs. Using these characteristics as guidelines, teachers and schools can design their own parent involvement programs that meet their specific needs. The characteristics can also be used to design assessment instruments to evaluate existing programs.

Use Proven and Effective Strategies

Too often, teachers ask parents and children to do educational activities of questionable value for improving academic performance. Drawing and coloring pictures or cutting out photographs from magazines may not be poor activity choices, but they may not be the best use of parents and children's time together at home. The amount of time that parents can devote to working with their children is often limited. Therefore, teachers and schools should ensure that suggested at-home activities are based on proven and appropriate methods for achieving academic success in reading. Many of the methods and strategies we described in earlier chapters can be readily adapted for home use.

Provide Training, Communication, and Support

Most parents lack teachers' instructional expertise. They need good and understandable training that includes demonstrations and opportunities for discussion and questions. Someone who is enthusiastic about and committed to parent involvement should provide the training. Teachers need to understand the realities of busy family life and be sensitive to educational barriers that may impede parent–child reading activity. Some parents may feel uncomfortable reading aloud to their children because of their own real or perceived lack of reading ability. Parents of second-language learners may not themselves be fluent readers of English. Parents whose own educational experiences were negative may hesitate to attend school functions. Yet, these parents want to help their children succeed. The teacher's challenge, then, is to find meaningful ways for all families to tackle home reading activities. Making books on tape available or suggesting that parents and children "read" wordless books are two ways to promote all families' involvement. With some thought, resourceful teachers can find many more.

Continuing communication and support in various forms should give parents timely feedback to their questions and concerns. This may be a regular informative newsletter, monthly training and support sessions in the school, encouraging and taking phone calls from parents, sending home informative articles from professional journals that might interest parents, and creating a parent lounge/library in the school where parents and teachers can chat and find professional resources. Ongoing support builds bonds between home and school and demonstrates to parents that other people care.

In addition to communication from school to home, teachers need to foster ongoing communication from home to school. Parents know a lot about their children—their likes and dislikes, as well as how they respond to at-school instruction. Effective teachers not only make it a point to inform parents about what is going on in school and how they can help, but also regularly ask parents to share information about their children that may help them become better teachers. This may mean something as simple as a questionnaire for parents that accompanies each report card or a periodic call to parents in order to ask them how their children are responding at home to classroom reading instruction. When parents realize that the teacher values their opinions and their knowledge about their children, they are more likely to invest themselves in supporting school learning at home. When this happens, authentic partnerships develop.

Real Reading

If this book has one theme, it is that authentic reading leads to reading growth. The research on real reading is quite clear. One of the best helps parents of all ages can give children of any age is to read to them. Research tells us that parents and teachers who read to their children regularly tend to have children with larger vocabularies and better comprehension. Similarly, when parents read with their children or listen to their children read, children grow as readers. Reading material should be relatively easy or include enough support from parents that children can read with ease. These simple activities—read to, read with, and listen to children—are powerful ways to promote student growth in reading.

Make Activities Easy and Consistent

Parents tell us that parent involvement activities fail if they are too complex, take inordinate amounts of time, or change from day to day or week to week. They have trouble developing a routine of working with their children under these conditions. Even in the best of situations, parents' time is limited. With all their other obligations, they must carefully ration their home time and energy.

Therefore, the instructional activities that teachers send home for parents need to be simple and quick to implement. Because parents are usually unfamiliar with elaborate instructional schemes, it is best to focus on simple, successful activities with some variation to keep interest high. Such activities make it easier for parents and children to develop predictable, time-efficient routines. These, in turn, increase the likelihood that the at-home activities will be conducted regularly and successfully.

Make Reading Enjoyable

For parents and children to persist in academic tasks over the long term, the instructional activities must be enjoyable for everyone. First, have parents and children read authentic and exemplary reading material. Second, ensure that activities can be successfully implemented and completed. Third, infuse a sense of informality and playfulness into the activities. Parents and children need to have fun as they play with written language. Fourth, encourage parents to be enthusiastic, provide positive encouragement, and support their children's attempts to read. Fifth, the texts children read should be easy; or, if the texts are challenging, design sufficient support for parents to offer their children while reading so that the children will be successful. Practiced or repeated readings, having the children hear their parents read a text before they are asked to do so, and having children and parents read a text together and aloud are just a few ways to make a more challenging text easier for children to read. Finally, allow children some control over the activity. For example, parents can allow children to choose the material to be read in an activity. If the reading is followed by some word games, children can choose the games as well as the words to include. We think that the best type of parent involvement activities are those in which parents and children share ownership.

Provide Parents with Texts and Other Instructional Materials

Some parent involvement plans fail because parents lack adequate materials, the time or resources to acquire them, or knowledge of where to acquire appropriate materials. Even with explicit directions about materials acquisition, many parents will fail to have the right materials at the right time. The easiest solution is to provide parents and children with the materials. When the materials are present—whether they are books, poems, diaries, or games—parents are more likely to remember to do the activities with their children. The materials themselves act as reminders to parents to do the job.

Provide Ways to Document Home Activities

Documenting at-home activity permits teachers and schools to monitor parent–child involvement and evaluate the program's success in achieving its goal. More important, perhaps, documentation gives parents tacit encouragement and reminds them to continue reading with their children.

Usually, documentation can be accomplished with a log sheet on which parents record their work with their children over a specified period of time. Parents tell us that they post the sheet in a prominent place to remind them to do the activity. At the end of the time period the log sheets are returned to the school (see Figure 12.1).

Be Consistent Over the Long Term

In chapter 11 we discussed the importance of teachers developing instructional routines that consist of a set of effective teaching activities implemented regularly and consistently over an extended period of time. This same notion applies to at-home programs. Once an effective instructional routine is introduced, it is best to avoid major changes or disruptions in the parent-child routine. Rather, allow families to develop a level of comfort with activities you know are effective. Create variety by changing the texts and the ways in which parents and children respond to what they read.

With these guidelines in mind, teachers or school administrators can design programs for parent involvement in reading that effectively supplement the instruction students receive in school. When home and school collaborate to provide enjoyable and authentic reading experiences, students benefit because they have multiple daily opportunities to grow as readers.

Successful Parent Involvement Programs

Communication

Communication is key to any successful educational program, including at-home reading programs. Effective teachers keep parents apprised of children's growth in reading, describe classroom activities, and suggest at-home literacy activities. While communication between classroom and home can occur in several ways, we think that written communication, particularly in the form of a regular newsletter, is especially effective. By its nature, written communication is permanent. Parents can read and reread newsletters and post them in a place that allows easy access and referral.

FAST START READING LOG

_____ Name   _____SEPTEMBER–OCTOBER_____ Month

_____ School   *Please return this log to your child's

teacher at the end of the month.

Date	Time spent on Lesson	Name of New Passage Introduced	Other Reading Activities
9-28			
9-29			
9-30			
10-1			
10-2			
10-3			
10-4			
10-5			
10-6			
10-7			
10-8			
10-9			
10-10			
10-11			
10-12			
10-13			
10-14			
10-15			
10-16			
10-17			
10-18			
10-19			
10-20			
10-21			
10-22			
10-23			
10-24			
10-25			
10-26			
10-27			
10-28			
10-29			
10-30			

Figure 12.1

Home Reading Log

We know many Title I and classroom reading teachers who send monthly or semimonthly newsletters home to parents. The better letters share what the children have done in school and what they will be encountering shortly. Teachers also include articles that describe ways in which parents can help their children, lists or brief reviews of appropriate and exemplary books for children, and descriptions of specific literacy-related games and activities that parents can share with their children.

Some newsletters include articles that children write and photographs of children at work. These offer added incentives for parents and children to read the newsletters, and preparing the articles gives children added practice in reading and writing. For example, the Title I program in a school near us publishes a newsletter made up largely of articles written by students enrolled in the program (see Figure 12.2). The teacher reports that student work makes parents look forward to upcoming issues. "Once I have their eyes and ears, I can share with them some of the things they can do at home to promote their children's learning."

Newsletters should be personal and informative. The personal touch is best achieved by including student work or descriptions of individual students' accomplishments. The informative is achieved by including information that helps parents help their children read. Book lists, instructional ideas and strategies, answers to questions that parents frequently ask, news about upcoming meetings and speakers, and practical tips will help many parents better meet the reading needs and interests of their children.

Parental involvement in reading should involve authentic literacy activities.

READING

Right to Read Week
March 3 - 7

A POTPOURRI OF READING

A Parent's Response

As a parent of a child in Chapter I reading, I have taken the opportunity to check out some of the reading material Mrs. Liu has available for parents. One of the books I have read is titled "Read to Me: Raising Kids Who Love to Read" by Bernice Cullinan. This book shares with parents the importance of reading aloud to kids. It explains how reading aloud helps teach children to love books. It includes tips for how to expand a child's imagination through reading, how to use television wisely, and how to interest children in writing. I would recommend this book to parents so they recognize how reading aloud to kids influences their motivation to read.

Sincerely

Cheryl

Mom & Johnathan

AUTHOR, AUTHOR!

Author Amy D will present an evening program for Chapter I students and their parents on March 1st. Students and parents will have an opportunity to do creative writing together.

Books written by Amy include "Me and My Friends," "The Ghost Man," "The Squirrel's Dinner," "No Homes," and others.

Figure 12.2
Reading Newsletter

The Moral of the Story is . . .

The farmer and the little boy think that nothing ever happens in the stories of *Hill of Fire* and *The Boy Who Cried Wolf*. The farmer and the little boy were bored. In the *Hill of Fire* there was a big explosion. In *The Boy Who Cried Wolf* the wolf came to eat the sheep for lunch. The people in the village got away to safety but the wolf ate the boy's sheep. I liked *The Boy Who Cried Wolf* the best because it was funny and the boy tricked the fisherman and the hunters.

by Rosa

Nobody believed the boy when he cried "wolf." The hunters and the fisherman believed him at first but after they were tricked and there really was a wolf, the sheep were eaten.

by Robert

I will never tell a lie so that I won't get in trouble because it is not fun.

Heidi

It is better to tell the truth because people will believe what you say when you tell the truth.

by Jo

Figure 12.2, *Continued*

A POTPOURRI OF READING

FUN READING
I Love A Story

Mouse Soup by Jacob S.

The mouse was reading a book under a tree. A wolf was behind a tree and caught the mouse and brought it home. The wolf put the mouse in a cage to save for supper. The mouse told the wolf four stories. The wolf believed the stories and got into trouble. The mouse got away.

The story was make-believe. The wolf should not have listened to the mouse.

George and Martha

The best part of the story was story number three. The Tub. George peeked in on Martha. It was funny.

By Kanika

Dreams
Hold fast to dreams
For if dreams die
Life is a broken-winged bird
That cannot fly.
Hold fast to dreams
for when dreams go
Life is a barren field
Covered with snow.

Langston Hughes

Poetry Surprise

I like to go sledding in the middle of winter.
Going down the hill at the cemetery, I hit the big snow ramp.
Elbows hitting the ground, I go up in the air—the best part.

Sijo —This verse pattern was developed in Korea. Its structure has three lines with 14 to 16 syllables to each line.

by Mathew

Figure 12.2, *Continued*

Make sure your newsletters avoid talking down to parents. Many parents complain that they feel intimidated or are made to feel inadequate at their children's schools. Newsletters should be informal and conversational, highlighting the notion of partnerships between home and school. (See Appendix M for an example of an introductory letter to parents.)

Encouragement and Incentive Programs

We discussed some incentive programs in chapter 3 as approaches to improving students' attitudes and motivation to read. The home is a great place to help nurture student reading, and incentive programs may offer a good connection between home and school.

Pizza Hut's *Book It* is a well-known incentive program designed to promote recreational reading. In the program, students read books on their own and receive certificates for pizzas if they meet certain teacher-established goals.

Book It is a nationwide program, but local reading encouragement programs can also be devised. Some teachers and schools contact local businesses to elicit support for at-home reading programs. A schoolwide project, called Reading Millionaires (O'Masta & Wolf, 1991) began when the staff at Diablo Elementary School in the Panama Region Department of Defense Schools wanted to increase students' out-of-school reading. They set a goal for students: reading for a million minutes by the end of the school year. An informational flier and newsletters about the program were sent to parents, who were asked to play an integral part in the project. Parents monitored children's reading at home, encouraged home reading, read to their children, and completed periodic reading logs of the number of minutes that children had read. Time spent reading to children also counted.

A display chart at school showed progress toward the reading goal. Teachers and the school principal constantly encouraged the children to read at home. In the end, they achieved their goal. Students felt a sense of community accomplishment, student reading at home increased and remained high throughout the school year, and parents felt better about helping their children in reading.

Similar programs have demonstrated similar results. Shanahan, Wojciechowski, and Rubik (1998) report that their school's year-long program to encourage students to read for a million minutes at home resulted in more reading, better reading, more interest in reading for students, and parents' greater enthusiasm for reading at home. One parent wrote at the end of the program that her two children "read more this year than ever before. Their interest in books was greater as were the variety of books they chose. They read more challenging books and were eager to discuss the stories and authors who wrote them. They became so well versed in a topic that I felt I was actually learning from them. Please continue this program . . . " (p. 96).

Paired Reading

Paired Reading, a reading-support program, is described in chapter 5. Although less able students can be matched with more proficient classmates, older students, teachers, parent volunteers, or other reasonably proficient readers, the program was initially intended for parents and children (Topping, 1987; 1995). In Paired Reading, parent and child sit side by side and read one text aloud together. (The child chooses the text.) The reading is done at a comfortable rate for the child, and either the parent or child points to the text as they read to draw both readers' attention to the print. In places where children feel comfortable reading alone, they signal parents nonverbally (perhaps with a nudge of an elbow). Parents stop reading aloud but continue to follow the reading and begin to read again if necessary. When children come to unfamiliar words and cannot decode them after a reasonable period, the parents simply say the words and the reading continues. Parents work with their children 5 to 10 minutes daily.

In England, where Paired Reading was first developed as a parent involvement program, research shows it to be a powerful method for improving students' reading. Students engaged in Paired Reading made gains in word recognition and comprehension three to five times above previous gains. That is an impressive achievement, especially given the small amount of time involved in the program.

Several schools in North America have incorporated Paired Reading as a parent involvement program. At Robinson School, an inner-city school, parents are invited to learn about Paired Reading at the beginning of each year. Because Robinson has used the program for several years, parents know about it and are anxious to participate. The gymnasium is full when the Title I teachers Sandra, Gail, and Nancy introduce Paired Reading in an hour-long training session that includes a live demonstration, a videotaped description and demonstration, and an explanation of how the program works at Robinson. Parents try out Paired Reading with their children during this training session while the teachers provide feedback. Parents learn that students choose books to bring home. They also learn to work daily with their children; to maintain a monthly log of their Paired Reading; and to contact Sandra, Gail, or Nancy if they have questions about how Paired Reading works. Parents receive a packet of information about the program for future reference. They sign a contract in which they agree to do Paired Reading with their children throughout the school year. The contracts, along with photographs of the children and parents taken at this session, are displayed on a bulletin board in a prominent location in the school.

Sandra, Nancy, and Gail consider Paired Reading a parent involvement program that actually works. Nancy says, "It works because parents know how they can help their children in a way that's easy, fun, and doesn't take the whole evening." Jackie, another veteran Title I teacher in the same school district, gives Paired Reading an enthusiastic and unconditional thumbs up:

"Paired Reading and Reading Recovery are the best things to have happened in the remedial reading programs" (Rasinski & Fredericks, 1991, p. 515).

Fast Start in Reading

Fast Start is a program we developed at Kent State University for involving parents of young readers (kindergarten through grade 2) and struggling readers. In Fast Start parents read short, highly predictable passages with their children. We have found that rhyming poetry, nursery rhymes, jokes and riddles for children, and short vignettes work well. Each day parents and their children spend about 15 minutes on one of the passages. What we ask of parents is specific and based on effective instructional principles:

1. The parent reads the passage to the child, and they talk about its content.

2. Parent and child read the passage together until the child is able to read it alone.

3. The parent listens to the child read and gives encouragement, support, and praise.

4. Parent and child choose a word or two from the passage, write them on index cards, add them to their word bank, and engage in word play and word bank activities. (See chapter 4 for a description of making and using word banks and word sorts.)

School personnel invite parents to attend Fast Start training sessions at the beginning of the school year. Several sessions are offered at each school, morning and evening, so that parents can choose which session to attend. We have found that this active encouragement and flexible scheduling helps more parents attend the meetings. We consistently have 85 to 100 percent participation in the training/introductory sessions. Parents leave the sessions with informational packets, enough passages for one month, and log forms for recording their work with their children. Each month from October through May, teachers send home new sets of readings and new log sheets. They also write and distribute a newsletter that answers common questions and concerns about the program, re-explains the program, describes other activities related to reading, and lists grade-appropriate books for children. Figures 12.3 and 12.4 show examples of Fast Start materials.

Parent participation in Fast Start has been exceptionally high, and student growth in reading is apparent and significant, especially among children who are most at risk for reading problems (Rasinski, 1995; Rasinski & Loudin, 1997; Stevenson, 2001). In as little as one month, we have detected noticeable and significant improvement in students' reading and word recognition when compared with students not part of the Fast Start program but receiving extra tutoring in reading. Recently, we worked with teachers in Seiberling Elementary School in Akron to implement Fast Start in kindergarten and first

Fast Start in Reading

Newsletter #1
Timothy Rasinski
Kent State University

Welcome to the **Fast Start in Reading** program. **Fast Start** is a simple yet effective way for parents to help their first grade children get off to a fast start in reading. Together with the instruction in reading your child receives in school, the Fast Start program helps to lay a solid foundation for continual growth and enjoyment in reading for your child. Parents are important, and in Fast Start parents are asked to work with their children a few minutes each day in a way that is enjoyable for both parents and children.

Fast Start employs short, highly readable passages that children will learn easily. Familiar rhymes, poetry, and other fun-to-read short passages form the core of materials that parents and children read in Fast Start.

The key activities in Fast Start are actually quite simple and easy to follow. We ask that you follow these four steps in every lesson.

1) Read the passage to your child.
2) Read the passage with your child.
3) Listen to your child read to you.
4) Choose and practice words from the passage.

This four-step procedure is extremely effective, in conjunction with regular classroom instruction, in helping children learn to read at an accelerated pace and diminishing the need for corrective or remedial instruction. Children who have been in the Fast Start program for as few as 4 weeks have demonstrated marked improvements in their reading as measured by various reading tests.

General Plan for Fast Start

In the Fast Start program, parents are asked to work with their children for about 10 minutes per day, every day. We realize that it isn't possible to work every single day with your child. Nevertheless, we want to set this as a goal and hope that all parents involved in Fast Start will be able to work with their first-grade child as much as possible.

We ask that you work with your child every day for about 10 minutes. The schedule for introducing new passages is as follows:

Monday: Introduce and read new reading passage or rhyme.
Tuesday: Introduce and read a second new passage.
Wednesday: Review and reread passages from Monday and Tuesday.
Thursday: Introduce and read a third new passage.
Friday: Introduce and read a fourth new passage.
Saturday and Sunday: Review passages introduced during the week.

We hope you will be able to keep as close to this schedule as possible throughout the year. Although you are asked to work each day with your child, the amount of time you need to devote to the Fast Start readings is only about 10 minutes. Remember, one of the most important aspects of this program—one that accounts for children's great progress in reading—is the consistent daily interaction between parent and child in reading.

In addition to doing the Fast Start program with your child throughout the school year, it is important that parents encourage and invite their children into reading in other ways as well. These other ways include reading interesting books to your child every day, making regular visits to the library to allow your child to choose books, having plenty of books and other reading materials around your home for you child to read, allowing your child to write by keeping a journal or diary, composing letters and notes to others, writing his or her own stories, providing your child with interesting experiences and discussing them with your child, and allowing your child to dictate stories to you that you then write down and read together. Above all, make sure your child knows that ***you think reading is important and fun.*** The best way to share your enthusiasm is to read to your child every day and talk about what you read together.

Figure 12.3

Fast Start in Reading Newsletter

Daily Fast Start Lesson

Parents: Please
1)   Read the rhyme to your child
2)   Read it with your child
3)   Listen to your child read
4)   Word play—write interesting words from the rhyme on this sheet; expand to other related words (dock—sock, rock, block)

Hickory, dickory, dock,
The mouse ran up the clock.
The clock struck one,
The mouse ran down,
Hickory, dickory, dock.

Figure 12.4
Daily Fast Start Lesson

grade. Results indicated that children who participated regularly made substantial and significant gains in reading achievement. Moreover, we found that both parents and children thoroughly enjoyed the passages that they read and the reading activities that they did as part of the Fast Start program.

The program is relatively inexpensive and time efficient. The major cost is duplication, and the major time commitment for teachers is in the initial training sessions. Fast Start has demonstrated to us that parents really do want to help their children in reading. In many cases, they just need to know what to do or what materials and programs to choose. When schools involve parents in a systematic way, using effective methods of instruction and providing support, materials, and communication, children make substantial and significant progress as readers.

Backpack Programs

Providing books, materials, and activities is critical to successful parent involvement. Backpack programs, in which students bring the materials and

Traveling Tales Instructions

Dear Parent(s),

Home writing activities are a great way to improve your child's reading and writing development. Traveling Tales is a backpack that includes a variety of writing materials for you to use with your child. We encourage you to work together with your child to create a story that we can share and enjoy at school.

Your child has been given this backpack for two nights. If you need more time, please call us at 672-2836.

We hope these guidelines will help you have a successful and enjoyable Traveling Tales experience with your child.

1. With your child, brainstorm a list of ideas or topics for writing. Ask questions that will invite your child to express ideas, interests, feelings, etc., about which he or she may wish to write. Stories about personal experiences (factual or fictional), information stories that tell of something your child finds interesting, stories about family members or others, and stories of science or history are great topics.

2. Next, help your child decide which of the writing materials included in the Traveling Tales backpack he or she will use to create the story. Suggest that the story may take several different forms. Some ideas include: (a) poetry, (b) fold-out book, (c) a play or skit, (d) puppet play, (e) dialogue, (f) pocket book, (g) backward book, and (h) shape book.

3. Help your child plan the story before beginning writing. You may wish to write down some of the ideas your child expresses for him or her to use in writing the first draft.

4. Remember, your child's first draft is a rough draft. It is all right for it to contain misspellings, poor handwriting, and incomplete ideas. Be available to answer questions as your child works on the first draft. Be careful to encourage him or her to keep writing and not worry about spelling, punctuation, etc. Ask your child just to do his or her best. Both of you can work on correctness later. Now is the time to develop ideas for writing.

5. Once the first draft is done, try to involve others at home by asking them to listen to it read aloud. Reading one's writing aloud helps writers determine the sense of the message. Be sure to tell those who listen to be encouraging rather than critical and to ask questions about ideas that were unclear or were poorly developed. Questions help a writer think about his or her writing without feeling bad.

6. Write out questions and suggestions made by the home audience. Talk with your child about how a second draft could use these suggestions to make the story easier to understand or more interesting. Remember to be supportive and encouraging! Offer your help, but encourage your child to make his or her best own efforts first.

7. After the second draft is completed, your child may want to read his or her writing to the family again for their response. If not, it is time to edit the writing. Now is the time to correct spellings, punctuation, etc. Praise your child for his or her attempts and tell your child that you want to help make his or her writing the best it can be. Show your child which words are misspelled and explain why. Do the same with punctuation and capitalization.

8. With the editing complete, the writing is ready to be revised for the final time. When writing the final draft, encourage your child to use neat handwriting. Feel free to help your child at any point during final revisions.

9. Once finished, encourage your family to listen to the final story and respond positively. This practice will help instill confidence in your child as he or she shares his or her writing at school.

10. We invite you to come to school with your child, if possible, to share the writing you have done together. Your child will appreciate the support, and we would enjoy talking with you.

Thank you for your help. We appreciate your involvement. If you are unable to come to school with your child, please call us or send a note with your child. We will be glad to call back or visit with you. Thanks again for your support. We hope you enjoy writing with your child!

Sincerely,

Ms. Robinson

Figure 12.5
Traveling Tales Instructions

Materials for the Traveling Tales Backpack	
Instructions and ideas in a notebook	Small stapler
Plain, unlined paper	Staples
Lined paper	Brass fasteners
Construction paper—multiple colors	Card stock
Drawing paper	Hole punch
Poster paper	Yarn
Crayons	Wallpaper for book covers
Watercolors	Glue stick
Water-base markers	Tape
Colored pencils	Paperclips
Pencils	Ruler
Felt-tip pens	Letter stencils
Scissors	Examples of other books done by students and parents

Figure 12.6

Contents of the Traveling Tales Backpack

Note: From "Traveling Tales: Connecting parents and children through writing," D. R. Reutzel, & P. C. Fawson, 1990, *The Reading Teacher, 44,* 222–227.

activities home with them, capitalize on this characteristic. Ray Reutzel and Parker Fawson (1990) describe a backpack program called Traveling Tales. Teachers develop backpacks that contain materials for writing, from various types of paper, to rulers and paper clips, to a letter of introduction and direction for parents (see Figures 12.5 and 12.6). The letter explains the program and invites parents to write a story with their children. It provides details for parents and children about the various stages of the writing process. When the writing is complete, parents come to school with their child and share the story. The backpack then goes home with the next child. Reutzel and Fawson found that parents were eager for specific guidance in working with their children and valued close working relationships with school personnel.

The Reutzel and Fawson model readily adapts for reading. Teachers decide what sort of activity to invite parents and children to do together, gather materials that allow parents and children to complete the activity successfully at home, provide parents with appropriate directions for the activity, and develop a management system that allows every family access to the backpack for enough time to complete the activity.

Many teachers consider backpack programs a great way to introduce parents to more extensive parent involvement activities. But even if this is the only parent involvement a teacher or school offers, everyone benefits. Parents have access to solid and enjoyable reading and writing activities as well as appropriate directions and materials. Children read and write in the warm, supportive environment of their home with their parents.

Remember, too, that students' at-school reading and writing activities can also work at home with only minor modifications, if any, and with some support and direction from the teacher. For example, children can be expected to read at home daily for a designated period of time. Nursery rhymes and childhood songs and chants that develop phonemic awareness can be shared between children and their parents. Parents can take dictation (language experience activity) from their children, and children can read the collaborative composition with their parents. Parents can keep dialogue journals with their children. Parents and children can talk about the books or stories children read in school. We have found that parents will go far to help their children, if they have the support and encouragement of teachers.

Although parent involvement may not be a cure-all for every difficulty that children encounter in reading, we know that it does make a difference—in some cases, a huge difference. Whether you are a classroom teacher or a special reading teacher, we strongly recommend that you strive to involve parents actively in children's literacy development. The potential benefits are simply too great to pass up.

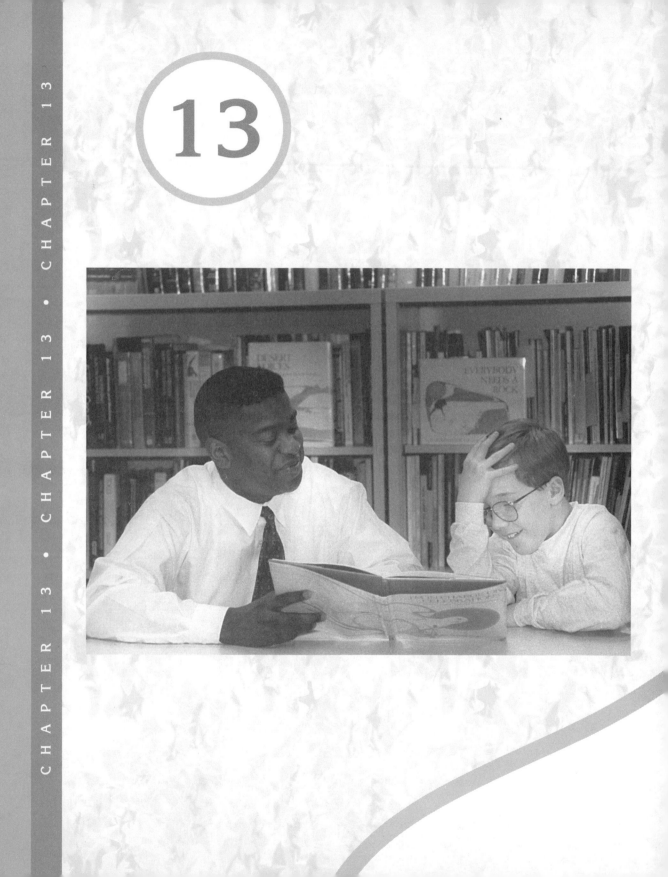

Determining Instructional Needs: Assessing Readers in Action

Sally Burtch's elementary school created a pre-first-grade class for students thought to be at risk for success in first grade. Sally volunteered to teach the class. During the summer before the new program began, Sally gathered available information about her students: their readiness test scores and brief anecdotal notes from their kindergarten teachers. As Sally examined the children's records, she realized that she had a problem—she didn't really know any of her students as readers or people. She worried about creating a classroom environment that would respond to children's needs with no idea of what those needs might be.

Sally considered what she needed to know about the children and how best to learn it. She wanted more than test scores because "when we contrive a reading or writing task, setting the topic and the purposes for reading or writing, what we observe may bear little resemblance to students' natural reading and writing behavior" (Rhodes & Dudley-Marling, 1988, p. 36). Sally, interested in these natural literacy behaviors, turned to the kindergarten teachers' anecdotal notes. She valued her colleagues' opinions but knew that her classroom would be different from theirs and that classroom contexts influence children's actions as readers. She also knew that her students would change over the summer.

Sally finally decided to create a reading portfolio for each student. An artist's portfolio is a sample of work collected to demonstrate the artist's breadth, depth, and flexibility. Likewise, a reader's portfolio is a sample of information about the reader. During the first few weeks of school, Sally began to develop reading portfolios for each child by observing, talking, and collecting reading and writing samples. During choice time, for example, she watched to see who would choose to read or write. During read-aloud time, she noted who paid attention and appeared to enjoy the story. She talked with children to discover their interest in books; these conversations also allowed her to evaluate their oral language development. She combined the insights she developed with other available information, such as the kindergarten teacher's notes and standardized test scores. In this way, she gained an in-depth and valuable perspective about each student as a reader and a person, which helped her develop a literacy program responsive to children's needs and interests.

Sally's situation was a bit atypical; after all, she was planning a new program. In many ways, however, her problem is one we all face. We need ways to find out about students as readers—what kinds of instructional opportunities to provide for them, what progress they are making, and what that progress means in terms of future instruction. These are important issues for all students but are particularly critical for struggling readers.

We believe that typical instruction offers many valuable opportunities to learn about students as readers. Throughout this book, we describe reading as the process of constructing meaning. We also detail several factors that influence reading, such as background knowledge, perceived purpose, instructional expectations, and type of materials or activities. All these factors vary among children, of course. But even for one child, they may vary throughout the school day or from one day to the next. This variation provides a strong rationale for basing assessment on daily routines.

In this chapter we develop that rationale. We also describe several informal, classroom-based techniques and strategies for learning about children who find reading difficult. We provide concrete suggestions for implementing each technique. Our overall goal is to present several systematic assessment and evaluation strategies that can serve as alternatives or additions to formal and informal tests. Rich descriptions of children involved in the day-to-day business of being readers can yield useful instructional insights.

The Classroom as Setting, the Reader as Informant

More and more often, teachers are turning to informal, in-process assessment and evaluation techniques to help them understand and plan instruction for struggling readers. This shift partly reflects advances in our understandings about the processes of reading and learning to read. We know that the reading process is fluid and flexible rather than static. We also know that children become readers in a variety of ways, with different learning tempos, and by using different strategies and styles when interacting with text.

For these reasons, many teachers and reading researchers (for example, Harp, 1994; Rhodes & Shanklin, 1993; Valencia & Pearson, 1987) question the assumptions that underlie standardized tests. They ask, "If the reading process is fluid, and growth in reading ability idiosyncratic, how can a single measure designed to compare students with each other (or to some prescribed set of expectations) provide useful instructional information?" Like many others seeking to understand at-risk readers, we think the answer is simple: Standardized tests alone cannot help teachers understand and assist struggling readers.

We know that standardized tests are facts of school life. Indeed, their use has proliferated during the past decade, and test results often figure in "high stakes" decisions such as student promotion or high school graduation. For these reasons, many teachers help students prepare for the particular type of comprehension they must demonstrate on standardized tests, which feature shorter (and often less interesting and engaging) text selections than students are accustomed to and response modes aimed toward "one right answer."

These tests may give an overall snapshot of how a class of students is doing in reading; however, from a teacher's instructional perspective, the results aren't terribly useful. Suppose Jeremy earned a stanine score of 3 on a standardized reading test or a percentile rank of 40. What should his teacher do to promote his reading achievement?

Fortunately, alternatives to standardized testing are available. In developing many of the techniques and strategies described in this chapter, we have borrowed ideas from naturalistic inquiry and qualitative research methods. The goal of naturalistic inquiry is to understand something from the perspective of those involved in the activity. Thus, our goal is to understand reading from the child's point of view. To achieve this goal, we need an evaluation plan.

A first step in developing the plan involves deciding where assessment should take place and what kinds of reading tasks children should complete as part of the assessment. We recommend that assessment and evaluation take place *in* the classroom rather than outside it. Moreover, assessment should focus on authentic (classroom-like) reading activities rather than artificial ones. Ideally, assessment and evaluation should be natural parts of the continuous learning process in classrooms. Indeed, good assessment methods maximize instruction and involve children in real reading activities (Tierney, 1998).

Next, we must decide whose opinions to seek. Because they are active participants who know students and activities better than anyone else, knowledgeable teachers may be the best evaluators. But in addition to the teacher, struggling readers should have some say in evaluating their own growth. In fact, students' ideas and opinions are crucial information in any assessment or evaluation. Self-evaluation can benefit both students and the teacher. Students can begin to take responsibility for their own learning, and teachers can learn about instruction from their students' points of view.

These ideas make good conceptual sense, and they also allay some of our concerns about conventional evaluation techniques. Beyond acknowledging their good sense, we must also find ways to implement these ideas. Assessment and evaluation plans aimed at creating reading portfolios for children who find reading difficult can provide a framework for successful implementation.

The Value of Portfolio Assessment

Portfolios can document what students think and do in situations involving reading. Teachers who use portfolios formulate questions about struggling readers and look to naturally occurring events in their classrooms to provide answers. They value the insights and interpretations that emerge from this process and realize that parents, children's previous teachers, and even friends can also be good sources of information about a child.

Successful portfolio assessment takes some initial planning, as the overview in Figure 13.1 shows. First, we must generate questions to be answered. These questions may relate to broad curricular goals or hunches about at-risk readers based on preliminary observations. Questions may be general: "What does Janey know about reading? What evidence shows that

Figure 13.1

An Overview of Assessment

- **Generate questions based on the following:**
    Broad curricular goals
    Observations
    Hunches

- **Decide on forms of evidence:**
    Observation
    Interaction
    Analysis

- **Develop a systematic and comprehensive plan for gathering information from and with the following sources:**
    Students
    Parents
    Other teachers
    Peers
    Yourself

- **Analyze information:**
    Look for patterns
    Form hypotheses

she is developing as a reader?" Or they may be more specific: "In what areas is Mikey experiencing reading difficulty?" "What does Ricky do when he encounters an unknown word?" Either way, theoretical understandings about reading and learning are critical. Just as a reading portfolio provides the physical framework for assessment and evaluation, the teacher's theoretical beliefs about reading and learning to read provide the conceptual framework.

Questions provide a focus for deciding upon the contents of the portfolio. The next step in planning involves deciding what kind of evidence belongs in the portfolio and how to obtain it. A student's reading portfolio might contain anecdotal notes and records of observations, conversations, and interviews; checklists or charts kept by the teacher or the student; and performance samples documenting reading behaviors and abilities. A variety of other documents may also be helpful in understanding the child as a reader: lists of books read, written self-evaluations, notes from parents, report cards or progress cards, records of at-home reading, tape recordings of oral reading, or selections from reading-response journals (Maxim & Five, 1997). All this variety means that teachers and students will create portfolios to fit the environments in which they teach and learn.

Whatever the focus and content of portfolios, the plan for gathering information must be systematic and comprehensive. Four broad kinds of activities can provide information for portfolios:

1. *Observation.* Teachers watch what struggling readers do, either independently or with others. The teachers are not directly involved but only observe.

2. *Conversations or interviews.* Informal conversations or planned reading conferences offer opportunities to talk with students in depth.

3. *Performance samples.* Lists of books read or written products such as excerpts from reading logs or notes made during instructional activities can yield useful information.

4. *Assessment activities.* Activities undertaken for assessment purposes, such evaluating oral reading for fluency or word recognition, can complement other information.

Each of these assessment activities can be formal; for example, teachers might plan specific times or activities for observation. Each can also be informal and incidental as teachers and students naturally come into contact during a school day. They can even occur simultaneously: Observing an interesting situation might lead to a conversation or some diagnostic teaching as the teacher seeks to understand the student more completely.

Standardized tests are often described in terms of their validity and reliability. The value of portfolio assessment can be determined by thinking about the same concepts. An assessment or evaluation is valid if it offers a true picture of the issue under study. Certainly, information gathered in natural classroom settings has the potential to offer true pictures of students as readers. Moreover, teachers ensure the reliability or consistency of portfolio data by developing a systematic and comprehensive plan for developing the portfolio. Thus, the diagnostic insights that emerge through portfolio analysis and interpretation yield valid and reliable conclusions about struggling readers.

The Importance of Observation

The best situations for assessing or evaluating attitudes, thoughts, and behaviors are integral parts of day-to-day instruction. This view of the relationship between assessment and instruction suggests the importance of observation as a tool for understanding struggling readers. Opportunities for observation are abundant. Over the course of any day, effective teachers observe in a variety of reading situations from free-choice activities through informal and incidental encounters with reading to more formal instructional situations. We learn a great deal about students by observing them as they read, write, and respond to instruction.

Yetta Goodman (1985) calls this approach "kidwatching." The informal name is purposeful because kidwatching is an informal but systematic process that aims to record naturally occurring behaviors in reading situations. Effective kidwatchers share a few critical beliefs and skills. First, they believe in observation as a valid and valuable tool for learning about struggling readers. They also believe that their own judgment is critical as they watch what children do, listen to what they say, and make decisions about

Good assessment demands close observation of students during reading.

what these observations mean. In other words, kidwatchers are comfortable as professional decision makers. Finally, kidwatchers are skilled observers who use several means of gathering and recording information. In the following sections we explore each of these characteristics in more detail.

Why Kidwatching?

This question has at least two good answers—one related to the nature of language use, the other to the nature of language learning. Harste, Woodward, and Burke (1984) describe the social nature of language use: "Language, whether oral or written, is a social event of some complexity. Language did not develop because of the existence of one language user, but of two. If we are to understand language, we must see it as an orchestrated transaction between [at least] two language users which has as its intent to convey meaning" (p. 28). Unlike more formal assessment procedures, kidwatching allows a teacher to record these natural and social language events for later examination and analysis.

Language use and language learning are also situational. Language and concepts grow and develop depending on the settings in which they occur and students' experiences in those settings—including interactions with texts, the teacher, and each other (Goodman, 1985). Kidwatching allows teachers to explore what happens when readers interact with genuine texts for real purposes. Moreover, the information derived from this sort of observation is easier to apply to instructional situations.

Professional Judgment in Making Diagnostic Decisions

Through kidwatching, we can learn about students as readers and develop insights about the effect of instruction on their growth. Professional judgment allows us to translate these observations into instructional improvements. Effective kidwatchers are comfortable making educational decisions. They trust their own professional judgment, even in the face of conflicting information. Unfortunately, many teachers lack this faith in their own judgment.

Sue is one such teacher. Not too long ago, we visited an elementary school for a day. During the lunch hour, we overheard a conversation between Sue and John, two fifth-grade teachers who were chatting about the results of the district-mandated standardized testing they had just received. The conversation went something like this:

Sue: I was really surprised by some of these results.

John: Me too.

Sue: Take Andy, for instance. I thought he was a pretty good reader. It seems as if he's always got his nose in a book. And the things he shares during our discussions are usually good—pretty insightful, actually.

Sue and John chatted about the results of the district-mandated testing program.

John: So?

Sue: Well, the test says he's reading at the 18th percentile. I wonder if I should ask Ms. D [the Title I teacher] to take a look at him.

Why didn't Sue trust her own observations about Andy? Why did she assume that he might need extra help in reading? We suspect that she does not trust her own professional judgment.

We also suspect that Sue is not alone. Where do these professional insecurities come from? Some people believe that researchers, theoreticians, and policymakers have sent negative messages about teachers' professionalism that have caused us to lose faith in ourselves (Harste, 1989). Professional uncertainty may also relate to an unexamined belief in the truth of statistical information such as standardized test scores. Yetta Goodman (1989) notes:

> Because numbers take on an aura of objectivity, which they do not intrinsically deserve, statistical data are equated with the development of knowledge and are valued more highly than the sense of an informed, committed professional who uses knowledge about the students, the community, and the context to make judgments. (p. 6)

Whatever the causes, teachers have traditionally received little respect as thinkers and decision makers. Therefore, educators who wish to become effective kidwatchers must learn to exercise professional judgment and trust themselves as decision makers (Tierney, 1998). To do so may involve considering, and perhaps altering, two sets of attitudes: attitudes toward themselves and attitudes toward their students.

Teachers who trust their professional judgment are a bit like detectives. They constantly and carefully observe, looking for clues to answer their questions about students. Like detectives, they base observations on the enormous amount of information they already have about students and the classroom community as well as their analyses of students' reading behavior. They are also careful not to jump to conclusions. They continually ask, "What do I think this means? What else might this mean?" They generate hypotheses about students and test them out. Experience with this process helps them learn to trust the results of their efforts.

Evidence of growth is often revealed through students' errors, so teachers' attitudes toward errors are also important. Dictionaries define *error* as "a usually ignorant or unintentional deviation." Wise kidwatchers acknowledge the occasional careless mistake but largely view errors as windows to students' current ways of thinking about language. They look for changes in patterns of errors as signs that students are developing as readers.

Brenda, a Title I teacher at the primary level, is a kidwatcher. Early in each school year, she gathers several samples of her students' oral reading behaviors, which she uses to determine how students deal with unknown words—an important developmental hurdle for young readers. Last year, she found several students who were "phonics bound": sounding words out seemed to be their only word identification strategy. Their oral reading errors or miscues (see Performance Samples section for more information) tended to look and sound like text words but often changed the author's meaning completely. Some children even made up nonsense words.

Brenda did not assume that these miscues were careless. Instead, she hypothesized that children were doing what they knew how to do or what they thought they should be doing. She made a conscious effort to help them broaden their repertoire for identifying words. She emphasized combining context ("What would make sense here?") with what the children already knew about phonics. After several weeks of instruction, Brenda made another informal check of her students' word identification strategies. She found evidence of growth in flexible use of strategies. Children were beginning to correct miscues that made no sense or changed the author's meaning.

Several of Brenda's actions and decisions are good examples of professional judgment. First, she understood the importance of gathering data about her Title I students in authentic reading situations. She knew that samples of children's oral reading obtained over several sessions could yield insights about their word identification strategies. Further, she viewed miscues as opportunities to explore how the children were currently organizing things (Goodman, 1985). She saw qualitative differences in errors—that is, patterns of graphophonically similar but nonsense miscues told her something different from patterns of self-corrections. She used her own professional judgment to make diagnostic decisions.

Professional judgment is critical to kidwatching, which in turn is key to effective observation. Professional judgment is at its best when teachers combine their concrete knowledge about the classroom and particular students with their theoretical knowledge about how students learn, what language is, and how language develops. This combination provides a useful framework for assessing struggling readers.

Observing Throughout the School Day

Effective kidwatchers are experts at recognizing and interpreting patterns of behavior. They differentiate between recurring behaviors and isolated ones. Patterns become evident when teachers observe over time and in various reading and reading-related activities. This, of course, requires a plan. Merriam (1998) describes general aspects of an event or situation that may be important for an observer to record. She also suggests questions that can help focus the observer's attention.

- *The participants.* Who's there? What are they doing? How are they working together? Although the struggling reader's behaviors may be the focal point for observation, it is equally important to note who else is in the general vicinity and what all the participants are doing.

- *Activities and interactions.* What's happening? What's the sequence of activities? How do people interact with the activity and each other? This is a particularly important aspect of an event or situation to note. Most of us have variable attitudes toward reading; we enjoy some reading activities and dislike others. Our students are no different. When we watch children within the context of particular reading activities, we can often discover the circumstances that promote and detract from positive reading experiences.

- *Frequency and duration.* How long does the activity last? Does it happen often? These questions can apply to indicators of student behavior in reading. For example, the teacher might note how frequently students choose to read during free periods or how long they sustain interest in reading on different days in different situations.

- *Subtle factors.* What unplanned, spontaneous events occur? What nonverbal signs and signals can be observed? These aspects can be revealing. Students who enjoy reading books, for example, may be impatient with disruptions when they are reading. Students who enjoy neither reading nor their books may be pleased with disruptions. To help understand subtle factors, talk with a student: "You look puzzled. What's the matter?" Effective kidwatchers are good listeners as well as keen observers.

Attention to all these aspects of classroom reading need not be complex or difficult. Observations can be brief; a few occasional minutes of concentrated effort ought to provide adequate data.

Matt, who offers extra support in the regular classroom for intermediate-grade students with learning disabilities, has been relying on observation for several years. He is particularly interested in watching his students interact with others.

> I watch pretty intensively at the beginning of a school year so I can get a feel for what students might need, and then I do "spot-checks" throughout the year. If I see something that surprises me, either good or bad, I observe more carefully again. It took me a while to get the hang of observing, especially organizing what I'd written, but I am convinced that I now know lots more about my students. And that makes it easier for me to help them, so the time and effort are worth it to me.

Techniques and Strategies

Karen Dalrymple (1989) is a kidwatcher. Here's how she describes the process as it operates in her classroom: "The ability to observe and record student learning, assess that learning, and make decisions about what experiences to offer a student is critical to my teaching. Good records allow easy reporting about an individual student; but they also reflect and store the many observations [a teacher] makes" (p. 115). Good records may take several forms, which we describe in this section. Information gleaned from any or all of these methods, when added to a student's reading portfolio, adds depth and detail to the picture of the student as a reader.

Anecdotal Notes

One way to learn about a struggling reader is to keep anecdotal records about informal, unplanned observations and the results of instruction. As all teachers know, classrooms are busy places; without making notes, important incidents are easily forgotten. Additionally, anecdotal notes guide instructional planning. We assess instructional impact as we plot students' progress in anecdotal notes and records.

Although any time can be the right time for making anecdotal notes, a plan or framework aids note taking. Using classroom routines as a framework for observation helps yield a representative sample of how children take advantage of classroom opportunities. (See chapter 2 for more about routines.) Teachers also need to consider the format for their anecdotal notes and records. Ultimately, this is an individual decision. Experiment with formats; fortunately, you have plenty of options to choose from.

Some teachers keep notebooks for recording general impressions of children or make brief observations on sticky notes or large adhesive-backed labels. Later, they expand on their notes and transfer them to students' portfolios. Jacobson (1989) uses a three-column sheet of paper for recording significant anecdotal information in her classroom. The columns are labeled "goals," "observations," and "instructional plans." This format allows her to make both objective ("What do I see or hear?") and subjective ("What do I think this means?") notes, which researchers suggest can yield more useful records (Merriam, 1998; Patton, 1990).

At the Fair Oaks School in Redwood City, California, teachers collaborate to gather and analyze anecdotal information. For example, they occasionally videorecord portions of instruction and later view the recordings together to share observations and insights. They also spend time in one another's classrooms and make notes about their observations for later discussion (Bird, 1989). Colleagues, then, can provide record-keeping assistance, as can video- or audiorecordings.

Any system or device for recording anecdotal information should first be field-tested to determine the level of specificity to include in notes. Matt, whom we introduced earlier, did this by looking at his notes a couple of weeks after they were taken. In reviewing the notes, he asked himself, "What doesn't make sense any more?" and "What do I want to know more about?" Answers to these questions helped him modify his note-taking strategies to ensure maximum usefulness.

Kidwatchers who are comfortable with their system for recording anecdotal information are convinced of the usefulness of this documentation technique. Teacher Mary Kitagawa puts it this way: "In spite of the after-school time they consume, anecdotal records seem to be the most accurate way to document the full picture of students' language development" (1989, p. 108).

Checklists and Charts

Many teachers use checklists or charts to keep their observations of struggling readers systematic and organized. For example, they develop charts that reflect curricular goals or specify instructional routines and include blocks of space for recording information about students. As Figures 13.2 and 13.3

Class Roster	Dates/Types of Mini-Lessons			
	9/3 Using Context			
Jenny	NE*			
Peter	D			
Amy	M			
Jimmy	M			

*NE: not evident during the week after the mini-lesson; D: appears to be developing; M: appears to be mastered

Figure 13.2
Checklist for Results of Mini-Lessons

Routines	Students				
	Mike	Matthew	Emily	Katy	Mary
SSR					
Sharing SSR books					
Small-group instruction					
Read aloud					
Free choice					
Library visits					

Figure 13.3

Chart for Noting Student Activity During Instructional Routines

show, charts or checklists can be completed with a coding system or brief notes.

Betsy, a first-grade teacher, uses both types of charts to provide a systematic focus for observing her students. Because she teaches reading skills only if her students need them, different children attend different mini-lessons on different days. Betsy uses the mini-lesson checklist (Figure 13.2) to record which students attended skill and strategy lessons and to evaluate lesson impact on children's reading. For this latter purpose, she observes carefully during the week after the mini-lesson when children have opportunities to use the new skill or strategy. She then codes the checklist with her conclusions about the children's use of the skill.

The chart in Figure 13.3 is more open ended. Over several days, Betsy makes brief notes about particular students in the boxes. Later, she elaborates on these notes and files them in students' reading portfolios. She keeps the chart on a clipboard; it is always nearby when she teaches. Betsy also uses the same chart format to explore other aspects of children's behavior and attitudes as readers, such as their engagement with different types of text material or their reactions to different types of activities.

Students can keep checklists or charts about their own reading. They record insights in reading logs or reading journals and keep lists of books they have read. Students also evaluate their own reading habits and behaviors by responding to questions in their logs: "How was my reading today?" and "Why do I think so?" Finally, students track their progress as strategic readers by maintaining a three-column chart: things I can do well, things I'm working on, and things I plan to learn (Hansen, 1987). Teachers who encourage students to evaluate aspects of their own reading find that this practice has several benefits: Students learn to take control of their reading behavior and become more aware of their growth as readers, and teachers have yet another source of information about students.

Conversations and Interviews

A few summers ago, we worked with Dale, a student who had just completed his first year in middle school. Dale's parents and some of his middle school teachers were concerned about his textbook reading. His parents were perplexed because he had done all his homework diligently in elementary school. They said that he had begun the school year with equal diligence but soon stopped reading assignments from his texts. When they asked him why, he always answered, "I don't need to." They feared that the middle-school textbooks were too difficult for him.

Terry, Dale's tutor, attempted to determine what aspects of textbook reading were giving Dale trouble. He seemed quite capable of reading and studying middle-school texts independently. Somewhat exasperated, Terry decided to talk to Dale about the situation. Here's how the conversation went:

Terry:　Your parents are concerned because you didn't read your textbook assignments last year. Did you read them?

Dale:　Well, I did at the beginning of the year, but then I stopped.

Terry:　Why did you stop?

Dale:　I figured, "Why bother?"

Terry:　What made you think that?

Dale:　Well, the teachers always told us all the stuff in the book the next day. I figured it didn't make much sense to do all that reading when they were going to tell us all of it anyway.

As you have probably guessed, this brief conversation was as helpful in understanding Dale's reading behavior as all the informal diagnosis that preceded it. The anecdote underscores the importance of conversations and interviews as ways of gathering information. By asking the right kinds of questions in the right ways and listening carefully to how students respond, teachers can learn about students' actions and attitudes as readers. Sometimes, as with Dale, we can obtain this information in no other way.

Other people's perceptions are also important. Parents and previous teachers, for example, often provide helpful information, as do regular teachers for children who receive assistance outside the classroom. By talking with students and their "significant educational others," we can add both depth and breadth to our understanding of children as readers.

Behavior during a conversation or interview influences responses. A good interviewer has rapport with the interviewee but remains neutral about the content of responses. For example, consider these two questions, one might ask to determine a student's opinion about a book:

"I really liked this book. Didn't you?"

"What did you think about this book?"

The first question offers cues or implicit suggestions toward a desirable response. Many students would simply agree with the first question, regardless of their true feelings. The second question is content-neutral; it sets up neither a positive nor a negative response. Neutral questions help create an environment in which students know they can share freely. Free sharing more often yields useful, accurate information.

A variety of content-neutral questions can enhance the value of an interview or conversation. Researchers who use interviews as a way to gather information have identified several beneficial types of questions (Merriam, 1998; Patton, 1990). The following work particularly well in conversations with children who struggle as readers:

- *Experience/behavior questions.* These questions aim at eliciting descriptions perhaps observable had the interviewer been present. Questions might include, "What's something you've learned to do in reading?" or "How did it go with this book?" or "What do you do when you come to a word that you don't know? How do you try to figure it out?"

- *Opinion/value questions.* These questions help determine what people think and their goals, intentions, desires, or values. Such questions include, "What's the best book you've read this month? Why did you like it?" and "What would you like to learn so that you can become a better reader?"

- *Feelings questions.* These questions elicit readers' feelings. They include, "How do you feel when you run into problems in your reading?" and "Do you like to read? Why?"

- *Hypothetical/future-oriented questions.* These "what if?" questions encourage speculations, including those about the future. Examples include, "If you could choose all the things you read in school, what would you choose?" and "What are your plans for this next month in reading? What do you hope to accomplish?"

- *Ideal-position questions.* These questions relate to readers' notions of perfection, such as, "What does someone have to do to be a good reader?" or "Who's the best reader you know? What does this person do as a reader?"

- *Interpretive questions.* These questions generally occur at the end of an interview or conversation. The teacher interprets and summarizes the interview and asks the student to validate the summary: "So, would you say that . . . ?" or "You seem to be saying. . . . Is that what you think?"

Conversations and interviews can be planned or spontaneous, general or focused on a certain aspect of reading. Preparing interview questions beforehand helps ensure that they will be comprehensive, content-neutral, and related to the area of interest. In use, however, questions should guide conversation rather than provide a rigid structure.

Some teachers take notes during interviews. Others prefer to record interviews so that they can actually converse with students. In any event, always prepare written summaries of these conferences about reading and add them to students' reading portfolios.

Performance Samples

Performance samples, as their name suggests, are samples of students' performance as readers. They also belong in students' reading portfolios. Because performance samples provide tangible evidence, they can complement data gathered through observation and conversations.

Instructional activities can provide performance samples to include in a student's reading portfolio. For example, reader-response entries from students' reading logs can be evaluated holistically, using procedures similar to holistic evaluation of writing, to explore growth in reading comprehension and response to reading. Writing samples can also document reading-related growth. For example, analyzing a young child's spelling strategies can yield important insights about her graphophonic knowledge. An early piece of writing can also be dictated back to a child. Then, the teacher, alone or with the child, analyzes the two pieces looking for evidence of development in spelling and other conventions of written language.

Teachers often obtain valuable information about students' comprehension abilities by listening in as students discuss their reading and by evaluating students' instructional products. Here are 10 quick ways to assess comprehension, some suitable for narrative, some for expository text, some for both:

- Make an *Important Book* page that reflects the content of the text (see chapter 10).
- Make a Venn diagram to compare and contrast key ideas from a text.
- Describe how something (or someone) in the text is the same or different from something (or someone) else.
- Draw a picture that reflects important content.
- Complete a cloze activity (see chapter 5).
- Tell "who" and "what happened."
- Write three sentences: beginning, middle, end.
- Make a list or order a list of important ideas.
- Write two sentences: problem and solution, as described in the text.
- Complete a Herringbone chart (see chapter 9) to represent the text.

These activities can be evaluated with a simple three-point scale: O (Outstanding), S (Satisfactory), or U (Unsatisfactory). Chart the results. None of these assessments alone offers a comprehensive look at comprehension, but patterns may become apparent when you view evaluation results across many of these performance samples.

Performance samples also result from planned, informal reading conferences with students. These conversations between teacher and student revolve around a book that the student is reading. Many teachers easily accept the theoretical value of basing conferences on real books but may be less comfortable, perhaps, about figuring out the real-world logistics. For example, what if the student reads a book unfamiliar to the teacher? In such a case, the teacher can evaluate comprehension and response to reading more generically or even read the book at a later time.

Teachers also must consider how much assistance to give students who encounter problems during the reading conference. We wish to discover what the student can do if left to his own resources. Frustrating students who encounter unsolvable problems, however, makes little sense. Our best advice is to wait a second or two and help if the student still needs it, noting the student's reaction to the assistance. In reviewing records from the conference, the teacher can ask, "Did the student profit from my help? How do I know?"

Reading conferences that last about 10 minutes every month or so should provide sufficient information about struggling readers, particularly when combined with observational and interview data. Some teachers plan conferences with all their at-risk readers on the same day and invite an adult helper (parent, grandparent, reading specialist, or the principal) to assist in the classroom on conference days.

Reading conferences offer important opportunities to learn how children interact with text and how they feel about reading and themselves as readers. Like other kidwatching techniques, the conference format varies according to the teacher's purpose. The student might read a page or two aloud, for example, or the student and teacher might simply discuss the book. Retelling might be an appropriate activity as well.

Assessment Situations

Occasionally, teachers may plan and conduct classroom-based assessments to focus directly on a particular reader's skills, strategies, or behaviors. For example, reading conferences or any time a child reads aloud can be used to find out about word identification. Teachers can note on a text copy miscues made during reading, track them on a separate piece of paper, or record the reading. Marking copy of the text a student reads is easiest. Most teachers develop a simple coding system to assist in this process, such as writing substitutions over words in the text, circling omissions, using the editor's caret (^) for insertions, and so forth.

After the reading conference, they analyze miscues by comparing them with words in the text. For each pair (i.e., miscue and text word), the teacher asks, "Do they look the same? Sound the same?" "Are they the same part of speech?" "Are their meanings similar?" "Does the child try to correct miscues that change meaning?" Looking for patterns in the answers to these questions allows the teacher to answer the broader question, "What does the reader do when encountering an unknown word?"

When a student rereads a book, comparing the two recorded versions reveals signs of increased fluency or changes in sight vocabulary or word identification strategies. Jacobson (1989) asks students to evaluate changes in their own reading by listening to recordings of the same text made at different times so that they become more aware of their growth as readers.

Curriculum-based assessments or evaluations (CBAs) offer another efficient way to gather several types of assessment information relatively quickly. CBAs use informal inventory procedures, which have long been used as a basic diagnostic technique. They differ from informal reading inventories in one important way—administering a CBA takes only one minute per student. Students read orally from a grade-level text. Because CBAs are ordinarily administered several times each year, many teachers select a text for students to read that will not be used in any other way. The teacher records oral reading errors and notes the number of words the student reads in one minute. After the reading, the teacher asks the student to retell the passage. From this information, the teacher can estimate the following:

- ■ *Overall difficulty of the text for the student.* Use this calculation: number of words read correctly (correct or corrected)/total number of words read. For example, if a student reads 145 words but makes 8 errors, the resulting equation would be 137/145 or 94.5 percent. Nearly perfect percentages (99 percent–100 percent) suggest that the material is easy for the student. Those slightly lower (91 percent– 98 percent) indicate instructional level performance, and percentages at or below 90 percent show that the material is too difficult.

- ■ *Oral reading fluency.* Compare the student's performance (words correct per minute) to the norms provided in chapter 6 (Hasbrouck & Tindal, 1992; Howe & Shinn, 2001).

- ■ *Comprehension.* Evaluate the student's retelling.

The three-point scale (O-S-U) works well to record performance in each of these areas. Most teachers keep class charts of all this information, which allows them to efficiently draw several conclusions. For example, we can track one student's reading strengths and weaknesses by examining performance at several points throughout the school year. Likewise, we can determine instructional focus for groups or the entire class by looking across all class records.

CBAs do not provide in-depth information about students, but they do provide a quick "status of the class" overview and a way to look at students' relative strengths and weaknesses in reading over time. As such, they are a powerful addition to the teacher's assessment plans.

Observing, Understanding, and Helping Students

In this chapter we have described both why and how to observe struggling readers in action. We have encouraged teachers to be kidwatchers, to observe and talk with children to understand their behaviors and attitudes as readers in the context of the classroom. The resulting data help us draw important conclusions about our students.

A final question about portfolio assessment relates to the quantity of evidence needed. When we talk with teachers about portfolios, they frequently ask, "How much information should I gather?" Our answer: "Enough to answer your questions." This answer is not flippant, but rather underscores the importance of questions that provide focus for evaluation and assessment and the variable nature of reading behaviors and reading growth.

One way to conceptualize an answer to this quantity-of-information question is to think in terms of three related layers of assessment data, as shown in Figure 13.4. At the top of this triangle belong the assessments to be administered to all students in the class. These techniques are selected to

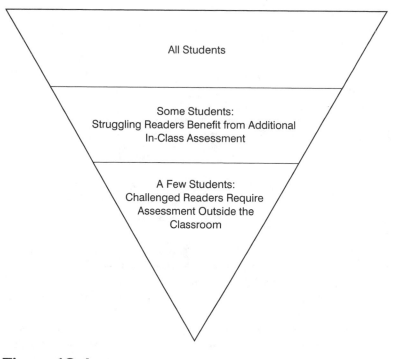

Figure 13.4
A Model for Classroom Assessment

parallel instructional goals—to enhance word identification abilities, comprehension strategies, fluency, and so on. Most of the evaluation techniques described in this chapter would be suitable for all students, perhaps several times each year.

These broad-brush views of students as readers will not provide enough information about all students, though; teachers may need additional information about some students, particularly struggling readers. For these, we may need additional information, also connected to curricular goals, such as more frequent observations, longer and more detailed oral reading assessments, or additional conversations or interviews.

Often, a student or two will need an even closer look at reading abilities and behaviors. These few students, represented by the tip of the triangle in Figure 13.4, may benefit from a diagnosis conducted by a reading specialist or other highly qualified educational professional. Such diagnoses, typically conducted outside of the classroom, also focus on curricular goals; they differ from classroom evaluations in depth. Using this classroom assessment model to organize and plan classroom evaluations ensures that we will indeed find enough information to answer questions about students as readers. Moreover, predicating decisions about particular assessment techniques for all levels of the model on curricular goals maintains a close link among the reading curriculum, classroom instructional routines, and evaluation.

Sally, whom we described at the beginning of the chapter, used many of the ideas we have outlined to create a systematic and comprehensive plan for learning about her pre–first-grade students. She says:

> I was interested in both a broad look, so I could get to know the kids, and some specific information that could guide instruction. When I tried to summarize all the information I had, I found some unevenness in students' behaviors and attitudes. But then I thought, "Well, we all have reading behaviors; we all have reading attitudes. Why should the kids be any different?"

Sally's goal became to gather data until patterns of strength and interest in different situations became apparent, until her questions about children had been answered. Thus, she found "enough was enough" when patterns became evident.

To find patterns and answer questions requires an open mind and a reflective posture. As Sally reviewed the contents of her students' reading portfolios, she thought about the evidence of learning using a problem-solving process that involved induction—the parts-to-whole search for patterns of behavior and attitudes. "I really tried to keep an open mind," she said. "I didn't want to jump to conclusions. I wanted to find the patterns." She found patterns and used them to form hypotheses about the children. She checked the value of these hypotheses in two ways. First, she reviewed portfolio contents one more time, looking for evidence that did not fit her hypotheses. When she found evidence, she reconsidered her thinking. "Sometimes I changed my mind, and sometimes I didn't," she commented. "But it was always worth it to think things through again." If she found no conflicting evidence, she checked the hypotheses with further observation. This, too, sometimes led her to modify her conclusions about children.

Good teachers have always acknowledged the potential of day-to-day activity for understanding their students. Nevertheless, the many demands on teachers' time and thoughts during a school day often leave observational data unrecorded. The processes and procedures in this chapter should help teachers develop a workable plan for observing, understanding, and helping struggling readers.

Appendix A

Award-Winning Books

Caldecott Award

Since 1938, the Association of Library Service to Children of the American Library Association has annually awarded the Caldecott Medal to the illustrator of the most distinguished picture book published in the United States in the preceding year. The recipient must be a citizen or resident of the United States. The medal was named in tribute to well-known English illustrator Randolph Caldecott (1846–1886).

2002 *The Three Pigs* by David Wiesner, Clarion/Houghton Mifflin. Honor Books: *The Dinosaurs of Waterhouse Hawkins* by Barbara Kerley, ill. by Brian Selznick, Scholastic; *Martin's Big Words: The Life of Dr. Martin Luther King, Jr.* by Doreen Rappaport, ill. by Bryan Collier, Jump at the Sun/Hyperion; *The Stray Dog* by Marc Simont, HarperCollins.

2001 *So You Want to Be President?* by Judith St. George, ill. by David Small, Philomel Books. Honor Books: *Casey at the Bat* by Ernest Lawrence Thayer, ill. by Christopher Bing, Handprint; *Click, Clack, Moo: Cows That Type* by Doreen Cronin, ill. by Betsy Lewin, Simon & Schuster; *Olivia* by Ian Flaconer, Atheneum.

2000 *Joseph Had a Little Overcoat*, by Simms Taback, Viking. Honor Books: *A Child's Calendar* by John Updike, ill. by Trina Schart Hyman, Holiday House; *Sector 7* by David Wiesner, Clarion; *When Sophie Gets Angry—Really, Really Angry . . .* by Molly Bang, Scholastic; *The Ugly Duckling* by Hans Christian Andersen, adapted by Jerry Pinkney, ill. by Jerry Pinkney, Morrow.

1999 *Snowflake Bentley* by Jacqueline Briggs Martin, ill. by Mary Azarian, Houghton Mifflin. Honor Books: *Duke Ellington: The Piano Prince and His Orchestra* by Andrea Davis Pinkney, ill. by Brian Pinkney, Hyperion; *No, David!* written and ill. by David Shannon, Blue Sky Press; *Snow* written and ill. by Uri Shule Vitz, Farrar, Strauss, Giroux; *Tibet Through the Red Box* written and ill. by Peter Sis, Farrar, Straus, Giroux.

1998 *Rapunzel* written and ill. by Paul O. Zelinsky, Dutton. Honor Books: *The Gardener* by Sarah Stewart, ill. by David Small, Farrar, Straus, Giroux; *There Was An Old Lady Who Swallowed a Fly* written and ill. by Simms Taback, Viking; *Harlem: A Poem* by Walter Dean Myers, ill. by Christopher Myers, Scholastic.

1997 *Golem* written and ill. by David Wisniewski, Clarion. Honor Books: *The Graphic Alphabet* written and ill. by David Pelletier, Orchard; *Hush! A Thai Lullaby* by Mingfong Ho, ill. by Holly Meade, Orchard; *The Paperboy* written and ill. by Dav Pilkey, Orchard; *Starry Messenger* written and ill. by Peter Sis, Farrar, Straus, Giroux.

1996 *Officer Buckle and Gloria* written and ill. by Peggy Rathman, Putnam. Honor Books: *Alphabet City* written and ill. by Stephen T. Johnson, Viking; *Zin! Zin! Zin! A Violin* by Lloyd Moss, ill. by Marjorie Priceman, Simon & Schuster; *The Faithful Friend* written and ill. by Robert San Souci, Simon and Schuster; *Tops and Bottoms* written and ill. By Janet Stevens, Harcourt.

1995 *Smoky Night* by Eve Bunting, ill. by David Diaz, Harcourt Brace. Honor Books: *Swamp Angel* by Anne Issacs, ill. by Paul O. Zelinsky, Dutton; *John Henry* by Julius Lester, ill. by Jerry Pinkney, Dial; *Time Flies* written and ill. by Eric Rohmann, Crown.

1994 *Grandfather's Journey* written and ill. by Allen Say, Houghton Mifflin. Honor Books: *In the Small Small Pond* written and ill. by Denise Fleming, Holt; *Owen* written and ill. by Kevin Henkes, Greenwillow; *Peppe the Lamplighter* by Elise Bartone, ill. by Ted Lewin, Lothrop; *Raven: A Trickster Tale* written and ill. by Gerald McDermott, Harcourt Brace; *Yo! Yes?* written and ill. by Chris Raschka, Orchard.

1993 *Mirette on the High Wire* written and ill. by Emily Arnold McCully, Putnam. Honor Books: *The Stinky Cheese Man* by Jon Scieszka, ill. by Lane Smith, Viking; *Working Cotton* by Sherley Anne Williams, ill. by Carole Byard, Harcourt Brace; *Seven Blind Mice* written and ill. by Ed Young, Philomel.

1992 *Tuesday* written and ill. by David Wiesner, Clarion. Honor Book: *Tar Beach* written and ill. by Faith Ringgold, Crown.

1991 *Black and White* written and ill. by David Macaulay, Houghton Mifflin. Honor Books: *"More More More," Said the Baby: 3 Love Stories* written and ill. by Vera B. Williams, Greenwillow; *Puss in Boots* by Charles Perrault, tr. by Malcolm Arthur, ill. by Fred Marcellino, Farrar, Straus.

1990 *A Red Riding-Hood Story* by Lon Po Po, tr. and ill. by Ed Young, Philomel. Honor Books: *Bill Peet: An Autobiography* written and ill. by Bill Peet, Houghton Mifflin; *Color Zoo* written and ill. by Lois Ehlert, HarperCollins; *Hershel and the Hanukkah Goblins* by Eric Kimmel, ill. by Trina Schart Hyman, Holiday; *The Talking Eggs* by Robert San Souci, ill. by Jerry Pinkney, Dial.

1989 *Song and Dance Man* by Karen Ackerman, ill. by Stephen Gammell, Knopf. Honor Books: *Free Fall* written and ill. by David Wiesner, Lothrop; *Goldilocks and the Three Bears* retold and ill. by James Marshall, Dial; *Mirandy and Brother Wind* by Patricia McKissack, ill. by Jerry Pinkney, Knopf; *The Boy of the Three-Year Nap* by Diane Snyder, ill. by Allen Say, Houghton Mifflin.

1988 *Owl Moon* by Jane Yolen, ill. by John Schoenherr, Philomel. Honor Books: *Mufaro's Beautiful Daughters* written and ill. by John Steptoe, Lothrop.

1987 *Hey, Al!* by Arthur Yorinks, ill. by Richard Egielski, Farrar, Straus. Honor Books: *The Village of Round and Square Houses* written and ill. by Ann Grifalconi, Little, Brown; *Alphabetics* written and ill. by Suse MacDonald, Bradbury; *Rumpelstiltskin* retold and ill. by Paul O. Zelinsky, Dutton.

1986 *The Polar Express* written and ill. by Chris Van Allsburg, Houghton Mifflin. Honor Books: *The Relatives Came* by Cynthia Rylant, ill. by Stephen Gammell, Bradbury; *King Bidgood's in the Bathtub* by Audrey Wood, ill. by Don Wood, Harcourt Brace.

1985 *St. George and the Dragon* retold by Margaret Hodges, ill. by Trina Schart Hyman, Little, Brown. Honor Books: *Hansel and Gretel* retold by Rika Lesser, ill. by Paul O. Zelinsky, Dodd, Mead; *Have You Seen My Duckling?* by Nancy Tafuri, Greenwillow; *The Story of Jumping Mouse* by John Steptoe, Lothrop.

1984 *The Glorious Flight: Across the Channel with Louis Blériot* by Alice Provensen and Martin Provensen, Viking. Honor Books: *Ten, Nine, Eight* by Molly Bang, Greenwillow; *Little Red Riding Hood* retold and ill. by Trina Schart Hyman, Holiday.

1983 *Shadow* by Blaise Cendrars, tr. and ill. by Marcia Brown, Scribner. Honor Books: *When I Was Young in the Mountains* by Cynthia Rylant, ill. by Diane Goode, Dutton; *A Chair for My Mother* by Vera B. Williams, Greenwillow.

1982 *Jumanji* written and ill. by Chris Van Allsburg, Houghton Mifflin. Honor Books: *Where the Buffaloes Begin* by Olaf Baker, ill. by Stephen Gammell, Warne; *On Market Street* by Arnold Lobel, ill. by Anita Lobel, Greenwillow; *Outside Over There* by Maurice Sendak, Harper & Row; *A Visit to William Blake's Inn* by Nancy Willard, ill. by Alice Provensen and Martin Provensen, Harcourt Brace.

1981 *Fables* written and ill. by Arnold Lobel, Harper & Row. Honor Books: *The Grey Lady and the Strawberry Snatcher* ill. by Molly Bang, Four Winds; *Truck* ill. by Donald Crews, Greenwillow; *Mice Twice* written and ill. by Joseph Low, Atheneum; *The Bremen-Town Musicians* ill. by Ilse Plume, Doubleday.

1980 *Ox-Cart Man* by Donald Hall, ill. by Barbara Cooney, Viking. Honor Books: *Ben's Trumpet* written and ill. by Rachel Isadora, Greenwillow; *The Garden of Abdul Gasazi* written and ill. by Chris Van Allsburg, Houghton Mifflin.

1979 *The Girl Who Loved Wild Horses* written and ill. by Paul Goble, Bradbury. Honor Books: *Freight Train* written and ill. by Donald Crews, Greenwillow; *The Way to Start a Day* by Byrd Baylor, ill. by Peter Parnall, Scribner.

1978 *Noah's Ark* ill. by Peter Spier, Doubleday. Honor Books: *Castle* written and ill. by David Macaulay, Houghton Mifflin; *It Could Always Be Worse* retold and ill. by Margot Zemach, Farrar, Straus.

1977 *Ashanti to Zulu: African Traditions* by Margaret Musgrove, ill. by Leo Dillon and Diane Dillon, Dial. Honor Books: *The Amazing Bone* written and ill. by William Steig, Farrar, Straus; *The Contest* retold and ill. by Nonny Hogrogian, Greenwillow; *Fish for Supper* written and ill. by M. B. Goffstein, Dial; *The Golem* written and ill. by Beverly Brodsky McDermott, Lippincott; *Hawk, I'm Your Brother* by Byrd Baylor, ill. by Peter Parnall, Scribner.

1976 *Why Mosquitoes Buzz in People's Ears* retold by Verna Aardema, ill. by Leo Dillon and Diane Dillon, Dial. Honor Books: *The Desert Is Theirs* by Byrd Baylor, ill. by Peter Parnall, Scribner; *Strega Nona* retold and ill. by Tomie dePaola, Prentice Hall.

1975 *Arrow to the Sun* adapted and ill. by Gerald McDermott, Viking. Honor Books: *Jambo Means Hello* by Muriel Feelings, ill. by Tom Feelings, Dial.

1974 *Duffy and the Devil* by Harve Zemach, ill. by Margot Zemach, Farrar, Straus. Honor Books: *Three Jovial Huntsmen* written and ill. by Susan Jeffers, Bradbury; *Cathedral: The Story of Its Construction* written and ill. by David Macaulay, Houghton Mifflin.

1973 *The Funny Little Woman* retold by Arlene Mosel, ill. by Blair Lent, Dutton. Honor Books: *Anansi the Spider* adapted and ill. by Gerald McDermott, Holt; *Hosie's Alphabet* by Hosea, Tobias, and Lisa Baskin, ill. by Leonard Baskin, Viking; *Snow White and the Seven Dwarfs* tr. by Randall Jarrell, ill. by Nancy Ekholm Burkert, Farrar, Straus; *When Clay Sings* by Byrd Baylor, ill. by Tom Bahti, Scribner.

1972 *One Fine Day* written and ill. by Nonny Hogrogian, Macmillan. Honor Books: *If All the Seas Were One Sea* written and ill. by Janina Domanska, Macmillan; *Moja Means One: Swahili Counting Book* by Muriel Feelings, ill. by Tom Feelings, Dial; *Hildilid's Night* by Cheli Duran Ryan, ill. by Arnold Lobel, Macmillan.

1971 *A Story, A Story* written and ill. by Gail E. Haley, Atheneum. Honor Books: *The Angry Moon* by William Sleator, ill. by Blair Lent, Atlantic/Little; *Frog and Toad Are Friends* written and ill. by Arnold Lobel, Harper & Row; *In the Night Kitchen* written and ill. by Maurice Sendak, Harper & Row.

1970 *Sylvester and the Magic Pebble* written and ill. by William Steig, Windmill. Honor Books: *Goggles!* written and ill. by Ezra Jack Keats, Macmillan; *Alexander and the Wind-Up Mouse* written and ill. by Leo Lionni, Pantheon; *Pop Corn and Ma Goodness* by Edna Mitchell Preston, ill. by Robert Andrew Parker, Viking; *Thy Friend, Obadiah* written and ill. by Brinton Turkle, Viking; *The Judge* by Harve Zemach, ill. by Margot Zemach, Farrar, Straus.

1969 *The Fool of the World and the Flying Ship* by Arthur Ransome, ill. by Uri Shulevitz, Farrar, Straus. Honor Book: *Why the Sun and the Moon Live in the Sky* by Elphinstone Dayrell, ill. by Blair Lent, Houghton Mifflin.

1968 *Drummer Hoff* by Barbara Emberley, ill. by Ed Emberley, Prentice Hall. Honor Books: *Frederick* written and ill. by Leo Lionni, Pantheon; *Seashore Story* written and ill. by Taro Yashima, Viking; *The Emperor and the Kite* by Jane Yolen, ill. by Ed Young, World.

1967 *Sam, Bangs & Moonshine* written and ill. by Evaline Ness, Holt. Honor Books: *One Wide River to Cross* by Barbara Emberley, ill. by Ed Emberley, Prentice Hall.

1966 *Always Room for One More* by Sorche Nic Leodhas, ill. by Nonny Hogrogian, Holt. Honor Books: *Hide and Seek Fog* by Alvin Tresselt, ill. by Roger Duvoisin, Lothrop; *Just Me* written and ill. by Marie Hall Ets, Viking; *Tom Tit Tot* written and ill. by Evaline Ness, Scribner.

1965 *May I Bring a Friend?* by Beatrice Schenk de Regniers, ill. by Beni Montresor, Atheneum. Honor Books: *Rain Makes Applesauce* by Julian Scheer, ill. by Marvin Bileck, Holiday; *The Wave* by Margaret Hodges, ill. by Blair Lent, Houghton Mifflin; *A Pocketful of Cricket* by Rebecca Caudill, ill. by Evaline Ness, Holt.

1964 *Where the Wild Things Are* written and ill. by Maurice Sendak, Harper & Row. Honor Books: *Swimmy* written and ill. by Leo Lionni, Pantheon; *All in the Morning Early* by Sorche Nic Leodhas, ill. by Evaline Ness, Holt; *Mother Goose and Nursery Rhymes* ill. by Philip Reed, Atheneum.

1963 *The Snowy Day* written and ill. by Ezra Jack Keats, Viking. Honor Books: *The Sun Is a Golden Earring* by Natalie M. Belting, ill. by Bernarda Bryson, Holt; *Mr. Rabbit and the Lovely Present* by Charlotte Zolotow, ill. by Maurice Sendak, Harper & Row.

1962 *Once a Mouse . . .* written and ill. by Marcia Brown, Scribner. Honor Books: *The Fox Went Out on a Chilly Night* written and ill. by Peter Spier, Doubleday;

Little Bear's Visit by Else Holmelund Minarik, ill. by Maurice Sendak, Harper & Row; *The Day We Saw the Sun Come Up* by Alice E. Goudey, ill. by Adrienne Adams, Scribner.

1961 *Baboushka and the Three Kings* by Ruth Robbins, ill. by Nicolas Sidjakov, Parnassus. Honor Books: *Inch by Inch* written and ill. by Leo Lionni, Obolensky.

1960 *Nine Days to Christmas* by Marie Hall Ets and Aurora Labastida, ill. by Marie Hall Ets, Viking. Honor Books: *Houses from the Sea* by Alice E. Goudey, ill. by Adrienne Adams, Scribner; *The Moon Jumpers* by Janice May Udry, ill. by Maurice Sendak, Harper.

1959 *Chanticleer and the Fox* adapted from Chaucer, ill. by Barbara Cooney, Crowell. Honor Books: *The House That Jack Built* written and ill. by Antonio Frasconi, Harcourt Brace; *What Do You Say, Dear?* by Sesyle Joslin, ill. by Maurice Sendak, Scott; *Umbrella* written and ill. by Taro Yashima, Viking.

1958 *Time of Wonder* written and ill. by Robert McCloskey, Viking. Honor Books: *Fly High, Fly Low* written and ill. by Donald Freeman, Viking; *Anatole and the Cat* by Eve Titus, ill. by Paul Galdone, McGraw-Hill.

1957 *A Tree Is Nice* by Janice May Udry, ill. by Marc Simont, Harper. Honor Books: *Mr. Penny's Race Horse* written and ill. by Marie Hall Ets, Viking; *I Is One* written and ill. by Tasha Tudor, Walck; *Anatole* by Eve Titus, ill. by Paul Galdone, McGraw Hill; *Gillespie and the Guards* by Benjamin Elkin, ill. by James Daugherty, Viking; *Lion* written and ill. by William Pène du Bois, Viking.

1956 *Frog Went A–Courtin'* ed. by John Langstaff, ill. by Feodor Rojankovsky, Harcourt Brace. Honor Books: *Play with Me* written and ill. by Marie Hall Ets, Viking; *Crow Boy* written and ill. by Taro Yashima, Viking.

1955 *Cinderella, or the Little Glass Slipper* by Charles Perrault, tr. and ill. by Marcia Brown, Scribner. Honor Books: *Book of Nursery and Mother Goose Rhymes* ill. by Marguerite de Angeli, Doubleday; *Wheel on the Chimney* by Margaret Wise Brown, ill. by Tibor Gergely, Lippincott; *The Thanksgiving Story* by Alice Dalgliesh, ill. by Helen Sewell, Scribner.

1954 *Madeline's Rescue* written and ill. by Ludwig Bemelmans, Viking. Honor Books: *Journey Cake, Ho!* by Ruth Sawyer, ill. by Robert McCloskey, Viking; *When Will the World Be Mine?* by Miriam Schlein, ill. by Jean Charlot, Scott; *The Steadfast Tin Soldier* by Hans Christian Andersen, ill. by Marcia Brown, Scribner; *A Very Special House* by Ruth Krauss, ill. by Maurice Sendak, Harper; *Green Eyes* written and ill. by A. Birnbaum, Capitol.

1953 *The Biggest Bear* written and ill. by Lynd Ward, Houghton Mifflin. Honor Books: *Puss in Boots* by Charles Perrault, ill. and tr. by Marcia Brown, Scribner; *One Morning in Maine* written and ill. by Robert McCloskey, Viking; *Ape in a Cape* written and ill. by Fritz Eichenberg, Harcourt; *The Storm Book* by Charlotte Zolotow, ill. by Margaret Bloy Graham, Harper & Row; *Five Little Monkeys* written and ill. by Juliet Kepes, Houghton Mifflin.

1952 *Finders Keepers* by Will, ill. by Nicolas, Harcourt Brace. Honor Books: *Mr. T. W. Anthony Woo* written and ill. by Marie Hall Ets, Viking; *Skipper John's Cook* written and ill. by Marcia Brown, Scribner; *All Falling Down* by Gene Zion, ill. by Margaret Bloy Graham, Harper; *Bear Party* written and ill. by William Pène du Bois, Viking; *Feather Mountain* written and ill. by Elizabeth Olds, Houghton Mifflin.

1951 *The Egg Tree* written and ill. by Katherine Milhous, Scribner. Honor Books: *Dick Whittington and His Cat* written and ill. by Marcia Brown, Scribner; *The Two Reds* by Will, ill. by Nicolas, Harcourt Brace; *If I Ran the Zoo* written and ill. by Dr. Seuss, Random House; *The Most Wonderful Doll in the World* by Phyllis McGinley, ill. by Helen Stone, Lippincott; *T-Bone, the Baby Sitter* written and ill. by Clare Newberry, Harper.

1950 *Song of the Swallows* written and ill. by Leo Politi, Scribner. Honor Books: *America's Ethan Allen* by Stewart Holbrook, ill. by Lynd Ward, Houghton Mifflin; *The Wild Birthday Cake* by Lavinia Davis, ill. by Hildegard Woodward, Doubleday; *The Happy Day* by Ruth Krauss, ill. by Marc Simont, Harper; *Bartholomew and the Oobleck* written and ill. by Dr. Seuss, Random House; *Henry Fisherman* written and ill. by Marcia Brown, Scribner.

1949 *The Big Snow* written and ill. by Berta Hader and Elmer Hader, Macmillan. Honor Books: *Blueberries for Sal* written and ill. by Robert McCloskey, Viking; *All Around the Town* by Phyllis McGinley, ill. by Helen Stone, Lippincott; *Juanita* written and ill. by Leo Politi, Scribner; *Fish in the Air* written and ill. by Kurt Wiese, Viking.

1948 *White Snow, Bright Snow* by Alvin Tresselt, ill. by Roger Duvoisin, Lothrop. Honor Books: *Stone Soup* written and ill. by Marcia Brown, Scribner; *McElligot's Pool* written and ill. by Dr. Seuss, Random House; *Bambino the Clown* written and ill. by George Schreiber, Viking; *Roger and the Fox* by Lavinia Davis, ill. by Hildegard Woodward, Doubleday; *Song of Robin Hood* ed. by Anne Malcolmson, ill. by Virginia Lee Burton, Houghton Mifflin.

1947 *The Little Island* by Golden MacDonald, ill. by Leonard Weisgard, Doubleday. Honor Books: *Rain Drop Splash* by Alvin Tresselt, ill. by Leonard Weisgard, Lothrop; *Boats on the River* by Marjorie Flack, ill. by Jay Hyde Barnum, Viking; *Timothy Turtle* by Al Graham, ill. by Tony Palazzo, Viking; *Pedro, the Angel of Olvera Street* written and ill. by Leo Politi, Scribner; *Sing in Praise: A Collection of the Best Loved Hymns* by Opal Wheeler, ill. by Marjorie Torrey, Dutton.

1946 *The Rooster Crows . . .* (traditional Mother Goose) ill. by Maud Petersham and Miska Petersham, Macmillan. Honor Books: *Little Lost Lamb* by Golden MacDonald, ill. by Leonard Weisgard, Doubleday; *Sing Mother Goose* by Opal Wheeler, ill. by Marjorie Torrey, Dutton; *My Mother Is the Most Beautiful Woman in the World* by Becky Reyher, ill. by Ruth Gannett, Lothrop; *You Can Write Chinese* written and ill. by Kurt Wiese, Viking.

1945 *Prayer for a Child* by Rachel Field, ill. by Elizabeth Orton Jones, Macmillan. Honor Books: *Mother Goose* ill. by Tasha Tudor, Walck; *In the Forest* written and ill. by Marie Hall Ets, Viking; *Yonie Wondernose* written and ill. by Marguerite de Angeli, Doubleday; *The Christmas Anna Angel* by Ruth Sawyer, ill. by Kate Seredy, Viking.

1944 *Many Moons* by James Thurger, ill. by Louis Slobodkin, Harcourt Brace. Honor Books: *Small Rain: Verses from the Bible* selected by Jessie Orton Jones, ill. by Elizabeth Orton Jones, Viking; *Pierre Pigeon* by Lee Kingman, ill. by Arnold E. Bare, Houghton Mifflin; *The Mighty Hunter* written and ill. by Berta Hader and Elmer Hader, Macmillan; *A Child's Good Night Book* by Margaret Wise Brown, ill. by Jean Charlot, Scott; *Good Luck Horse* by Chic-Yi Chan, ill. by Plao Chan, Whittlesey.

1943 *The Little House* written and ill. by Virginia Lee Burton, Houghton Mifflin. Honor Books: *Dash and Dart* written and ill. by Mary Buff and Conrad Buff, Viking; *Marshmallow* written and ill. by Clare Newberry, Harper.

1942 *Make Way for Ducklings* written and ill. by Robert McCloskey, Viking. Honor Books: *An American ABC* written and ill. by Maud and Miska Petersham, Macmillan; *In My Mother's House* by Ann Nolan Clark, ill. by Velino Herrera, Viking; *Paddle-to-the-Sea* written and ill. by Holling C. Holling, Houghton Mifflin; *Nothing at All* written and ill. by Wanda Gág, Coward.

1941 *They Were Strong and Good* written and ill. by Robert Lawson, Viking. Honor Books: *April's Kittens* written and ill. by Clare Newberry, Harper.

1940 *Abraham Lincoln* written and ill. by Ingri and Edgar Parin d'Aulaire, Doubleday. Honor Books: *Cock-A-Doodle Doo . . .* written and ill. by Berta and Elmer Hader, Macmillan; *Madeline* written and ill. by Ludwig Bemelmans, Viking; *The Ageless Story* ill. by Lauren Ford, Dodd, Mead.

1939 *Mei Li* written and ill. by Thomas Handforth, Doubleday. Honor Books: *The Forest Pool* written and ill. by Laura Adams Armer, Longmans; *Wee Gillis* by Munro Leaf, ill. by Robert Lawson, Viking; *Snow White and the Seven Dwarfs* written and ill. by Wanda Gág, Coward; *Barkis* written and ill. by Clare Newberry, Harper; *Andy and the Lion* written and ill. by James Daugherty, Viking.

1938 *Animals of the Bible* by Helen Dean Fish, ill. by Dorothy P. Lathrop, Lippincott. Honor Books: *Seven Simeons* written and ill. by Boris Artzybasheff, Viking; *Four and Twenty Blackbirds* by Helen Dean Fish, ill. by Robert Lawson, Stokes.

Newbery Award

Named in honor of John Newbery (1713–1767), the first English publisher of children's books, this medal has been given annually since 1922 by the American Library Association's Association for Library Service to Children. The recipient is recognized as author of the most distinguished book in children's literature published in the United States in the preceding year. The award is limited to citizens or residents of the United States.

2002 *A Single Shard* by Linda Sue Park, Clarion/Houghton Mifflin. Honor Books: *Everything on a Waffle* by Polly Horvath, Farrar, Straus, Giroux; *Carver: A Life in Poems* by Marilyn Nelson, Front Street.

2001 *A Year Down Yonder* by Richard Peck, Dial. Honor Books: *Because of Winn-Dixie* by Kate DiCamillo, Candlewick Press; *Hope Was Here* by Joan Bauer, Putnam; *Joey Pigza Loses Control* by Jack Gantos, Farrar, Straus, Giroux; *The Wanderer* by Sharon Creech, Joanne Cotler Books, HarperCollins.

2000 *Bud, Not Buddy* by Christopher Paul Curtis, Delacorte. Honor Books: *Getting Near to Baby* by Audrey Couloumbis, Putnam; *Our Only May Amelia* by Jennifer L. Holm, HarperCollins; *26 Fairmount Avenue* by Tomie dePaola, Putnam.

1999 *Holes* by Louis Sachar, Farrar, Straus, Giroux. Honor Books: *A Long Way from Chicago* by Richard Peck, Dial.

1998 *Out of the Dust* by Karen Hesse, Scholastic. Honor Books: *Lily's Crossing* by Patricia Reilly Giff, Delacorte; *Ella Enchanted* by Carson Levine, HarperCollins; *Wringer* by Jerry Spinelli, HarperCollins.

1997 *The View from Saturday* by E. L. Konisburg, Atheneum. Honor Books: *A Girl Named Disaster* by Nancy Farmer, Orchard; *Moorchild* by Eloise McGraw, Simon & Schuster; *The Thief* by Megan Whalen Turner, Greenwillow; *Belle Prater's Boy* by Ruth White, Farrar, Straus, Giroux.

1996 *The Midwife's Apprentice* by Karen Cushman, Bantam. Honor Books: *What Jamie Saw* by Carolyn Coman, Front St.; *The Watsons Go to Birmingham: 1963* by Christopher Paul Curtis, Delacorte; *Yolanda's Genius* by Carol Fenner, Simon & Schuster; *The Great Fire* by Jim Murphy, Scholastic.

1995 *Walk Two Moons* by Sharon Creech, HarperCollins. Honor Books: *Catherine, Called Birdy* by Karen Cushman, Clarion; *The Ear, the Eye, and the Arm* by Nancy Farmer, Orchard.

1994 *The Giver* by Lois Lowry, Houghton Mifflin. Honor Books: *Crazy Lady* by Jane Conly, HarperCollins; *Dragon's Gate* by Lawrence Yep, HarperCollins; *Eleanor Roosevelt: A Life of Discovery* by Russell Freedman, Clarion.

1993 *Missing May* by Cynthia Rylant, Orchard. Honor Books: *What Hearts* by Bruce Brooks, HarperCollins; *The Dark-Thirty: Southern Tales of the Supernatural* by Patricia McKissack, Knopf; *Somewhere in the Darkness* by Walter Dean Myers, Scholastic.

1992 *Shiloh* by Phyllis Reynolds Naylor, Atheneum. Honor Books: *Nothing but the Truth: A Documentary Novel* by Avi, Orchard; *The Wright Brothers: How They Invented the Airplane* by Russell Freedman, Holiday.

1991 *Maniac Magee* by Jerry Spinelli, Little, Brown. Honor Books: *The True Confessions of Charlotte Doyle* by Avi, Orchard.

1990 *Number the Stars* by Lois Lowry, Houghton Mifflin. Honor Books: *Afternoon of the Elves* by Janet Taylor Lisle, Orchard; *Shabanu: Daughter of the Wind* by Suzanne Fisher Staples, Knopf; *The Winter Room* by Gary Paulsen, Orchard.

1989 *Joyful Noise: Poems for Two Voices* by Paul Fleischman, HarperCollins. Honor Books: *In the Beginning: Creation Stories from Around the World* by Virginia Hamilton, Harcourt Brace; *Scorpions* by Walter Dean Myers, HarperCollins.

1988 *Lincoln: A Photobiography* by Russell Freedman, Clarion. Honor Books: *Hatchet* by Gary Paulsen, Bradbury; *After the Rain* by Norma Fox Mazer, Morrow.

1987 *The Whipping Boy* by Sid Fleischman, Greenwillow. Honor Books: *On My Honor* by Marion Dane Bauer, Clarion; *A Fine White Dust* by Cynthia Rylant, Bradbury; *Volcano* by Patricia Lauber, Bradbury.

1986 *Sarah, Plain and Tall* by Patricia MacLachlan, HarperCollins. Honor Books: *Commodore Perry in the Land of Shogun* by Rhoda Blumberg, Lothrop; *Dogsong* by Gary Paulsen, Bradbury.

1985 *The Hero and the Crown* by Robin McKinley, Greenwillow. Honor Books: *The Moves Make the Man* by Bruce Brooks, HarperCollins; *One-Eyed Cat* by Paula Fox, Bradbury; *Like Jake and Me* by Mavis Jukes, Knopf.

1984 *Dear Mr. Henshaw* by Beverly Cleary, Morrow. Honor Books: *The Wish Giver: Three Tales of Coven Tree* by Bill Brittain, HarperCollins; *A Solitary Blue* by Cynthia Voigt, Atheneum; *The Sign of the Beaver* by Elizabeth George Speare, Houghton Mifflin; *Sugaring Time* by Kathryn Lasky, Macmillan.

1983 *Dicey's Song* by Cynthia Voigt, Atheneum. Honor Books: *The Blue Sword* by Robin McKinley, Greenwillow; *Dr. De Soto* by William Steig, Farrar, Straus; *Graven*

Images by Paul Fleischman, HarperCollins; *Homesick: My Own Story* by Jean Fritz, Putnam; *Sweet Whispers, Brother Rush* by Virginia Hamilton, Philomel.

1982 *A Visit to William Blake's Inn: Poems for Innocent and Experienced Travelers* by Nancy Willard, Harcourt Brace. Honor Books: *Ramona Quimby, Age 8* by Beverly Cleary, Morrow; *Upon the Head of the Goat: A Childhood in Hungary, 1939–1944* by Aranka Siegel, Farrar, Straus.

1981 *Jacob Have I Loved* by Katherine Paterson, Crowell. Honor Books: *The Fledgling* by Jane Langton, HarperCollins; *A Ring of Endless Light* by Madeleine L'Engle, Farrar, Straus.

1980 *A Gathering of Days: A New England Girl's Journal, 1830–32* by Joan Blos, Scribner. Honor Books: *The Road from Home: The Story of an Armenian Girl* by David Kherdian, Greenwillow.

1979 *The Westing Game* by Ellen Raskin, Dutton. Honor Books: *The Great Gilly Hopkins* by Katherine Paterson, Crowell.

1978 *Bridge to Terabithia* by Katherine Paterson, Crowell. Honor Books: *Anpao: An American Indian Odyssey* by Jamake Highwater, Lippincott; *Ramona and Her Father* by Beverly Cleary, Morrow.

1977 *Roll of Thunder, Hear My Cry* by Mildred D. Taylor, Dial. Honor Books: *Abel's Island* by William Steig, Farrar, Straus; *A String in the Harp* by Nancy Bond, Atheneum/McElderry.

1976 *The Grey King* by Susan Cooper, Atheneum/McElderry. Honor Books: *The Hundred Penny Box* by Sharon Bell Mathis, Viking; *Dragonwings* by Lawrence Yep, Harper & Row.

1975 *M. C. Higgins, The Great* by Virginia Hamilton, Macmillan. Honor Books: *Figgs and Phantoms* by Ellen Raskin, Dutton; *My Brother Sam Is Dead* by James Lincoln Collier and Christopher Collier, Four Winds; *The Perilous Guard* by Elizabeth Marie Pope, Houghton Mifflin; *Philip Hall Likes Me, I Reckon Maybe* by Bette Greene, Dial.

1974 *The Slave Dancer* by Paula Fox, Bradbury. Honor Books: *The Dark Is Rising* by Susan Cooper, Atheneum/McElderry.

1973 *Julie of the Wolves* by Jean George, Harper & Row. Honor Books: *Frog and Toad Together* by Arnold Lobel, Harper & Row; *The Upstairs Room* by Johanna Reiss, Crowell; *The Witches of Worm* by Zilpha Keatley Snyder, Atheneum.

1972 *Mrs. Frisby and the Rats of NIMH* by Robert C. O'Brien, Atheneum. Honor Books: *Incident at Hawk's Hill* by Allan W. Eckert, Little, Brown; *The Planet of Junior Brown* by Virginia Hamilton, Macmillan; *The Tombs of Atuan* by Ursula K. Le Guin, Atheneum; *Annie and the Old One* by Miska Miles, Atlantic/Little, Brown; *The Headless Cupid* by Zilpha Keatley Snyder, Atheneum.

1971 *Summer of the Swans* by Betsy Byars, Viking. Honor Books: *Kneeknock Rise* by Natalie Babbitt, Farrar, Straus; *Enchantress from the Stars* by Sylvia Louise Engdahl, Atheneum; *Sing Down the Moon* by Scott O'Dell, Houghton Mifflin.

1970 *Sounder* by William H. Armstrong, Harper & Row. Honor Books: *Our Eddie* by Sulamith Ish-Kishor, Pantheon; *The Many Ways of Seeing: An Introduction to the Pleasures of Art* by Janet Gaylord Moore, World; *Journey Outside* by Mary Q. Steele, Viking.

1969 *The High King* by Lloyd Alexander, Holt. Honor Books: *To Be a Slave* by Julius Lester, Dial; *When Shlemiel Went to Warsaw and Other Stories* by Isaac Bashevis Singer, Farrar, Straus.

1968 *From the Mixed-Up Files of Mrs. Basil E. Frankweiler* by E. L. Konigsburg, Atheneum. Honor Books: *Jennifer, Hecate, Macbeth, William McKinley, and Me, Elizabeth* by E. L. Konigsburg, Atheneum; *The Black Pearl* by Scott O'Dell, Houghton Mifflin; *The Fearsome Inn* by Isaac Bashevis Singer, Scribner; *The Egypt Game* by Zilpha Katley Snyder, Atheneum.

1967 *Up a Road Slowly* by Irene Hunt, Follett. Honor Books: *The King's Fifth* by Scott O'Dell, Houghton Mifflin; *Zlateh the Goat and Other Stories* by Isaac Bashevis Singer, Harper & Row, *The Jazz Man* by Mary H. Weik, Atheneum.

1966 *I, Juan de Pareja* by Elizabeth Borten de Trevino, Farrar, Straus. Honor Books: *The Black Cauldron* by Lloyd Alexander, Holt; *The Animal Family* by Randall Jarrell, Pantheon; *The Noonday Friends* by Mary Stolz, Harper & Row.

1965 *Shadow of a Bull* by Maia Wojciechowska, Atheneum. Honor Books: *Across Five Aprils* by Irene Hunt, Follett.

1964 *It's Like This, Cat* by Emily Cheney Neville, Harper & Row. Honor Books: *Rascal* by Sterling North, Dutton; *The Loner* by Esther Wier, McKay.

1963 *A Wrinkle in Time* by Madeleine L'Engle, Farrar, Straus. Honor Books: *Thistle and Thyme* by Sorche Nic Leodhas, Holt; *Men of Athens* by Olivia Coolidge, Houghton Mifflin.

1962 *The Bronze Bow* by Elizabeth George Speare, Houghton Mifflin. Honor Books: *Frontier Living* by Edwin Tunis, World; *The Golden Goblet* by Eloise McGraw, Coward; *Belling the Tiger* by Mary Stolz, Harper & Row.

1961 *Island of the Blue Dolphins* by Scott O'Dell, Houghton Mifflin. Honor Books: *America Moves Forward* by Gerald W. Johnson, Morrow; *Old Ramon* by Jack Schaefer, Houghton Mifflin; *The Cricket in Times Square* by George Selden, Farrar, Straus.

1960 *Onion John* by Joseph Krumgold, Crowell. Honor Books: *My Side of the Mountain* by Jean George, Dutton; *America Is Born* by Gerald W. Johnson, Morrow; *The Gammage Cup* by Carol Kendall, Harcourt Brace.

1959 *The Witch of Blackbird Pond* by Elizabeth George Speare, Houghton Mifflin. Honor Books: *The Family Under the Bridge* by Natalie S. Carlson, Harper; *Along Came a Dog* by Meindert DeJong, Harper; *Chucaro: Wild Pony of the Pampa* by Francis Kalnay, Harcourt Brace; *The Perilous Road* by William O. Steele, Harcourt Brace.

1958 *Rifles for Watie* by Harold Keith, Crowell. Honor Books: *The Horsecatcher* by Mari Sandoz, Westminster; *Gone-Away Lake* by Elizabeth Enright, Harcourt Brace; *The Great Wheel* by Robert Lawson, Viking; *Tom Paine, Freedom's Apostle* by Leo Gurko, Crowell.

1957 *Miracles on Maple Hill* by Virginia Sorensen, Harcourt Brace. Honor Books: *Old Yeller* by Fred Gipson, Harper; *The House of Sixty Fathers* by Meindert DeJong, Harper; *Mr. Justice Holmes* by Clara Ingram Judson, Follett; *The Corn Grows Ripe* by Dorothy Rhoads, Viking; *Black Fox of Lorne* by Marguerite de Angeli, Doubleday.

1956 *Carry On, Mr. Bowditch* by Jean Lee Latham, Houghton Mifflin. Honor Books: *The Secret River* by Marjorie Kinnan Rawlings, Scribner; *The Golden Name Day* by Jennie Lindquist, Harper; *Men, Microscopes, and Living Things* by Katherine Shippen, Viking.

1955 *The Wheel on the School* by Meindert Dejong, Harper. Honor Books: *The Courage of Sarah Noble* by Alice Dalgliesh, Scribner; *Banner in the Sky* by James Ullman, Lippincott.

1954 *. . . and Now, Miguel* by Joseph Krumgold, Crowell. Honor Books: *All Alone* by Claire Huchet Bishop, Viking; *Shadrach* by Meindert DeJong, Harper; *Hurry Home, Candy* by Meindert DeJong, Harper; *Theodore Roosevelt, Fighting Patriot* by Clara Ingram Judson, Follett; *Magic Maize* by Mary Buff and Conrad Buff, Houghton Mifflin.

1953 *Secret of the Andes* by Ann Nolan Clark, Viking. Honor Books: *Charlotte's Web* by E. B. White, Harper; *Moccasin Trail* by Eloise McGraw, Coward; *Red Sails to Capri* by Ann Weil, Viking; *The Bears of Hemlock Mountain* by Alice Dalgliesh, Scribner; *Birthdays of Freedom* (vol. 1) by Genevieve Foster, Scribner.

1952 *Ginger Pye* by Eleanor Estes, Harcourt Brace. Honor Books: *Americans Before Columbus* by Elizabeth Baily, Viking; *Minn of the Mississippi* by Holling C. Holling, Houghton Mifflin; *The Defender* by Nicholas Kalashnikoff, Scribner; *The Light at Tern Rock* by Julia Sauer, Viking; *The Apple and the Arrow* by Mary Buff and Conrad Buff, Houghton Mifflin.

1951 *Amos Fortune, Free Man* by Elizabeth Yates, Aladdin. Honor Books: *Better Known as Johnny Appleseed* by Mabel Leigh Hunt, Lippincott; *Gandhi, Fighter Without a Sword* by Jeanette Eaton, Morrow; *Abraham Lincoln, Friend of the People* by Clara Ingram Judson, Follett; *The Story of Appleby Capple* by Anne Parrish, Harper.

1950 *The Door in the Wall* by Marguerite de Angeli, Doubleday. Honor Books: *Tree of Freedom* by Rebecca Caudill, Viking; *The Blue Cat of Castle Town* by Catherine Coblentz, Longmans; *Kildee House* by Rutherford Montgomery, Doubleday; *George Washington* by Genevieve Foster, Scribner; *Song of the Pines* by Walter Havighurst and Marion Havighurst, Winston.

1949 *King of the Wind* by Marguerite Henry, Rand McNally. Honor Books: *Seabird* by Holling C. Holling, Houghton Mifflin; *Daughter of the Mountains* by Louise Rankin, Viking; *My Father's Dragon* by Ruth S. Gannett, Random House; *Story of the Negro* by Arna Bontemps, Knopf.

1948 *The Twenty-One Balloons* by William Pène du Bois, Lothrop. Honor Books: *Pancakes-Paris* by Claire Huchet Bishop, Viking; *Li Lun, Lad of Courage* by Carolyn Treffinger, Abingdon; *The Quaint and Curious Quest of Johnny Longfoot* by Catherine Besterman, Bobbs-Merrill; *The Cow-Tail Switch and Other West African Stories* by Harold Courlander, Holt; *Misty of Chincoteague* by Marguerite Henry, Rand McNally.

1947 *Miss Hickory* by Carolyn Sherwin Bailey, Viking. Honor Books: *Wonderful Year* by Nancy Barnes, Messner; *Big Tree* by Mary Buff and Conrad Buff, Viking; *The Heavenly Tenants* by William Maxwell, Harper; *The Avion My Uncle Flew* by Cyrus Fisher, Appleton; *The Hidden Treasure of Glaston* by Eleanore Jewett, Viking.

1946 *Strawberry Girl* by Lois Lenski, Lippincott. Honor Books: *Justin Morgan Had a Horse* by Marguerite Henry, Rand McNally; *The Moved-Outers* by Florence Crannell Means, Houghton Mifflin; *Bhimsa, The Dancing Bear* by Christine Weston, Scribner; *New Found World* by Katherine Shippen, Viking.

1945 *Rabbit Hill* by Robert Lawson, Viking. Honor Books: *The Hundred Dresses* by Eleanor Estes, Harcourt Brace; *The Silver Pencil* by Alice Dalgliesh, Scribner; *Abraham Lincoln's World* by Genevieve Foster, Scribner; *Lone Journey: The Life of Roger Williams* by Jeanette Eaton, Harcourt Brace.

1944 *Johnny Tremain* by Esther Forbes, Houghton Mifflin. Honor Books: *These Happy Golden Years* by Laura Ingalls Wilder, Harper; *Fog Magic* by Julia Sauer, Viking; *Rufus M.* by Eleanor Estes, Harcourt Brace; *Mountain Born* by Elizabeth Yates, Coward.

1943 *Adam of the Road* by Elizabeth Janet Gray, Viking. Honor Books: *The Middle Moffat* by Eleanor Estes, Harcourt Brace; *Have You Seen Tom Thumb?* by Mabel Leigh Hunt, Lippincott.

1942 *The Matchlock Gun* by Walter D. Edmonds, Dodd, Mead. Honor Books: *Little Town on the Prairie* by Laura Ingalls Wilder, Harper; *George Washington's World* by Genevieve Foster, Scribner; *Indian Captive: The Story of Mary Jemison* by Lois Lenski, Lippincott; *Down Ryton Water* by Eva Roe Gaggin, Viking.

1941 *Call It Courage* by Armstrong Sperry, Macmillan. Honor Books: *Blue Willow* by Doris Gates, Viking; *Young Mac of Fort Vancouver* by Mary Jane Carr, Crowell; *The Long Winter* by Laura Ingalls Wilder, Harper; *Nansen* by Anna Gertrude Hall, Viking.

1940 *Daniel Boone* by James Daugherty, Viking. Honor Books: *The Singing Tree* by Kate Seredy, Viking; *Runner of the Mountain Tops* by Mabel Robinson, Random House; *By the Shores of Silver Lake* by Laura Ingalls Wilder, Harper; *Boy with a Pack* by Stephen W. Meader, Harcourt Brace.

1939 *Thimble Summer* by Elizabeth Enright, Farrar & Rhinehart. Honor Books: *Nino* by Valenti Angelo, Viking; *Mr. Popper's Penguins* by Richard Atwater and Florence Atwater, Little, Brown; *"Hello, the Boat!"* by Phyllis Crawford, Holt; *Leader by Destiny: George Washington, Man and Patriot* by Jeanette Eaton, Harcourt Brace; *Penn* by Elizabeth Janet Gray, Viking.

1938 *The White Stag* by Kate Seredy, Viking. Honor Books: *Pecos Bill* by James Cloyd Bowman, Little, Brown; *Bright Island* by Mabel Robinson, Random House; *On the Banks of Plum Creek* by Laura Ingalls Wilder, Harper.

1937 *Roller Skates* by Ruth Sawyer, Viking. Honor Books: *Phebe Fairchild: Her Book* by Lois Lenski, Stokes; *Whistler's Van* by Idwal Jones, Viking; *Golden Basket* by Ludwig Bemelmans, Viking; *Winterbound* by Margery Bianco, Viking; *Audubon* by Constance Rourke, Harcourt Brace; *The Codfish Musket* by Agnes Hewes, Doubleday.

1936 *Caddie Woodlawn* by Carol Brink, Macmillan. Honor Books: *Honk, The Moose* by Phil Strong, Dodd, Mead; *The Good Master* by Kate Seredy, Viking; *Young Walter Scott* by Elizabeth Janet Gray, Viking; *All Sail Set* by Armstrong Sperry, Winston.

1935 *Dobry* by Monica Shannon, Viking. Honor Books: *Pageant of Chinese History* by Elizabeth Seeger, Longman; *Davy Crockett* by Constance Rourke, Harcourt Brace; *Day on Skates* by Hilda Van Stockum, Harper.

1934 *Invincible Louisa* by Cornelia Meigs, Little, Brown. Honor Books: *The Forgotten Daughter* by Caroline Snedeker, Doubleday; *Swords of Steel* by Elsie Singmaster, Houghton Mifflin; *ABC Bunny* by Wanda Gág, Coward; *Winged Girl of Knossos* by Erik Berry, Appleton; *New Land* by Sarah Schmidt, McBride; *Big Tree of Bunlaby* by Padraic Colum, Macmillan; *Glory of the Seas* by Agnes Hewes, Knopf; *Apprentice of Florence* by Anne Kyle, Houghton Mifflin.

1933 *Young Fu of the Upper Yangtze* by Elizabeth Foreman Lewis, Winston. Honor Books: *Swift Rivers* by Cornelia Meigs, Little, Brown; *The Railroad to Freedom* by Hildegarde Swift, Harcourt Brace; *Children of the Soil* by Nora Burglon, Doubleday.

1932 *Waterless Mountain* by Laura Adams Armer, Longmans. Honor Books: *The Fairy Circus* by Dorothy P. Lathrop, Macmillan; *Calico Bush* by Rachel Field, Macmillan; *Boy of the South Seas* by Eunice Tietjens, Coward; *Out of the Flame* by Eloise Lownsbery, Longmans; *Jane's Island* by Marjorie Allee, Houghton Mifflin; *Truce of the Wolf and Other Tales of Old Italy* by Mary Gould Davis, Harcourt Brace.

1931 *The Cat Who Went to Heaven* by Elizabeth Coatsworth, Macmillan. Honor Books: *Floating Island* by Anne Parrish, Harper; *The Dark Star of Itza* by Alida Malkus, Harcourt Brace; *Queer Person* by Ralph Hubbard, Doubleday; *Mountains Are Free* by Julia Davis Adams, Dutton; *Spice and the Devil's Cave* by Agnes Hewes, Knopf; *Meggy Macintosh* by Elizabeth Janet Gray, Doubleday; *Garram the Hunter* by Herbert Best, Doubleday; *Ood-Le-Uk the Wanderer* by Alice Lide and Margaret Johansen, Little, Brown.

1930 *Hitty, Her First Hundred Years* by Rachel Field, Macmillan. Honor Books: *Daughter of the Seine* by Jeanette Eaton, Harper; *Pran of Albania* by Elizabeth Miller, Doubleday; *Jumping-Off Place* by Marian Hurd McNeely, Longmans; *Tangle-Coated Horse and Other Tales* by Ella Young, Longmans; *Vaino* by Julia Davis Adams, Dutton; *Little Blacknose* by Hildegarde Swift, Harcourt Brace.

Coretta Scott King Award

Established in 1969, this award commemorates the life and work of Martin Luther King Jr., and honors Mrs. King for continuing the work for peace and world brotherhood. It is presented annually by the American Library Association to a Black author (A) and illustrator (I) whose works encourage and promote world unity and peace and serve as an inspiration to young people in the achievement of their goals.

2001 *Miracle's Boys* by Jacqueline Woodson, Putnam (A); *Uptown* by Bryan Collier, Henry Holt (I).

2000 *Bud, Not Buddy* by Christopher Paul Curtis, Delacorte (A); *In the Time of the Drums* by Kim L. Siegelson, ill. by Brian Pinkney, Jump at the Sun/Hyperion (I).

1999: *Heaven* by Angela Johnson, Simon & Schuster (A); *I See the Rhythm* by Michele Wood, Children's Book Press (I).

1998 *Forged by Fire* by Sharon Draper, Atheneum (A); *In Daddy's Arms I Am Tall* ill. by Javaka Steptoe, Lee & Low (I).

1997 *Slam!* by Walter Dean Myers, Scholastic (A); *Minty: A Story of Young Harriet Tubman* by Alan Schroeder, ill. by Jerry Pinkney, Dial (I).

1996 *Her Stories* by Virginia Hamilton, Scholastic (A); *The Middle Passage: White Ships Black Cargo* ill. by Tom Feelings, Dial (I).

1995 *Christmas in the Big House, Christmas in the Quarters* by Patricia McKissack and Frederick McKissack, Scholastic (A); *The Creation* by James Weldon Johnson, ill. by James Ransome, Holiday House (I).

1994 *Toning the Sweep* by Angela Johnson, Orchard (A); *Soul Looks Back in Wonder* written and ill. by Tom Feelings, Dial (I).

1993 *The Dark-Thirty: Southern Tales of the Supernatural* by Patricia McKissack, Knopf (A); *The Origin of Life on Earth: An African Myth* by David Anderson, ill. by Katherine Atkins Wilson, Sight Productions (I).

1992 *Now Is Your Time: The African American Struggle for Freedom* by Walter D. Myers, HarperCollins (A); *Tar Beach* by Faith Ringgold, ill. by Faith Ringgold, Crown (I).

1991 *Aida* by Leontyne Price, ill. by Leo Dillon and Diane Dillon, Harcourt Brace (I); *Road to Memphis* by Mildred D. Taylor, ed. by Phyllis Fogelman, 1990, Dial (A).

1990 *Long Hard Journey* by Patricia McKissack and Frederick McKissack, Walker (A); *Nathaniel Talking* by Eloise Greenfield, ill. by Jan S. Gilchrist, Black Butterfly (I).

1989 *Fallen Angels* by Walter D. Myers, Scholastic (A); *Mirandy and Brother Wind* by Patricia C. McKissack, ill. by Jerry Pinkney, Knopf (I).

1988 *The Friendship* by Mildred D. Taylor, ill. by Max Ginsburg, Dial (A); *Mufaro's Beautiful Daughter: An African Tale* ed. and ill. by John Steptoe, Lothrop (I).

1987 *Justin and the Best Biscuits in the World* by Mildred P. Walter, ill. by Catherine Stock, Lothrop (A); *Half a Moon and One Whole Star* by Crescent Dragonwagon, ill. by Jerry Pinkney, Macmillan (I).

1986 *The People Could Fly* by Virginia Hamilton, ill. by Leo Dillon and Diane Dillon, Knopf (A); *Patchwork Quilt* by Valerie Flournoy, ill. by Jerry Pinkey, Dial (I).

1985 *Motown and Didi: A Love Story* by Walter D. Myers, Viking (A).

1984 *Everett Anderson's Goodbye* by Lucille Clifton et al., ill. by Ann Grifalconi, Holt (A); *My Mamma Needs Me* by Mildred P. Walter, ill. by Pat Cummings, Lothrop (I).

1983 *Sweet Whispers, Brother Rush* by Virginia Hamilton, Philomel (A); *Black Child* written and ill. by Peter Magubane, Knopf (I).

1982 *Let the Circle Be Unbroken* by Mildred D. Taylor, Dial (A); *Mother Crocodile: An Uncle Amadou Tale from Senegal* adapted by Rosa Guy, ill. by John Steptoe, Delacorte (I).

1981 *This Life* by Sidney Poitier, Knopf (A); *Beat the Story-Drum, Pum-Pum* written and ill. by Ashley Bryan, Atheneum (I).

1980 *The Young Landlords* by Walter Dean Myers, Viking (A); *Cornrows* by Camille Yarbrough, ill. by Carole Byard, Coward (I).

1979 *Escape to Freedom* by Ossie Davis, Viking (A); *Something on My Mind* by Nikki Grimes, ill. by Tom Feelings, Dial (I).

1978 *Africa Dream* by Eloise Greenfield, ill. by Carole Byard Day/HarperCollins (A, I).

1977 *The Story of Stevie Wonder* by James Haskins, Lothrop (A).

1976 *Duey's Tale* by Pearl Bailey, Harcourt Brace (A).

1975 *The Legend of Africana* by Dorothy Robinson, ill. by Herbert Temple, Johnson (A, I).

1974 *Ray Charles* by Sharon Bell Mathis, ill. by George Ford, HarperCollins (A, I).

Boston Globe–Horn Book Award

These awards have been given annually in the fall since 1967 by the *Boston Globe* and *Horn Book Magazine*. Through 1975, two awards were given: for outstanding text and outstanding illustration. In 1976 the award categories were changed to outstanding fiction or poetry, outstanding nonfiction, and outstanding illustration.

2001 Fiction: *Carver: A Life in Poems* by Merilyn Nelson, Front Street; Nonfiction: *The Longitude Prize* by Joan Dash, ill. by Dusan Petricic, Foster/Farrar; Illustration: *Cold Feet* by Cynthia DeFelice, ill. by Robert Andrew Park, DK Ink.

2000 Fiction: *The Folk Keeper* by Franny Billingsley, Atheneum; Nonfiction: *Sir Walter Ralegh and the Quest for El Dorado* by Marc Aronson, Clarion; Illustration: *Henry Hikes to Fitchburg* written and ill. by D. B. Johnson, Houghton.

1999 Fiction: *Holes* by Louis Sachar, Foster/Farrar; Nonfiction: *The Top of the World: Climbing Mount Everest* written and ill. by Steve Jenkins, Houghton Mifflin; Illustration: *Red-Eyed Tree Frog* by Joy Cowley, ill. with photographs by Nic Bishop, Scholastic. Special Citation: *Tibet: Through the Red Box*, written and ill. by Peter Sis, Foster/Farrar.

1998 Fiction: *The Circuit: Stories From the Life of a Migrant Child* by Francisco Jimenez, University of New Mexico Press; Nonfiction: *Leon's Story* by Leon Walter Tillage, Farrar, Straus, Giroux; Illustration: *And If the Moon Could Talk* by Kate Banks, ill. by Georg Hallensleben, Farrar, Straus, Giroux.

1997 Fiction: *The Friends* by Kazumi Yumoto, Farrar, Straus, Giroux; Nonfiction: *A Drop of Water: A Book of Science and Wonder* by Walter Wick, Scholastic; Illustration: *The Adventures of Sparrow Boy* written and ill. by Brian Pinkney, Simon and Schuster.

1996 Fiction: *Poppy* by Avi, Orchard; Nonfiction: *Orphan Train Rider: One Boy's True Story* by Andrea Warren, Houghton Mifflin; Illustration: *In the Rain with Baby Duck* by Amy Hest, ill. by Jill Barton, Candlewick.

1995 Fiction: *Some of the Kinder Plants* by Tim Wynne-Jones, Orchard; Nonfiction: *Abigail Adams: Witness to a Revolution* by Natalie S. Bober, Atheneum; Illustration: *John Henry* by Julius Lester, ill. by Jerry Pinkney, Dial.

1994 Fiction: *Scooter* by Vera Williams, Greenwillow; Nonfiction: *Eleanor Roosevelt* by Russell Freedman, Clarion; Illustration: *Grandfather's Journey* written and ill. by Allen Say, Houghton Mifflin.

1993 Fiction: *Ajeemah and His Sons* by James Berry, HarperCollins; Nonfiction: *Sojourner Truth: Ain't I a Woman* by Patricia McKissack and Frederick McKissack, Scholastic; Illustration: *The Fortune-Tellers* by Lloyd Alexander, ill. by Trina Schart Hyman, Dutton.

1992 Fiction: *Missing May* by Cynthia Rylant, Orchard; Nonfiction: *Talking with Artists* by Patricia Cummings, Bradbury; Illustration: *Seven Blind Mice* written and ill. by Ed Young, Philomel.

1991 Fiction: *The True Confessions of Charlotte Doyle* by Avi, ill. by Ruth E. Murray, Orchard; Nonfiction: *Appalachia: The Voices of Sleeping Birds* by Cynthia Rylant, ill. by Barry Moser, Harcourt Brace; Illustration: *Tale of the Mandarin Ducks* by Katherine Paterson, ill. by Leo Dillon and Diane Dillon, Lodestar.

1990 Fiction: *Maniac Magee* by Jerry Spinelli, Little, Brown; Nonfiction: *Great Little Madison* by Jean Fritz, Putnam; Illustration: *Lon Po Po: A Red Riding Hood Story from China* by Ed Young, Philomel.

1989 Fiction: *Village by the Sea* by Paula Fox, Orchard; Nonfiction: *The Way Things Work* written and ill. by David Macaulay, Houghton Mifflin; Illustration: *Shy Charles* written and ill. by Rosemary Wells, Dial.

1988 Fiction: *The Friendship* by Mildred Taylor, Dial; Nonfiction: *Anthony Burns: The Defeat and Triumph of a Fugitive Slave* by Virginia Hamilton, Knopf; Illustration: *The Boy of the Three-Year Nap* by Diane Snyder, Houghton Mifflin.

1987 Fiction: *Rabble Starkey* by Lois Lowry, Houghton Mifflin; Nonfiction: *Pilgrims of Plimouth* by Marcia Sewall, Atheneum; Illustration: *Mufaro's Beautiful Daughters* by John Steptoe, Lothrop.

1986 Fiction: *In Summer Light* by Zibby O'Neal, Viking/Kestrel; Nonfiction: *Auks, Rocks and the Odd Dinosaur* by Peggy Thomson, Crowell; Illustration: *The Paper Crane* by Molly Bang, Greenwillow.

1985 Fiction: *The Moves Make the Man* by Bruce Brooks, Harper & Row; Nonfiction: *Commodore Perry in the Land of the Shogun* by Rhoda Blumberg, Lothrop; Illustration: *Mama Don't Allow* by Thatcher Hurd, Harper & Row.

1984 Fiction: *A Little Fear* by Patricia Wrightson, Atheneum/McElderry; Nonfiction: *The Double Life of Pocahontas* by Jean Fritz, Putnam; Illustration: *Jonah and the Great Fish* retold and ill. by Warwick Hutton, Atheneum/McElderry.

1983 Fiction: *Sweet Whispers, Brother Rush* by Virginia Hamilton, Philomel; Nonfiction: *Behind Barbed Wire: The Imprisonment of Japanese Americans During World War II* by Daniel S. Davis, Dutton; Illustration: *A Chair for My Mother* by Vera B. Williams, Greenwillow.

1982 Fiction: *Playing Beatie Bow* by Ruth Park, Atheneum; Nonfiction: *Upon the Head of the Goat: A Childhood in Hungary, 1939–1944* by Aranka Siegal, Farrar, Straus; Illustration: *A Visit to William Blake's Inn: Poems for Innocent and Experienced Travelers* by Nancy Willard, ill. by Alice Provensen and Martin Provensen, Harcourt Brace.

1981 Fiction: *The Leaving* by Lynn Hall, Scribner; Nonfiction: *The Weaver's Gift* by Kathryn Lasky, Warne; Illustration: *Outside Over There* by Maurice Sendak, Harper & Row.

1980 Fiction: *Conrad's War* by Andrew Davies, Crown; Nonfiction: *Building: The Fight Against Gravity* by Mario Salvadori, Atheneum/McElderry; Illustration: *The Garden of Abdul Gasazi* by Chris Van Allsburg, Houghton Mifflin.

1979 Fiction: *Humbug Mountain* by Sid Fleischman, Atlantic/Little, Brown; Nonfiction: *The Road From Home: The Story of an Armenian Girl* by David Kherdian, Greenwillow; Illustration: *The Snowman* by Raymond Briggs, Random House.

1978 Fiction: *The Westing Game* by Ellen Raskin, Dutton; Nonfiction: *Mischling, Second Degree: My Childhood in Nazi Germany* by Ilse Koehn, Greenwillow; Illustration: *Anno's Journey* by Mitsumasa Anno, Philomel.

1977 Fiction: *Child of the Owl* by Laurence Yep, Harper & Row; Nonfiction: *Chance Luck and Destiny* by Peter Dickinson, Atlantic/Little, Brown; Illustration: *Ganfa' Grig Had a Pig and Other Rhymes* by Wallace Tripp, Little, Brown.

1976 Fiction: *Unleaving* by Jill Paton Walsh, Farrar, Straus; Nonfiction: *Voyaging to Cathay: Americans in the China Trade* by Alfred Tamarin and Shirley Glubok, Viking; Illustration: *Thirteen* by Remy Charlip and Jerry Joyner, Parents.

1975 Text: *Transport 7–41–R* by T. Degens, Viking; Illustration: *Anno's Alphabet* by Mitsumasa Anno, Crowell.

1974 Text: *M. C. Higgins, The Great* by Virginia Hamilton, Macmillan; Illustration: *Jambo Means Hello* by Muriel Feelings, ill. by Tom Feelings, Dial.

1973 Text: *The Dark Is Rising* by Susan Cooper, Atheneum/McElderry; Illustration: *King Stork* by Trina Schart Hyman, Little, Brown.

1972 Text: *Tristan and Iseult* by Rosemary Sutcliff, Dutton; Illustration: *Mr. Gumpy's Outing* by John Burningham, Holt.

1971 Text: *A Room Made of Windows* by Eleanor Cameron, Atlantic/Little, Brown; Illustration: *If I Built a Village* by Kazue Mizumura, Crowell.

1970 Text: *The Intruder* by John Rowe Townsend, Lippincott; Illustration: *Hi, Cat!* by Ezra Jack Keats, Macmillan.

1969 Text: *A Wizard of Earthsea* by Ursula K. Le Guin, Houghton Mifflin; Illustration: *The Adventures of Paddy Pork* by John S. Goodall, Harcourt Brace.

1968 Text: *The Spring Rider* by John Lawson, Crowell; Illustration: *Tikki Tikki Tembo* by Arlene Mosel, ill. by Blair Lent, Holt.

1967 Text: *The Little Fishes* by Erik Christian Haugaard, Houghton Mifflin; Illustration: *London Bridge Is Falling Down* by Peter Spier, Doubleday.

Appendix B

Poetry and Rhymes for Reading

Adoff, Arnold. (1995). *Slowdance heartbreak blues*. New York: Macmillan.

Bagert, Brod. (1992). *Let me be the boss*. Honesdale, PA: Boyds Mills.

Bagert, Brod. (1999). *Rainbows, head lice, and pea-green tile: Poems from the voice of the classroom teacher*. Gainesville, FL: Maupin.

Bagert, Brod. (2002). *Giant children*. New York: Dial.

Benjamin, Alan. (1993). *A nickel buys a rhyme*. New York: Morrow.

Brown, Marc. (1980). *Pickle things*. New York: Putnam.

Carle, Eric. (1989). *Eric Carle's animals animals*. New York: Philomel.

Cofer, Judith O. (1995). *An island like you*. New York: Orchard.

Cole, Joanne, & Calmenson, Stephanie. (1995). *Yours till banana splits: 201 autograph rhymes*. New York: Beech Tree.

dePaola, Tomie. (1985). *Tomie de Paola's Mother Goose*. New York: Putnam.

dePaola, Tomie. (1988). *Tomie de Paola's book of poems*. New York: Putnam.

de Regniers, Beatrice S., Moore, Eva, & White, Mary M. (1969). *Poems children will sit still for*. New York: Citation.

de Regniers, Beatrice S., Moore, Eva, & White, Mary M. (1988). *Sing a song of popcorn: Every child's book of poems*. New York: Scholastic.

Dyer, Jane. (1996). *Animal crackers: A delectable collection of pictures, poems, and lullabies for the very young*. Boston: Little, Brown.

Fleischman, Paul. (1988). *Joyful noise: Poems for two voices*. New York: Harper & Row.

Fleming, Denise. (1996). *Where once there was a wood*. New York: Henry Holt.

Florian, Denise. (1994). *Bing, bang, bong*. New York: Harcourt, Brace.

Florian, Douglas. (1994*). Beast feast*. New York: Harcourt Brace.

Goldstein, Bobbye. (1992). *What's on the menu?* New York: Viking.

Hale, Glorya. (1997). *Read-aloud poems for young people*. New York: Black Dog & Leventhal.

Hopkins, Lee Bennett. (Ed.). (1992). *Pterodactyls and pizza.* New York: Trumpet.

Hopkins, Lee Bennett. (1995). *Small talk: A book of short poems.* New York: Harcourt Brace.

Lansky, Bruce. (1994). *A bad case of the giggles.* New York: Meadowbrook Press.

Lansky, Bruce. (1996). *Poetry party.* New York: Meadowbrook Press.

Lewis, J. Patrick. (1998). *Doodle dandies: Poems that take shape.* New York: Atheneum.

Livingston, Myra C. (1987). *Cat poems.* New York: Holiday.

Livingston, Myra C. (1988). *Space songs.* New York: Holiday.

Lobel, Arnold. (1983). *The book of pigericks.* New York: Harper & Row.

Lobel, Arnold. (1986). *The Random House book of Mother Goose.* New York: Random House.

London, Jonathan. (1993). *Eyes of Grey Wolf.* San Francisco: Chronicle.

Martin, Rafe. (1996). *Mysterious tales of Japan.* New York: Putnam.

Medearis, Angela S. (1995). *Skin deep.* New York: Macmillan.

Moss, Jeff. (1989). *The butterfly jar.* New York: Bantam.

Moss, Jeff. (1991). *The other side of the door.* New York: Bantam.

Nye, Naomi S. (1995). *The tree is older than you are.* New York: Simon Schuster.

O'Neill, Mary. (1961). *Hailstones and halibut bones: Adventures in color.* Garden City, NY: Doubleday.

Opie, Iona. (Ed.). (1996). *My very first Mother Goose.* Cambridge, MA: Candlewick.

Opie, Iona, & Opie, Peter. (Eds.). (1992). *I saw Esau: The schoolchild's pocket book.* Cambridge, MA: Candlewick.

Patten, Brian. (1999). *The Puffin twentieth-century collection of verse.* London: Penguin.

Prelutsky, Jack. (Ed.). (1983). *The Random House book of poetry for children.* New York: Random House.

Prelutsky, Jack. (1984). *New kid on the block.* New York: Greenwillow.

Prelutsky, Jack. (Ed.). (1986). *Read-aloud rhymes for the very young.* New York: Knopf.

Prelutsky, Jack. (1986). *Ride a purple pelican.* New York: Greenwillow.

Prelutsky, Jack. (1990). *Something big has been here.* New York: Greenwillow.

Prelutsky, Jack. (1999). *The twentieth century children's poetry treasury.* New York: Knopf.

Silverstein, Shel. (1974). *Where the sidewalk ends.* New York: HarperCollins.

Silverstein, Shel. (1981). *A light in the attic.* New York: HarperCollins.

Slier, Deborah. (Ed.). (1991). *Make a joyful sound: Poems for children by African-American poets.* New York: Checkerboard.

Sword, Elizabeth Hauge. (1995). *A child's anthology of poetry.* Hopewell, NJ: Ecco Press.

Viorst, Judith. (1981). *If I were in charge of the world and other worries.* New York: Atheneum.

Wildsmith, Brian. (1964). *Brian Wildsmith's Mother Goose.* New York: Franklin Watts.

Appendix C

Classic Predictable Pattern Books

Pattern or predictable books contain distinct language patterns that make them easy for children to learn to read. Moreover, since the repetitive and predictable language patterns give children an enjoyable way to play with sounds, words, phrases, and sentences, reading pattern books to children can enhance their phonemic awareness.

In general, pattern books should be read several times to allow children to learn them thoroughly. This can be done over several days or even weeks. Once the children learn the text, the teacher begins to direct their attention to individual sentences, phrases, words, letters, and letter combinations. This natural progression from whole to part allows students to discover how smaller units of language work without distorting or disrupting the process of reading and enjoying the story. Teachers use tools such as sentence strips, word banks, and word sort activities to direct students' attention to words, phrases, and sentences in the stories.

Because of the predictable and patterned nature of the stories, they are well suited for students who write their own versions of these stories using the language patterns in the original text as a guide or scaffold. Students find it fun and satisfying to compose stories similar to those they hear and read and to share their compositions with their classmates.

Adams, Pam. (1974). *This old man*. New York: Grosset & Dunlap.

Alborough, Jez. (2000). *Duck in the truck*. New York: Harper.

Aliki. (1989). *My five senses*. New York: Crowell.

Allenberg, Janet, & Allenberg, Allan. (1978). *Each peach, pear, plum*. New York: Viking Press.

Baer, Gene. (1989). *Thump, thump, rat-a-tat-tat*. New York: Harper & Row.

Becker, John. (1973). *Seven little rabbits*. New York: Scholastic.

Brown, Marcia. (1957). *The three billy goats gruff*. New York: Harcourt Brace Jovanovich.

Brown, Margaret Wise. (1947). *Goodnight moon*. New York: Harper & Row.

Brown, Margaret Wise. (1964). *The important book*. New York: Parents' Magazine.

Brown, Ruth. (1981). *A dark, dark tale*. New York: Dial.

Carle, Eric. (1969). *The very hungry caterpillar*. New York: Philomel.

Carle, Eric. (1977). *The grouchy ladybug*. New York: Crowell.

Chapman, Cheryl. (1994). *Snow on snow on snow*. New York: Dial.

Cowley, Joy. (1987). *Mrs. Wishy-Washy*. Bothell, WA: Wright Group.

Downey, Lynn. (2000). *The flea's sneeze*. New York: Holt.

Emberley, Ed. (1974). *Klippity klop*. Boston: Little, Brown.

Ets, Marie Hall. (1972). *Elephant in a well*. New York: Viking.

Fox, Mem. (1990). *I went walking*. New York: Harcourt.

Fox, Mem. (1992). *Hattie and the fox*. New York: Bradbury.

Gág, Wanda. (1928). *Millions of cats*. New York: Coward-McCann.

Galdone, Paul. (1973). *The little red hen*. New York: Scholastic.

Guarino, Deborah. (1989). *Is your mama a llama?* New York: Scholastic.

Hennessy, B. G. (1990). *Jake baked the cake*. New York: Viking.

Hill, Eric. (1980). *Where's Spot?* New York: Putnam.

Hoberman, Mary Ann. (1978). *A house is a home for me*. New York: Viking.

Hutchins, Pat. (1968). *Rosie's walk*. New York: Macmillan.

Hutchins, Pat. (1971). *Titch*. New York: Collier.

Hutchins, Pat. (1972). *Good-night owl*. New York: Macmillan.

Hutchins, Pat. (1982). *1 hunter*. New York: Greenwillow.

Hutchins, Pat. (1986). *The doorbell rang*. New York: Greenwillow.

Jonas, Ann. (1989). *Color dance*. New York: Greenwillow.

Keats, Ezra Jack. (1971). *Over in the meadow*. New York: Scholastic.

Kent, Jack. (1971). *The fat cat*. New York: Scholastic.

Kovalski, Maryann. (1987). *The wheels on the bus*. Little, Brown.

Kraus, Robert. (1970). *Whose mouse are you?* New York: Macmillan.

Langstaff, John. (1974). *Oh, a-hunting we will go*. New York: Atheneum.

Martin, Bill. (1983). *Brown bear, brown bear*. New York: Holt.

Martin, Bill. (1991). *Polar bear, polar bear*. New York: Holt.

McKissack, Patricia. (1986). *Who is coming?* Chicago: Children's Press.

McKissack, Patricia, & McKissack, Fredrick. (1988). *Constance stumbles*. Chicago: Children's Press.

McNaughton, Colin. (1994). *Suddenly!* New York: Harcourt.

Numeroff, Laura Joffe. (1985). *If you give a mouse a cookie*. New York: Harper & Row.

Numeroff, Laura Joffe. (1991). *If you give a moose a muffin*. New York: HarperCollins.

Peek, Merle. (1985). *Mary wore her red dress*. New York: Clarion.

Pomerantz, Charlotte. (1994). *Here comes Henny*. New York: Greenwillow.

Raffi. (1987). *Down by the bay*. New York: Crown.

Roffey, Maureen. (1988). *I spy at the zoo*. New York: Macmillan.

Rosen, Michael. (1992). *We're going on a bear hunt*. New York: Atheneum.

Rounds, Blen. (1989). *Old MacDonald had a farm*. Holiday.

Sendak, Maurice. (1962). *Chicken soup and rice*. New York: Williams.

Sendak, Maurice. (1963). *Where the wild things are*. New York: Scholastic.

Seuss, Dr. (1957). *The cat in the hat*. New York: Random House.

Seuss, Dr. (1965). *Green eggs and ham*. New York: Random House.

Shaw, Nancy. (1989). *Sheep in a jeep*. Boston: Houghton Mifflin.

Shaw, Nancy. (1989). *Sheep on a ship*. Boston: Houghton Mifflin.

Viorst, Judith. (1972). *Alexander and the terrible, horrible, no good, very bad day*. New York: Atheneum.

Waddell, Martin. (1993). *Farmer duck*. Cambridge, MA: Candlewick.

Wescott, Nadine Bernard. (1980). *I know an old lady who swallowed a fly*. Boston: Houghton Mifflin.

Williams, Sue. (1992). *I went walking*. Orlando, FL: Harcourt Brace Jovanovich.

Winter, Jeanette. (2000). *The house that Jack built*. New York: Dial.

Wood, Audrey. (1984). *The napping house*. New York: Harcourt Brace Jovanovich.

Zemach, Margot. (1965). *The teeny tiny woman*. New York: Scholastic.

Zemach, Margot. (1976). *Hush, little baby*. New York: Dutton.

Appendix D

Series Books

Beginning Readers

Adler, David. CAM JANSEN AND YOUNG CAM JANSEN ADVEN-TURE SERIES. New York: Penguin Group.

Allard, Harry. MISS NELSON BOOKS. Boston: Houghton Mifflin.

Asch, Frank. BEAR BOOKS. New York: Scholastic.

Bridwell, Norman. CLIFFORD (the dog) BOOKS. New York: Scholastic.

Bright, Robert. GEORGIE BOOKS. New York: Doubleday.

Brown, Marc. ARTHUR BOOKS. Boston: Little, Brown.

Cameron, Ann. JULIAN BOOKS. New York: Random House.

Caseley, Judith. HARRY AND ARNEY BOOKS. New York: Greenwil-low.

Clifton, Lucille. EVERETT ANDERSON BOOKS. New York: Holt, Rinehart, & Winston.

dePaola, Tomie. 26 FAIRMOUNT AVENUE AND SEQUELS. New York: Putnam.

Giff, Patricia Reilly. THE KIDS OF THE POLK STREET SCHOOL. Bantam Doubleday, Dell Books for Young Readers, Delacorte Press.

Hill, Eric. SPOT BOOKS. New York: Putnam.

Hoban, Russell. FRANCES (the badger) BOOKS. New York: Harper & Row.

Lobel, Arnold. FROG AND TOAD BOOKS. New York: Harper & Row.

McDonnell, Christine. DON'T BE MAD, IVY and others. New York: Dial.

Parrish, Peggy. AMELIA BEDELIA BOOKS. New York: Harper & Row.

Pilkey, Dav. DRAGON BOOKS. New York: Orchard.

Rey, H. A., & Rey, Margaret. CURIOUS GEORGE BOOKS. Boston: Houghton Mifflin.

Rylant, Cynthia. HENRY AND MUDGE BOOKS. Scarsdale, NY: Bradbury.

Rylant, Cynthia. THE HIGH-RISE PRIVATE EYES. New York: Green-willow.

Rylant, Cynthia. MR. PUTTER AND TABBY BOOKS. New York: Harcourt Brace & Company.

Sharmat, Marjorie Weinman. NATE THE GREAT BOOKS. New York: Random House International.

Zion, Gene. HARRY (the dirty dog) BOOKS. New York: Harper & Row.

Transitional and Maturing Readers

Byars, Betsy. BINGO BROWN BOOKS. New York: Viking.

Cleary, Beverly. HENRY HUGGINS BOOKS. New York: Morrow.

Cleary, Beverly. RAMONA BOOKS. New York: Morrow.

Danziger, Paula. AMBER BROWN BOOKS. New York: Putnam.

Haas, Dorothy. PEANUT BUTTER AND JELLY BOOKS. New York: Scholastic.

Haywood, Carolyn. BETSY BOOKS. San Diego: Harcourt Brace.

Haywood, Carolyn. EDDIE BOOKS. San Diego: Harcourt Brace.

Herman, Charlotte. MAX MALONE BOOKS. New York: Henry Holt.

Howe, James. SEBASTION BARTH MYSTERIES. New York: Atheneum.

Hurwitz, Johanna. ALDO BOOKS. New York: Morrow.

Hurwitz, Johanna. RUSSELL BOOKS. New York: Morrow.

Kline, Suzy. HERBIE JONES BOOKS. New York: Putnam.

Lisle, Janet Taylor. THE GOLD DUST LETTERS and others. New York: Orchard.

Lowry, Lois. ANASTASIA KRUPNIK BOOKS. Boston: Houghton Mifflin.

Martin, Ann. BABY-SITTERS BOOKS. New York: Scholastic.

Naylor, Phillis Reynolds. ALICE BOOKS. New York: Atheneum.

Osborne, Mary Pope. MAGIC TREE HOUSE BOOKS. New York: Random House, Scholastic.

Park, Barbara. JUNIE B. JONES BOOKS. New York: Random House.

Peck, Robert Newton. SOUP BOOKS. New York: Knopf.

Sanchar, Louis. WAYSIDE SCHOOL BOOKS. New York: Morrow.

Simon, Seymour. EINSTEIN ANDERSON BOOKS. New York: Puffin.

Stine, R. L. GOOSEBUMPS BOOKS. New York: Scholastic.

Warner, Gertrude Chandler. BOXCAR CHILDREN BOOKS. New York: Scholastic.

Wilder, Laura Ingalls. LITTLE HOUSE BOOKS. New York: Harper & Row.

Appendix E

Alphabet, Number, and Other Concept Books

ABC Books

Anno, Mitsumasa. (1974). *Anno's alphabet*. New York: Crowell. (Ages 5–7).

Aylesworth, Jim. (1992). *The folks in the valley: A Pennsylvania Dutch ABC*. HarperCollins. (Ages 3–7).

Base, G. (1986). *Animalia*. New York: Abrams. (Ages 6+).

Bridwell, Norman. (1984). *Clifford's ABC*. New York: Scholastic. (Ages 5–7).

Ehlert, Lois. (1989). *Eating the alphabet: Fruits and vegetables from A to Z*. Harcourt. (Ages 2–7).

Feelings, Muriel L. (1974). *Jambo means hello*. New York: Dial. (Ages 5–7).

Folsom, Marcia, & Folsom, Michael. (1985). *Easy as pie: A guessing game of sayings* (Ill. by Jack Kent). New York: Clarion. (Ages 7–10).

Gardner, Beau. (1986). *Have you ever seen . . .? An ABC book*. New York: Dodd, Mead. (Ages 3–6).

Geisert, Arthur. (1986). *Pigs from A to Z*. Boston: Houghton Mifflin. (Ages 2–8).

Grimes, Nikki. (1995). *C is for city*. Lothrop, Lee & Shepard. (Ages 6–10).

Gustafson, Scott. (1994). *Alphabet soup: A feast of letters*. New York: Greenwich. (Ages 3–8).

Hawkins, Colin, & Hawkins, Jacqui. (1987). *Busy ABC*. New York: Viking. (Ages 4–6).

Hoban, Tana. (1987). *26 letters and 99 cents*. New York: Greenwillow. (Ages 5–7).

Hughes, Shirley. (1987). *Lucy and Tom's a.b.c.* New York: Puffin. (Ages 4–7).

Johnson, Stephen. (1995). *Alphabet city*. New York: Viking. (Ages 3–8).

Jordan, Tanis. (1996). *Amazon alphabet*. New York: Kingfisher. (Ages 3–8).

Kitamura, Satoshi. (1985). *What's inside: The alphabet book*. New York: Farrar, Straus, & Giroux. (Ages 3–8).

Kitchen, Bert. (1984). *Animal alphabet*. New York: Dial. (Ages 2–5).

Laidlaw, Ken. (1996). *The amazing I spy ABC*. New York: Dial. (Ages 3–8).

Lobel, Anita, & Lobel, Arnold. (1981). *On Market Street*. New York: Greenwillow. (Ages 4–7).

Marshall, James. (1995). *Look once look twice*. New York: Ticknor and Fields. (Ages 3–8).

Martin, Bill, Jr., & Archambault, John. (1989). *Chicka chicka boom boom* (Ill. by Lois Ehlert). New York: Simon & Schuster. (Ages 4–6).

Meddaugh, Susan. (1996). *Martha blah blah*. Boston: Houghton Mifflin. (Ages 3–8).

Musgrove, Margaret W. (1976). *Ashanti to zulu*. New York: Dial. (Ages 5–8).

Neumeier, Marty, & Glaser, Byron. *Action alphabet*. New York: Greenwillow. (Ages 3–8).

Pelham, David. (1991). *A is for animals*. New York: Simon & Schuster. (Ages 3–8).

Pelletier, David. (1996). *Graphic alphabet*. New York: Orchard. (Ages 3–8).

Potter, Beatrix. (1987). *Peter Rabbit's ABC*. New York: Warne. (Ages 2–4).

Sanders, Marilyn, & Sanders, Eve. (1995). *What's your name?* Holiday. (Ages 6–10).

Steig, William. (1968). *CDB!* New York: Simon & Schuster. (Ages 5–8).

Tapahonso, Luci, & Schick, Eleanor. (1995). *Navajo ABC*. Little, Brown. (Ages 6–12).

Van Allsburg, Chris. (1987). *The Z was zapped: A play in twenty-six acts*. Boston: Houghton Mifflin. (Ages 5–8).

Colors

Boynton, Sandra. (1984). Blue hat, green hat. New York: Simon & Schuster. (Ages 2–5).

Chocolate, Debbi. (1996). *Kente colors*. New York: Walker. (Ages 3–8).

Crews, Donald. (1978). *Freight train*. New York: Greenwillow. (Ages 2–7).

Ehlert, Lois. (1988). *Planting a rainbow*. New York: Harcourt Brace Jovanovich. (Ages 4–8).

Henkes, Kevin. (1996). *Lily's purple plastic purse*. New York: Greenwillow. (Ages 3–8).

Hill, Eric. (1986). *Spot looks at colors*. New York: Putnam. (Ages 3–6).

Hoban, Tana. (1978). *Is it red? Is it yellow? Is it blue?* New York: Greenwillow. (Ages 4–8).

Hoban, Tana. (1988). *Of colors and things*. New York: Greenwillow. (Ages 4–8).

Imershein, Betsy. (1989). *Finding red finding yellow*. New York: Harcourt Brace Jovanovich. (Ages 4–8).

Jonas, Ann. (1989). *Color dance*. New York: Greenwillow. (Ages 2–5).

Johnson, Crockett. (1955). *Harold and the purple crayon*. New York: HarperCollins. (Ages 3–8).

Lionni, Leo. (1959). *Little blue, little yellow.* New York: Astor. (Ages 4–8).

Lionni, Leo. (1976). *A color of his own.* New York: Pantheon. (Ages 4–8).

Martin, Bill. (1983). *Brown bear, brown bear* (Ill. by Eric Carle). New York: Holt. (Ages 3–7).

McMillan, Bruce. (1988). *Growing colors.* New York: Lothrop. (Ages 2–5).

Peck, Merle. (1985). *Mary wore her red dress, Henry wore his green sneakers.* New York: Clarion. (Ages 4–8).

Reasoner, Charles. (1996). *Color crunch!* New York: Putnam. (Ages 2–5).

Samton, Sheila White. (1987). *Beside the bay.* New York: Philomel. (Ages 3–5).

Sawicki, Norma. (1989). *The little red house* (Ill. by Toni Goffe). New York: Lothrop. (Ages 3–7).

Serfozo, Mary. (1988). *Who said red?* (Ill. by Keiko Narahashi). New York: McElderry. (Ages 3–6).

Seuss, Dr. (1996). *My many colored days.* New York: Random House. (Ages 3–8).

Sis, Peter. (1989). *Going up.* New York: Greenwillow. (Ages 4–7).

Walsh, Ellen Stoll. (1989). *Mouse paint.* New York: Harcourt Brace. (Ages 3–8).

Yumilteo. (1996). *The green frogs: A Korean folktale.* Boston: Houghton Mifflin. (Ages 3–8).

Counting Books

Addshead, Paul. (1995). *One odd old owl.* New York: Child's Play. (Ages 3–8).

Aylesworth, Jim. (1988). *One crow: A counting rhyme* (Ill. by Ruth Young). Philadelphia: HarperCollins. (Ages 2–6).

Bang, Molly. (1983). *Ten, nine, eight.* New York: Greenwillow. (Ages 3–6).

Bertrand, Lynne. (1996). *Dragon naps.* New York: Viking. (Ages 2–6).

Boon, Emilie. (1987). *1 2 3, how many animals can you see?* New York: Orchard. (Ages 3–6).

Bowen, Betsy. (1995). *Gathering: A northwoods counting book.* Boston: Little, Brown. (Ages 3–8).

Boynton, Sandra. (1995). *Doggies.* New York: Simon & Schuster. (Ages 2–5).

Burningham, John. (1980). *The shopping basket.* New York: Crowell. (Ages 3–7).

Christelow, Eileen. (1989). *Five little monkeys jumping on the bed.* New York: Clarion. (Ages 2–7).

Crews, Donald. (1986). *Ten black dots.* New York: Greenwillow. (Ages 3–6).

de Regniers, Beatrice Schenk. (1985). *So many cats!* (Ill. by Ellen Weiss). New York: Clarion. (Ages 3–5).

Falwell, Cathryn. (1993). *Feast for ten.* New York: Clarion. (Ages 4–7).

Garne, S. T. (1994). *One white sail.* New York: Simon & Schuster. (Ages 6–8).

Fowler, Richard. (1987). *Mr. Little's noisy 1 2 3.* New York: Grosset & Dunlap. (Ages 3–8).

Giganti, Paul. (1992). *Each orange had eight slices: A counting book.* New York: Greenwillow. (Ages 3–8).

Gustafson, Scott. (1995). *Animal orchestra: A counting book*. New York: Greenwich. (Ages 3–8).

Hoban, Tana. (1972). *Count & see*. New York: Macmillan. (Ages 3–6).

Hoban, Tana. (1985). *1, 2, 3*. New York: Greenwillow. (Ages 3–6).

Hutchins, Pat. (1982). *1 hunter*. New York: Greenwillow. (Ages 3–6).

Inkpen, Mick. (1987). *One bear at bedtime*. Boston: Little, Brown. (Ages 3–7).

Kitchen, Bert. (1987). *Animal numbers*. New York: Dial. (Ages 3–5).

Long, Lynette. (1996). *Domino addition*. Watertown, MA: Charlesbridge. (Ages 3–8).

Mack, Stan. (1974). *10 bears in my bed*. New York: Pantheon. (Ages 3–6).

McGrath, Barbara. (1994). *The M&Ms brand counting book*. Watertown, MA: Charlesbridge. (Ages 3–6).

McMillan, Bruce. (1995). *Jelly beans for sale*. New York: Scholastic. (Ages 3–8).

Merriam, Eve. (1996). *12 ways to get to 11*. New York: Alladin. (Ages 3–8).

Pallotta, Jerry. (1992). *The icky bug counting book*. Watertown, MA: Charlesbridge. (Ages 3–8).

Peek, Merle. (1981). *Roll over*. New York: Clarion. (Ages 3–6).

Potter, Beatrix. (1988). *Peter Rabbit's 1 2 3*. New York: Warne. (Ages 3–5).

Ryan, Pam Munoz. (1994). *One hundred is a family*. New York: Hyperion. (Ages 5–10).

Sis, Peter. (1989). *Going up! A color counting book*. New York: Greenwillow. (Ages 4–7).

Stobbs, William. (1984). *1, 2 buckle my shoe*. Oxford: Oxford University Press. (Ages 3–6).

Tafuri, Nancy. (1986). *Who's counting?* New York: Greenwillow. (Ages 3–6).

Wadsworth, Olive A. (1985). *Over in the meadow: A counting out rhyme* (Ill. by Mary Maki Rae). New York: Viking. (Ages 2–5).

Other Concepts

Adlerman, David. *Africa calling nighttime falling*. New York: Whispering Coyote. (Ages 3–8).

Alhberg, Janet, & Ahlberg, Allen. (1978). *Each peach pear plum: An I spy book*. New York: Viking. (Ages 5–7).

Barton, Byron. (1986). *Airplanes*. New York: Crowell. (Ages 3–6).

Barton, Byron. (1986). *Boats*. New York: Crowell. (Ages 3–6).

Barton, Byron. (1986). *Trains*. New York: Crowell. (Ages 3–6).

Barton, Byron. (1986). *Trucks*. New York: Crowell. (Ages 3–6).

Brown, Margaret Wise. (1995). *Big red barn*. New York: HarperCollins. (Ages 2–8).

Carle, Eric. (1969). *The very hungry caterpillar*. New York: Philomel. (Ages 4–8).

Clifton, Lucile. (1978). *Some of the days of Everett Anderson* (Ill. by Evangeline Ness). New York: Holt. (Ages 5–8).

Demi. (1987). *Demi's opposites: An animal game book*. New York: Grosset & Dunlap. (Ages 3–8).

Dunrea, Olivier. (1989). *Deep down underground*. New York: Macmillan. (Ages 5–8).

Finelli, Sara. (1995). *My map book*. New York: HarperCollins. (Ages 3–8).

Gundersheimer, Karen. (1986). *Shapes to show*. New York: Harper & Row. (Ages 2–6).

Hill, Eric. (1986). *Spot looks at shapes*. New York: Putnam. (Ages 3–5).

Hoban, Tana. (1985). *Is it larger? Is it smaller?* New York: Greenwillow. (Ages 3–6).

Hooper, Meredith. (1986). *Seven eggs* (Ill. by Terry McKenna). New York: Harper & Row. (Ages 3–5).

Isadora, Rachel. (1985). *I see, I hear, I touch*. New York: Greenwillow. (Ages 2–4).

Kunhardt, Dorothy. (1968). *Pat the bunny*. Racine, WI: Western. (Ages 2–5).

Lionni, Leo. (1995). *On my beach there are many pebbles*. New York: Morrow. (Ages 3–8).

McMillan, Bruce. (1991). *Eating fractions*. New York: Scholastic. (Ages 6–10).

Nikola-Lisa, W. (1994). *Bein' with you this way*. New York: Lee & Low. (Ages 3–8).

Onyefulu, Ifeoma. (1995). *Emeka's gift: An African counting story*. Cobblestone.(Ages 6–10).

Pilkey, Dav. (1997). *Big dog and little dog getting into trouble*. New York: Harcourt Brace. (Ages 2–6).

Provenson, Alice, & Provenson, Martin. (1978). *The year at Maple Hill Farm*. New York: Atheneum. (Ages 4–7).

Rogers, Fred. (1987). *Making friends* (Photos by Jim Judkis). New York: Putnam/First Experience. (Ages 3–6).

Rogers, Fred. (1987). *Moving* (Photos by Jim Judkis). New York: Putnam/First Experience. (Ages 3–6).

Roy, Ron. (1987). *Whose hat is that?* (Photos by Rosemarie Hausherr). New York: Clarion. (Ages 4–8).

Scieszka, Jon. (1995). *Math curse*. New York: Viking. (Ages 6–12).

Ward, Cindy. (1988). *Cookie's week* (Ill. by Tomie de Paola). New York: Putnam. (Ages 4–6).

Wells, Tony. (1987). *Puzzle doubles*. New York: Macmillan/Aladdin. (Ages 2–5).

Yetkai, Niki. (1987). *Bears in pairs* (Ill. by Diane deGroat). New York: Bradbury. (Ages 2–6).

Ziefert, Harriet. (1986). *All clean!* (Ill. by Henrik Drescher). New York: Harper & Row. (Ages 3–6).

Ziefert, Harriet. (1986). *All gone!* (Ill. by Henrik Drescher). New York: Harper & Row. (Ages 3–6).

Ziefert, Harriet. (1986). *Bear all year: A guessing-game story* (Ill. by Arnold Lobel). New York: Harper & Row. (Ages 3–5).

Ziefert, Harriet. (1986). *Run! Run!* (Ill. by Henrik Drescher). New York: Harper & Row. (Ages 3–6).

Appendix F

Common Word Families

Teachers use word families (letter patterns or phonograms) as an alternative strategy for recognizing or decoding unknown words. One instructional approach is to focus on one or two word families at a time. Brainstorm short and long words that belong to the particular word families. List the words on chart paper and display the charts around the room for easy reading and spelling. When students come to unknown words, cue them to look for word families they know. Because words in word families rhyme, an excellent complement to word family instruction is reading and writing poetry.

ab: tab, drab
ace: race, place
ack: lack, track
ad: bad, glad
ade: made, shade
ag: bag, flag
age: page, stage
ail: mail, snail
ain: rain, train
ake: take, brake
alk: talk, chalk
all: ball, squall
am: ham, swam
ame: name, blame
amp: camp, clamp
an: man, span
and: land, gland
ane: plane, cane
ang: bang, sprang
ank: bank, plank
ant: pant, chant
ap: nap, snap
ape: tape, drape
ar: car, star
are: care, glare
ark: dark, spark

art: part, start
ash: cash, flash
ast: past, blast
at: fat, scat
ate: gate, plate
ave: gave, shave
aw: saw, draw
ay: hay, clay
eak: leak, sneak
eal: real, squeal
eam: team, stream
ean: mean, lean
ear: year, spear
eat: beat, cheat
eck: peck, check
ed: bed, shed
eed: need, speed
eel: feel, kneel
een: seen, screen
eep: keep, sheep
eet: feet, sleet
eg: leg
ell: fell, swell
elt: felt, belt
en: Ben, when
end: tend, send

ent: sent, spent
ess: less, bless
est: rest, chest
et: get, jet
ew: flew, chew
ib: bib, crib
ice: rice, splice
ick: kick, stick
id: hid, slid
ide: wide, pride
ig: pig, twig
ight: tight, bright
ike: Mike, spike
ill: fill, chill
im: him, trim
in: tin, spin
ind: kind, blind
ine: mine, spine
ing: sing, string
ink: sink, shrink
ip: hip, flip
ipe: ripe, swipe
ire: tire, sire
ish: dish, swish
it: hit, quit
ite: bite, write
ive: five, hive
oat: boat, float
ob: job, throb
ock: lock, stock
og: fog, clog
oil: boil, broil
oke: woke, spoke
old: gold, scold
ole: hole, stole

oll: droll, roll
one: cone, phone
ong: long, wrong
ool: cool, fool
oom: room, bloom
oop: hoop, snoop
oot: boot, shoot
op: top, chop
ope: hope, slope
ore: bore, snore
orn: horn, thorn
ose: rose, close
oss: boss, gloss
ot: got, trot
ought: bought, brought
out: pout, about
ow: bow, throw
ow: how, chow
ox: fox, pox
oy: boy, ploy
ub: cub, shrub
uck: duck, stuck
ud: mud, thud
uff: puff, stuff
ug: dug, plug
um: sum, thumb
ump: bump, plump
un: run, spun
unch: bunch, scrunch
ung: hung, flung
unk: sunk, chunk
unt: hunt, grunt
ush: mush, crush
ust: dust, trust
ut: but, shut

Appendix G

Maze and Cloze Activities

Maze and cloze activities are powerful ways to help students strengthen their abilities to use meaningful context to guide their word recognition. Teachers can develop maze and cloze activities by finding an exemplary text that students may be familiar with and deleting selected words from the passage. Words chosen for deletion should be those that can be identified using the context preceding or following the deletion. After students work in groups or alone to determine missing words, teacher and students should discuss how they were able to determine selected words. Several variations of the maze and cloze are possible, as the following examples show.

Maze

In a maze activity, deleted words are provided at the end of the passage so that students' task is less challenging. In effect, it is a multiple-choice cloze.

> Abraham Lincoln wasn't the sort of man who could lose himself in a _____. After all, he stood _____ feet four inches tall, and to top it off, he _____ a high silk _____.
>
> His height was mostly in his _____ bony legs. When the _____ sat in a _____, he seemed no taller _____ anyone else.
>
> Choices: (than, six, president, wore, chair, long, crowd, hat)

Note: From Friedman, R. (1987). *Lincoln: A photobiography.* New York: Clarion.

Cloze

> Wintertime was _____ quiet in the little town in Calabria where Strega Nona (Grandma Witch) and her helper Big Anthony _____. People came _____ Strega Nona to help them _____ their troubles. Big Anthony did _____ chores and tried to behave _____. And

every morning Bambolona, the baker's daughter, came to deliver the
_____.

Note: From dePaola, T. (1979). *Big Anthony and the magic ring.* New York: Harcourt Brace.

Modified Cloze

This approach marks deleted words with initial letters.

Caleb the carpenter and Kate the weaver l_____ each other, b_____
not every single minute. O_____ in a while, they'd differ about this
or th_____ and wind up in such a fierce quarrel you'd never believe
they were h_____ and w_____.

Note: From Steig, W. (1977). *Caleb and Kate.* New York: Farrar, Straus, and Giroux.

Modified Cloze

Here deleted words are marked with length-of-word cues.

Though his father was fat and merely owned _ candy and nut _____,
Harry Tillian liked his papa. Harry stopped liking _____ and nuts
when he was around seven, but __ in spite of this, __ and Mr. Tillian
had remained friends the ___ Harry turned twelve.

Note: From Rylant, C. (1985). *Every living thing.* New York: Bradbury.

Appendix H

Internet Sites

The Internet contains an extraordinary wealth of information for teachers, students, parents, and others interested in literacy education. The following are some of our favorite Web sites. In parentheses after each description, we have noted audiences for the sites: teachers (T), students (S), and parents (P). These sites were active as of Spring 2003.

Access Excellence

<http://www.accessexcellence.org>

A resource for integrating science instruction. (T)

A&E Resource

<http://www.aetv.com>

The Arts & Entertainment television channel guide to upcoming biographies and documentaries about famous people and world events. (T, S, P)

Amazon.com

<http://www.amazon.com>

An online bookstore that offers a wealth of free information about children's literature, including professionally published book reviews, reviews written by children and teachers, and search engines by age range and topic. (T, S, P)

Ask the Author

<http://www.ipl.org/kidspace/AskAuthor/>

A question-and-answer service for anyone interested in authors and illustrators of children's and young adult books; includes author biographies and links to other author and illustrator sites. (T, S, P)

Association for Library Service to Children

<http://www.ala.org/alsc/>

Lists Newbery, Caldecott, and other book awards, and many notable books. Links to useful sites, including author home pages. (T, S, P)

Book Rap

<http://rite.ed.qut.edu.au>

A site for cyber-literature discussions. (T, S)

Boston Globe–Horn Book Award

<http://www.hbook.com/bghb.shtml>

Complete list of the Boston Globe–Horn Book Award winners. (T, S, P)

Cambridge Library for Kids

<http://www.ci.cambridge.ma.us/~CPL/kids>

Eclectic mix of resources with many links to book sites. (T, S, P)

Carol Hurst's Children's Literature Site

<http://www.carolhurst.com/profsubjects/reading/parentreading.html>

<http://www.carolhurst.com/profsubjects/reading/emergentreaders.html>

Great books for children and lots of ideas for their instructional use. (T)

Children's Literature Web Guide

<http://www.ucalgary.ca/~dkbrown/index.html>

Lists Internet resources related to books for children and young adults. Offers discussion boards, book lists, and links. (T, S, P)

The Crayola Crayon Company

<http://www.crayola.com>

Fun activities from the makers of Crayola crayons. (T, S, P)

Creative Classroom

<http://www.creativeclassroom.org>

Ideas and advice for K–8 teachers. (T)

Discover

<http://discover.com>

Discover magazine's Web site; great for science information. (T, S, P)

Education Index

<http://www.educationindex.com>

An annotated guide to the best education-related sites on the Web sorted by subject and children's ages. (T)

Education World

<http://www.education-world.com>

A variety of lesson plans and activities. (T)

ERIC

<http://www.eric.ed.gov>

All the ERIC clearinghouses and AskERIC; great resources for reviewing educational research. (T)

Four Blocks

<http://www.wfu.edu/~cunningh/fourblocks/>

Help with planning language arts curricula, especially for primary teachers. (T)

Free Federal Resources for Educational Excellence

<http://www.ed.gov/free>

Choose a subject area, and this site will provide you with links to many resources. (T, P)

The Global School House

<http://www.gsn.org>

Offers posting of collaborative projects, communication tools, and professional development. (T)

The Graphic Organizer

<http://www.graphic.org>

Many examples of graphic organizers. (T)

Great Sites

<http://www.ala.org/Content>

Search for "Online Resources for Parents and Children"; developed by the American Library Association. This site includes more than 700 outstanding locations for children. (T, P)

Helping Your Child Series

academic/udp

<http://www.ed.gov/~~pubs~~/parents/hyc.html>

Resources for parents who want to assist their children in school learning. Brochures are also available in Spanish. (T, P)

The Idea Box

<http://www.theideabox.com>

Online stories and activities for young children. (T, S, P)

Index to Internet Sites: Children's and Young Adults' Authors and Illustrators

<http://falcon.jmu.edu/~ramseyil/biochildhome.htm>

A searchable site that focuses on authors. (T, P, S)

Intercultural E-mail Classroom Connections

<http://www.iecc.org>

Free service to help teachers and classes link with partners in other countries for e-mail classroom pen pals (sometimes called "key pals") and project exchanges. (T)

International Reading Association

<http://www.reading.org>

IRA's home page. Also contains links to *Reading Online,* IRA's electronic professional journal. (T)

Kathy Schrock's Guide for Educators

<http://school.discovery.com/schrockguide/>

Links to resources; updated daily. (T)

KidPub

<http://kidpub.com>

A place for children to publish stories on the World Wide Web and to read stories published by others, with an ongoing collaborative story to which children are invited to contribute. (T, S, P)

Kids' Farm

<http://www.kidsfarm.com/>

An entertaining site for younger children, centered on the barnyard. (T, S, P)

Kid's Search Tools

<http://www.rcls.org/ksearch.htm>

An excellent research tool, this site gives quick access to searches using Ask Jeeves for Kids, ThinkQuest Library, Awesome Library, KidsClick, GEM Gateway to Educational Materials, Yahooligans, and Education World. (T, S, P)

Los Angeles County Office of Education

<http://teams.lacoe.edu/documentation/places/language.html>

Links to other reading and writing sites. (T)

NASA On-line Educational Resources

<http://www.gsfc.nasa.gov/>

A sampling of science resources affiliated with NASA and related organizations. (T, S, P)

National Council of Teachers of English

<http://www.ncte.org>

NCTE's home page. (T)

PBS Teachersource

<http://www.pbs.org/teachersource>

Current events, lesson plans, and other sources of interest. (T)

Research

<http://www.nuevaschool.org/~debbie/library/research/research.html>

A site developed by two teachers to help other teachers and their students research on the Internet. (T, S)

Stories from the Grimm Brothers

<ftp://ftp.std.com/obi/Fairy.Tales/Grimm/>

A complete resource for introducing the Grimm brothers' fairy tales to young readers. (T, S, P)

Teachers Helping Teachers

<http://www.pacificnet.net/~mandel/>

Resource links for teachers from all fields. (T)

Teacher Links

<http://www.geocities.com/Heartland/4251/teacher.html>

A useful site for locating links to other education-related Internet sites. (T)

The Teacher's Toolbox

<http://trc.org>

Useful information for teachers from all fields; includes links to many sites for K–12 teachers. (T)

Virtual Literary Café

<http://library.thinkquest.org/17500/data/cafe.html>

Everything from a guide to literary terms to biographies of authors. (T, S)

Web 66

<http://web66.coled.umn.edu/schools.html>

An international registry of schools. (T)

Appendix I

Sources of Information on Word Histories and Word Play

Allington, Richard. (1990). *Reading and science words.* Austin, TX: Raintree Steck-Vaughn. ISBN: 081722498X.

Almond, Jordan. *Dictionary of word origins: A history of the words, expressions, and cliches we use.* Secaucus, NJ: Carol Publishing. ISBN: 0-80651-713-1.

Ayto, John. (1998). *Oxford dictionary of slang.* Oxford, UK: Oxford University Press. ISBN: 019863157X.

Bromberg, Murray, & Liebb, Julius. *601 words you need to know to pass your exam.* Barrons Educational Series. ISBN: 0-81209-645-2.

Dalzell, Tom. (1996). *Flappers 2 rappers: American youth slang.* Springfield, MA: Merriam-Webster. ISBN: 0-87779-612-2.

Ehrlich, Ida. (1968). *Instant Vocabulary.* New York: Simon & Schuster. ISBN: 0-671-67727-6.

Flavell, Linda, & Flavell, Roger. (1992). *Dictionary of idioms and their origins.* London: Kyle Cathie. ISBN: 1856261298.

Fry, Edward; Kress, Jacqueline; & Fountoukidis, Dona Lee. (1997). *The reading teacher's book of lists.* Upper Saddle River, NJ: Prentice Hall. ISBN: 0-13-0348937.

Funk, Charles. (1950). *Thereby hangs a tale: Stories of curious word origins.* New York: Harper & Row. ISBN: 0-06272-049-Y.

Funk, Charles. (1955). *Heavens to Betsy! And other curious sayings.* New York: HarperCollins. ISBN: 0060913533.

Gwynne, Fred. (1970). *The King who rained.* New York: Simon & Schuster. ISBN: 0-440-84127-5.

Gwynne, Fred. (1976). *A chocolate moose for dinner.* New York: Simon & Schuster. ISBN: 0-440-84330-8.

Gwynne, Fred. (1988). *A little pigeon toad.* New York: Simon & Schuster. ISBN: 0-440-84798-2.

Hendrickson, Robert. (1997). *The facts on file encyclopedia of word and phrase origins, revised and expanded edition.* New York: Facts on File. ISBN: 0-81603-266-1.

Hoad, T. F. (1996). *Oxford concise dictionary of English etymology.* Oxford, UK: Oxford University Press. ISBN: 019861182X.

Kennedy, John. (1996). *Word stems: A dictionary.* New York: Soho Press. ISBN: 1569470510.

Knowles, Elizabeth (Ed.). (1997). *The Oxford dictionary of phrase, saying, and quotation.* Oxford: Oxford University Press. ISBN: 0-19-886229-7.

Lederer, Richard. (1988). *Get thee to a punnery.* Charleston, SC: Wyrick. ISBN: 0440204992.

Lederer, Richard. (1991). *The play of words: Fun and games for language lovers.* New York: Pocket Books. ISBN: 0671689088.

Lederer, Richard. (1996). *Pun and games.* Chicago: Chicago Review Press. ISBN: 1556522649.

Moore, Bob, & Moore, Maxine. (1997). *NTC's dictionary of Latin and Greek origins.* Chicago: NTC Publishing. ISBN: 0844283215.

Muschell, David. (1996). *What in the word? Origins of words dealing with people and places.* Bradenton, FL: McGuinn & McGuire. ISBN: 1-88111-714-6.

Simon, Seymour. (1995). Earth words: A dictionary of the environment. New York: Harpercrest. ISBN: 0-06020-234-3.

Terban, Marvin. (1988). *Guppies in tuxedos: Funny eponyms.* New York: Houghton Mifflin. ISBN: 0-89919-509-1.

Terban, Marvin. (1982). *Eight ate: A feast of homonym riddles.* New York: Houghton Mifflin. ISBN: 0-89919-086-3.

Terban, Marvin. (1983). *In a pickle: And other funny idioms.* New York. Houghton Mifflin. ISBN: 0-60600-812-8.

Terban, Marvin. (1984). *I think I thought: And other tricky verbs.* New York: Houghton Mifflin. ISBN: 0-89919-290-4.

Terban, Marvin. (1985). *Too hot to hoot: Funny palindrome riddles.* New York: Houghton Mifflin. ISBN: 0-89919-320-X.

Terban, Marvin. (1986). *Your foot's on my feet: And other tricky nouns.* New York: Houghton Mifflin. ISBN: 0-89919-413-3.

Terban, Marvin. (1987). *Mad as a wet hen: And other funny eponyms.* New York: Houghton Mifflin. ISBN: 0-89919-479-6.

Note: A good dictionary and thesaurus are absolutely essential among any list of resources for word study.

Meaningful Prefixes, Suffixes, and Word Parts

Prefixes	Meanings	Examples
ante	before	antebellum
anti (ant)	against	antitoxin
archi (arch)	chief	archenemy
auto	self	autobiography
bene	good	benefit
bi	two	bicycle
centi	one hundred	centigrade
circum	around	circumnavigate
co	together	coauthor
com	with	combine
contra	against	contradiction
deca (dec, deka, dek)	ten	decade
ex	out	exodus
extra	beyond	extraordinary
hetero	different	heterosexual
homo	same	homophone
hyper	above	hyperactive
hypo	under	hypodermic
im	not	immature
inter	between	interurban
intra	within	intrastate
kilo	one thousand	kilowatt
macro	large	macrobiotic
mal	bad	maladjust
mega	large	megaphone
micro	small	microscope

mid	middle	midway
mis	bad	misbehave
mono (mon)	one	monologue
multi	many	multitude
omni	all	omnivorous
penta (pent)	five	pentagon
peri	all around	perimeter
phono	voice, sound	phonograph
poly	many	polysyllabic
post	after	postdoctoral
pre	before	prefix
re	again	rewrite
semi	half, partly	semicircle
super	over	supervisor
tele	distant	television
trans	across	transatlantic
tri	three	tricycle
ultra	beyond	ultramodern
un	not	unbeaten

Suffixes	*Meaning*	*Examples*
arium	place for	planetarium
ary	place for	library
ation	state of	starvation
cule	small	minuscule
dom	state of	freedom
enne	female	comedienne
er	comparative	smarter
ess	female	actress
est	comparative	smartest
ette	female	majorette
ette	little	cigarette
ful	full of	careful
ism	doctrine of	capitalism
ite	mineral	granite
less	without	worthless

ment	state of	amazement
ology	study of	biology
orium	place for	emporium
ory	place for	laboratory
phobia	fear of	claustrophobia

Word Parts	*Meaning*	*Examples*
aero	air	aeronautics
alt	high	altitude
ambul	move	ambulance
anthr	man	anthropology
ast	star	asterisk
aud	hear	audience
belli	war	antebellum
biblio	book	Bible
bio	life	biology
cardi	heart	cardiology
chron	time	chronic
cycl	circle	bicycle
dem	people	epidemic
derm	skin	hypodermic
gam	marriage	monogamy
gram	written	grammar
graph	write	autograph
homo	man	homicide
hydr	water	hydrant
lab	work	laboratory
mania	madness	kleptomania
max	greatest	maximum
mort	death	immortal
narr	tell	narrate
neo	new	neonatal
nov	new	novice
opt	eye	optician
ped	foot	pedestal
phil	love	Philadelphia

phon	sound	phonics
photo	light	telephoto
port	carry	portable
psych	mind	psychiatrist
scop	see	microscope
scribe	write	inscribe
solv	loosen	dissolve
struct	build	construction
term	end	terminator
terr	land	Mediterranean
therm	heat	thermos
urb	city	urban
vag	wander	vagrant
ver	truth	verify
volv	roll	revolver
vor	eat	herbivorous

Appendix K

Magazines for Children

Some of these magazines also publish student writing. Web addresses current as of Fall 2002.

American Girl

Girls, ages 7–12
<www.americangirl.com>
Pleasant Company Publications, Inc.
8400 Fairway Place
P.O. Box 620984
Middleton, WI 53562-0984
(800) 234-1278

Boys' Life

Boys, ages 7–17
<www.boyslife.org>
P.O. Box 152079
Irving, TX 75015-2079
(214) 580-2366

Chickadee: The Canadian Magazine for Young Children

Ages 6–9
<www.owlkids.com/chickadee>
OWL
25 Boxwood Lane
Buffalo, NY 14227-2707
(800) 551-6957

Children's Digest

Ages 10–12
<www.cbhi.org/magazines/childrensdigest/index.shtml>
Children's Better Health Institute
1100 Waterway Blvd.
P.O. Box 567
Indianapolis, IN 46206
(800) 558-2376

Children's Playmate

Ages 6–8
<www.cbhi.org/magazines/childrensplaymate/index.shtml>
Children's Better Health Institute
1100 Waterway Blvd.
P.O. Box 567
Indianapolis, IN 46206
(800) 558-2376

Cobblestone: The History Magazine for Young People

Ages 9–14
<www.cobblestonepub.com>
Cobblestone Publishing Co.
30 Grove St., Suite C
Peterborough, NH 03458
(800) 821-0115

Creative Kids

Ages 8–14
<www.prufrock.com/prufrock_jm_createkids.cfm>
Prufrock Press
P.O. Box 8813
Waco, TX 76714-8813
(800) 998-2208

Cricket: The Magazine for Children

Ages 7–14
<www.cricketmag.com>
Cricket Magazine Group
P.O. Box 7434
Red Oak, IA 52591-0434
(800) 827-0227

Current Science

Ages 10–14
<www.weeklyreader.com/teens/current_science/>
200 First Stamford Place
P.O. Box 120023
Stamford, CT 06912-0023
(800) 446-3355

Faces: The Magazine about People

Ages 9–14
<www.cobblestonepub.com/pages/facemain.htm>
Cobblestone Publishing Co.
30 Grove St., Suite C
Peterborough, NH 03458
(800) 821-0115

Highlights for Children

Ages 2–12
<www.Highlights.com>
803 Church St.
Honesdale, PA 18431
(800) 603-0349

Hopscotch: The Magazine for Young Girls

Girls, ages 6–12
<www.hopscotchmagazine.com>
Bluffton New Publishing and Printing Company
P.O. Box 164
Bluffton, OH 45817-0164
(800) 358-4732

Jack and Jill

Ages 7–10
<www.jackandjillmag.org>
Children's Better Health Institute
1100 Waterway Blvd.
P.O. Box 567
Indianapolis, IN 46206
(800) 558-2376

Ladybug: The Magazine for Young Children

Ages 2–6
<www.cricketmag.com>
Cricket Magazine Group
P.O. Box 7434
Red Oak IA 51591-0434
(800) 827-0227

Merlyn's Pen: Fiction, Essays, and Poems by America's Teens

Ages 12–18
<www.merlynspen.com>
P.O. Box 910
East Greenwich, RI 02818
(800) 247-2027

Muse

Ages 10–14
<www.cricketmag.com/productdetail.asp?pid=12>
332 S. Michigan Ave., Suite 1100
Chicago, IL 60614
(800) 821-0115

National Geographic World

Ages 8–14
<www.nationalgeographic.com/ngkids/>
1145 17th St. N.W.
Washington, DC 20036
(202) 857-7000

Odyssey

Ages 8–14
<www.odysseymagazine.com>
Cobblestone Publishing Co.
30 Grove St., Suite C
Peterborough, NH 03458
(800) 821-0115

Owl: The Discovery Magazine for Children

Ages 9+
<www.owlkids.com>
The Owl Group
49 Front Street East, 2nd Floor
Toronto, ON
Canada, M5E 1B3
(800) 551-6957

Plays: The Drama Magazine for Young People

Ages 6–17
<www.playsmag.com>
Kalmbach Publishing Co.
21027 Crossroads Circle
P.O. Box 1612
Waukesha, WI 53187-1612
(800) 446-5489

Ranger Rick

Ages 7–12
<www.nwf.org/rangerrick>
National Wildlife Foundation
8925 Leesburg Pike
Vienna, VA 22184-0001
(800) 822-9919

Skipping Stones: A Multicultural Magazine

Ages 7–14
<www.efn.org/~skipping>
Skipping Stones
P.O. Box 3939
Eugene, OR 97403
(541) 342-4956

Sports Illustrated for Kids

Ages 7–14
<www.siforkids.com>
SI for Kids
P.O. Box 60001
Tampa, FL 33660-0001
(800) 992-0196

Stone Soup: The Magazine by Young Writers and Artists

Ages 6–14
<www.stonesoup.com>
P.O. Box 83
Santa Cruz, CA 95063
(800) 447-4569

Zoobooks

Ages 5–12
<www.zoobooks.com>
Wildlife Education Limited
3590 Kettner Blvd.
San Diego, CA 92101
(800) 992-5034

Appendix L

Bookmaking Ideas

Basic Materials

Paper & Covers	Fasteners	Tools
heavy cardboard	metal rings	scissors
boxes	yarn, thread	glue
oak tag	ribbon, twine	1" and 2" tape
newspaper	staples	paper cutter
construction paper	brass fasteners	needles
newsprint	nuts, bolts, & washers	stapler
manila paper	elastic bands	
wallpaper sample books		
flat boxes		
paper towel tubes		
clear contact paper		
tie-dye, batik		

Large Class Books

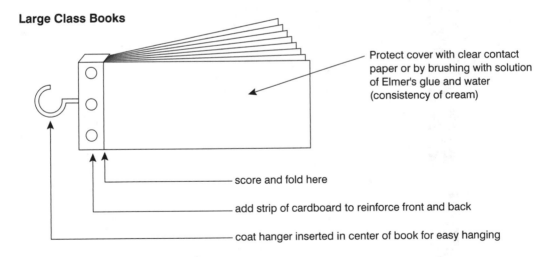

Protect cover with clear contact paper or by brushing with solution of Elmer's glue and water (consistency of cream)

— score and fold here

— add strip of cardboard to reinforce front and back

— coat hanger inserted in center of book for easy hanging

— cut heavy cardboard covers to suit large sheets of paper.
   — punch holes and fasten with nuts, washers, and bolts.
     (These can easily be removed to add pages.)

Small Books for Individual Use

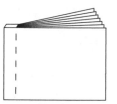

Staples

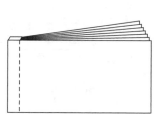

Stitch with yarn or thread

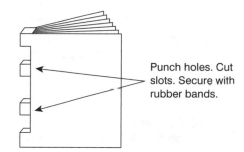

Punch holes. Cut slots. Secure with rubber bands.

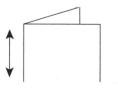

Apply Scotch tape to front and back covers. Punch holes through tape. Fasten with rings, brass fasteners, twists from plastic bags, shoe laces, etc.

Saddle Stitch Signature

1. Fold paper in half.
2. Bone (sharpen) fold using a folding bone or blunt stick.

3. Jog the signature (set of folded pages) by tapping the top end on a table or flat surface.
4. Mark an odd number of holes on the fold. Mark the center hole first, then the two end holes the same distance from the top and bottom edges. Mark other holes if needed.

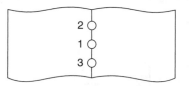

5. Punch holes using an awl, needle, or nail.
6. Cut thread 2 times longer than the signature. Wax thread. Thread needle. Knot the thread.

7. Sew signature pages together using a saddle stitch. Begin sewing in the center hole of the folio.

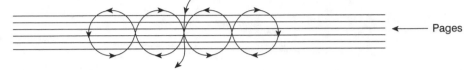

Pages

8. On the third time through the center hole, loop thread under the beginning stitch and then go back through the center hole.

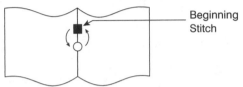

Beginning
Stitch

9. Tie a knot and clip extra thread. The knot will be on the inside of the book.

Creative Blank Books

Pages that have holes of varying sizes and numbers
Pages that are shaped
Pages that have different textures
Pages that fold out
Pages that have windows and doors
Pages that indicate direction (up-down-over-in)
Pages that progress in color (light-bright-dark-dull)
Pages that pop up

Experiment with Lettering

Appendix M

Sample Letter to Parents

This letter should be sent at the beginning of the school year.

Dear Parents:

One of the most important things we know about how children learn to read is that children who read the most tend to be the best readers. The more you read, the better reader you become! For this reason I am asking you to take a few minutes (15–20 would be great) each day to read to or with your child.

The time you give to reading will allow your child to practice reading strategies and skills he or she will be learning here at school. More important, however, is the message you will send to your child. Through your actions you will say that reading is important in your life and in your child's life and that you want him or her to become the best reader possible.

You can read to or with your child in many ways. Here are a few suggestions:

Have your child sit next to you or on your lap as you read a good story to him or her. Be sure to read with an expressive voice and make sure your child can see the words and pictures.

Read together. Sitting side by side, read aloud together a story that your child has chosen. Let your voices blend together to create a real partnership in reading. If your child can read a section on his or her own without trouble, allow your voice to fade. On those sections that challenge your child, let your voice lead the way by reading slightly louder and ahead of your child. This has proven to be a superb way to improve children's reading.

Echo reading. Allow your child to read back, phrase for phrase, a short text that you read to him or her.

Alternate reading. Switch who does the reading after every page or paragraph.

Repeat reading. Read a short story or poem to your child. (You can read the passage several times if you like, over several days.) Then allow your child to read the same passage to you.

Spend your time together quietly reading material of your own choosing. Although your child may be reading on his or her own, the fact that you are in the same room reading sends a strong message to your child about the importance of reading.

Try to read with your child every day. Develop a routine for reading that will last a lifetime. Be sure to praise your child for good reading. And when he or she struggles over a word or phrase while reading, simply say the unknown word and continue. Don't make a lesson out of every mistake. (You can go back to the word after you've read.) Finally, don't just read—talk about the stories you read together and discuss your own reading habits and interests with your child. He or she needs to know that reading is an important part of everyday life.

Thank you for your help in making this year a successful one for your child in reading. Working together, we can help your child become a successful and lifelong reader.

Sincerely,

Ms. Summers, Teacher

Appendix N

Professional Resources

Book Links

(6 issues per year)
American Library Association
50 E. Huron St.
Chicago, IL 60611

Journal of Adolescent and Adult Literacy (formerly Journal of Reading)

(8 issues per year)
International Reading Association
800 Barksdale Road
P.O. Box 8139
Newark, DE 19714-8139

Language Arts

(6 issues per year)
National Council of Teachers of English
1111 W. Kenyon Rd.
Urbana, IL 61801-1096

The Reading Teacher

(8 issues per year)
International Reading Association
800 Barksdale Rd.
P.O. Box 8139
Newark, DE 19714-8139

Reading Online

The electronic journal of the International Reading Association. Available without charge at http://www.readingonline.org/home.html/

Reading and Writing Quarterly

(4 issues per year)
Taylor and Francis, Inc.
325 Chestnut St., Suite 800
Philadelphia, PA 19106

Voices from the Middle

(4 issues per year)
National Council of Teachers of English
1111 W. Kenyon Rd.
Urbana, IL 61801-1096

The WEB (Wonderfully Exciting Books)

(3 issues per year; back issues available for purchase)
Ohio State University
200 Ramseyer Hall
29 W. Woodruff Ave.
Columbus, OH 43210

Appendix O

The Essential Primary Grade Sight Word List

We developed this list of 400 essential words from the high-frequency-word lists created by Dolch (1955), Fry (1980), and Cunningham and Allington (1999). It also includes words that represent the most common phonograms (Fry, 1998) and words selected by primary-grade teachers as words every student should recognize by sight and know by the end of third grade.

We recommend that primary-grade teachers in a school work together to determine the words that should be learned at each grade level. Kindergarten children might learn 25 words, and 125 words might be learned during each of the primary years, first, second, and third grade. The list could easily be covered in 25 weeks by presenting and teaching five words each week.

There is no best way to teach these words. They should be put on the class word wall and practiced regularly. Students can add them to their personal word banks and use them for practice and word games. Class word games work well in teaching these words. It is also a good idea to send the words home at the beginning of the school year and ask parents to regularly work with their children in helping them learn to know and recognize the words. Because these are high-frequency words, the absolute best way to provide plenty of exposure to them is through regular and wide reading.

about	bell	cut	fly
above	below	dad	follow
add	best	day	food
after	better	did	for
again	between	different	found
air	big	do	four
all	black	does	friend
almost	blue	done	from
along	book	don't	full
also	both	down	fun
always	bottom	draw	funny
am	boy	drink	gave
America	bring	drum	get
and	brother	earth	girl
animal	bug	eat	give
another	but	eight	glow
answer	buy	end	go
any	by	enough	goes
are	call	even	good
around	came	every	got
as	can	example	grade
ask	can't	eye	great
at	car	face	green
ate	carry	fake	group
away	cat	family	grow
back	change	far	had
bag	chill	farm	hand
bank	children	fast	hard
be	city	father	has
because	clean	favorite	have
bed	close	feed	he
been	cold	feet	head
before	come	few	hear
began	could	find	help
begin	country	first	her
being	crab	five	here

hill	leave	move	part
him	left	much	people
high	let	must	pick
his	letter	my	picture
hold	life	myself	place
home	lip	name	plant
hop	light	near	play
hot	like	need	please
house	line	new	point
how	list	never	pretty
hug	little	·next	pull
hum	live	new	put
hurt	lock	nice	ran
I	look	nine	read
idea	long	night	red
if	luck	no	really
important	made	not	ride
in	mail	now	right
into	main	number	river
is	make	of	rock
it	man	off	round
its	many	often	run
it's	map	old	said
jam	may	on	same
job	me	once	saw
jump	mean	one	say
junk	men	only	school
just	might	open	sea
keep	mile	or	second
kind	mine	other	see
know	miss	our	seed
land	mom	out	seem
large	more	over	sentence
last	most	own	set
later	mother	page	seven
learn	mountain	paper	shall

she	story	to	were
show	study	today	what
should	such	together	when
shout	take	too	where
sick	talk	took	which
side	tap	top	while
sing	teacher	tree	white
sink	tell	try	who
sister	ten	turn	why
sit	than	two	win
six	thank	under	will
sleep	that	until	wish
slow	the	up	with
small	their	upon	without
so	them	us	write
some	then	use	wrong
something	there	very	won't
sometimes	these	walk	word
song	they	want	work
soon	they're	warm	world
sound	thing	was	would
spell	think	wash	write
stand	this	watch	year
start	those	water	yellow
state	thought	way	yes
still	three	we	you
stop	through	well	young
store	time	went	your

References

Adams, M. J. (1990). *Beginning to read: Thinking and learning about print.* Cambridge, MA: MIT Press.

Allington, R. L. (1977). If they don't read much, how they ever gonna get good? *Journal of Reading, 21,* 57–61.

Allington, R. L. (1978, March). *Are good and poor readers taught differently? Is that why poor readers are poor readers?* Paper presented at the meeting of the American Educational Research Association, Toronto.

Allington, R. L. (1980). Teacher interruption behaviors during primary grade oral reading. *Journal of Educational Psychology, 72,* 371–377.

Allington, R. L. (1983). Fluency: The neglected reading goal. *The Reading Teacher, 36,* 556–561.

Allington, R. L. (1983). The reading instruction provided readers of differing abilities. *Elementary School Journal, 83,* 548–559.

Allington, R. L. (1984). Content coverage and contextual reading in reading groups. *Journal of Reading Behavior, 26,* 85–96.

Allington, R. L. (1987, July/August). Shattered hopes: Why two federal reading programs have failed to correct reading failure. *Learning, 87,* 60–64.

Allington, R. L. (1994). The schools we have. The schools we need. *The Reading Teacher, 48,* 14–29.

Allington, R. L. (2000). *What really matters for struggling readers: Designing research-based programs.* New York: Longman.

Allington, R. L. (2002). What I've learned about effective reading instruction. *Phi Delta Kappan, 83,* 740–747.

Allington, R. L., & McGill-Franzen, A. (1989). Different programs, indifferent instruction. In A. Gardner & D. Lipsky (Eds.), *Beyond separate education.* New York: Brookes.

Allington, R. L., Stuetzel, H., Shake, M., & Lamarche, S. (1986). What is remedial reading? A descriptive study. *Reading Research and Instruction, 24,* 15–30.

Allington, R. L., & Walmsley, S. A. (Eds.) (1995). *No quick fix: Rethinking literacy programs in America's elementary schools.* New York: Teachers' College Press.

Alvermann, D. E. (1991). The discussion web: A graphic aid for learning across the curriculum. *The Reading Teacher, 45,* 92–99.

American Library Association. (1989). *American Library Association Presidential Committee on Information Literacy.* Chicago: Author.

Ames, C. (1992). Classrooms: Goals, structures, and student motivation. *Journal of Educational Psychology, 84*, 261–271.

Anderson, B. (1981). The missing ingredient: Fluent oral reading. *Elementary School Journal, 81*, 173–177.

Anderson, R. C., & Freebody, P. (1981). Vocabulary knowledge. In J. Guthrie (Ed.), *Comprehension and teaching: Research reviews* (pp. 77–117). Newark, DE: International Reading Association.

Anderson, R. C., Hiebert, E., Scott, J., & Wilkinson, I. (1985). *Becoming a nation of readers.* Washington, DC: U.S. Department of Education.

Anderson, R. C., Wilson, P. T., & Fielding, L. G. (1988). Growth in reading and how children spend their time outside of school. *Reading Research Quarterly, 23*, 285–303.

Armbruster, B., Lehr, F., & Osborn, J. (2001). *Put reading first.* Washington, DC: U.S. Department of Education.

Aslett, R. (1990). *Effects of the oral recitation lesson on reading comprehension of fourth grade developmental readers.* Unpublished doctoral dissertation, Brigham Young University, Provo, UT.

Atwell, N. (1987). *In the middle: Writing, reading, and learning with adolescents.* Portsmouth, NH: Heinemann.

Baker, L., Afflerbach, P., & Reinking, D. (Eds.). (1996). *Developing engaged readers in school and home communities.* Mahwah, NJ: Erlbaum.

Ball, E., & Blachman, B. A. (1991). Does phoneme awareness training in kindergarten make a difference in early word recognition and developmental spelling? *Reading Research Quarterly, 26*, 49–66.

Barksdale–Ladd, M. A., & Nedeff, A. R. (1997). The worlds of a reader's mind: Students as authors. *The Reading Teacher, 50*, 564–573.

Baumann, J., & Duffy, A. (1997). *Engaged reading for pleasure and learning: A report from the National Reading Research Center.* Athens, GA: National Reading Research Center.

Baumann, J., Hooten, H., & White, P. (1999). Teaching comprehension through literature: A teacher-research project to develop fifth graders' reading strategies and motivation. *The Reading Teacher, 53*, 38–51.

Baumann, N. (1995). Reading millionaires—It works! *The Reading Teacher, 48*, 730.

Bear, D. R., Invernizzi, M., Templeton, S., & Johnston, F. (2000). *Words their way* (2nd ed.). Upper Saddle River, NJ: Prentice Hall.

Billmeyer, R., & Barton, M. (1998). *Teaching reading in the content areas* (2nd ed.). Aurora, CO: Mid-Continent Regional Educational Laboratory.

Bird, L. B. (1989). The art of teaching: Evaluation and revision. In K. S. Goodman, Y. M. Goodman, & W. J. Hood (Eds.), *The whole language evaluation book* (pp. 15–24). Portsmouth, NH: Heinemann.

Bleich, D. (1978). *Subjective criticism.* Baltimore: Johns Hopkins University Press.

Block, C., & Mangieri, J. (2002). Recreational reading: Twenty years later. *The Reading Teacher, 55*, 572–580.

Bottomley, D., Henk, W., & Melnick, S. (1997/1998). Assessing children's views about themselves as writers using the Writer Self-Perception Scale. *The Reading Teacher, 51*, 286–296.

Brabham, E. G., Murray, B. A., & Hudson, S. (2001, December). *Effects of interactive reading aloud and multimedia interactions with alphabet books on phoneme awareness, letter knowledge, and vocabulary.* Paper presented at the annual meeting of the National Reading Conference, San Antonio, Texas.

Bradley, L., & Bryant, P. (1983). Categorizing sounds and learning to read: A causal connection. *Nature, 271*, 746–747.

Bradley, L., & Bryant, P. (1985). Rhyme and reason in reading and spelling. Ann Arbor, MI: University of Michigan Press.

Brown, M. (1949/1999). *The important book.* New York: HarperCollins.

Burke, J. (2002). The Internet reader. *Educational Leadership, 60*(3), 38–42.

Callaghan, M. (1935). All the years of her life. *New Yorker, 11*(17), 17–19.

Cambourne, B. (1995). Towards an educationally relevant theory of literacy learning: Twenty years of inquiry. *The Reading Teacher, 49,* 182–190.

Carbo, M. (1978). Teaching reading with talking books. *The Reading Teacher, 32,* 267–273.

Catts, H. W. (1991). Early identification of reading disabilities. *Topics in Language Disorders, 12,* 1–16.

Cazden, C. (1981). Social context of learning to read. In J. Guthrie (Ed.), *Comprehension and teaching: Research reviews* (pp. 118–139). Newark, DE: International Reading Association.

Clarke, L. (1988). Invented versus traditional spelling in first graders' writing: Effects on learning to spell and read. *Research in the Teaching of English, 22,* 281–309.

Clay, M. M. (1985). *The early detection of reading difficulties* (3rd ed.). Portsmouth, NH: Heinemann.

Clay, M. M. (1986). Constructive processes: Talking, reading, writing, art, and craft. *The Reading Teacher, 39,* 764–770.

Clay, M. M. (1993). *Reading Recovery: A guidebook for teachers in training.* Portsmouth, NH: Heinemann.

Clymer, T. (1996). The utility of phonics generalizations in the primary grades. *The Reading Teacher, 50,* 182–187 (originally published in *The Reading Teacher, 16,* 1963)

Cohen, D. (1968). The effect of literature on vocabulary and reading achievement. *Elementary English, 45,* 209–213, 217.

Commission on Chapter I. (1993). *Making schools work for children of poverty: A new framework.* Washington, DC: Author.

Cooper, H. (1977). Controlling personal rewards: Professional teachers' differential use of feedback and the effects of feedback on the students' motivation to perform. *Journal of Educational Psychology, 69,* 419–427.

Cunningham, A. E., & Stanovich, K. E. (1998). What reading does for the mind. *American Educator, 22,* 8–15.

Cunningham, P. M., & Allington, R. L. (1999). *Classrooms that work* (2nd Ed.). New York: Longman.

Cunningham, P. M., & Cunningham, J. W. (1992). Making words: Enhancing the invented spelling–decoding connection. *The Reading Teacher, 46,* 106–115.

Cunningham, P. M., Hall, D. P., & Defee, M. (1991). Nonability grouped, multilevel instruction: A year in a first-grade classroom. *Reading Teacher, 44,* 566–571.

Cunningham, P. M., Hall, D. P., & Defee, M. (1998). Nonability-grouped, multilevel instruction: Eight years later. *The Reading Teacher, 51,* 652–664.

Curtis, C. (1999). *Bud, not Buddy.* New York: Delacorte.

Dahl, K., & Scharer, P. (2000). Phonics teaching and learning in whole language classrooms: New evidence from research. *The Reading Teacher, 53,* 584–594.

Dalrymple, K. S. (1989). "Well, what about his skills?" Evaluation of whole language in the middle school. In K. S. Goodman, Y. M. Goodman, & W. J. Hood (Eds.), *The whole language evaluation book* (pp. 111–130). Portsmouth, NH: Heinemann.

Daniels, H. (2002). *Literature circles: Voice and choice in book clubs and reading groups* (2nd ed.). Portland, ME: Stenhouse.

Davidson, J. (1982). The group mapping activity for instruction in reading and thinking. *Journal of Reading, 26,* 52–56.

Davidson, J. (1986). The teacher–student generated lesson: A model for reading instruction. *Theory into Practice, 25,* 84–90.

Davidson, J. (1987, June). *Writing across the curriculum.* Paper presented at the meeting of the Language Experience Special Interest Council, DeKalb, IL.

Davis, F. B. (1944). Fundamental factors of comprehension in reading. *Psychometrika, 9,* 185–197.

DePaola, T. (1982). *Strega Nona's magic lessons.* New York: Harcourt Brace Jovanovich.

Doiron, R. (1994). Using nonfiction in a read-aloud program: Letting the facts speak for themselves. *The Reading Teacher, 47,* 616–624.

Dolch, E. (1955). *Methods in reading.* Champaign, IL: Garrand.

Dowhower, S. L. (1987). Effects of repeated reading on second-grade transitional readers' fluency and comprehension. *Reading Research Quarterly, 22,* 389–407.

Dowhower, S. L. (1994). Repeated reading revisited: Research into practice. *Reading and Writing Quarterly, 10,* 343–358.

Dugan, J. (1997). Transactional literature discussions: Engaging students in the appreciation and understanding of literature. *The Reading Teacher, 51,* 86–96.

Durkin, D. (1966). *Children who read early.* New York: Teachers College Press.

Dyson, A. (1984). "N spell my grandmama": Fostering early thinking about print. *The Reading Teacher, 38,* 262–271.

Eldredge, J. L., & Baird, J. E. (1996). Phonemic awareness training works better than whole language instruction for teaching first graders how to write. *Reading Research and Instruction, 35,* 193–208.

Eldredge, J. L., Reutzel, D. R., & Hollingsworth, P. M. (1996). Comparing the effectiveness of two oral reading practices: Round-robin reading and the Shared Book Experience. *Journal of Literacy Research, 28,* 201-225.

Elley, W. (1992). *How in the world do students read?* Hamburg, Germany: International Association for the Evaluation of Educational Achievement.

Ericson, L., & Juliebo, M. F. (1998). *The phonological awareness handbook for kindergarten and primary teachers.* Newark, DE: International Reading Association.

Evans, C. (1984). Writing to learn in math. *Language Arts, 61,* 828–835.

Fernald, G. M. (1943). *Remedial techniques in basic school subjects.* New York: McGraw-Hill.

Fielding–Barnsley, R. (1997). Explicit instruction in decoding benefits children high in phonemic awareness and alphabet knowledge. *Scientific Studies of Reading, 1,* 85–98.

Fisher, B. (1991). *Joyful learning.* Portsmouth, NH: Heinemann.

Fountas, I., & Pinnell, G.S. (2001). *Guiding readers and writers.* Portsmouth, NH: Heinemann.

Fresch, M. J., & Wheaton, A. (1997). Sort, search, and discover: A spelling in the child-centered classroom. *The Reading Teacher, 51,* 20–31.

Fry, E. (1980). The new instant word list. *The Reading Teacher, 34,* 284–289.

Fry, E. (1998). The most common phonograms. *The Reading Teacher, 51,* 620–622.

Fry, E. B., Fountoukidis, D. L., & Polk, J. K. (2000). *The new reading teacher's book of lists* (4th ed.). Upper Saddle River, NJ: Prentice Hall.

Gambrell, L. (1996). Creating classroom cultures that foster reading motivation. *The Reading Teacher, 50,* 14–25.

Gambrell, L. (1998, November). *Motivating readers.* Paper presented at the annual Kent State University Reading Conference, Kent, OH.

Gaskins, I. W. (1998). There's more to teaching at-risk and delayed readers than good reading instruction. *The Reading Teacher, 51,* 534–547.

Gaskins, I. W., Ehri, L. C., Cress, C., O'Hara, C., & Donnelly, K. (1997). Procedures for word learning: Making discoveries about words. *The Reading Teacher, 50,* 312–327.

Gere, A. (Ed.). (1985). *Roots in the sawdust: Writing to learn across the disciplines.* Urbana, IL: National Council of Teachers of English.

Gillet, J., & Kita, M. (1979). Words, kids, and categories. *The Reading Teacher, 32,* 538–542.

Good, T. (1987). Two decades of research on teacher expectations: Findings and future directions. *Journal of Teacher Education, 38,* 32–47.

Goodman, Y. (1985). Kidwatching: Observing children in the classroom. In A. Jaggar & M. T. Smith-Burke (Eds.), *Observing the language learner* (pp. 9–18). Newark, DE: International Reading Association.

Goodman, Y. (1989). Evaluation of students: Evaluation of teachers. In K. S. Goodman, Y. M. Goodman, & W. J. Hood (Eds.), *The whole language evaluation book* (pp. 3–14). Portsmouth, NH: Heinemann.

Goodman, Y., & Watson, D. (1977). A reading program to live with: Focus on comprehension. *Language Arts, 54,* 868–879.

Graves, D. (1983). *Writing: Teachers and children at work.* Portsmouth, NH: Heinemann.

Graves, D., & Stuart, V. (1985). *Write from the start.* New York: Dutton.

Griffith, P., & Klesius, J. P. (1990, November). *The effect of phonemic awareness ability and reading instructional approach on first grade children's acquisition of spelling and decoding skills.* Paper presented at the annual meeting of the National Reading Conference, Miami, FL.

Griffith, P., & Olson, M. (1992). Phonemic awareness helps beginning readers break the code. *The Reading Teacher, 45,* 516–523.

Guthrie, J., Schafer, W., Wang, Y., & Afflerbach, P. (1995). Relationships of instruction to amount of reading: An exploration of social, cognitive, and instructional connections. *Reading Research Quarterly, 30,* 8–25.

Hall, D. (1994). *I am the dog, I am the cat.* New York: Dial.

Hansen, J. (1987). *When writers read.* Portsmouth, NH: Heinemann.

Hanser, C. (1986). The writer's inside story. *Language Arts, 63,* 153–159.

Harp, B. (Ed.). (1994). *Assessment and evaluation for student-centered learning.* Norwood, MA: Christopher–Gordon.

Harste, J. C. (1989). *New policy guidelines for reading: Connecting research and practice.* Urbana, IL: National Council of Teachers of English.

Harste, J. C., Woodward, V. A., & Burke, C. L. (1984). *Language stories and literacy lessons.* Portsmouth, NH: Heinemann.

Hartman, D., & Hartman, J. (1993). Reading across texts: Expanding the role of the reader. *The Reading Teacher, 47,* 202–211.

Hasbrouck, J. E. & Tindal, G. (1992). Curriculum-based oral reading fluency forms for students in grades 2 through 5. *Teaching Exceptional Children, 24*(3), 41–44.

Heald–Taylor, B. G. (1996). Three paradigms for literature instruction in grades 3 to 6. *The Reading Teacher, 49,* 456–466.

Heald–Taylor, B. G. (1998). Three paradigms of spelling instruction in grades 3–6. *The Reading Teacher, 51,* 404–413.

Heap, J. (1980). What counts as reading: Limits to certainty in assessment. *Curriculum Inquiry, 10,* 265–292.

Heckelman, R. G. (1969). A neurological impress method of reading instruction. *Academic Therapy, 4,* 277–282.

Henderson, A. T. (1988). Parents are a school's best friend. *Phi Delta Kappan, 70,* 148–153.

Henk, W., & Melnick, S. (1995). The Reader Self-Perception Scale (RSPS): A new tool for measuring how children feel about themselves as readers. *The Reading Teacher, 48,* 470–482.

Henk, W., & Melnick, S. (1998). Upper elementary-aged children's reported perceptions about good readers: A self-efficacy influenced update in transitional literacy contexts. *Reading Research and Instruction, 38,* 57–80.

Herber, H. (1978). *Teaching reading in content areas* (2nd ed.). Englewood Cliffs, NJ: Prentice Hall.

Herman, P. A. (1985). The effect of repeated readings on reading rate, speech pauses, and word recognition accuracy. *Reading Research Quarterly, 20,* 553–564.

Hiebert, E. H., Pearson, P. D., Taylor, B. M., Richardson, V., & Paris, S. G. (1998). *Every child a reader: Concepts of print, letter naming, and phonemic awareness.* Ann Arbor, MI: Center for the Improvement of Early Reading Achievement.

Hoffman, J. V. (1987). Rethinking the role of oral reading in basal instruction. *Elementary School Journal, 87,* 367–373.

Hoffman, J. V., & Crone, S. (1985). The oral recitation lesson: A research-derived strategy for reading basal texts. In J. A. Niles & R. A. Lalik (Eds.), *Issues in literacy: A research perspective. Thirty-fourth yearbook of the National Reading Conference* (pp. 76–83). Rochester, NY: National Reading Conference.

Holdaway, D. (1979). *The foundations of literacy.* Sydney, Australia: Ashton Scholastic.

Holdaway, D. (1981). Shared book experience: Teaching reading using favorite books. *Theory into Practice, 21,* 293–300.

Howe, K. B., & Shinn, M. M. (2001). *Standard reading assessment passages (RAPS) for use in general outcome measurements: A manual describing development and technical features.* Eden Prairie, MN: Edformations.

Ivey, G., & Broaddus, K. (2001). "Just plain reading": A survey of what makes students want to read in middle school classrooms. *Reading Research Quarterly, 36,* 350–377.

Jacobson, D. (1989). The evaluation process—in process. In K. S. Goodman, Y. M. Goodman, & W. J. Hood (Eds.), *The whole language evaluation book* (pp. 177–188). Portsmouth, NH: Heinemann.

Jewell, T., & Pratt, D. (1999). Literature discussions in the primary grades: Children's thoughtful discourse about books and what teachers can do to make it happen. *The Reading Teacher, 52,* 842–850.

Johnson, A. (1992). *Tell me a story, mama.* New York: Orchard.

Kear, D., Coffman, G., McKenna, M., & Ambrosio, A. (2000). Measuring attitude toward writing: A new tool for teachers. *The Reading Teacher, 54,* 10–23.

Kitagawa, M. M. (1989). Guise, son of the shoemaker. In K. S. Goodman, Y. M. Goodman, & W. J. Hood (Eds.), *The whole language evaluation book* (pp. 101–109). Portsmouth, NH: Heinemann.

Koch, K. (2000). At play with words. *American Educator, 24*(3), 11-15.

Koskinen, P. S., & Blum, I. H. (1984). Repeated oral reading and the acquisition of fluency. In J. A. Niles & L. A. Harris (Eds.), *Changing perspectives on research in reading/language processing and instruction. Thirty-third yearbook of the National Reading Conference* (pp. 183–187). Rochester, NY: National Reading Conference.

Koskinen, P. S., & Blum, I. H. (1986). Paired repeated reading: A classroom strategy for developing fluent reading. *The Reading Teacher, 40,* 70–75.

Koskinen, P. S., Blum, I. H., Bisson, S. A., Phillips, S. M., Creamer, T. S., & Baker, T. K. (1999). Shared reading, books, and audiotapes: Supporting diverse students in school and at home. *The Reading Teacher, 52,* 430–444.

Kuhn, M., & Stahl, S. (2000). *Fluency: A review of developmental and remedial reading practices.* CIERA Report #2–008. Ann Arbor, MI: University of Michigan, Center for the Improvement of Early Reading Achievement.

Lancia, P. (1997). Literary borrowing: The effects of literature on children's writing. *The Reading Teacher, 50,* 470–475.

Lansky, B. (1996). *Poetry party.* New York: Meadowbrook Press.

Lederer, R. (1987). *Anguished english: an anthology of accidental assaults upon our language.* Charleston: Wyrick.

Lehman, B., & Scharer, P. (1996). Reading alone, talking together: The role of discussion in developing literary awareness. *The Reading Teacher, 50,* 26–35.

Maclean, M., Bryant, P., & Bradley, L. (1987). Rhymes, nursery rhymes, and reading in early childhood. *Merrill–Palmer Quarterly, 33,* 255–281.

Manzo, A. (1975). The guided reading procedure. *Journal of Reading, 18,* 287–291.

Martinez, M., Roser, N. L., & Strecker, S. (1999). "I never thought I could be a star": A readers theater ticket to reading fluency. *The Reading Teacher, 52,* 326–334.

Marzano, R. (2003). *What works in schools: Translating research into action.* Alexandria, VA: Association for Supervision and Curriculum Development.

Marzano, R., Pickering, D., & Pollock, J. (2001). *Classroom instruction that works: Research-based strategies for increasing student achievement.* Alexandria, VA: Association for Supervision and Curriculum Development.

Maxim, D., & Five, C. L. (1997). Classroom practices that monitor and inform learning. *School Talk, 3*(2), 1.

McCormick, S. (1994). A nonreader becomes a reader: A case study of literacy acquisition by a severely disabled reader. *Reading Research Quarterly, 29,* 156–176.

McCormick, S. (1995). *Instructing students who have literacy problems.* Upper Saddle River, NJ: Prentice Hall.

McDermott, R. (1978). Pirandello in the classroom: On the possibility of equal educational opportunity in American culture. In M. Reynolds (Ed.), *Futures of exceptional children: Emerging structure* (pp. 41–64). Reston, VA: Council for Exceptional Children.

McKenna, M., & Kear, D. (1990). Measuring attitude toward reading: A new tool for teachers. *The Reading Teacher, 43,* 626–629.

McKeon, C. (1999). The nature of children's e-mail in one classroom. *The Reading Teacher, 52,* 698–706.

McMahon, S., & Raphael, T. (1997). *The book club connection: Literacy learning and classroom talk.* New York: Teachers College Press.

Menon, M., & Mirabito, J. (1999). "Ya' mean all we hafta do is read?" *The Reading Teacher, 53,* 190–196.

Merriam, S. B. (1998). *Qualitative research and case study applications in education* (2nd ed.). San Francisco: Jossey-Bass.

Mervar, K., & Hiebert, E. H. (1989). Literature-selection strategies and amount of reading in two literacy approaches. In S. McCormick & J. Zutell (Eds.), *Cognitive and social perspectives for literacy research and instruction. Thirty-eighth yearbook of the National Reading Conference* (pp. 529–535). Chicago: National Reading Conference.

Moffett, J., & Wagner, B. (1992). *Student-centered language arts, K–12* (4th ed.). Portsmouth, NH: Boynton/Cook.

Moore, P. W., & Moore, S. A. (1986). Possible sentences. In E. K. Dishner, T. W. Bean, J. E. Readence, & P. W. Moore (Eds.), *Reading in the content areas: Improving classroom instruction,* 2nd ed. (pp. 174–179). Dubuque, IA: Kendall/Hunt.

Morris, D. (1998, December). *Research address: Preventing reading failure in the primary grades.* Paper presented at the annual meeting of the National Reading Conference, Austin, Texas.

Morris, D., & Nelson, L. (1992). Supported oral reading with low-achieving second graders. *Reading Research and Instruction, 31,* 49–63.

Moss, B., & Hendershot, J. (2002). Exploring sixth graders' selection of nonfiction trade books. *The Reading Teacher, 56,* 6–17.

Nagy, W. E. (1988). *Teaching vocabulary to improve reading comprehension.* Urbana, IL: National Council of Teachers of English.

National Assessment of Educational Progress. (2000). Available online at http://nces.ed.gov/nationsreportcard/reading.

National Center for Education Statistics. (2001). *Fourth-grade reading highlights 2000.* Washington, DC: U.S. Department of Education, Office of Educational Research and Improvement.

National Reading Panel. (2000). *Report of the National Reading Panel: Teaching children to read. Report of the subgroups.* Washington, DC: U.S. Department of Health and Human Services, National Institutes of Health.

Nelson, O., & Linek, W. (Eds.). (1999). *Classroom applications of language experience.* Boston: Allyn & Bacon.

Nicholson, T. (1998). The flashcard strikes back. *The Reading Teacher, 52,* 188–192.

Noe, K., & Johnson, N. (1999). *Getting started with literature circles.* Norwood, MA: Christopher Gordon.

Ogle, D. (1986). K–W–L: A teaching model that develops active reading of expository text. *The Reading Teacher, 38,* 564–570.

Oldfather, P., & Wigfield, A. (1996). Children's motivations for literacy learning. In L. Baker, P. Afflerbach, & D. Reinking (Eds.), *Developing engaged readers in school and home communities* (pp. 89–113). Mahwah, NJ: Erlbaum.

O'Masta, G. A., & Wolf, J. A. (1991). Encouraging independent reading through the reading millionaires project. *The Reading Teacher, 44,* 656–662.

Padak, N. (1987). *Reading placement and diagnosis: A guide for elementary teachers.* Springfield: Illinois State Board of Education.

Palmer, B., Codling, R., & Gambrell, L. (1994). In their own words: What elementary students have to say about motivation to read. *Reading Teacher, 48,* 176–178.

Patton, M. Q. (1990). *Qualitative evaluation methods* (2nd ed.). Newbury Park, CA: Sage.

Paulsen, G. (1999). *Hatchet* New York: Aladdin Paperbacks.

Perfetti, C., Beck, I., Bell., L., & Hughes, C. (1987). Phonemic knowledge and learning to read are reciprocal: A longitudinal study. *Merrill–Palmer Quarterly, 33,* 283–319.

Pikulski, J. J. (1994). Preventing reading failure: A review of five effective programs. *The Reading Teacher, 48,* 30–39.

Pinnell, G. S. (1989). Reading Recovery: Helping at-risk children learn to read. *Elementary School Journal, 90,* 161–183.

Pinnell, G. S., Fried, M. D., & Estice, R. M. (1990). Reading Recovery: Learning how to make a difference. *The Reading Teacher, 43,* 282–295.

Pinnell, G. S., Pikulski, J. J., Wixson, K. K., Campbell, J. R., Gough, P. B., & Beatty, A. S. (1995). *Listening to children read aloud.* Washington, DC: U.S. Department of Education, Office of Educational Research and Improvement.

Postlethwaite, T. N., & Ross, K. N. (1992). *Effective schools in reading: Implications for educational planners.* The Hague: International Association for the Evaluation of Educational Achievement.

Prescott, J. O. (2003). The power of reader's theater. *Instructor, 112*(5), 22–26+.

Pressley, M., Allington, R., Wharton-McDonald, R., Block, C., & Morrow, L. (2001). *Learning to read: Lessons from exemplary first grades.* New York: Guilford.

Rasinski, T. V. (1989). Fluency for everyone: Incorporating fluency in the classroom. *The Reading Teacher, 42,* 690–693.

Rasinski, T. V. (1990). *The effects of cued phrase boundaries in texts.* Bloomington, IN: ERIC Clearinghouse on Reading and Communication Skills (ED 313 689).

Rasinski, T. V. (1992). Promoting recreational reading. In K. Wood (Ed.), *Exploring literature in the classroom: Content and methods* (pp. 85–109). Norwood, MA: Christopher-Gordon.

Rasinski, T. V. (1995). Fast Start: A parent involvement reading program for primary grade students. In W. Linek & E. Sturtevant (Eds.), *Generations of literacy: 17th Yearbook of the College Reading Association* (pp. 301–312). Harrisonburg, VA: College Reading Association.

Rasinski, T. V. (1999). Making and writing words. *Reading Online,* an electronic journal of the International Reading Association (www.readingonline.org/articles/art_index.ap?HREF=/articles/words/rasinski_index.html)

Rasinski, T. V. (2003). *The fluent reader: Oral reading strategies for building word recognition, fluency, and comprehension.* New York: Scholastic.

Rasinski, T. V., & Fredericks, A. D. (1991). The Akron Paired Reading project. *The Reading Teacher, 44,* 514–515.

Rasinski, T. V., & Linek, W. (1993). *Do students in whole language classrooms really like reading?* Paper presented at the annual meeting of the College Reading Association, Richmond, VA.

Rasinski, T. V., & Loudin, M. (1997). *Fast Start: A parent involvement program in reading for primary grade students in an urban school.* Unpublished manuscript. Kent, OH: Kent State University.

Rasinski, T. V., & Padak, N. D. (1998). How elementary students referred for compensatory reading instruction perform on school-based measures of word recognition, fluency, and comprehension. *Reading Psychology: An International Quarterly, 19,* 185–216.

Rasinski, T. V., Padak, N. D., Linek, W. L., & Sturtevant, E. (1994). Effects of fluency development on urban second-grade readers. *Journal of Educational Research, 87,* 158–165.

Rasinski, T. V., & Zutell, J. B. (1996). Is fluency yet a goal of the reading curriculum? In E. G. Sturtevant and W. M. Linek (Eds.), *Growing literacy: 18th Yearbook of the College Reading Association* (pp. 237–246). Harrisonburg, VA: College Reading Association.

Read, C. (1971). Pre-school children's knowledge of English phonology. *Harvard Educational Review, 41,* 1–34.

Reutzel, D. R., & Fawson, P. C. (1990). Traveling Tales: Connecting parents and children through writing. *The Reading Teacher, 44,* 222–227.

Reutzel, D. R., & Hollingsworth, P. M. (1993). Effects of fluency training on second graders' reading comprehension. *Journal of Educational Research, 86,* 325–331.

Reutzel, D. R., Hollingsworth, P. M., & Eldredge, J. L. (1994). Oral reading instruction: The impact on student reading development. *Reading Research Quarterly, 29,* 40–62.

Rhodes, L., & Dudley-Marling, C. (1988). Readers and writers with a difference. Portsmouth, NH: Heinemann.

Rhodes, L., & Shanklin, N. (1993). *Windows into literacy.* Portsmouth, NH: Heinemann.

Richek, M. A., & McTague, B. K. (1988). The "Curious George" strategy for students with reading problems. *The Reading Teacher, 42,* 220–226.

Rose, M. (1995). *Possible lives.* Boston: Houghton Mifflin.

Rosenblatt, L. (1938). *Literature as exploration.* New York: Modern Language Association.

Rosenblatt, L. (1978). *The reader, the text, and the poem.* Carbondale, IL: Southern Illinois University Press.

Rupley, W., Wise, B., & Logan, J. (1986). Research in effective teaching: An overview of its development. In J. Hoffman (Ed.), *Effective teaching of reading: Research and practice* (pp. 3–36). Newark, DE: International Reading Association.

Samuels, S. J. (1979). The method of repeated readings. *The Reading Teacher, 32,* 403–408.

Schreiber, P. A. (1980). On the acquisition of reading fluency. *Journal of Reading Behavior, 12,* 177–186.

Schreiber, P. A. (1991). Understanding prosody's role in reading acquisition. *Theory into Practice, 30,* 158–164.

Schwartz, R., & Raphael, T. (1985). Concept of definition: A key to improving students' vocabulary. *The Reading Teacher, 39,* 198–205.

Shanahan, S., Wojciechowski, J., & Rubik, G. (1998). A celebration of reading: How our school read for one million minutes. *The Reading Teacher, 52,* 93–96.

Shanahan, T. (2000, November). *The literacy teaching framework.* Paper presented at the annual Kent State University Reading Conference, Kent, Ohio.

Shimron, J. (1994). The making of readers: The work of Professor Dina Feitelson. In D. Dickinson (Ed.), *Bridges to literacy* (pp. 80–99). Cambridge, MA: Blackwell.

Sidelnick, M., & Svoboda, M. (2000). The bridge between drawing and writing: Hannah's story. *The Reading Teacher, 54,* 174-184.

Silvers, P. (1986). Process writing and the reading connection. *The Reading Teacher, 39,* 684–688.

Slavin, R. E., Madden, N. L., Karweit, N. L., Dolan, L., & Wasik, B. A. (1992). *Success for All: A relentless approach to prevention and early intervention in elementary schools.* Arlington, VA: Educational Research Service.

Smith, F. (1992). Learning to read: The never-ending debate. *Phi Delta Kappan, 73,* 432–441.

Smith, J., & Elley, W. (1997). *How children learn to read: Insights from the New Zealand experience.* Katonah, NY: Richard C. Owen.

Snow, C. E., Burns, M. S., & Griffin, P. (1998). *Preventing reading difficulties in young children.* Washington, DC: National Academy Press.

Sowers, S. (1985). Learning to write in a workshop: A study in grades one through four. In M. Farr (Ed.), *Advances in writing research. Vol. 1: Children's early writing development* (pp. 297–342). Norwood, NJ: Ablex.

Spurlin, J., Dansereau, D., Larson, C., & Brooks, L. (1984). Cooperative learning strategies in processing descriptive text: Effects of role and activity level of the learner. *Cognition and Instruction, 1,* 451–463.

Stahl, S. A. (1986). Three principles of effective vocabulary instruction. *Journal of Reading, 29,* 662–671.

Stahl, S. A. (1992). Saying the "p" word: Nine guidelines for exemplary phonics instruction. *The Reading Teacher, 45,* 618–625.

Stahl, S. A., & Clark, C. H. (1987). The effects of participatory expectations in classroom discussion on the learning of science vocabulary. *American Educational Research Journal, 24,* 541–556.

Stahl, S. A., & Heubach, K. (in press). Fluency-oriented reading instruction. *Elementary School Journal.*

Stahl, S. A., & Kapinus, B. A. (1991). Possible sentences: Predicting word meanings to teach content vocabulary. *The Reading Teacher, 45,* 36–43.

Stahl, S. A., & Vancil, S. J. (1986). Discussion is what makes semantic maps work in vocabulary instruction. *The Reading Teacher, 40,* 62–69.

Stanovich, K. E. (1986). Matthew effects in reading: Some consequences of individual differences in the acquisition of literacy. *Reading Research Quarterly, 21,* 360–407.

Stanovich, K. E. (1994). Romance and reality. *The Reading Teacher, 47,* 280–289.

Stauffer, R. (1980). *The language-experience approach to the teaching of reading* (2nd ed.). New York: Harper & Row.

Stevenson, B. (2001). *The effects of the Fast Start parent tutoring program in the acquisition of reading skills by first-grade students.* Unpublished doctoral dissertation. Columbus, OH: The Ohio State University.

Sullivan, J. (1998). The electronic journal: Combining literacy and technology. *The Reading Teacher, 52,* 90–93.

Sweet, A., & Guthrie, J. (1996). How children's motivations relate to literacy development and instruction. *The Reading Teacher, 49,* 660–662.

Tancock, S. M. (1994). A literacy lesson framework for children with reading problems. *The Reading Teacher, 48,* 130–140.

Taylor, B., Frye, M., & Maruyama, K. (1990). Time spent reading and reading growth. *American Educational Research Journal, 27,* 351–362.

Taylor, B., Pearson, P. D., Clark, S., & Walpole, S. (2000). Effective schools and accomplished readers: Lessons about primary-grade reading instruction in low-income schools. *Elementary School Journal, 101,* 121–165.

Templeton, S., & Morris, D. (1999). Questions teachers ask about spelling. *Reading Research Quarterly, 34,* 102–112.

Tierney, R.(1998). Literacy assessment reform: Shifting beliefs, principled possibilities, and emerging practices. *The Reading Teacher, 51,* 374–390.

Topping, K. (1987). Paired Reading: A powerful technique for parent use. *The Reading Teacher, 40,* 608–614.

Topping, K. (1989). Peer tutoring and Paired Reading: Combining two powerful techniques. *The Reading Teacher, 42,* 488–494.

Topping, K. (1995). *Paired reading, spelling, and writing.* New York: Cassell.

Turner, J., & Paris, S. (1995). How literacy tasks influence children's motivation for literacy. *The Reading Teacher, 48,* 662–673.

U.S. Department of Education, National Center for Educational Statistics. (1996). *Almanac: Reading from 1984–1994*. Washington, DC: Author.

Vacca, R. T., & Vacca, J. L. (2001). *Content area reading* (7th ed.). Boston: Allyn & Bacon.

Valencia, S., & Pearson, P. D. (1987). Reading assessment: Time for a change. *The Reading Teacher, 40,* 726–733.

Vygotsky, L. (1962). *Thought and language.* Cambridge, MA: MIT Press.

Vygotsky, L. (1978). *Mind in society.* Cambridge, MA: Harvard University Press.

Watson, B., & Konicek, R. (1990). Teaching for conceptual change: Confronting children's experience. *Phi Delta Kappan, 71,* 680–685.

Watson, D. (1987). *Ideas and insights.* Urbana, IL: National Council of Teachers of English.

Weiner, B. (1979). A theory of motivation for some classroom experiences. *Journal of Educational Psychology, 71,* 3–25.

Wells, G. (1986). *The meaning makers.* Portsmouth, NH: Heinemann.

Wigfield, A., & Asher, S. (1984). Social and motivational influences on reading. In R. Barr, M. Kamil, P. Mosenthal, & P. D. Pearson (Eds.), *Handbook of reading research* (Vol. 1) (pp. 423–452). New York: Longman.

Winograd, P., & Smith, L. (1987). Improving the climate for reading comprehension instruction. *The Reading Teacher, 41,* 304–310.

Worthy, J., & Prater, K. (2002). "I thought about it all night": Readers theater for reading fluency and motivation. *The Reading Teacher, 56,* 294–297.

Yopp, H. (1992). Developing phonemic awareness in young children. *The Reading Teacher, 45,* 696–703.

Yopp, H. K. (1995a). A test for assessing phonemic awareness in young children. *The Reading Teacher, 49*(1), 20–29.

Yopp, H. K. (1995b). Read-aloud books for developing phonemic awareness: An annotated bibliography. *The Reading Teacher, 48,* 538–543.

Name Index

Subject Index

About the Authors

Timothy Rasinski and Nancy Padak are Professors of Curriculum and Instruction at Kent State University, where they teach courses in literacy education. They also served as editors of *The Reading Teacher,* the most widely read professional journal in reading education, and currently edit the *Journal of Literacy Research.*

Previously a classroom and Title I teacher in Nebraska, Tim Rasinski received his Ph.D. from The Ohio State University and has taught at the University of Georgia. He has written and edited several books on literacy education including *Case Studies in Whole Language* (coauthored with Rich Vacca), *Sensitive Issues: An Annotated Guide to Children's Literature, K–6* (coauthored with Cindy Gillespie), *Parents and Teachers: Helping Children Learn to Read and Write,* and *Good-bye Round Robin* (coauthored with Michael Opitz). Tim has also conducted research and written many articles on reading and writing education published in *Reading Research Quarterly, Reading Psychology, Reading Research and Instruction, Journal of Experimental Education, Education Forum,* and *The Reading Teacher,* among others.

Nancy Padak received her Ed.D. from Northern Illinois University, and has worked as a classroom teacher, Title I administrator, and a school district reading and language arts curriculum director in Illinois. She is Director of the University Reading and Writing Center at Kent State and Principal Investigator at the Ohio Literacy Resource Center. Nancy's extensive research in literacy education has been published in *Journal of Reading, Journal of Educational Research, Language Arts, The Reading Teacher,* and the *Yearbooks of the National Reading Conference* and the *College Reading Association,* among others. Nancy was recently named Distinguished Professor by Kent State University.

Tim and Nancy have worked intensively with children in public schools and in university reading clinics who have experienced difficulty in learning to read. The reading clinical program that they direct won an Ohio's Best Award for its innovative practices in helping children learn to read. They wrote this book in the hope that teachers who work with struggling readers can make reading a successful, exciting, and lifelong experience for those children.